COLUMBIA HOUSE / New York

understanding human behavior
An Illustrated Guide to Successful Human Relationships

COLUMBIA HOUSE / New York

Editor	Nicolas Wright
Deputy Editor	Susan Joiner
Senior Designer	Stewart Cowley
Art Editor	Mary Cooper
Art Assistant	Jeff Gurney
Editorial Assistants	Mundy Ellis
	Sarie Forster
	John Moore
	Michael McIntyre
Picture Research	Diane Rich
	Hazel Robinson
	Paul Snelgrove
Editorial Director	Graham Donaldson
Production Manager	Warren E. Bright

contents

introduction

There are few things more devastating for a child than being rejected by his parents. Rejection works in many ways; it ranges from callous indifference to extreme physical cruelty. But why do some parents behave in this way? And what happens to the child thus treated? Volume Nineteen of *Understanding Human Behavior* examines the child-rejection syndrome; it shows how a child's whole personality can be shaped by his first two years of life and it sounds a warning note: parents who reject their children are in turn rejected by them. They are ignored, rebelled against and finally in old age — when they need the support of their children most — they are left to fend for themselves.

We all swear — some of us more than others! In fact, swearing has become so commonplace that the words which once caused a shudder now don't even raise an eyebrow. The naughtiest words of yesteryear are so well established in our daily vocabulary that their effect is nil.

And yet, as you will learn from Volume Nineteen, though the effect of an expletive may have been lost, it is still subject to a great many social taboos. No matter how much we might swear ourselves we would be shocked to the core if a respected public figure suddenly let fly.

(continued)

Every time you drive your car you are contributing to a sequence of atmospheric changes which may cause the polar ice caps to melt and eventually flood the road you're driving on. Every time you throw away a plastic bag, flush detergent down the sink, or spray your garden with insecticide, you are helping upset nature's delicate balance.

Volume Nineteen of *Understanding Human Behavior* discusses pollution which — together with overpopulation — is possibly the greatest threat facing our own survival and, ultimately, the future of our frail planet. The solution lies with ourselves: the human element is still the decisive factor.

Students are always being criticized: they're dubbed sexually permissive, drug crazy and work shy. But how many people realize the strain most students are under. Volume Nineteen shows that the student's lot is not always the happy one it might at first appear.

— The Editor

BBC

Monkey business

Language is an ability which distinguishes man from other animals. But now that psychologists can successfully teach it to chimpanzees are we heading for the planet of the apes?

It is difficult to visualize a modern society without a spoken and written language. This ability distinguishes us from other animals which have evolved systems of communication. Yet, at the same time, it shows very clearly our affinity with less sophisticated creatures.

The ape, our nearest relative, can convey to other individuals his state of mind, emotions, moods, and desires. He cannot, however, relate abstract ideas; neither can he name objects or individuals around him. His verbal communications are simple, consisting of screams, hoots, grunts, chattering, and various other noises, none of which contain an element of

speech. The main method of communication is by gesticulations and facial expressions. Indeed, the naked face of the ape has probably evolved to make facial expressions more easily visible.

Once more, our affinities are demonstrated by the similarities of facial expression between man and ape. The astonishingly mobile face of a chimpanzee often parodies human emotion. We are close enough to the ape to need no interpreter for such chimpanzee "language." The emotions and moods of the chimpanzee are made explicit to us by grimaces which almost exactly parallel those of a human in the same frame of mind.

Above: Washoe was brought up like a human by adults using only sign language. Now telling Dr. Roger Fouts she wants food is simply child's play.

This "primitive" part of human language is one which we still use to add force and nuances of meaning to our conversation. A slight smile, or a raised eyebrow, can impart a totally different meaning to the spoken word. And we can still use this faculty in the manner of an ape, without the aid of the spoken word. Parents often convey complex messages by grimacing and gesticulating, in the vain hope that their child will not comprehend.

Far from being in an evolutionary backwater as had long been assumed, it appears that chimpanzees in particular are still able to make advances in their mental evolution. In the wild, troops of chimpanzees have been observed to create simple tools, and have even improvized clubs with which to attack stuffed leopards, strategically placed by an experimenter. In other troops, the growth of an organized hunting technique has been noted. It may well be that at this point in their evolution, acquiring a language could help them make a giant evolutionary stride.

Both physically and mentally, the young chimpanzee and the human child have a great deal in common. They develop physically in a similar manner, and they acquire similar physical and mental skills. Examining the behavior of animals who parallel human development so closely may shed light on how we learn to talk.

Resonant Cavities

Early attempts at using chimpanzees as experimental models for human language learning proved a dismal failure, due to two basic misapprehensions. First, the animals were being taught to read detailed meanings into verbal sounds that normally have no meaning to chimpanzees, and more fundamentally, the chimpanzee's vocal apparatus is incapable of reproducing such complex sounds. Birds can be taught to speak, as opposed to talk, for they simply repeat words and phrases without any attempt to use them appropriately. But the chimpanzee can do neither, for it lacks the large resonant cavities in the mouth region which give our speech its richness; their vocal cords are different in structure and their tongue and palate do not lie in the same relative positions as ours. Despite these handicaps, success of a sort has been achieved.

In the 1940s a chimpanzee called Viki was raised as a member of the family by Keith and Cathy Hayes, who succeeded, after six years of intensive training, in teaching her to say four simple words: "mama," "papa," "up," and "cup." To an impartial observer, however, it is doubtful if these words would be recognizable. Earlier work showed that chimpanzees were quite capable of recognizing and understanding English words. In the 1930s, a couple named Kellogg raised a female chimpanzee called Gua together with their own child. At the age of 18 months, it was estimated that Gua understood 100 words,

although she never learned to speak.

Apart from the anatomical problems, another difficulty in teaching language to chimpanzees is that gesticulation is more natural to them than vocalization. In efforts to overcome the problem, more recent research has concentrated on the development of synthetic languages which can be used and understood by chimpanzees, and which take advantage of their natural tendencies. So far, three distinct "languages" have been created, all of which have proved highly successful and have caused many researchers to think again about our supposedly unique ability to use language.

Experience has shown that strict controls need to be built into any learning program to ensure that the animals are not simply picking up almost imperceptible cues from the trainer. This had proved to be the explanation for the success of a number of performing horses and dogs who appeared to be able to count, but in fact were provided with the answer by their trainer, quite unconsciously. A "talking" chimpanzee must be able to converse with anyone who has learned the language.

The most spectacular success has been achieved by Allen and Beatrice Gardner, both professors of psychology at the University of Nevada. They have taken advantage of observations made during the relatively unsuccessful attempts to teach Viki to speak intelligibly, when it was noted that each "word" was accompanied by a particular gesture. So the Gardners used an existing sign language— American Sign Language, or ASL. This sign language has been used for many years by the deaf and dumb. It has proved capable of expressing all of the complex nuances of the English language, and yet can be built up into a vocabulary, through a number of extremely simple stages, just as an infant learns normal spoken English. So the chimpanzee can itself select the items of language which it is able to grasp, exactly like a human child, and the researcher can make direct comparisons between the rate of learning in children and chimpanzees.

Deaf and Dumb Language

The Gardner's pioneering work began with Washoe, a female chimpanzee born in the wild, who was about a year old when her training began. Her physical and mental abilities were similar to those of a child of the same age. Washoe was treated almost exactly like a human

child. To avoid confusing her, the Gardners and their colleagues used only ASL when within earshot of Washoe, so she learned by copying them, in precisely the same way as would the child of deaf parents.

In ASL, each sign signifies a complete word, unlike finger spelling, which is another language used by the deaf. To a human, many signs are self-explanatory, such as that for baby (cradling the arms and rocking them from side to side) and for drink (clenching the fist with thumb extended and placing the thumb to the lips). Washoe seemed to find them equally obvious, for within less than a year she was stringing signs together into sentences, such as "Open food drink" to ask for a drink which she knew was in the refrigerator.

Spontaneous Sentences

Her ability to name an object or activity using signs was not unexpected; what was surprising was the ease with which she demonstrated an ability to transfer the name to other objects or situations, which she considered to be related. For example, Washoe was taught the sign for "open," which she used when she wanted the door of her room opened. But in rapid succession she transferred use of the sign to the refrigerator door, boxes, jars, drawers, and, more intelligently, to the water faucet. Obviously her concept of the meaning of "open" was precisely that of a normal human child.

Many of the more interesting insights into her learning abilities came from her mistakes. She was taught the sign for "flower," which she used correctly, and transferred to mean the odor of cooking or of tobacco. So she was taught "smell," and learned to differentiate the two. But she still sometimes confused "smell" and "flower"; perhaps indicating that a chimpanzee's idea of a pleasant smell is radically different from our own. Washoe showed a remarkable ability to recognize photographs of familiar objects, a very rare ability in animals. At first, she called them all "baby," but later showed that she also recognized them as the required object. "Baby" seems to mean "duplicate," or "model" in chimpanzee terms.

After 21 months of training, she had 34 signs which could be recognized by anyone conversant in ASL. By now

Chimpanzees use facial expressions to convey their feelings. Top right: A pout of greeting. Right: Teeth bared in a temper tantrum.

she had progressed to concepts rather than names, using signs like "funny" and "hurt" in the correct circumstances. Instead of tapering off, her learning rate now accelerated; within three years she knew 85 signs, and within another year nearly twice as many. She could now spontaneously produce sentences as complex as "Baby (doll) in my cup," using the individual signs in the appropriate order. Washoe had now mastered some simple rules of grammar as well as the signs for names and meanings.

At this stage in Washoe's education, she was handed over to Roger Fouts, another psychologist, at a research institute in Oklahoma. There she was introduced to other primates and

learned to call them "monkey." But when she was threatened by a rhesus monkey, he immediately became "dirty monkey," a remarkably human reaction. "Dirty" was a term she had previously used to describe her own feces, and just like many a human child she used the word with great glee. Another apt invention was her coining of the term "water bird" to describe a duck.

Washoe now has a number of colleagues being taught ASL, although at first she was disconcerted at the inability of other apes to understand her. Already, the beginnings of conversation between these young chimpanzees has been observed, although so far their vocabulary is too limited to

The language experiment with Washoe was successful because her teachers concentrated on communication, not sound.

allow much more than two-word "sentences." Some of these young chimpanzees have already shown an advance on Washoe's learning skills. The Gardners taught Washoe by showing her an object and simultaneously demonstrating the appropriate sign. But some of the chimpanzees at the institute already understood the names of many objects in spoken English. These animals learned to use a sign correctly when the trainer spoke the word and demonstrated the sign, without seeing the object. They were able to recognize an object visually, by spoken English (which is a totally alien and supposedly unattainable ability for a chimpanzee), and in ASL.

Lucy, another young chimpanzee at the institute, has her own pet, a ginger cat. Her games with the cat may have deep significance for the future study of language learning in the chimpanzee, for she attempted to teach the cat to use sign language. Lucy sat the cat in front of her, held up an object, and signed "what that" to the reluctant animal. With a cat, the response was nonexistent; with a chimpanzee infant, the result could have been dramatic.

Plastic Symbols

In complete contrast to the research initiated by the Gardners, with its adoption of a previously existing language with the same grammatical rules as English, other researchers have created artificial languages which they feel may be more appropriate to the intellectual capabilities of the chimpanzee. One such researcher is David Premack, of the University of California, Santa Barbara, who has trained Sarah, an African-born chimpanzee, with a "written" language. Sarah's language lessons began when she was about six years old, well past the equivalent age at which a human child most easily absorbs language.

Unlike Washoe, Sarah was not raised in a "family" environment, but lived and was taught in an ordinary laboratory pen. Washoe was continuously exposed to humans, as is a human infant, but Sarah had close human contact for only one hour a day, five days a week. Yet, despite this, she learned to master the language which Premack created for her, and, given the limitations under which she was trained, her accomplishments are remarkable.

Sarah's language consists of manipulating small colored plastic shapes on a magnetized board, arranging them in a vertical column. There are certain advantages to this system, in that the words or sentences constructed are semipermanent and not subject to the experimenter's interpretation, as must sometimes happen in the case of sloppily produced ASL. When a question is posed, Sarah remains aware of the problem, because it is on her work board—she cannot pretend that she has not noticed it.

Her education began in 1966, and she has since learned the meanings of about 130 of her plastic symbols.

Sarah's training was conducted by standard conditioning techniques. A stimulus was presented to her; if she responded correctly, she was rewarded; if a false response was offered, no reward was forthcoming, but she was not punished in any way. The meaning of the varied symbols was rapidly acquired, and Sarah went on to master simple rules of grammar and syntax, which Washoe used only in a rudimentary form.

By manipulation of her plastic symbols, Sarah has learned to ask questions, make plural constructions, and discuss abstract concepts. She has also learned to follow quite complex instructions, such as "Sarah insert apple pail Sarah insert banana disk," demonstrating that she can decide, by applying the appropriate grammatical rules, the exact sequence of operations she is being asked to follow.

About two years ago, Sarah's physical strength outgrew her trainers' determination to continue with her education. The training program is now continuing with two five-year-old chimpanzees, each of whom have so far learned to use about 50 signs. The question remains, Will they talk to each other? Unfortunately the spontaneity of ASL is lacking, and their conversation is more akin to that of deaf persons writing notes to each other with pencil and paper.

Yet another technique has been developed at the Yerkes Primate Research Center, in Atlanta. This program is conducted by Duane Rumbaugh of Georgia State University, who feels that although Washoe used combinations of words successfully, her understanding of the rules of grammar and syntax was not clear.

Punching the Keys

The Yerkes program revolves about Lana, a three-year-old chimpanzee who is being studied to learn the extent of her grasp of sentence meaning and structure, rather than her ability simply to learn names. Like Premack's Sarah, Lana spends her time in the laboratory, but her "tools" are much more sophisticated. Lana communicates by punching the 50 keys of a typewriter, which connects directly with a series of visual display screens and a PDP-8 computer. Every communication she makes is recorded by the computer, for later study.

Lana's learning and environment are all controlled by the computer. By punching the appropriate keys, she can request, "Please machine give piece of apple," followed by a symbol to indicate that she has completed the

message. As she types, the message is repeated on the illuminated display panel, where colored symbols matching those on the keys light up. If she makes her request accurately, the computer operates the machinery which drops a piece of apple into her feeding tray—or opens a viewing window, plays music, provides a drink, or whatever. If she makes an error, no reward is forthcoming. Lana then examines her message, deletes the offending words with a "cancel" button, and tries again.

Mobile Faces

There is no doubt that Lana can construct her own sentences correctly, but she can also correct "mistakes" made by the computer or the operator. When a part-sentence is typed into the visual displays by the operator, Lana will complete it accurately. If she considers the sentence to be inappropriate or inaccurate, she cancels it and then produces a corrected version.

These three totally different approaches to the problem of teaching chimpanzees to "talk" have shown their hitherto unsuspected abilities and demonstrated how their capacity to learn language closely parallels that of a human child. The gap between human and ape widens with increasing age, but this may result partly from the use of inappropriate languages, for it is likely that researchers have yet to hit upon the type of language most suited to the chimpanzee's personality. Indeed, it is possible that *we* would be unable to communicate with a chimpanzee in the language which comes to him most naturally. Unlike theirs, our human faces are not sufficiently mobile to communicate accurately highly complex messages solely by grimacing.

The next stage in research is to discover if chimpanzees will teach their own offspring the artificial language they have themselves been taught. Given time, would such a language spread spontaneously throughout a colony of chimpanzees? And more speculatively, if a colony of "talking" chimpanzees were returned to the wild, would their new ability to communicate with each other provide them with such an advantage over normal chimpanzees that they might become dominant by natural selection? If so, we could be providing an artificial spur to the evolution of the chimpanzee, which might result in the eventual appearance of another "intelligent" species.

Home sour home

They say there's no place like home, but when you're not wanted there it's not all peaches and cream. For the kid who's been discarded by his parents and thrown out with the garbage, life is more like a squashed tomato than the proverbial bowl of cherries.

There cannot be many worse fates for a child than to be born into a home where he is rejected by his parents. For many children, rejection means callous and indifferent neglect or positive hostility and cruelty from the parents. However, cruelty does not always take a physical form: it may be emotional and so subtle that the child comes to believe he is an unmitigated nuisance, that his very existence makes his parents unhappy, that he is something that is unwanted.

It is of vital importance for a child to identify with an adult and model himself on that adult's behavior. This means that he must form an attachment—a bond of love and dependency—with his parents. As the psychologists McCord and McCord put it, almost all social scientists believe that the development of conscience takes place primarily through the child's acceptance of his parents. The child and the parents strike an unconscious bargain: in return for the child's conformity to social restrictions, the parents give the child love. If the child fails to conform, he is momentarily rejected.

Unholy Alliance

In time, the child looks ahead to the consequences of his acts. If he is about to misbehave, a gnawing fear warns that his parents might stop loving him. Thus, the inner anxiety eventually results in internationalization of the parents' morality. The child has developed a conscience.

There is, of course, a more positive aspect to the formation of inner controls: not only does the child fear withdrawal of love, he also identifies with his parents. He loves them, and wishes to emulate them. As. personality theorist Gordon Allport has pointed out, children who fear the loss of love develop the concept of "must"; but the "ought" of behavior comes only through identification with parents and other moral symbols.

These developments are subverted if the parents fail to love the child. Parental rejection usually involves a combination of lax discipline and hostility. This unholy alliance produces very aggressive and poorly controlled behavior in the offspring. The lax parent is one who gives in to the child, acceding to his demands, indulging him, allowing him a great deal of freedom, being submissive and inconsistent and, in extreme cases, neglecting and deserting him.

Kim Sayer

The hostile parent is mainly unaccepting and disapproving of the child, failing to give affection, understanding or explanations. He or she tends to use a lot of physical punishment without giving reasons for exerting authority—something he does erratically and unpredictably. Over a long period of time this combination produces rebellious, irresponsible and aggressive children; they tend to be disorderly in the classroom and lacking in sustained concentration.

No Bonds

Psychologists have come to realize that extreme rejection or prolonged separations from mother or an adequate mother substitute (especially in the first two years of life when the child is becoming a social being) can have serious consequences for his personality development. The child psychiatrist Michael Rutter concludes from his exhaustive review of the evidence (in the book *Maternal Deprivation Reassessed*), "Distorted intrafamilial relationships involving both lack of affection and hostility or discord are associated with the development of later antisocial behavior and delinquency. Although the presence of a deviant parental model and inefficient discipline may be contributing factors, the lack of a stable, persistent, harmonious relationship with a parent appears to be the crucial variable.

"Less is known about the syndrome of 'affectionless psychopathy' but the little evidence available suggests that the most tenable hypothesis is that a failure to develop attachments (or bonds) in early childhood is the main factor. A bond to one or other parent, usually the mother, is the strongest attachment formed by most normal young children. Whether this is to the mother seems irrelevant in this connection and indeed it is doubtful whether it even has to be an adult."

Rejection, in its extreme forms, is an invidious kind of deprivation. The different forms of juvenile delinquency which have been related to different patterns of rejection include the unsocialized aggressive delinquent. This is the youth who is defiant of authority, malicious, sullen and characteristically hostile and coercive to the people around him, showing little guilt or remorse. Most often he comes from a family in which the parent-child relationships are filled with mutual suspicion, hostility and rejection. The parents punish severely and are inconsistent and unjust. It is difficult for the child to identify with

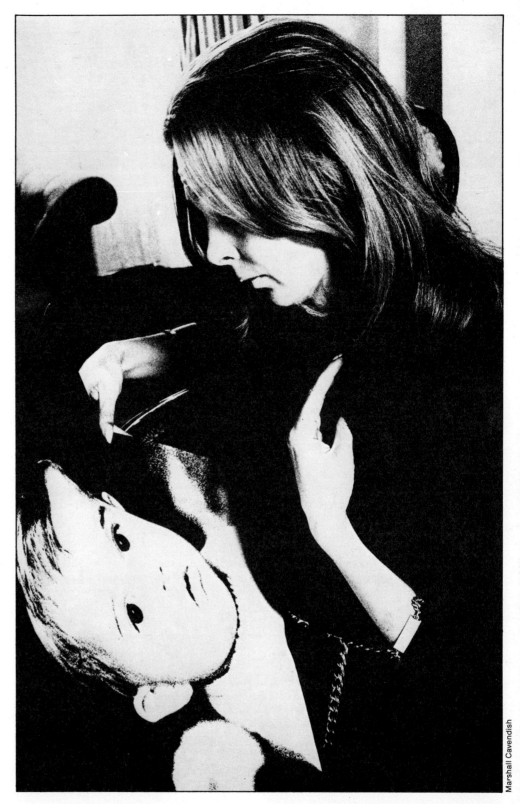

Marshall Cavendish

such parents, and thus the aggression they provoke is not directed against the self—as it is in the case of a child with a conscience—but is turned outwards on society.

Whereas punishments which evoke anxiety are likely to result later on in self-control, those producing an aggressive reaction in the child do not—though of course they may well make him wary of being caught. For this reason physical punishments are among the least effective as far as the development of the child's conscience

The mother who rejects her child at an early age may have regrets when he grows up a total stranger.

is concerned. The normal reaction to any physical assault is anger and aggression, though the expression of anger may be inhibited by fear.

Some parents reserve physical chastisement as a penalty for bullying. But a smacking is least suitable in this context if in the end the parent wishes the child to stop bullying, even when he cannot be found out. On the contrary, physical punishment may be confusing from the child's point of view. He is being beaten by a parent whom he is normally expected to imitate but who is now setting an example of the very behavior for which the child is blamed. As a general rule, physical punishment stimulates feelings of aggression. It bypasses the more subtle sense of anxiety which results in resistance to temptation by self-control not fear of punishment.

Phantom Parents

It is almost a law of human nature that punishment leads to self-control only when the child is on the side of the person punishing. Since he loves his mother, the child is partly on his mother's side. Because of this identification with his mother, he will share her condemnation of himself. In the case of a loveless child this assumption cannot be made. Although loving attachment makes the development of conscience possible, it also places in the hands of the mother a power which could be detrimental to the child. If a child is strongly and exclusively attached to a mother who sets impossibly high standards and is deeply "hurt" when her child fails to live up to them, it is probable that the child will acquire a sense of conscience so severe and restrictive that his instincts are crippled and much of his creative energy will remain unused.

Parental rejection takes many forms. Abandonment is an extreme form of rejection and is only too often the fate of illegitimate children, though this is not necessarily the case. A study of a thousand unmarried mothers in California showed that they were fairly representative, socioeconomically, of all females of equivalent age, race, and marital status in that state. The majority of the mothers reported either a love relationship or a close friendship with their sexual mates, who also seemed quite typical of men in general. The personalities of the mothers ranged from very positive to very negative, but the majority represented the norm for females of similar age and showed little evidence of subnormal mentality or emotional instability. In fact, the only thing that unmarried mothers seem to have in common is an illegitimate child.

There has been a dramatic liberalizing of social attitudes, as well as public policies, in many countries during the twentieth century. But however liberal the present-day policies may be, there are serious personal problems remaining for the child of the unmarried mother. The

illegitimate child is made to feel different. He may hear certain insinuations: "after all, he wasn't wanted by them," "he was a mistake," or "he's their punishment." These stereotyped attitudes may be only unconsciously felt, but they can still have a profound influence on the sensitive child's growing self-esteem.

To those who have grown up within a family it is nearly impossible to comprehend fully what it must be like to know nothing of one's family—either of one parent (if the mother keeps the child) or both of them (if the child is placed in care). Diana Dewar, introducing her book *Orphans of the Living,* describes this lack of a sense of family as the greatest human grief apart from death—when forlorn, loveless children mourn for phantom parents. The problem is mitigated to a large extent when illegitimate babies have substitute parents, as in adoption, but there are many more illegitimate children of all races than childless couples who want to provide a family life for them.

Many illegitimate children accept the popular myth (and stigma) that they come from "bad blood." One of the most difficult handicaps of all for them to bear is their feeling of inferiority, of being unwanted by at least one parent (if not both). And another burden is the lack of a family history to give them a niche in society. Boys find it much harder than girls to accept that their mother was unmarried when they were born and never married their father. In these matters, the truth has a way of coming out, and if it is not explained to a child in a humane and sensitive way, it may come out in a crude jest or some other traumatic discovery.

Dog in the Manger

Those children whose mothers have no hope of making a home, or who may not even wish to acknowledge the baby, remain the hard core of youngsters in long-term care. The extramarital offspring of married women are often admitted to orphanages because the husband will "forgive" his wife her unfaithfulness only if she gives up the child. These are often very sad cases, since the mothers sometimes have strong maternal feelings and agree to part with the new baby only to preserve the home for the children of the marriage. Later on, such children may long to be in touch with their mothers but the husbands will seldom allow this, even after many years.

The illegitimate child who suffers

most is the one whose future home is continually undecided, usually because of the unstable personality of the mother. She may tenaciously hang onto the child as a symbol of the wrong she feels has been done her. On the other hand, she may have convinced herself, no matter how unlikely the prospects, that she will one day sort things out and make a satisfactory home for the child. In the meantime the child may suffer from severe early emotional deprivation, never knowing a real home. Many countries have introduced legislation to protect children from the mother who fails to assume a maternal role but will not permit anyone else to do so.

Struggle to Survive

There is a familiar pattern in the lives of this type of mother and child. The mother had an unhappy childhood (perhaps being illegitimate herself) and no loving parents to stand by her when she was in trouble. Feeling herself an outcast, she has to face up to the responsibility of a child when her way of life shows her she is incapable of being responsible for herself. She is probably torn between a desire to shelve her burdens and have the baby adopted and an even greater desire to possess at least one human being to love and be loved by in return. She compromises, finding some way to keep the child and at the same time work to support him. She is likely to stay in lodgings where a landlady or registered child-minder cares for him while she is at work, but lodgings of this kind are hard to come by and difficult to keep. She may use a day nursery. If the child gets sick and she has to take time off from work, she could lose her job. Then living on some form of welfare, she may slide into debt. If the rent is not paid, she could end up on the street.

There are several courses of action at this point, such as a casual liaison with a man or prostitution—both tragic for her own and the child's well-being. If she is not successful in finding alternative accommodation or resources quickly, she may give up the struggle of keeping the child with her. He will end up in care, torn from the small bit of security he has so far known. This may be the last the child sees of the mother. She may, however, struggle to get him back, and visit him regularly at the children's home with presents and treats. Only too often these visits become less regular or taper off completely.

Children in this situation may show great loyalty to the rejecting parent and weave elaborate fantasies as to why she cannot visit and when they will be reunited. The effects of such instability and insecurity on a child's life are incalculable.

Most social workers, in the course of their work, come into contact with the problems of the neglected child, the youngster who is a victim of emotional deprivation.

"Failure to thrive" is a sociologist's term describing the result of parental neglect and physical abuse, yet another aspect of a breakdown in the mothering function. There have been reports of deliberate withholding of food from children; recent studies in

hospitals draw attention to the fact that there is a regular, though small, incidence in hospital admissions of babies under the age of three years who repeatedly return to hospital for failure to thrive and develop properly, or with broken limbs or severe internal and external bruising.

As early as 1946 a connection between fractures of the long bones and severe head injuries in children was noted by a radiologist, but it was another six years before it was accepted that these were not accidents. Dr. Silverman, American radiologist, reported, "Many individuals responsible for the care of infants and chil-

dren (who cannot give their own history) may permit trauma, but forget or be reluctant to admit it, or may deliberately injure the child and deny it." But apart from scattered reports, it was not until the early 1960s that further research was undertaken and given publicity.

In general there was a good deal of complacency—despite the publicizing of a few notorious and tragic cases of child deaths—in connection with this serious form of child abuse. It was for this reason that Professor Henry Kempe (coeditor of the book *Helping the Battered Child and his Family*) used the emotive term "battered child." In June, 1972, in the *British Medical Journal,* Dr. Graham Jackson at King's College Hospital, London, reported on the tendency for medical personnel still to overlook the syndrome. He reported his findings in one hundred case records of children aged two or less, admitted for physical injury. When cases where the cause of the injury was clear were excluded, eighteen children still remained. According to Dr. Jackson, in each of these eighteen cases there was enough objective evidence to suggest a strong possibility that the child was being abused, but this diagnosis seems not to have been considered.

Double-edged Weapon

The battered baby syndrome is no new phenomenon, but an awareness of its extent, in possibly all strata of society, is only now dawning. Many of the causal factors in this problem can be traced to the parents' own childhood, uncovering a cycle of deprivation. Physically violent parents have often suffered severe emotional deprivation themselves and have had their dependency needs frustrated. As a result many grow up unable to nurture their offspring or to empathize with them; they tend to be highly dependent and very low in self-esteem. Many of the parents of battered children have personality disorders ranging from extreme emotional immaturity and neurosis to psychopathy.

Rejection, of course, is a double-edged weapon. Parents who reject their children are rejected by them in turn. Eventually they are ignored, rebelled against, and even abandoned by their unhappy youngsters, so that in their old age these unstable parents lose the one prop that might make their lives worth living.

Sun Gravure

Little girl lost: a child who is not loved by her parents may withdraw and have difficulty making friends.

The madding crowd

Multiplication—that's the name of the game, but if we go on like this we will soon be standing shoulder to shoulder, fighting for food and a breath of fresh air.

The population explosion presents one of the greatest threats ever to face mankind. The very word "population" is almost invariably linked with other words like "problem," "crisis," "dilemma," "emergency."

The mere number of people on this earth is not only a problem in itself, but it is also the root cause of most of the other evils with which humanity has to grapple on a world scale—pollution, lack of resources and energy, starvation, poverty, disease, crime, war, and the many other scars on the face of civilized life. It is hard to face the facts and figures and remain neutral and dispassionate; they turn you into an alarmist and propagandist. The simple fact is there are already far too many people on this planet.

This seems an absurd impression to the man who leaves his home in a spacious suburb and gets on a plane which flies him over mile upon mile of open countryside. How can he equate what he sees with the predictions of the doomsayers who warn that every habitable part of the globe has already been settled, and that by the end of the next century we will be standing shoulder to shoulder? The aircraft cabin is probably the worst possible viewpoint from which to contemplate the population problem. It belies the facts of the matter, facts which mean different things to different people.

To the demographer—the statistician with his charts, graph, and slide rule—the overpopulation problem is a set of figures confronting him with an insoluble equation. The figures, which are out-of-date before they are even collated, show that there are nearly 4 billion people in the world and that 75 million are added every year. It was not until 1650 that we reached our first half-billion, and the next 300 years brought 2 billion more—around 2.5 billion in 1950. But the next two billion, so it is predicted, will take only a tenth of that time—4.5 billion in 1980. At the present growth rate we should have a population of 6.5 billion by the turn of the century, possibly reaching 8 billion less than ten years after that.

Breaking Point

What appear to be the wildest prognostications are rooted in these facts. One of them comes from a British physicist who calculates that before the end of the next century there will be 60 billion people spread over the globe; that is 100 per square yard of the earth's land and sea surface. This is obviously an inconceivable situation, and breaking point will have been reached long before that. Already we cannot feed our present population adequately. There are limits to the amount of space available and obstacles to the fair distribution of food, materials and energy. The only unlimited capacity we have seems to be in reproducing our species. This is the statisticians' insoluble equation.

For the affluent suburban man of the wealthier nation, the population problem means the "agony" of rush-hour travel, urban congestion, the "misery" of shopping on Christmas Eve, going on waiting lists, and the occasional shortage of some consumer commodity. It is a mild inconvenience. But these are the things which bring the problem home to him rather than the Sunday paper reports on how the other half lives, or television documentaries which can be switched off.

But for these others—the majority of the world's population—the crisis is a stark reality. Half the world is hungry and several million people—mostly children—die of starvation every year, the victims of famine or natural disaster. From the rural areas of India and Ethiopia to the shanty towns of Calcutta or Jakarta survival

is the best life can offer. The problem is the same: too many people and not enough to go around. It takes a walk down an Indian city street for even the most enlightened demographer to begin to "get the feel" of the real magnitude of the problem.

It is not just a matter of numbers alone, or the allocation of people to a given number of square miles. This is what the air traveler, zooming over acres of uninhabited open space, would fail to take into account. The problem arises because every person has to be fed, clothed, and sheltered, a task which the world's present resources—and the economic systems by which they are produced and distributed—cannot adequately perform. People also need to be educated, they need health and welfare services, they need jobs and demand exceeds supply.

Our present resources are not up to the job, and in the absence of either an unpredictable catastrophe which would effectively reduce numbers, or a miracle of science which would unearth new resources, the future promises a situation in which twice as many people are using up half the resources. The steps we are taking about it now are at best stopgap contingency measures to deal with the present emergency: we cannot put much by for the future.

Imbalance of Nature

Another illusion held by our air passenger is that the populations of the world are evenly spread over the landmasses of the globe. If they were, he might see more people scattered around the vast wasteland area which his view commands. But some countries are crammed to saturation point while others, like parts of Africa and South America, reckon themselves to be deficient. Geographical and climatic factors make other places utterly uninhabitable. The expanses of open space in the saturation countries of Asia are accounted for by people's migration from the rural areas and their concentration in the cities.

By an accident of history the earth is now divided into two parts. One is composed of the developed countries, the wealthy nations with advanced technologies, like North America, Europe, the U.S.S.R., Japan and Australasia. The other consists of the rest—the poor countries, undeveloped and not so much as self-sufficient in resources. The imbalance of nature also endows these poorly provided nations with far more than their fair share of the world's population. They are caught in a vicious circle; as long

as they lag behind in industrial development, go short of materials and energy, and maintain poor medical and educational services—which taken together create the conditions which favor small families—the population will be ever-increasing.

Redistribution of Resources

The developed nations are made up of about one-third of the total world population. The growth rate—the percentage of births over deaths—averages at about 1 percent a year in the biggest two nations, the United States and the U.S.S.R. In the undeveloped countries live the remaining two-thirds. Their growth rate, however, is 2.5 percent, and in some places as high as 3.4 percent. At this rate they will have to accommodate 5½ billion people by the end of this century, 28 billion fifty years later, and adding a billion a year by the end of next century. At present the peoples of these countries consume 8 times less per head than do the people of developed nations. Another estimate claims that the average Westerner is eating into the world's pool of resources 500 times faster than, say, an Asian living on the breadline.

These few statistics are enough to show that, in considering population problems, you have two sets of figures to deal with: one tells a story of glaring poverty, the other of unashamed affluence. The disparity of population density may not have been the initial cause of the discrepancy between living standards of the two groups, but it has certainly exaggerated the problems. We know that 30 percent of the world's population consumes 75 percent of its resources. On the one hand we have vast populations eking out a meager existence on poor resources, or starving for complete lack of them. On the other hand we have affluent nations with overfed populations, huge surpluses, and appalling waste. This is the problem.

On the face of it, the answer looks simple. You just channel the surplus to the countries which do not have enough and if that still fails to meet the demand you constrain the wealthy nations at least not to consume more than they need. Then you have even distribution of resources. But we should not think of resources as some single substance which can be packaged and transported from places where it is in excess to places where it is in short supply. Even if this were so there would be no reason to think that the problem had been solved. The problem is overpopulation, and any humanitarian gesture to redeploy supplies will not solve it.

Another obstacle to any easy solution is human nature. Over the centuries man has come to think of himself as a member of separate ethnic or national groups living apart from others. In the days before he had explored his planet to its limits and before developments in science and communications made global and international activity possible, that was good enough. But now he has to think of himself as a member of the whole human race—a great responsibility to have thrust on him all of a sudden. Wherever he is, his activities have direct repercussions in the far corners of the earth. But he is as irrational as ever; life is still arranged so that a man in a wealthy nation can consume twice as much as he needs in the full knowledge that someone on the other side of the world is starving, while the undernourished man will go on having children in total disregard of the certainty that he will be unable to provide for them.

Reproduction is a basic human urge. At one time having large families presented the only hope for the survival of the species. High infant mortality, short life expectancy, and the ever present hazards of life—disease, famine, war, accident, overexertion—compounded to make a higher deathrate than birthrate a very real possibility. Evolution by natural selection allowed only for the survival of the fittest. We are descended from those with the greatest resistance to the calamities of life and we have inherited their high degree of immunity. We also issue from those with the greatest capacity to reproduce, and we are endowed with that too.

Science Plays Its Part

Long after the survival of the human race was assured there was a remarkable leap forward in medical science. This, according to population expert Dr. Paul Erlich, was the straw which broke the camel's back. It happened about 1800 when populations, in the developed countries at least, stood at a level which promised a decent standard of living for all. It lowered the infant mortality rate, reduced the number of deaths due to disease and injury, arrested the process of aging, and lengthened the span of years in which a woman could be expected to reproduce. Meanwhile the march of science and technology took much of the donkey work out of life, which became less hard and lasted longer.

Forgetting for the moment that medical science can be applied to the reduction of population, we can see that together with our strong sexual urge and the generous allocation of fertile periods in the female reproductive system, advances in medicine have made propagation harder to avoid than to achieve. This is where man's other unique genetic endowment might have come in useful—his capacity for rational thought and intellectual appraisal of his predicament for exercising some measure of control over his destiny. But in this matter it did not. Mankind has gone on reproducing as though he had no thought for tomorrow.

Return of the Four Horsemen

The first authoritative warnings of the dangers of uncontrolled population growth came from the social economist Thomas Malthus in about 1800, although the subject had been previously broached by Franklin and Hume. Malthus' pessimistic treatise *An Essay on the Principle of Population* pointed out the natural tendency of populations to increase faster than their means of subsistence. With man, he said, propagation could be controlled by reason, although the ultimate check was want of food. It could be prevented by moral restraint and by prophylactic methods but, failing that, other factors would emerge to discourage population growth or to reduce numbers: unwholesome occupations, severe labor, extreme poverty, bad nursing, large towns, excesses of all kinds, diseases, wars and famine.

On reading Malthus' work, Charles Darwin said that natural selection was an inevitable result of rapid increase of all organic beings, as such a rapid growth in numbers necessarily leads to a struggle for existence. But the intensity of that struggle was considerably mitigated by breakthroughs in science, technology, and agriculture, which were occurring at that time in response to the social demands. They confounded Malthus' gloomy prophecy that "the power of population is so superior to the power of the earth to produce subsistence to man that premature death must in some shape visit the human race."

The stages of a population explosion are very simple. Once you have a sudden upward swing, a snowballing process has started which only some catastrophe can significantly reverse. Plain for all to see is the fact that on the whole children outnumber parents. From there on it is a matter of elementary arithmetic. A man with two children has, in numerical terms, reproduced himself and his wife. A number of grandchildren and even great-grandchildren will be born before he himself dies, by which time he will have reproduced himself many times over. If the birthrate exceeds the deathrate the population continues to grow—and the longer this situation persists the faster that growth proceeds, as each generation provides a broader base for the creation of the next.

A growth rate of 1 percent doubles a population in 70 years, 2 percent doubles it in 35 years, 3 percent in 23 years, and so on, assuming that everybody survives and not allowing for deaths by famine, war, accident, disease or misadventure which on a large scale relieve the situation. This rate does not take into account immigration and emigration, male-female ratios, and so on, which obviously have a bearing on any population statistics within any given country.

In the United States, where the rate of growth is as modest and well controlled as anywhere in the world, it is felt that an ideal situation would be achieved if every couple limited itself to two children. If this were achieved, by some having more and others less, it would not be until the end of the next century that the country's population would stabilize, when it would stand at between 370 and 400 million. If it could be achieved throughout the world, by about the year 2040, the total world population would level off at just under 16 billion, over four times greater than today.

Pessimistic Predictions

Just as the world can be subdivided into two, so each nation can, in a sense, be regarded as two nations—the rural population and the city dwellers. In the developed countries, 80 percent of the population live in towns, and in the undeveloped nations, the migration into the urban centers is steady and unrelenting. It is estimated that by 1980 3½ billion will be living in the cities of these countries.

Aristotle once said that people came to the cities in search of the "good life." That may have been true in his day, but now it is importunity which drives them there and which their new environment does little to relieve. They come in search of jobs for themselves and education for their children, or they come just to stay alive.

Every city is in reality two cities: each has its affluent, fashionable central areas and its elegant suburban fringes, but it also has its slum areas, its twilight zones and shanty towns.

It is here that the majority of migrants converge in far greater numbers than can be absorbed. They have to be fed, employed, educated, transported, entertained. It is in the cities that the problems of overpopulation are most harshly felt. Overcrowding makes for problems of health, sanitation, and hygiene. Health and welfare services are often overwhelmed by the persistent influx of people and can do little to maintain a decent standard of living. Unable to provide enough resources, housing, education, medical care or employment, they fight a losing battle against the deterioration of conditions, and the way is left wide open for the increase of crime, violence, squalor, vagrancy, poverty, hardship, and all the concomitant ills of overcrowded conditions.

This is happening now, and a recent survey has shown how much more likely to increase are the populations of the cities which are at present most densely inhabited. Djakarta, a city in Indonesia built for two million people, already has four million. It tops the table of projected growth with a 93 percent increase by 1985. By then, Calcutta, which now has a population of nearly 7 million, will have swelled its numbers by 75 percent. Tokyo's projected increase will bring its population to over 25 million. How will these people be living then?

Like rats? This may not seem too wide of the mark if we consider how rats do live in overcrowded conditions. A few years ago an American psychologist, John B. Calhoun, conducted a series of extensive experiments with a confined rat population. For a time he allowed the population to increase at its natural rate. When it reached a manageable limit, it stabilized. What might have expanded to a colony of 5,000 animals in the prescribed time span remained at 150. But this was not achieved as a result of any wisdom or forbearance on the part of the rats.

Sardines in a Can

The stabilization was the result of their violent perversion of the course of nature. Most of the deaths were due to the negligence of the mothers, who refused to build nests for their young or deserted them if they did. Other deaths were due to fierce territorial contests between males, and some to cannibalism. What was left of the colony became either unnaturally aggressive, paranoid, withdrawn, overdefensive, hyperactive, sexually perverted or generally neurotic.

What Dr. Calhoun had done was to create a miniature overcrowded city. Even with the added advantage of reason and intelligence, man has done little better in his congested environment than his rodent counterpart. We have a natural psychological aversion to living at too close quarters and do not remain sociable in this predicament for long. Figures for acts of violence, crime, arson, sexual perversion, suicide and other disruptive behavior are higher per capita for the densely populated cities than elsewhere: they are daily occurrences. As with the rats, violent, antisocial and wayward behavior becomes the norm.

Whichever way you look at it, the population explosion appears to have set us on a course for self-destruction —economic, biological, psychological, social, and environmental. Man's struggle for existence has always involved maintaining the balance between the demands of populations and the supply of the earth's natural resources. Until that equilibrium is achieved something has got to give. We can either reduce the rate of population growth, or allow it to increase and reduce the standard of living for all or increase the yield of nature. At present, the burden of overpopulation is being met in all three ways: some populations are being allowed to die; others are condemned to a pitifully impoverished standard of living; others are turning the full force of technology into an assault on the land to maximize its produce. Ultimately, man's survival depends on how long his natural environment can hold out.

Too many demands are being made on the world's limited resources: soon our nest egg may crack.

David Levin/Jancis Cowley

Birds and bees

All too often sex education just means passing on one generation's hang-ups to the next.

Throughout history, the typical family has lived in no more than one or two rooms, in many cases sharing their beds or sleeping mats. Some of the more primitive tribes still do. Children brought up under these circumstances have no embarrassment or ignorance about the human body. By comparison, people in the developed nations suffer great inhibitions, ritually concealing their bodies from each other, segregating the sexes, and assigning different activities to certain rooms.

In Western society, children in peasant communities are traditionally less inhibited about sex and the human body. Any child brought up in the country is likely to pick up facts about the nature of sexual activity from the mating of farm animals.

The habits of European rural society towards the end of the nineteenth century shocked Scottish novelist Robert Louis Stevenson. On a walking tour of rural France (reported in his *Travels with a Donkey*) he found that innkeepers assumed that he would share a bedroom with others. And on the first occasion, to his embarrassed astonishment, he found that one of his compulsory bedroom companions was a woman—he was to share a room with a married couple and their small child. One bed for them, the other for him. "I kept my eyes to myself, and knew nothing of the woman except that she had beautiful arms, and seemed no whit embarrassed."

The compartmentalization of everyday activities within the Western home

is relatively recent. Before the industrial revolution, the family home was also often the "unit of production"—some or all of the produce for sale or for the family's own needs, was made at home, by both men and women. The center of domestic activity was the hall of the house, the entrance space. Meals were cooked there, some of the family slept there, and some sort of productive labor was done there. In England, separate rooms for separate activities—a cooking room, sleeping rooms, and so on—were not common in working-class homes until towards the end of the nineteenth century.

A Western child now experiences many barriers in the home. He (or she) is unlikely to have seen his parents naked; probably he has never slept in the same room with them; nor, perhaps, has he ever seen other children's bodies—if, as is typical, he is a member of a small family. He almost certainly has to be formally instructed about the nature of the human body, its changes as it matures, and the sexual act. And he is likely to feel great shock and temporary disbelief at the thought of his parents indulging in an activity so alien to all he knows about them.

In most of the world's societies, sex "education" is a more automatic process than it is in Western industrial societies. The anthropologist Margaret Mead, who has carried out extensive studies into the behavior of primitive societies, suggests that a child needs to be able to observe the constant, gradual physical changes among many other children, adolescents and adults.

Early Awareness

"What the child receives in a primitive society," she writes, "is the assurance that there is a continuous series of steps between his small body and that of an adult. The little boy needs to see the changes in body form and hair, the gradually developing genitals . . . the first soft facial down." To see these things will bind his sense of himself to the man he will become.

And the little girl, Dr. Mead feels, needs to be able to observe, and to identify with, a series of girls—from "the nubile girl with budding breasts to the mature young woman, and finally to the just pregnant, the fully pregnant, and the postparturient and suckling mother. This is what happens in those primitive societies in which the body is hardly covered at all. . . . The full pageant of human development from early childhood to full maturity is visible."

In primitive societies, the child is, as it were, surrounded by continuous sex education. A lot of the ceremony and celebration in tribal life is concerned with sexual matters, and children hear and see explicitly sexual behavior between adults. Accustomed to this from the first, sexual knowledge is acquired gradually.

In some societies where the virginity of a bride is important, proof of her virginity is shown publicly. A woman who is a virgin has a thin membrane covering the entrance to the vagina, and the first penetration of the vagina will break this membrane and often cause a drop or two of blood to be shed. After the couple have gone to their marriage bed, in some societies, a large white cloth stained with blood will be hung outside the house, as "proof" of the bride's virginity (a practice of doubtful value: cheating with chicken blood is commonly contrived).

Girls and boys growing up with such customs must acquire sexual knowledge as a matter of course. Some societies praise the sexual parts of a child's body very early. Dr. Mead cites the Balinese, who tease a baby boy's penis, crying, "Handsome, handsome, handsome," as they do so, and pat a little girl's vulva gently, crying, "Pretty, pretty, pretty." And a little girl of two or three walking with her belly thrust out might be poked playfully and teased about being pregnant.

The passing from childhood to maturity is also almost invariably a matter for celebration in primitive societies. In many societies there is a specific time at which a boy is understood to become a man and when he must pass initiation tests to be admitted to manhood. And whereas in Western society a girl's first menstruation is usually a matter for secrecy, embarrassment, and shame, in primitive societies the occasion is usually marked with a public celebration. A girl is also liable to be betrothed some years before menstruation. Sometimes she goes to live with her "husband's" family, both of them fully accepting of their future together, both waiting unquestioningly for sexual maturity and the correct time for their actual mating.

Although people in such societies enjoy what seems to us a lot of sensuous freedom, untainted by shame, in fact their taboos and strictures are very strong. Some societies, for instance, prohibit sexual intercourse while a wife is nursing a child —and since she may nurse him for three years, this is a considerable restriction. Every society has its rules.

A child in a primitive society may have to learn complicated gradations governing his behavior with other people, according to their relationship to him. Rules governing sexual relationships are complicated and incest taboos particularly stringent. A boy avoiding proscribed contacts with a "sister" may find that a third of the girls of the village fit into this category, though genealogical "records" are so unreliable and bewildering that it may be difficult for a man to be sure whether a particular woman is in a forbidden relationship to him or not.

Changes in life at adolescence are sometimes as difficult as in our own society. Initiation tests for boys are often very demanding, sometimes painful. There can be pain for girls, too, as in one society's ceremonies surrounding a girl's first menstruation, in which the older women of her family instruct her in rolling stinging nettle leaves and inserting them into

There was no room for privacy or modesty in the average family home of only a century ago.

Radio Times

Alan Hutchinson

An initiation ceremony in Ghana. In many primitive societies a boy becomes a man in the space of a few hours of public ritual.

her vulva to make her breasts grow.

Restriction and inhibition at puberty are taught particularly to the girl. She learns protective measures like keeping her legs crossed or tucking her heels under her; she must dress to protect her sexual areas, with a grass skirt carefully concealing her; she will probably tend more and more to be chaperoned.

Boys may also suffer a sudden loss of freedom. Margaret Mead writes of one New Guinea society in which, after a carefree childhood, boys in their early teens are whisked away to be initiated: then they may spend several miserable months, or sometimes years, during which they are chased away by the women, though they are not yet anxious to join the men. In one society, boys are sent away in early childhood to their maternal grandparents to lead a life of ease; then, when the time for initiation arrives, they are sent back to encounter the harshness of a father to push them into manhood.

In any society, the pattern of social organization is what trains a child in his social and sexual behavior and his expectations of the behavior of others. And different societies have very different patterns of social organization. In some, there is little emphasis on distinctions between men and women. Boys and girls play the same games; fathers show tenderness to children; sexual relationships may be initiated by females as well as by males; dominance and competitiveness are not admired, and neither are violence and aggression.

In another society, both men and women may be expected to be violent and aggressive, children may be treated harshly, and there may be hostility and competition within the family— between parents and children, between man and woman. And again, elsewhere, women may be taught to be self-reliant, dominant, and sexually aggressive, while the men are relaxed and submissive. Most peoples lie somewhere between these extremes, and their "sex-education"— one of the ways a society conveys its own nature to its children—reflects this considerable variation.

The Samoan culture and its ap-

proach to sex was the one which Margaret Mead considered particularly desirable. Samoans expected sex to be a delightful experience, and unashamedly considered sexual expertise a desirable skill. They disapproved of great passions, however, regarding them as threats to the social order. Parents did not discuss sex with children, although parents and children might together attend dances of uninhibited frankness. As a girl became ready for sexual experience, she would be chosen for her first love affair by an older boy, who had himself been initiated into full sexual experience by older girls. Marriages were arranged between families, though the parents would take the wishes of the young people into consideration as well, and thereafter the girl was expected to become pregnant only by her betrothed, although this must sometimes have turned out to be wishful thinking. Children were treated indulgently, but without any passionate or possessive mother-child relationships and marriages were stable. Samoans were also able to adjust to change, weaving Christianity lightly into the fabric of the native culture without damage.

In marked contrast to the Samoan culture, Margaret Mead notes modern society's difficulty in absorbing change into its attitudes to sex. "In a changing society, the parts of the system get out of step; a childhood suited for an expressive adolescence may be followed by a restricted one, or a restricted childhood be followed by a demand for an expressive adolescence. Then the patterns become confused; more children fail to experience the sequence of events which, in that culture, are the appropriate prelude to adulthood."

Element of Choice

When, as today, procreation is no longer accepted as the sole purpose of adult life, and the biological purpose of sexual intercourse is no longer its sole function, establishing and passing on sexual values becomes very difficult: simple certainties disappear. The fact that a future of pregnancies is no longer the morally approved future for a woman puts painful elements of choice and decision making into sex education. The small girl in a primitive society sees all about her examples of the single norm for adult women. In an urban, industrial society, the small girl sees adult women living in a variety of ways: some of them unmarried, some of them childless—and some of them apparently achieving status or fulfillment in spite of this.

It may indeed be comfortable to have a single norm of behavior in a society. But it is impossible to transplant customs evolved within a simple, exclusive culture into a complex, industrial, literate and mobile society, where people tend to question simple, time-honored assumptions. At the same time, medicine has greatly increased life span and saves millions of babies that would otherwise die. A responsible woman in an industrial society cannot regard herself as nothing but a baby machine—if for no other reason than that within a very brief time the country's population would reach untenable proportions. The modern child needs to know that contraception can give him control over the size of his future family, and that this control is necessary for the sake of social order.

Fertility is Not Enough

Sex education regarding contraception is more difficult in industrial societies in another way: in primitive societies, if a man is fertile, he is sexually successful. Now, fertility is not enough, because as a rule the couple will want only two children. With contraception, the purpose of sexual intercourse is demonstrably one of pure pleasure and love, and the man must consider his lover's pleasure, must learn sexual skill. Plentiful evidence showing that women have, if anything, a greater capacity for orgasm than men feeds this obligation. Many men, with either puritan or domineering attitudes towards women, find this difficult to face: for them, a wife who rejoices in sexual intercourse, and experiences orgasm, is not entirely desirable. Some women, with either puritan or submissive attitudes towards men, feel the same way. Contraception, for some, has destroyed the "moral" reason for the sensual act.

Western society has inhibited sensuality—touching each other is largely forbidden in almost every social situation, except in very small children. Margaret Mead refers to the "lack of skin sensuousness of Americans" and attributes to this the great emphasis on looks and appearance in American love and love-making. This visual emphasis multiplies the difficulties resulting from the way we conceal our bodies. We hide erogenous areas,

A relaxed attitude to nakedness and sexuality is an important part of informal sex education.

forbid touching, deny sensuality, and yet expose children to extraordinary gigantic, technological versions of the female body—an endlessly repeated breast-and-thigh diet of visual erotica on television screens, in advertising, and in sexual fantasy films—most of them recreating "primitive" male and female stereotypes.

Redress the Balance

It seems that we have contrived a peculiarly difficult society which combines a prohibition of sensuous contact between most people with a life-long visual stimulus of sexual desires. It may be that we need to adjust the balance, to reduce belief in the importance of sexual achievement and relearn sensuous contact between people in normal everyday social situations.

Writing on psychosexual development, William Simon and John H. Gagnon suggest that the power of

sexuality may have been promoted and overemphasized by man himself for various social reasons. "It is possible that, given the historical nature of human societies, we are victim to the needs of earlier social orders." For earlier societies, it may not have been a matter of severely *constraining* a powerful sexual impulse in order to maintain social stability; rather, it may have been a need to *invent* an importance for sexuality—not only to ensure high levels of reproductive activity, but also to provide a "socially available reward." And this reward could be used to achieve social order in a variety of ways. "A part of the legacy of Freud is that we have all become relatively adept at seeking out the sexual ingredient in many forms of nonsexual behavior."

We do not know for certain what our "sexual nature" is. Every society strongly directs its members and educates its young to a particular

If you don't tell them they'll find out about sex somehow. Many of the pitfalls of teenage sex could be avoided if parents could only talk frankly to their children about sex.

sexual nature, which serves that society's social order. Because our society is so diverse, it does not promote one set of sexual values and accords more importance to the individual, and to his development, than primitive societies have done.

Today's child has a great variety of life-styles open to him, and a great many confusing choices to make. On one hand, we protect him from contact of any kind with real bodies, real sexual relationships, and at the same time feed him with highly colored photographic fantasy. Compared with the sexual training of a primitive child, the sex education of a child in modern industrialized society is complicated and contradictory.

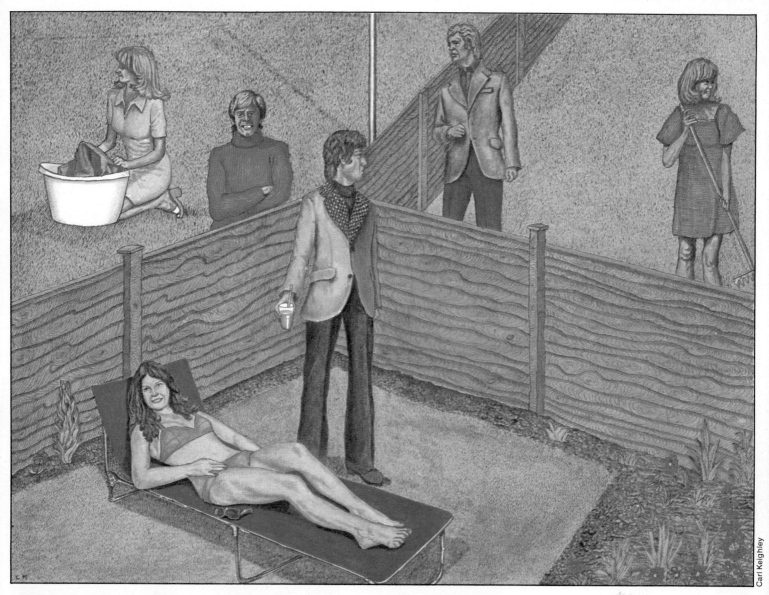

Carl Keighley

Pastures new

The other man's grass is always greener—and his wife is usually sexier too.

The desire to explore is part of man's nature; it is this—along with his ability to think, reason, conceptualize and feel emotion—that distinguishes him from the rest of the animal kingdom. The lion, for instance, contrary to old beliefs, has no desire to stray off his territory provided he has a mate and sufficient food for his family.

Competitive Spirit

Man, on the other hand, continues to seek new pastures. If this were not so, entire populations would have remained isolated, ignorant of the existence of others; war would have been a rarity, and so would trade; and the entire structure of our civilization would have been different. As it is, in spite of our "nesting," consolidating

instincts, we still continue to look ahead, or over our shoulders, where the grass, we are certain, *is* greener.

Though we may have beautiful homes ourselves, someone always seems to have a better one. Though we have delightful, intelligent children, the woman down the street seems to be the mother of an angelic genius. And though our own husband, wife, or lover suits us fine, there is often the lingering suspicion that somewhere there exists one who would make us even happier. As long as the thought remains a passing one, there is little harm in it, but when we find ourselves obsessed by comparisons the situation becomes dangerous.

Literature and the media are, to a large extent, responsible for our wist-

fulness and bent for comparison. Most small children are fed on a literary diet which includes some fairy tales, be they the classics like "Cinderella" or modern versions on the same theme—the cousin who married a millionaire, the boy down the street who became a boxing champion, the girl your mother was at school with who is now a famous movie star. To want to be like these heroes is natural enough, but it is a stage we should grow out of, certainly by the time we are adults—and most of us do.

But the media do not help, particularly commercial advertising. We may for instance be quite happy with our looks, homes, life-style—but the advertisers work hard at creating a certain discontent, a desire to improve ourselves and our way of life. After all, if we accepted our lot without question much of the merchandise on the market now, especially so-called "luxury" goods, would not sell.

Nevertheless the majority of people keep some sense of proportion, and though they may dream of being the one girl singled out to accompany the virile, handsome pipe-smoking play-boy, or the man chosen for the way his hair shines and the irresistible smell of his after-shave, they do not translate idle daydreams into genuine striving. As always, however, there are a few men and women who constantly seek something better.

Unable to Keep Up

People in any form of show business are often heard to blame the failure of relationships on their sudden success, and it is easy to see why. Success *is* exhilarating, and when your fans prove how desirable you are it is understandable that you are tempted to believe their exalted opinion of you. The man who marries when he is an office clerk or delivery boy, and later metamorphoses into a pop star may feel it unfair that he should be saddled with one woman, when thousands—often prettier or younger—are clamoring for his attention. The show-biz marriage that fails because one partner can not keep up with the other's rise to fame is common.

One young actor who has achieved considerable acclaim explained how easily the rift developed. "When I first became 'noticed' I was living with a super bird. We were actually thinking of getting married. Then it all started to happen—reviews, film offers—everyone seemed to want to know me. Susie was a quiet girl, but she was delighted with what promised to be the start of some kind of fame. I suppose I just took her for granted. To begin with she always came to parties and things with me, never pushed herself forward as some girls would, knowing their man was in the limelight. Of course I was flattered by all the attention I got, and I certainly fell for some of the girls I met. They were a breed I had only ever read about before in flashy magazines—rich, pretty and downright brazen.

"The inevitable happened: I started staying out later and later, eating in

Another time, another place, another body, another face: if only she could escape from all this or emerge from those endless beauty treatments a new woman, her sex life would be much better.

Coty (UK) Ltd

Mark Edwards

2188

expensive restaurants, going to all the 'in' places, and Susie was with me less and less. You know, she never made a fuss, never blamed me. I did actually sleep around quite a bit, too — the first time I felt enormously guilty, but it got easier and I told myself it was all right, that Susie and I weren't married after all. Then I came home to our apartment—we had moved to a terrific one by then—after a two-day fling and found Susie gone. She left a note saying she still loved me and always would, but she knew she was a stone around my neck now and she didn't want to tie me down. It shows how arrogant I had become when I tell you I even felt a little annoyed that she should leave.

You Can't Turn Back the Pages

"It's easy to be wise now and see how stupid I was, but at the time I was very young and very bigheaded. I never found another girl like Susie. The ones I mixed with were like me— out for what they could get, always on the make. When all the fuss about me being the 'new' man died down, they didn't want to know me anymore. By this time, of course, I was used to being flattered, used to good living. I've had more 'success' since then, and I've lived with four different birds, but they never last.

"About six months ago I had this awful moment of truth when I knew, without being nostalgic, that Susie was the best thing that ever happened to me and that I would never find anyone better. I tried to trace her then. She had gone to Australia months before and I know I will never find her now, and I guess I don't deserve to. I might know she was my 'ideal', but though I'm older and you could say wiser, I'm still a selfish bastard and if she ever did reappear I would still behave in the way I did."

A well-known radio personality, twenty years older than this young actor, reinforced the view that once the change of life-style has taken place, it is almost impossible to go back to a previous one. "I have been married three times. I don't think I'm either foolish or unpleasant, but like many people in television and radio— those who have made it I mean—I find it hard to feel the property of just one person. It may sound a cliché, but I belong far more to my public be-cause, like it or not, I am 'known' to thousands; they are my job, and because the job is exacting, they are my life as well. Each of my wives has been a really nice person—it's me that's to blame."

Whether we identify with it or not, it is not difficult to appreciate that such a man or woman (or, in fact, any cele-brity) is more prone to indulge in "greener grass" speculation. But it also happens to people suffering from no such pressures. A psychiatrist ex-plained that in many cases it has to do with a person's inability to deal with the reality of any given situation.

"Some of us, thank goodness only relatively few, are totally unable to live in the present, to recognize a situation for what it is. It is, of course, perfectly normal and healthy to em-ploy fantasy from time to time. To cry for the moon occasionally is some-thing we all do, but if we truly believe we can get it, there is something amiss with our psychological make-up. It would be facile to say that all men and women who have been married more than twice are guilty of infantile, or unreasoning attitudes to life and what a partnership implies, but I have cer-tainly seen a number of people who fit that description.

"One woman in particular I remem-ber. She was referred to me because she was obsessed with the desire to have plastic surgery. She wanted a face-lift, mammoplasty (surgery on the breasts), and her nose reshaped. In fact she was a good-looking woman of 42 with a body that any other woman of her age would have been glad to possess. She was in her third marriage and she thought it was in danger. Her sole reason for believing this was some inkling that her hus-band might prefer younger girls, and if she could have her appearance fixed she felt she would be able to compete.

Over The Hill

"Subsequent talks revealed that she had a history of wanting something better than what she had at the time: men, jobs, home, looks. She truly believed that the grass was greener over the hill, even though an observer would have said that her own couldn't be better. She had been an over-indulged child with wealthy parents who refused her nothing. In addition, her father had worshiped her and thought no man good enough for his only daughter. And her mother had constantly told her that there was nothing in this life you couldn't get if you wanted it badly enough.

"Another girl in a similar situation might have reacted in quite a different way, but she had taken her parents' assessment of her unquestioningly. So now approaching middle age, with two broken marriages behind her and a history of disappointments, she was

looking for another magical solution, still believing that change was the way to improvement.

"Unfortunately, though she was in many ways an intelligent woman, I was unable to guide her to a new assessment of herself, and she left my office in a huff one day, telling me I didn't understand her, and proving my point conclusively by saying she was going to another psychiatrist whom a friend had told her 'would work wonders'.

"She may be an extreme case, but in not being able to face up to her situation she has quite a few com-panions. Many of us run away from reality, and the ways we escape differ enormously. But believing it is our circumstances that are at fault and not ourselves is a fairly common condition, though it becomes serious when it is an unshakeable belief."

Keeping Up with the Joneses

Many of us have to suffer compari-son, sometimes unfavorable, from time to time. The housebound wife with limited funds, two or three chil-dren, and a husband who spends five days a week away from home is bound to wonder whether, given a wealthier husband, she might not still be as glamorous as the models she looks at in her weekly magazine. And her hus-band could be forgiven for occasion-ally wishing that he had a female com-panion as cool and sophisticated as his boss's personal assistant. But it is an immature man or woman who does not realize that even with more money to spend, there would still be grass that looked greener somewhere else.

One young wife almost lost her hus-band because he was prey to this kind of longing all the time. "No matter how pretty I made myself, or how good the meal I had prepared for our friends, he always managed to sug-gest that some other woman would have done better. He really was a classic case of someone trying to keep up with the Joneses. One woman in particular he seemed to admire above everyone else. She was married to one of his colleagues—always looked im-maculate, kept a beautiful home, and seemed unable to do any wrong, at least in my husband's eyes. There were times when I could have torn her hair out, though she was always per-fectly charming to me.

"At first I tried to keep up, to always be as good as her, but then after awhile my resentment took hold of me and I began to let everything go—my looks, the house, even the children suffered from lack of attention. If he had upped and left me at this point, an outside observer would have said he had every reason to. My mother put me on the right track again though, thank goodness. She could see what I was doing and she sympathized but told me I was doing it all wrong, and *would* lose him if I carried on in this way. She helped me get the house and the children back into shape again and insisted I buy some new clothes, get my hair done and generally pretty myself up. Then she enlisted the help of one of her younger friends. He started paying a lot of attention to me—at dinner parties he would not take his eyes off me, and kept telling my husband what a lucky dog he was to have a wife like me. Then I started to be out sometimes when my husband expected me to be home and would rush in looking flustered, but happy.

Constant Comparison

"It could all have gone hideously wrong, as such games can, but thankfully the ploy worked. My husband became quite violently jealous and finally insisted we talk about my 'affair'. I didn't actually deny that I was very flattered by all the attention I was getting, but implied it hadn't *yet* gone too far. I told him the truth then about the fact that I was fed up with constant comparison and had decided that I too was due for some admira-

tion. I think he was pretty chastened by the whole thing. Anyway, he stopped raving about his friend's wife. For awhile we cut down on entertaining, even though we both enjoyed having people to dinner or to play cards, and when we started being sociable I did see a difference in his behavior.

"Once or twice he would be on the point of suggesting that some other woman was superb, but he usually stopped before his praise got out of hand; we even laughed together as he was doing it. Part of his trouble is that he does have very high standards in everything. His parents brought him up to believe that your best is never good enough, and I think they are largely to blame for his constant striving towards perfection. I think we have our marriage pretty steady again now, but we would have failed if I hadn't worked very hard to make him see that the grass just isn't greener next door."

Sadly, however, it sometimes is. If a relationship is really threatened because one or both partners are immutably dissatisfied with the situation, then inevitably another man or woman may seem, and actually be, far more attractive. If love and physical attraction are dead, or irreversibly on the wane, then longing for someone else, be he real or imaginary, becomes part of the cause of the final breakup. One 30-year-old woman—whose marriage

had been "dead" two years before she finally made a move—put it like this: "At first you think it only might be greener over there but after awhile you *know* it is. Mine was the typical case of the out-of-love wife who transfers all her longings and aspirations onto one particular man. In my case he was totally unsuitable, as everyone except me could see. But he served a useful purpose in helping me to finally quit an outworn marriage. He was a schoolteacher and married to someone else—unhappily I thought, but only because I wanted it to be. He was tall, thickset, and quiet with huge brown eyes and a habit of staring at people in a way that made your stomach turn over. What I took to be veiled lust was in fact pure cogitation, but then I wanted to see love there. I bored everyone rigid with my infatuation, mostly because I endowed him with such godlike qualities.

A Shrewd Move

"I left my husband and moved so that I could see him every day going to and from school. I think, looking back, that he did genuinely like me, maybe desired me a little even, but he certainly wasn't in love with me, as he finally explained in a way that even I could understand. It took me a year to get over the pain of not being able to live with him in the paradise I had built up in my mind, but one day I realized that I still had a lot of life to look forward to and was only wasting time wishing I could be with him. I am married again now, and happily, but I would never knock the person who tells you that they yearn to be somewhere else, or with someone else, if they truly mean it. It was only by imagining that the grass *was* greener that I managed to get out of a relationship that was as dead as straw."

A psychiatrist would probably say that this woman did know the difference between dreaming and reality, that her longing for something better than she had was healthy because what she had was not good enough. But it is only by knowing how to differentiate between a pipe dream—an escape into fantasy that happens because you cannot deal with the present reality—and a true need to improve your lot that you can find out whether the grass is really greener over there, or whether it just appears so because your eyes are out of focus.

Keystone

The main attraction of the pop star is his unattainability. Most fans would be struck dumb if they met their idol, face to face.

ENCYCLOPEDIA OF HUMAN BEHAVIOR

ORNITHOPHOBIA
An abnormal fear of birds.

Zip Art

Zip Art

ORTHOGENESIS
The theory that evolution is proceeding in a definite direction, in other words that life is evolving with a purpose.

OSCILLOSCOPE
A device used for amplifying and measuring electrical energy, used extensively in physiology. Electrical signals from the nervous system are projected onto a cathode-ray tube something like a TV set.

OSMOSIS
The process by which substances are absorbed through a membrane, as when food passes through the stomach lining.

OTOLITHS
Minute deposits of calcium in the inner ear which react to movement of the head and help in the maintenance of balance.

OTOLOGY
The study of the anatomy, function, and diseases of the ear.

OUIJA BOARD
A device which fits under the hand and moves freely on a flat surface, used by spiritualist mediums to spell out messages allegedly coming from the spirit world. Messages achieved by this and similar devices are almost always caused through partly unconscious interference from the operator.

OVARY
The organ inside the female which produces the egg and the female sex hormones.

OVERCOMPENSATION
Excessive effort, activity or other behavior which is a conscious or unconscious attempt by the individual to mask or make up for a deficiency within himself.

OVERDETERMINED
Refers to something which is caused by numerous, and possibly too many, factors. Dreams often fall into this category, which may be why they are often so difficult to interpret.

PACING
Controlling or directing the speed at which a task is learned or performed.

PACINI CORPUSCLE
A tiny, unusually shaped nerve cell which is believed to be sensitive to pressure stimulation.

PAIN
An unpleasant sensation of varying degrees of intensity, generally considered to be the opposite of pleasure. No totally satisfactory theory of pain has been developed. At one time it was thought that there were special cells in the skin and other parts of the body which dispatched pain signals when they were stimulated. Another theory postulated that pain was felt when any nerve cell was over-stimulated. It was also once believed that pain would occur whenever a nerve cell was damaged. None of these hypotheses seem to measure up to the facts, and the most recent view is that pain is a kind of amplification of nervous impulses, controlled by some center in the brain.

PAIN SPOT
A point on the skin particularly sensitive to pain.

PALEOMNESIS
Memory for events which took place in the early part of one's life.

PALEOPSYCHOLOGY
The study of psychological processes which were present in our ancestors and which may still exist in modern man even if they are no longer appropriate.

PALILALIA
The constant repetition of particular words or meaningless phrases. It is often associated with serious brain disorders.

PALINLEXIA
Reading backwards, such as "step" for "pets." It is more commonly found in children.

PALLIUM
An obsolete term for the *cerebral cortex,* the densely-packed layer of nerve cells on the outer part of the brain.

PALMAR REFLEX
The instinctive grasping response of a newborn baby.

PALMISTRY
An attempt to read the future or tell someone's character from the lines on his hands. It has never been shown to have any scientific validity.

PALPABLE
Touchable; has also come to mean directly observable.

PALPITATION
An extremely rapid beating of the heart, generally caused by anxiety.

PALSY
Paralysis of the limbs accompanied by a characteristic shaking of the hands.

PANCREAS
A large gland near the stomach secreting gastric juices and hormones.

PANIC
An overwhelming feeling of helplessness and fear which may lead to reckless or dangerous action. It is often associated with phobias.

PANPSYCHISM
The belief that mind or spirit is universal and the only reality.

PANSEXUALISM
The belief that the sexual drive is the basis of all behavior, motives and activity. Freud is often, quite incorrectly, assumed to have supported this theory.

PANTHEISM
The belief that God is everywhere and exists in all natural objects.

PAPILLAE
Tiny protuberances on body organs, often containing sensory nerves.

PARA-
A prefix which generally means "alongside, outside or beyond."

PARABIOSIS
Temporary loss of function in a nerve.

PARACUSIA
The apparent ability of slightly deaf people to be particularly good at picking out speech from a background of noise or chatter.

PARADOX
A statement which contradicts itself.

PARADOXICAL COLD
The sensation of coldness which can be felt when a hot object touches certain areas of the skin.

PARADOXICAL SLEEP
A phase of sleep in which the animal or human shows all the signs of being deeply asleep, although there is still considerable electrical activity of the brain. Paradoxical sleep is often accompanied by rapid eye movements (REMs), which in humans are associated with dreaming.

PARAGEUSIA
A hallucination of taste.

PARAGRAPHIA
A tendency to include incorrect or nonsense words in speech or writing. This is a common symptom of brain disorder.

PARAHYPNOSIS
The vague sleeplike state associated with the so-called hypnotic trance. The electrical activity of the brain in this state is indistinguishable from that of wakefulness.

PARALLAX
The apparent movement of two objects at different distances from the eyes when the head is moved from side to side. The nearer object seems to move in the direction opposite to the head movement.

PARALOGICAL THINKING
Fallacious thinking or argument in which the individual is unaware of the inconsistencies.

PARALYSIS
Loss of function in a muscle or muscles. It is most commonly due to disease or damage in the motor areas of the brain or spinal cord and is rarely due to muscle damage itself.

PARAMNESIA
A false memory of some kind, including the sensation known as *déjà vu*.

PARAMECIUM
A minute single-celled organism which some psychologists have claimed is capable of showing the most rudimentary form of learning.

PARANOIA
A severe mental disorder or psychosis in which the most characteristic symptom is a delusion or set of delusions. The patient may believe that he is famous, powerful, or divine or, perhaps more commonly, he may feel that overwhelming forces in the world are plotting to destroy him.

PARANOID PERSONALITY
Someone who, while not actually psychotic and requiring hospital treatment, tends to suffer from delusions of grandeur or extreme suspicion and oversensitivity.

PARANORMAL
Refers to anything which cannot be accounted for by the standard or established scientific laws.

PARAPHILIA
Any kind of sexual perversion or severe disruption of normal sexual behavior.

PARAPHRENIA
An obsolete term for *paranoia*.

PARAPLEGIA
Paralysis of the legs, often caused by damage to the spinal cord, but also sometimes related to emotional problems.

PARAPRAXIS
The technical term for slips of the tongue and momentary losses of memory.

PARAPSYCHOLOGY
Literally "on the edge of psychology," but technically the scientific investigation of paranormal phenomena and alleged powers of the mind, such as telepathy, precognition, and psychokinesis (the ability of the mind to move objects at a distance). The scientific study of such phenomena began in England in the nineteenth century when it was known as *psychical research* and concentrated on spirit mediumship, the investigation of ghosts and other dramatic happenings. In the 1920s the world's first officially sanctioned university department in parapsychology was founded in Duke University in North Carolina under Dr. J. B. Rhine. For over thirty years, until it was formally closed with Rhine's retirement in 1964, the department supported an active program of research and in many scientific papers claimed clear-cut evidence for the existence of various extrasensory powers in man. Despite these claims, the topic has made only limited headway among other scientists,

particularly psychologists. Recent exaggerated claims that the U.S.S.R. was making a big investment in para-psychology are no longer taken seriously by Western scientists. In the view of most authorities the scientific investigation of ESP is unlikely to make much headway until telepathy experiments can be repeated satisfactorily by skeptical researchers.

PARASEXUALITY
Sexual deviations or perversions.

PARASYMPATHETIC NERVOUS SYSTEM
The part of the *autonomic nervous system* which concerns itself with controlling digestive and sexual processes.

PARATHYMIA
Showing an emotional response which is opposite to the appropriate one—for example, laughing at a tragic situation. It is a common schizophrenic symptom.

Zip Art

PARATHYROIDS
Four tiny glands in the neck close to the thyroid glands.

PARENT IMAGE
A fantasy figure which is used as a substitute for a parent.

PARESIS
A psychotic condition caused by syphilis, which leads to a steadily progressing paralysis. Otherwise known as GPI *(general paralysis of the insane)*, once among the most common forms of insanity.

PARIETAL BRAIN
The part of the brain at the top and center of the skull. The parietal cortex handles information connected with bodily sensations such as touch and balance.

PARKINSON'S DISEASE
A disorder of the nervous system, almost entirely a feature of old age, of which the characteristic symptom is an uncontrolled trembling of the limbs and head. The disease is progressive and slow in onset.

PAROREXIA
An abnormal desire to eat strange or peculiar foods.

PAROSMIA
A disorder of the sense of smell.

PAROTID GLAND
The gland situated at the top of the jawbone which secretes saliva.

PAROXYSM
A severe convulsion of a muscle. It also sometimes denotes a violent, emotional state.

PARTHENOGENESIS
"Virgin birth": the development of a living being from an unfertilized egg. It occurs in certain simple animals such as worms.

PARTIAL REINFORCEMENT
Rewarding or reinforcing only *some* correct responses in a training situation. For instance, if a rat is being taught to press a lever in order to obtain a pellet of food, partial reinforcement would mean that the pellet was delivered only after certain bar presses, and not after every one. It is something of a surprise to learning theorists that partial reinforcement is often more effective than regular reinforcement in establishing a habit.

PART OBJECT
A psychoanalytic term which refers to some part of an individual which becomes the focal point for love instead of the whole person. Hair color, breast size or shape, or even intellectual qualities are possible examples.

PARTURITION
The act of giving birth.

PASSION
An emotional state which momentarily goes beyond conscious control.

PASSIVE
Relates to behavior or attitudes which are determined almost exclusively by outside forces.

PASSIVISM
A personality type which tends to be extremely submissive. It refers particularly to sexual submissiveness in males.

PASTORAL PSYCHIATRY
An approach to psychotherapy in which a definite religious element is incorporated as an aid to treatment. The technique is fairly widely used in the United States by ministers of religion specially trained in psychiatric methods.

PATELLAR REFLEX
A completely automatic muscle jerk in response to a sharp tap on the kneecap. The reflex vanishes in certain nervous disorders.

PATERNALISM
The tendency to adopt a fatherly attitude and treat other people like children.

PATHIC
Anything relating to a disease.

PATHOGEN
A microorganism which can cause disease or infection.

PATHOLOGICAL
Refers to an abnormality, particularly when caused by a disease.

PATHOLOGICAL LIAR
Someone who, while not recognizably insane, nevertheless lies without clear motive and in a way which is easily detected.

PATHOS
Extreme suffering or unhappiness of any kind.

PATRIARCHY
A society ruled by males. A patrilineal society is one in which descent is through the male line—that is, children are named after their fathers.

PATTERN
A collection of objects or markings which appear to the brain to form a recognizable and memorable unit.

PAVLOV, IVAN PETROVICH (1849-1936)
The outstanding Russian physiologist who discovered the conditioned reflex and made a gallant attempt at explaining all cerebral and psychological processes in terms of it. In so-called Pavlovian conditioning, an animal is taught to associate a previously meaningless or insignificant stimulus (say, a bell) with the presentation of food, which itself normally brings a behavioral response (salivation). After a given number of presentations the bell alone will bring on salivation, and Pavlov assumed that some kind of connection of nerve cells had been formed so that the first stimulus now automatically triggered the conditioned response. Pavlovian ideas were taken up in the United States by J. B. Watson, and a whole school of psychology known as behaviorism emerged. It still has strong supporters, including B. F. Skinner, but it seems to have little to say about consciousness or mental processes and the present view of psychology is that it can at best be only a partial solution to the problem of the brain and mind. Nevertheless, Pavlov's influence on both psychology and physiology was tremendous, and in 1904 he received a Nobel Prize for his work. The greater part of modern Russian psychology is still based on his theories.

PAVOR NOCTURNUS
The medical name for night terrors, vivid hallucinatory states which often afflict very young children.

PEARSON, KARL (1857-1936)
A British mathematician who was one of the first people to develop statistical methods for use in psychology. In one remarkable experiment, he analyzed a long sequence of the numbers generated by the roulette tables at Monte Carlo and noted that they did not appear to be random. From this he decided that roulette as played at Monte Carlo was not really a game of chance.

PECCATOPHOBIA
An abnormal fear of committing a sin.

PECKING ORDER
A curious behavioral phenomenon noticed among many animals, and in particular among birds such as chickens confined in an enclosed space, in which a kind of order of dominance builds up, with a "boss bird," who may peck or bully all others, at the top and a submissive bird, who is pecked or bullied by everyone, at the bottom. The mechanism by which animals organize themselves in this way is not clearly understood, and it is not a matter of physical strength, for tough, muscular animals may often be relatively low down the pecking order. Furthermore, "superior" animals from one group become totally submissive when transferred into a new group. Many sociologists see in man's love of rank, privilege and status, clear evidence of human acceptance of pecking order rituals.

PEDAGOGY
The study of educational methods, teaching and training.

PEDANTRY
Overconscientious and rigid attitudes to teaching and presenting knowledge.

PEDERASTY
Anal sexual intercourse with a young male person.

PEDIATRICS
The branch of medicine dealing with the illnesses of childhood.

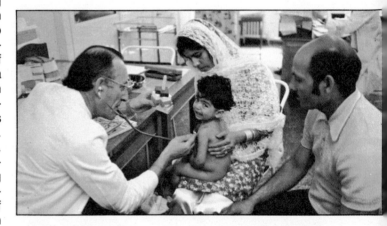

PEDOPHILIA
Sexual interest in young children.

PEER GROUP
A group with whom one normally associates. It refers particularly to a child and its friends.

PEKING MAN
An extinct species of man whose remains were found in China and who was living in caves and making simple tools about a million years ago.

PENIS ENVY
An emotional response experienced, according to Freud, by young girls when they discover that they are sexually different from males. They apparently unconsciously attribute their own lack of a penis to castration and wish to have it returned to them.

PENOLOGY
The science of punishment and deterrence for social and criminal violations.

PENTOTHAL
The trade name for the drug thiopental. A powerful and quick-acting general anesthetic, it is frequently used in preparation for surgery and dental operations. When given in small doses, it induces a drowsy, rambling state with a reduction in inhibition. For this reason it has been called a "truth drug."

PEPTIC ULCER
An ulcer in some part of the stomach.

PERCEIVED SELF
The individual as he sees himself: all the experiences and feelings which are normally grouped under the heading "I."

PERCEPT
Any perceived event.

PERCEPTION
The process or processes in the brain which involve the interpretation of messages coming through the senses. The topic of perception is one of the most important in psychology, though its meaning is frequently misunderstood and it is often confused with sensation. Sensation relates to the reception of information from the outside world at the senses—eyes, ears, and so on—and the transmission of this information onto the brain. Once it reaches the brain, then the perceptual mechanisms come into action, and these involve the recognition of the sensory material and its interpretation by conscious processes. Perception therefore could be looked upon as the conversion of sensory data into meaningful experiences. Needless to say, it relates to all the senses and may even involve integrating material from different senses.

PERCEPTION TIME
The delay between the reception of information in the brain by the senses and its interpretation or recognition.

PERCEPTUAL DEFENSE
The brain process which prevents unpleasant or unacceptable information from passing into consciousness. In the classic experiments demonstrating this effect in the 1950s, college students were shown a mixture of neutral and "taboo" (obscene or highly emotional) words for very brief exposures. At the same time the electrical resistance of their skin (this changes significantly when an individual is emotionally disturbed) was recorded. The results showed that while the subjects claimed not to be able to read or recognize any of the words, their automatic skin response reacted sharply when the taboo words were presented.

PERCEPTUAL FIELD
That proportion of the information brought to the brain by the senses which is within the realm of conscious awareness.

PERCEPTUAL LEARNING
The process by which the brain learns to interpret unfamiliar information. An obvious simple example is learning to read print in a mirror. The important point is that the information actually reaches the brain perfectly, but the mechanisms for recognizing it do not exist and must be acquired.

PERCIPIENT
Someone who perceives something; more particularly in parapsychology someone who receives information by extrasensory means.

PERFECT PITCH
Also known as *absolute pitch*, the unusual ability to identify musical notes by sound—say, middle C—without comparing them to other notes.

PERIMETER
The outside area of something. In psychology, this refers to a device which allows one to plot the visual sensitivity and color perception of the noncentral areas of the retina.

PERIPHERAL VISION
Seeing something with the outer edge of the retina. This vision is almost entirely color-free.

PERISTALSIS
A contraction of the stomach and intestine which progresses from one end of the system to the other in the form of a wave. Its function is to move food and waste matter down the alimentary tract.

PERITONEUM
A tissuelike lining of the inside of the abdomen.

PERMEABILITY
The capacity of something, such as the stomach wall or a cell membrane, to allow substances to pass through it without causing damage to it.

PERMISSIVENESS
In educational psychology, the tendency to allow children to express themselves quite openly and without restraint, provided that the things they do are appropriate to their age and general background. Because in the case of young adults this would include relative freedom of sexual behavior, permissiveness has tended to become associated in popular terms with sexual *promiscuity*.

PERSEVERATION
The desire to finish a task once it has begun or a tendency to "press on regardless" once an action has been initiated. Reluctance to stop for gas on a long drive is a common—and unrewarding—example.

PERSONA
An aspect of personality roughly corresponding to all conscious experience. The word was coined by Jung and is the approximate equivalent of the *ego* in Freudian terms.

PERSONALITY
The sum total of the conscious and unconscious characteristics of an individual which give him an identity, not only to himself but also to other human beings.

PERSONALITY DISORDERS
Disorganizations of personality, also known as *character disorders*, which generally have a long-term rather than a short-term course and frequently have their roots in early childhood maladjustments.

PERSONALITY TYPING
Any one of a number of ways in which psychologists have attempted to classify or group human beings according to their personality. These include introversion and extroversion types, Sheldon's ectomorphs and endomorphs, and some of the psychoanalytic types (anal, oral, aggressive) put forward by Freud.

PERSONAL UNCONSCIOUS
A concept used by Jung to refer to those basic features of the unconscious which can, by using techniques like psychoanalysis and dream interpretation, be brought into consciousness.

PERSONNEL PSYCHOLOGY
One of the earliest approaches to industrial psychology, principally concerned with selecting people for jobs, evaluating their effectiveness at work, and attempting to deal with problems arising as the result of their work.

Time bomb

Half the world guzzles and gorges while the other half suffers and starves.

"Population Year"—1974—was observed by a gathering in Bucharest of demographers, economists, environmentalists, civil servants and social administrators from 135 nations intent on thrashing out the whole matter of the menace of world overpopulation.

It was the first conference of its kind and it held the promise that some kind of international plan might emerge to bring the rapid growth of the world's population under control. After two weeks of discussion the delegates produced a policy document recommending that each nation should by 1985 have set itself a population "target" and decide how to stick to it.

By that year, 1985, the population of the world will be well over 4 billion at its present rate of growth, and the number of people living in some of our already most overcrowded cities will

have doubled. Yet this rather tenuous "target" resolution was the most positive plank of what was to have been the basis of a World Plan of Action. It was obviously difficult to come up with any less nebulous proposal which could command the support of representatives of such diverse nationalities. And perhaps the real achievement of the conference was that the differences between national attitudes to the population explosion are now better understood.

The Future of Mankind

The delegates split into two camps—broadly, the developed and the undeveloped nations—and to begin with could not agree on the nature of the problem. To one group the problem was that there were too many people; to the other, that resources were in-

sufficiently exploited and unevenly distributed. Their answers were on the one side to curb the growth of population, and on the other to concentrate on economic development.

Much of the wrangling was fired by differences of political ideology which always come to the fore whenever nations gather to discuss such a broad concept as "the future of mankind": an international conference, convened in response to a global emergency, provides both an admirable platform and a captive audience for political harangue. It happened at Caracas at the conference on the future exploitation of ocean resources; it happened in Rome at the World Food Conference; and it happened in Bucharest at the World Population Conference. Delegates never lost sight of their own national

interests, even in deference to the needs of the world as a whole.

We can well understand how the wealthier countries might inspire fierce resentment in the poorer over-populated nations in the grips of famine and drought, suffering wide-spread starvation and undernourish-ment. They do not take kindly to pres-sure to curb their numbers when it comes from nations which comprise only a third of the total population but consume 75 percent of the world's resources. If anything, they say their problem is not having *enough* people to develop their economies to bring their standards of living into line with those of the industrialized societies.

Smaller Families

Their preference for economic growth as opposed to population con-trol is born of the fact that it promises quicker results. The various depriva-tions of their peoples call for imme-diate measures, while the objective of reducing the birthrate would take generations to achieve. Reinforcing this view is the disappointing record of government-sponsored family

planning programs. But there is no reason why these two approaches to the problem should be mutually ex-clusive. The conference was told by John D. Rockefeller III, a staunch advocate of family planning, that population control programs only work within a context which makes couples *want* to have small families.

That social context already exists in the highly developed industrialized countries. Here the desire to have fewer children is nurtured, and the provision of family planning services on a large scale makes it possible. The nations where the growth rate has fallen most dramatically are those where these services have been com-bined with rapid rises in agricultural modernization, industrial growth, and urban expansion. The inclination to-wards smaller families is a natural and beneficial spin-off.

Family size is not so much a matter of choice as of social tradition and cultural habit. These are not easily abandoned and can be transformed only gradually. A new social environ-ment, such as comes with industria-lization, can be created long before

people's ideas and attitudes have adjusted to it. The migration of rural families into the cities of a developing country is not going to change their breeding habits significantly. But immigrants from countries with tradi-tions for large families have scaled down their families within one genera-tion to a size acceptable to their host nation.

Planned Parenthood

What is it then about developed so-cieties which favor a reduction in family size? For a start, birth control services are readily available, and contraception does not, by and large, infringe upon traditional or religious taboos. Admittedly the Roman Catho-lic church, with its worldwide influ-ence, has yet to be persuaded—but on the whole family planning is socially and politically reinforced. The "new morality" allows for people to have as many children as they can provide for.

But the actual effectiveness of con-traception as a means of population control has not gone unchallenged. It allows people to have as many child-ren as they want, which is not the

same thing as the number which is socially desirable. By offering only the means for *individual couples* to control fertility, family planning neglects the means for *societies* to do so. But there are fewer parents in developed societies who *plan* large families.

National Preoccupation

The emancipation of women is one reason for this. Better education and increasing employment opportunities offer them a whole new range of positive interests which many consider preferable to a life of regular childbirth and interminable child rearing. And increased leisure time and a higher income make room for entertainment and recreational pursuits. A surfeit of children is time-consuming; it restricts mobility and eats into the family budget.

In materialistic societies, where "keeping up with the Joneses" is the national preoccupation, the pressure is on to maintain a high standard of living. With a fixed family income each extra child contributes to a decline of that standard, as parents find they can afford less and less. Furthermore they feel greater responsibility to-

wards their children, wanting to give them material advantages, education and recreational amenities. The more children there are to a family the more they have to forego luxuries in order to meet needs. In an economy of rising expectations people are being urged to want more for themselves and their children: advertisers remind them of the things they can have, which, in a family stretching its resources to the limit, have to be sacrificed.

Contrast this with the situation of a poorer population in a developing country. Where the activities of children are one of the few pleasures in life, reducing the family size is not so easy when there are no positive or apparent advantages in doing so. This is one, but not the main, reason why population control programs in poorer communities have not been particularly successful.

The primary obstacles to the successful introduction of family planning are ignorance and superstition. This was certainly so in India where the birthrate was reaching a crisis point that called for government action in the early 1950s. Sex education, contraceptives and vasectomy operations

Commuters in Tokyo would rather be crushed to death than late for work.

were made available. Inducements to take advantage of them were offered. Such a comprehensive scheme was easy to administer and, considering what was at stake, relatively cheap.

Financial Reward

But the program met with suspicion. Rumors circulated about the physical ill effects of contraception. It was put about that some methods caused cancer, some locked couples together, and others caused excessive bleeding. The apathy towards the government's initiative was increased by religious scruples and moral doubts. Financial reward for volunteering for contraceptive treatment or sterilization did not produce the expected results. Some women took out their intrauterine devices so that they could collect the bounty for having them fitted once again. The result is that the population in India, now standing at about 600 million, continues to edge upwards, probably reaching 717 million by 1980 and 808 million in the following five years.

The appeal of family planning depends very much on the type of community in which it is being introduced. For instance, in some territories of Kenya the demand for fertility clinics is greater than for birth control clinics. This is partly because the infant mortality rate is still high, but mainly because each birth provides another pair of hands, which can contribute more to the family income than it takes from it. Where this is still the case parents have a strong motive for not cooperating with a population policy.

Primitive agricultural economies still show a net gain from increasing the labor force; industrial economies with their emphasis on mechanization and automation do not. The transition from one to the other produces a surplus of labor and creates a situation in which children become a drain on family resources. The process of industrial development sets off a chain reaction: agricultural modernization reduces the need for a vast rural labor force; industry lures people out of rural areas into cities to earn their living. But technology demands skilled and semiskilled workers rather than unskilled labor, and factories and offices need a higher proportion of administrative and clerical staffs. This increases the demand for education, which many people see as the key to a real population solution. Education takes children out of the labor force so that they no longer contribute to the family income. These children, who might once have been an economic advantage, are now a liability, and the motive for family planning is established.

Mixed Blessing

It is therefore clear that economic development and industrial expansion are not just a means of providing for large numbers but actually a means of reducing them. They also offer a way to exploit resources. Industrial advance therefore seems to be the solution to both the problem of "too many people" and that of "not enough to go around." But this is questionable. It is naive to suppose that resources of food, materials and energy are themselves unlimited and that it is only lack of equipment and know-how which stops them from being sufficiently tapped.

Farm workers in South Africa are paid wages below starvation level.

Technology is a mixed blessing, a treacherous friend. Its purpose is to increase the yield of natural resources and to decrease the workload of man. But in doing so, it uses up more resources than any population, so in order to justify itself it has to increase productivity correspondingly beyond the demands of an expanding population—a vicious circle.

Some thirty years ago the visionary futurologist Buckminster Fuller estimated that the average American had the technological equivalent of 150 slaves working for him. Now these human substitutes number 400, which, in terms of strain on resources, is like having 400 extra mechanical mouths to feed. Unless technology can guarantee to provide itself with a reasonable standard of upkeep, it will have defeated its own purpose.

Technology reaches beyond city boundaries and into the fields: the modernization of agriculture brings with it the fear that artificial stimulants to the land—chemical fertilizers and pesticides—may in the long run inhibit output by interfering with the time-honored cycles of nature. Meanwhile industry—and the cities in which it flourishes—contributes to the deterioration of the environment by disgorging waste and pollutants into the land, into coastal and inland waters and into the atmosphere. In short, unless industry and technology can support themselves, and over-compensate for their own deleterious by-products, they will cease to pay their way, cease to be the servant of the population. And even if they can support themselves, they also have to allow for both the rapid depletion of resources and the greater demands of a rising population.

In poorer nations, with vast populations, labor is the most abundant resource: any reduction of the human workload as a result of technological advance can often make the situation worse. Assuming that technology can find all the food the people need, their most pressing demand is for jobs to produce incomes for their families. What is needed here, according to one economist, Dr. E. F. Schumacher, is not "high technology," but "intermediate technology"—a system which utilizes the excess manpower, keeps pace with the population's technical expertise, and enables people to make the best use of their own natural resources. His message to the developing nations is "think small." This scaling down of operations to fit the real capacity of individual nations will ultimately increase productivity and profit, will avoid wastage, reduce pollution, provide full employment, and raise the standard of living. It will also redress the imbalance between the demands of huge populations and the exploitation of the environment. The accepted answer to the population problem—in economic terms—has shifted in the last few years from "proceed at all costs" to "proceed with caution."

Inalienable Right
There is a wide measure of agreement on this line of thought, but it is not easy to put into practice. The Bucharest conference was at least an indication that we are finally aware of our danger. The experts are unanimously worried about the state of our planet, but few are without hope. However, if their advice and warnings go completely unheeded, we must either expect the worst or be prepared to reduce our consumption and curb our population.

To have children is an inalienable human right. Family size is a personal

matter, so any attempts to reduce numbers by force of law would be regarded as a gross infringement of individual liberty. But even that seems preferable to some of the "natural" ways in which populations throughout history have been periodically cut down: war, famine, disease, and, to a lesser degree, accident, which wipe out whole segments of any population. War and disease are often the result of overpopulation, and while drought, famine, natural disasters such as floods and earthquakes, and

Famine is one of nature's ways of cutting down the world's population.

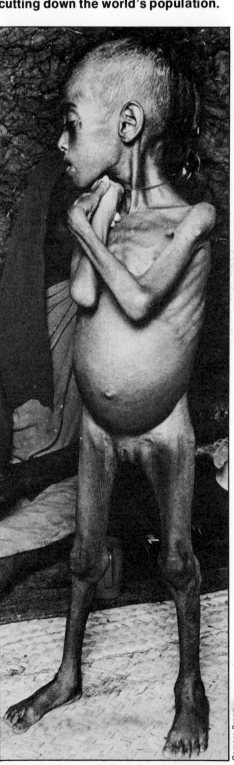
Camera Press

other "acts of God" are not related to population size, they often occur in the most thickly populated areas.

War reduces populations by more than just the "death toll" (which the two world wars of recent history brought to unprecedented levels). As the majority of casualties are young fighting men who, if they survived, would father children, the loss is more significantly felt in the following generation. But postwar periods are often marked by an acceleration of growth as the nation consciously strives to restore its depleted population and regain its strength—often for yet another war. In more belligerent times it was a constant cause of anxiety to mothers that the sons they were producing were more "cannon fodder."

Question Mark
Diseases which assume epidemic proportions—cholera, yellow fever, malaria, smallpox—do not bring death on the same scale as they used to. During the 1930s, malaria was the cause of as many as half the deaths on the island of Ceylon (now Sri Lanka) but, when DDT was introduced in 1946 to bring the disease-carrying mosquitoes under control, the death-rate fell immediately. Since then the deathrate has halved and the birthrate has doubled. But the control of disease depends on medical treatment and supplies, and densely populated areas of poorer countries—the seedbeds of disease and infection—are the very places where medical services are likely to be inadequate.

No one likes to believe that the only solution to the population problem is a disaster of cataclysmic proportions: a global famine, an uncontrollable epidemic, or a nuclear holocaust. But we can be certain that, sooner or later, one or the other will occur if we continue to propagate with such abandon. Equally certain is that such a catastrophe can be avoided if we aim purposefully at a reduction of birthrate and equity in the sharing of resources. What is uncertain, however, is whether we are at all capable of being sensible, unselfish, restrained and global-minded.

A big question mark also hangs over the ability of science, technology, and medicine to come up with new resources and from these to create the "more" needed by future populations —or to make the "less" go farther. So far they have succeeded, but there is no reason to think that they will necessarily do so forever, and it is wisest not to bank on it.

Bob Harvey

Gift of the gab

We rely heavily on language as a means of communicating with our fellows, but we come unstuck when we want to talk to someone who doesn't speak the *same* language.

The Hebrews considered language to be a gift from God. Many other ancient races recognized that the uniqueness of human language separated us from the lower animals, and so decided that their own language had been handed to them a completely fashioned divine ability.

Tower of Babel

The Bible laid down that until God punished the race of man for his presumption in building the Tower of Babel, all men spoke the same God-given language. This was widely supposed to have been Hebrew, and King James IV of Scotland is said to have raised two children in isolation to test the hypothesis. They spoke in "very guid Ebrew," although we may suspect that King James' translators were not the best.

At other times in history, a number of similar attempts have been made: the Egyptian Pharaoh Psammitichos found that the first word spoken by his experimental subjects was the Phrygian word for "bread."

The study of language is very complex, encompassing a number of separate disciplines. Linguistics, psychology, sociology, anthropology, brain structure and function, and the anatomy of the vocal apparatus must all be taken into account in language study. This situation is made even more complex by disputes as to what actually constitutes a language.

Danish, Swedish, and Norwegian can be understood, to a large extent, by natives of any of these countries but are universally considered to be different languages. Local dialects, however, in a country as small as Italy can differ among each other far more than do the Scandinavian languages, yet they are still considered to be dialects of the "Italian" language.

With few exceptions, we find that a language does not suddenly cease to be heard beyond the limit of territory inhabited by its speakers. Language crosses national boundaries and merges imperceptibly into the one spoken by the adjacent peoples. Only in highly developed nations where all the inhabitants are exposed to a consistent radio or television language does a standard language emerge.

This has resulted in the disappearance or suppression of many local dialects, although in Britain, at least, the reverse tendency is now emerging. From the Greek and Roman empires to the modern day, a "rustic" accent was not socially acceptable in urban areas. Now, however, dialects are more acceptably renamed "regional accents," and are becoming a source of local pride.

It is agreed that language is a universal ability. Every race or national grouping has a spoken language (about 10,000 in all, plus an unknown number of extinct languages), and many have evolved a written language.

But how each person goes about learning his language is not completely understood. The group of language psychologists founded by Noam Chomsky has postulated that at certain stages of a child's mental development there exists a sort of "intellectual vacuum" in which part of the brain becomes available for language learning. This so-called rationalist school holds that the child has an innate tendency to produce language, and that experience of the environment has a minimal effect.

On the other hand, the influential behaviorist school of thought, founded by B. F. Skinner, holds that language, together with almost all other human abilities, must be learned as a result of experience of the environment. Experience will then determine all subsequent behavior.

Both groups agree that children need only limited exposure to spoken language during their development; this is sufficient to enable them to comprehend and learn effectively. Which school of thought is correct? As in so many similar disputes, the answer is both or neither.

Coo and Chuckle

There is much evidence to confirm the rationalist view, that the tendency to develop language is built into the brain, but the theory holds only for the acquisition of a spoken language, and many sophisticated races of the past have conducted their civilizations satisfactorily by means of a spoken language only. In these circumstances, a written language first comes into being as a reminder to help in commercial transactions, or as a record for taxation or religious purposes. Methods such as the knotted strings used by ancient South American Indians to convey messages are a simple form of mnemonic, or memory-jogging device. Pictographs, the pictorial symbols used by the ancient Egyptians, convey more complex ideas but still do not approach the true alphabets used today, where every letter conveys a specific sound.

In a human child, the first signs of speech, or attempts at speech, seem to appear spontaneously. By the age of four months, a normal child will be cooing and chuckling. At this age he can sit, supported by a pillow, and his neck muscles support his head firmly enough to allow him to view his environment. Significantly, the child's first vocal attempts are usually directed at its mother.

By six to nine months, the child almost instinctively produces a speech-like babble. He will mimic sounds which interest him and form simple words like "mama" and "dadda." This stage of spontaneous babbling is very important in the development of language and appears to reflect a child's innate ability to produce language, rather than his degree of learning. Children who are born deaf begin to babble at this age, but soon cease. It seems that the sound is produced automatically, but without the feedback normally obtained by

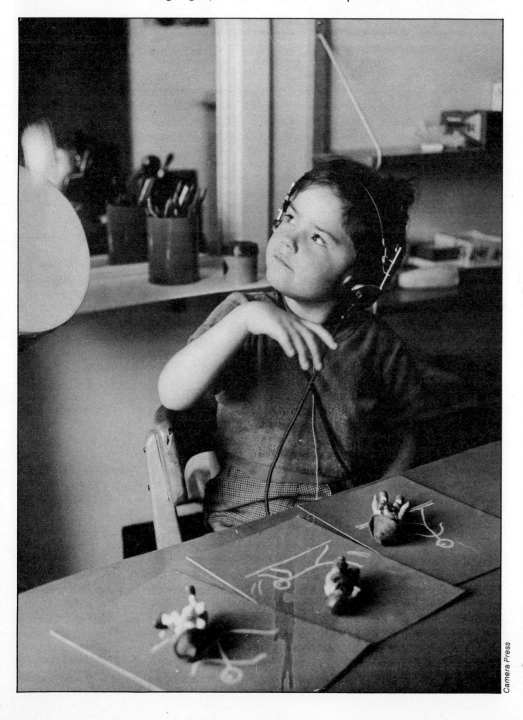

A three-year-old deaf girl is taught to speak at the Voldslokka Clinic in Norway. She is able to hear sounds on electro-acoustic earphones and is taught the meaning of the sounds by pictures and dolls.

Camera Press

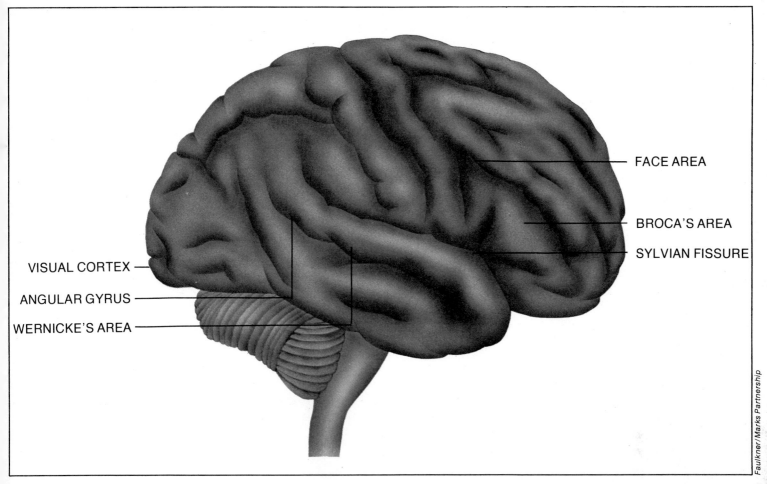

VISUAL CORTEX

ANGULAR GYRUS

WERNICKE'S AREA

FACE AREA

BROCA'S AREA

SYLVIAN FISSURE

Faulkner/Marks Partnership

hearing the responses of the mother or other individuals, the child is unable to refine his babblings into proper speech. This childlike chatter has been likened to a violinist tuning his instrument by comparison with notes produced by other instruments.

Largely Gibberish

One 14-month-old child was unable to make any sound for six months because of surgery on his throat. Immediately after his throat was repaired, he was able to make the general sounds (but not proper words) which were appropriate to his actual age, without ever going through the stage of babbling. His brain had evidently developed past the stage at which babble is generated.

At 12 to 18 months, the child knows a few simple words and can respond to some straightforward commands. By about 21 months, he should know around 200 words and will ask to be told appropriate names by pointing to objects and looking questioningly at an onlooker. He can now put together simple two-word phrases.

The biggest spurt in the child's language-learning ability comes at about two-and-a-half, when sentences are constructed, word order is established, and the child forms his own peculiar rules of grammar. By

three years, most children have a vocabulary of 1,000 words and are beginning to respond to generally accepted grammatical rules, rather than their own constructions.

This sequence holds for all languages, however complex, but the timetable varies enormously between individuals. Some children do not coo until six months. This does not mean that they are mentally retarded; however, since the age at which a child starts to coo and chuckle will coincide with the time he begins to support his head without letting it flop back, his mental development at this age is closely tied to his physical development. His ability to produce "language" does not appear to be closely tied to the amount of practice he has had, although in an impoverished environment, where the child is never able to copy adult speech, his own language is liable to be largely gibberish.

The part played by auditory feedback, or hearing our own voices, is critical, supported by the deaf child who never progresses beyond the babbling stage. Auditory feedback is continuously used to monitor our speech, and whenever this is interrupted, speech disturbances may occur. When an adult who has learned to speak fluently becomes deaf, the

Language areas of the brain are thought to be on the left side. If Broca's area is damaged, speech is affected; if Wernicke's area is damaged, comprehension is lost.

quality of his speech rapidly deteriorates, unless special training is undertaken, because this feedback is no longer received.

If speech is played back through earphones after a momentary delay of about 0.2 seconds, the rate of speaking first slows, then may deteriorate into stuttering. By modifying the input so that the auditory feedback is concentrated in one ear or the other, it can be demonstrated that sounds presented to the right ear have greater effect on speech. The input from the right ear is channeled to the left side of the brain, and this confirms the view which has long been held, that the language center of the human brain is situated in the left hemisphere.

Brain Damage

Until this simple demonstration had been devised, it was possible to study the part played by the brain in language behavior only under unnatural conditions—during brain surgery, by observing the behavior of people with brain damage, or by postmortem examination of the brain. Through

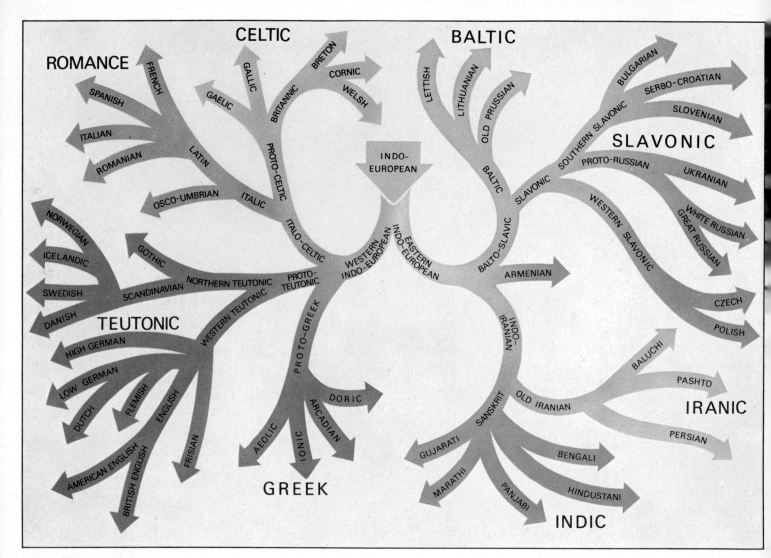

study of the brain under these conditions, as well as study of various types of language disorders, particular areas of the brain associated with the ability to understand and reproduce language have been identified.

One of the commonest language disorders is aphasia, a loss or impairment of the ability to use words which usually results from rupture of blood vessels in the brain. In 1861, Paul Broca, a French scientist, pointed out the correlation between aphasia and damage to a specific part of the left side of the brain (subsequently called Broca's area). This "language" area lies just in *front* of the part of the cortex controlling the muscles of the face, tongue, and palate—those responsible for producing speech.

Verbal Shorthand

In Broca's aphasia, speech becomes very slow and words are abbreviated into a sort of verbal shorthand. Sufferers reply to questions with poorly articulated phrases or often merely with a single word. It might be supposed that aphasia is simply muscular paralysis resulting from damage to this region. But facial muscles, un-

like the language facilities controlled by Broca's area, can be controlled quite effectively by the *other* half of the brain. Damage to this area results in weakness in the facial muscles.

Broca soon discovered that damage to the corresponding "language" area on the right side of the brain did not affect language ability. This is an example of cerebral dominance, where one side of the brain effectively takes over a particular function. Subsequent work has shown that 97 percent of brain-damaged patients with permanent language defects have sustained injury to the left side.

Damage to Broca's area results in slow and incomplete speech, but it was found that damage in other areas could produce quite different types of speech disorder. In 1874, Carl Wernicke found that damage to an area farther towards the back of the brain, on the left side, caused a rapid and sometimes incoherent babble. Wernicke's aphasia results in speech which, superficially, sounds perfectly fluent, with apparently normal grammar and rhythm. But when the content of this speech is examined it is found to be almost meaningless. The

Many of the world's major languages developed over a period of 5,000 years from Indo-European roots.

sufferer talks quite readily about nothing in particular and may drop totally inappropriate words into his conversation ("I drove to work in my table"). Even more disconcertingly, he coins neologisms, inventing a new and meaningless word. Another difference between these two basic types of aphasia is that where damage to Broca's area does not affect comprehension of language, in Wernicke's aphasia the sufferer may no longer understand language.

Roses Are Red

With Wernicke's aphasia, the sufferer can no longer comprehend either spoken or written language and will be unable to reproduce these forms of communication correctly. Conversely, when Broca's area is damaged, the patient retains full understanding but is unable to articulate his messages. Apparently, comprehension of language is accomplished in Wernicke's area, and communication via the vocal apparatus is actually effected by Broca's area. This implies that the two areas are connected, and other forms of aphasia resulting from damage to the connections can be predicted.

Such forms of aphasia do occur, and they cast more light on the function of the brain in producing language. In one study, a woman remained completely comatose for nine years, after suffering from carbon monoxide poisoning. During that time, she never spoke spontaneously but could complete phrases spoken by others. If she heard, "Roses are red," she would repeat the phrase and complete it: "Roses are red, violets are blue, sugar is sweet, and so are you." If a song was played to her, she would eventually sing along with the music, and finally would sing the entire song unaccompanied after having been cued in by the first few bars.

Flash Cards
After her death, brain examination showed a most unusual injury which isolated her speech center from the rest of her cortex. But it did not seem to matter to the type of speech she could produce. Both Broca's and Wernicke's areas remained intact, and these turn out to be "switching stations" of a sort. Apparently, Wernicke's area recognized the chant and Broca's area took it up automatically: she could repeat speech independently of the areas of the brain which initiate original speech. The brain appears to treat poetry and singing—both measured and semiautomatic verbal expression—as something quite separate from actual language, as in all these types of aphasia comprehension of song seems to be normal.

In some patients, damage to other brain areas results in specific forms of aphasia: alexia and agraphia—the loss of ability to read and write—while full comprehension and use of spoken language is retained. They are in the anomalous position of understanding a word when it is spoken to them, but not when it is spelled out. That is, they recognize the word as a complete sound, rather than as a collection of separate symbols and sounds. This child can learn to "read" by identifying individual words visually, in the form of the "flash cards" often used in primary schools. In this form of teaching, the child has no idea of the alphabet, or of the sounds portrayed by each letter, but merely recognizes the word by its visual shape. The individual sounds are learned much later. The loss of the ability to read and write results from a separation of

the visual and auditory language areas, which produces a superficial resemblance to the language learning ability of a young child. Dyslexia, which is a congenital difficulty in reading unrelated to intelligence, may also be associated with a disturbance in the neural pathways connecting the language ability parts of the brain.

As the child's brain develops, the complexity of the connections between nerve cells in the cortex increases, and with it the ability to comprehend more of the hidden structure of language. Children aged five to six usually assume that any person or object named in a sentence is taking an active part in the subject being discussed. For example, when children were presented with sentences like "The wolf is happy to bite," or "The duck is fun to bite," and asked to explain which of the two animals involved was actually biting, they thought both wolf and duck were biting. But around six to six and a half years of age they begin to comprehend the deeper structure of the sentence, but by no means reliably. By age ten the normal child can comprehend all such sentences.

Wind Instrument
The human vocal apparatus is capable of producing only a limited number of sounds, although these can be given distinctive treatment by different national groupings. All vocal sounds are produced in the same way, by liberating air compressed in the lungs. As we exhale, air is forced past the vocal cords in the larynx. These are a pair of flaplike membranes stretched across the larynx, which can be tensed by small muscles. The vocal cords vibrate like the reed in a wind instrument.

Varying the muscles' tension produces higher or lower notes, but producing the characteristic sounds of speech is more complex. The lips, tongue, and the soft palate at the back of the throat can all move to produce a characteristic sound. Interruption of the air streams or a sudden release of pressure can produce "hard" sounds, such as *t, p,* or the "hard" sound of *ch.* When the soft palate diverts air through the nasal passages, the English *m* or *n* is produced. Apart from the characteristic forms of the English language, there are a number of more unusual sounds, such as the guttural *rs* of German, the trilled *rs* found in French, and the clicks found in some African languages, which are almost impossible for a European or American to reproduce.

In describing a language, it may be broken down into simple sounds, or phonemes. These are the minimal recognizable component sounds of a word, but do not necessarily represent a single letter (for example, *th* in English). In a perfect alphabet, each phoneme could be represented by a different letter. The nearest to this ideal situation are the Welsh and the Finnish languages, while the worst is probably the English language.

Detective Work
Local dialects result when the phonemes in a word vary slightly in pronunciation. Then the change is usually consistent through a number of other words. There is an almost imperceptible but continuous change from dialect to a distinct language, as permanent and distinctive pronunciation shifts occur. These can often be traced back to some ancient people who left their linguistic mark on the areas they once inhabited.

The largest language family of all is the Indo-European group from which many of the world's major languages are descended. By complicated detective work, tracing shifts in phonemes and words over long periods of time, linguists can make close guesses at the original Indo-European words which give rise to their modern successors. The word "father" has many related variants: *pita* (Sanskrit, an ancient Indian language), *pater* (Greek and Latin), and *fadar* (Gothic). These four words are all obviously related, but there has been a change from the *p* sound to *f* in languages which are known to be recent. So it is probable that the original word began with *p*, or a sound like it.

Recent languages which have evolved naturally are Pidgin English and Creole French; both are complex mixtures of other languages, superimposed on a very simple framework of native words. They have gradually become established as true languages in their own right, but still have a haunting familiarity to speakers of some of the original tongues. "Mi gat trifela buk" is Melanesian Pidgin English for "I have three books." These languages are a direct outgrowth of colonization in the eighteenth and nineteenth centuries and the resulting need to provide easy communication between the colonizers and colonized. As such, they reflect the basic function of all languages: to communicate with others as naturally and spontaneously as possible within a mutually recognizable system.

Three's a crowd

Some men can't do anything without their buddy, and when the best man goes on the honeymoon too it's time to part the pals. We all need friends, but the guy who's wedded to his cronies is no hot tip in the marriage stakes. If love is to survive, sidekicks must be kicked aside.

Friendship can mean more than love. A marital relationship built around amity and a comfortable sexual tie may easily outlast the white-hot romance that conceals basic incompatibility. And, over the years, companionship can come to seem more valuable than sexual fervor.

Friendships outside the marriage, too, can help to stabilize the relationship and provide support for the couple at moments when they find it difficult to communicate. But there can be a dark side to the coin when friendship interferes with a couple's life together—even drives them apart.

Not Enough

Friendship between a man and a woman can cement them together for the wrong reasons and become a time bomb threatening to blow apart an apparently amicable relationship because the two people are confused about the nature of their desires.

A lonely boy and girl meet and find they enjoy sharing activities, knowing they will have each other's company where before they were solitary. Perhaps love dawns—perhaps it does not. But they drift into marriage because neither can face the future alone.

Life may be very pleasant, but friendship is not love, so the niggly problems of living together and the resulting emotional quarrels that lovers indulge in and overcome may cause resentments to build beneath the tranquil facade. Instead of sharing, the partners may begin to exploit each other as their original friendship crumbles under the strain of day-to-day living. Eventually one, possibly the one who feels most frightened of loneliness, becomes an emotional appendage of the other.

"When I met Georgia," said John, "I didn't know any other women at all —my time went on hobbies which I shared with a few other guys. Georgia was a cousin of one of the guys who'd just moved into town. We found we shared an interest in hypnotism, tarot cards and that kind of thing. We'd spend hours up in my room talking —I even hypnotized Georgia—and eventually we ended up in bed.

"The silly thing was just how little it meant to us—for me it was partially curiosity to see what Georgia's body looked like, and years later she told me that it had been a favor on her part which she thought I'd like. But we got ourselves caught on an escalator of expectations. Because we were making love we felt we had to tell each other we were in love.

"But once we were married, what was the point? We couldn't spend all day reading each other's cards. Neither of us wanted children and we didn't really want the responsibility of buying a house and so on. After a while we virtually made a pact to play at marriage—it was more like sharing an apartment with a friend of the opposite sex. On that level we'd have

Dave Smith

been fine, but the problem, of course, was that we were committed to each other in all sorts of ways—sharing a bed each night, for example. There were times when I resented Georgia intensely because she made it clear she wanted me to stimulate her physically. I sort of liked our being in bed together, being cozy, but I'd just lost interest in the idea of a sexual relationship with her.

"Curiously enough, we were both widening our contacts with others. I was getting to know Georgia's girl-friends, she was spending time with my pals. It's something that should have happened *before* we contemplated marriage. Eventually we decided to separate and our divorce is through now. We're still friendly—but we've both learned that we're looking for more than that."

Friendship can seduce two people into an unsuccessful marriage; when turned outside the relationship it can also bring another possibility of breakdown. Jealousy is the basic danger. Although psychologists know that the partners in a successful marriage are likely to have more friends—both in common and separately—than the partners in a rocky relationship, it is exactly those whose marriage could benefit from an open attitude who fear the threat of friendship.

Escape Clause

Sometimes this jealousy is sexual—a man or woman, unsure of his or her partner's affections, may be disturbed by the idea of a friendship with someone of the opposite sex. Even if the friendship is, in fact, based on non-sexual attraction, it can produce strains in a marriage just because the insecure partner is unable to accept its platonic basis. In this view, all male-female relationships lead to sex, and a married man or woman must give up any idea of a nonsexual friendship. And when a marriage is precariously based, uncertainties in the relationship between husband, wife and friend generate tensions that can themselves lead to awareness of the sexual possibilities outside marriage.

Resentment often builds, however, against the time and emotional effort expended on friends whether of the same or the opposite sex, rather than against a possible sexual involvement. Sometimes this time and effort really is excessive. In other situations the resentment stems more from a false idea of marriage as an all-exclusive partnership; one partner makes such neurotic and compulsive demands for love that they prevent

Marshall Cavendish

the other partner from entering any external relationships. In both cases the marriage comes under strain.

A man or woman may use friendships as an excuse for evading a full commitment to marriage. Drifting off to spend an occasional evening with the boys, giving up a few hours to advise a friend on personal problems, or helping a girlfriend with a tricky piece of dressmaking may be reasonable activities in themselves, but when they begin happening every evening and Saturdays and Sundays too it suggests something is wrong.

Talking over marital problems with a friend may be seen as a betrayal of trust by the marriage partner.

Taking refuge in these undemanding pastimes—and compared to making a marriage work this is what they are, however much effort the person concerned claims to be putting in—reveals the urge to act as though the marriage does not exist as a binding emotional relationship.

The man who appears wedded to his cronies or the woman who spends all her time with her canasta-playing friends may never have seen more in the marriage than a simple and socially acceptable guarantee of intermittent sexual release linked to a meal ticket or housekeeping arrangement. With such an arid relationship it is no wonder one or both partners look for more congenial outlets.

In other cases, escape into outside friendships is an immature reaction to the problems of marriage. A young man or woman may have grown used to a reasonably active social life without realizing how much of it depended on being part of a group of single people. When this apparently ceases with marriage—because conflicting wishes, household tasks, and caring for a baby intervene—there is a gap unfilled by a different kind of mutually enjoyable social life that takes into account the constraints of marriage. Sooner or later arises the temptation to fall back into the only kind of social round so far experienced—and this one-sided plunge exerts a divisive influence on the marriage.

Subtler pressures develop when friends are used as safety valves for the emotional pressures building within a marriage. A full partnership implies that the two people involved try to share and face up to their problems together—doing this may include seeking professional guidance or, at a less formal level, talking individually or together with friends. But some people step away from problems that they might be able to cope with if they faced up to them and substitute talking to friends for real action.

Like the Weather
Complaining about the wife's deficiencies over drinks in a bar or exposing a husband's failing at morning coffee is meaningless and can become embarrassing for all involved. If there are real difficulties, the only person worth talking to is the partner—for matters to improve, both partners probably have to change the way they behave towards each other and this cannot happen if they are not communicating. And revealing problems in the semi-public setting of a group of acquaintances reduces them to the status of an inevitable burden which can be lightened slightly by joking about it. Like the weather, they have to be accepted rather than dealt with.

"That Harry can be a real pain," said Randy. "Half a dozen of us used to meet for a couple of hours in a local bar after work on a Friday evening. You know how it goes—a few beers, chew the fat a little, some work problems maybe that could be sorted out,

since we're all in the same line. It's just a matter of relaxing a little in readiness for the weekend.

"Harry really threw me when he asked me to stay behind after the others left one Friday. He bought another round and we shifted over to a booth. He put his face real close to mine and said, 'What do you do when your wife's frigid?' 'Get yourself another broad,' I replied. 'No, no. I'm being serious. Peggy just isn't interested in making love. I can hammer away for hours and she doesn't react.'

"What can you say? I told him they ought to see a marriage counselor. There's no future in trying to give advice. It's crazy to say, 'Have you tried this, or that?' and anything else is sympathy which may or may not be helpful if it leaves things just like they are. Peggy, the couple of times I met her, was OK—pretty, not neurotic or anything. I'd have gotten in the sack with her myself if it was going to help.

Innocent Party
"We left it at that. But then a couple of months later Tony gave me a call. Harry had converted him—he really thought we ought to be in there laying on broads and lawyers for Harry, marriage manuals or something for Peggy. Tony's Eagle Scout mentality can run wild at times. Harry had been talking to all of us one by one until he found someone who'd go along with his conviction that Peggy was the wrong woman for him.

"That Friday night session quietly stopped happening. Drinking friends just aren't the same as an encounter group or marriage forum. We weren't geared up to handling a real problem —whatever it was that was going wrong in Harry's marriage."

Even if friends and acquaintances do interest themselves in each other's marital difficulties, this can be more dangerous than helpful. Closing ranks around one or other of the partners may reinforce the view that one is to blame for what is going on while the other is an innocent party. The reality is likely to be a confused mixture of sad failures. Advice given in these situations is likely to present a false stereotype of the nature of men and women and of marriage itself. Even people who themselves have satisfying and sincere relationships with others may still talk in a way that suggests all relationships depend on exploitation to some extent.

People are usually flattered to be asked for help and, sometimes, may become heavily involved in a situation which can only worsen as a result

of their meddling. Curiosity may impel an outsider to ask deep, searching questions about sexual and emotional aspects of the relationship, and a person in difficulty may find some cathartic release in revealing the most intimate secrets to a third party. A desire to tamper—linked to a false belief that it is possible to "impose" a happy solution on other people—may lead the confidant to map out a course of action that has little connection with the real needs of the couple.

A simplistic idea put forward by a forceful personality may persuade a vacillating husband or wife to do something he or she will later regret. Worse, suggesting that the "guilty" party requires a good talking to is but a short step from offering to do the job. However well known he is to both partners, an outsider taking on this kind of responsibility is treading on very dangerous ground. He is extremely likely to have a one-sided view of what is going on, and there is no guarantee that the "errant" partner will be interested in his opinions anyway. And most upsetting, as soon as the third party makes an active move, there is no disguising the fact that marital secrets have been bandied about. Whatever their view of the situation, there are few people who would not be upset to find that their partner has been discussing matters that they thought were private.

Advice may not be as disinterested as it sounds, either. A man hoping to have an affair with an abandoned wife may feed a husband's conviction that he should seek a separation. An older woman may compensate for a sense of failure in her own marriage by maliciously advising a young wife to take revenge on the whole of mankind.

Sidekick Syndrome
"Have an affair yourself," was Yvette's suggestion when Carole told her she thought Gerald was seeing another woman. "Men are after what they can get. Why shouldn't you enjoy yourself too? Get yourself proof that Gerald really does have a mistress and you'll have him exactly where you want him—under your thumb. That's the way I dealt with Philip." If Carole's dismayed anger at Gerald's suspected infidelity had persisted, she might well have taken Yvette's distorted advice and followed her into a loveless and unproductive relationship.

Same-sex friendships that drain vitality from a person's relationships can start well before marriage, and establish a pattern that interferes with the search for a partner and later with

the development of a marriage itself. These friendships become two-sided mutual exploitation associations that trap both friends into attitudes that are ultimately destructive. In this "sidekick syndrome" one apparently leads, the other follows, but each is, in a way, dependent on the other and unconsciously begins to assume that manipulating others is natural. The duo face the world together because they are frightened of the responsibilities of initiating a serious relationship as an individual.

The tough-guy adolescent comes to depend on the admiration of his timid sidekick, just as this timid teenager needs the protection of his boastful companion. A beautiful girl uses her plainer friend as an excuse for sliding away from apparently firm sexual commitments she does not feel mature enough to handle, while her girl-friend, who might otherwise remain in the social shadows, basks in the attention of the group of boys attracted not initially by her but by the more beautiful half of the partnership.

The satisfaction of these symbiotic relationships can, however, interfere with the progress towards full emotional maturity. In some cases, the notion that a relationship is exploitative yet dependent is easily transferred to a sexual or marital partnership. Unfortunately, what works for a teenage pair can prove disastrous in the long-term context of marriage. In other cases the sidekick relationship is so strong that it effectively prevents those involved from establishing the kind of relationships that would ultimately lead to marriage.

False Friends

Two buddies who insist on bolstering each other's opinion that women are lesser beings fit only for sexual release after a Saturday night's drinking may drift into a lonely and resentful middle age. Two girls who find themselves giggling together at the local teenagers' crude efforts at seduction may still find themselves ridi-

In the early days, she always took her friend on dates with her, but now she wishes she'd kept this date to herself because it looks as though her "friend" is edging her out.

culing men in general—and men in the throes of sexual desire in particular—when all their other friends are long since married. Even when their behavior is upsetting to each other it serves to put off people who would like to know them as individuals.

Threats from false friendships highlight the importance of establishing real friendships. Where false friends exploit and manipulate, real friends can offer the kind of sympathetic neutrality that helps a marriage survive the bad patches that happen in every relationship. The couple who can treat each other as friends as well as lovers, who have a network of friends in common, and who accept that each will have friends the other knows little about will find their marriage is strengthened.

The facts of life

A growing child is curious about all facets of life, but while adults are happy to answer most questions they are often untruthful or evasive about sex.

Sooner or later every parent finds himself face to face with the problem of sex education and the curiosity his child shows in the manifestations of sexuality in the world around him.

And while most parents try to give satisfactory answers to the endless and difficult "general" questions of their children (such as "Where does the wind come from?") none seem quite so embarrassing to them as queries about sex, reproduction and intimate marital relationships.

There will probably be some parents who object to the suggestion that children have any sexual interest or sex life at all. But to believe this is to shut our eyes and ears to what children do and say as they grow up. Before Sigmund Freud's work, it was commonly believed that children are sexually neutral until their sex glands mature at adolescence. In fact, from early on, youngsters enjoy exposing their bodies and looking at others. There is pleasure in touching and examining themselves and others, and some experience orgasm. The questions about sex that they dart at their harassed parents are likely to be searching ones: "What is that?"— "Why doesn't a girl have a penis?"—

"Why is Daddy's penis bigger than mine?"—"Where does a baby come from?"—"Where does a baby come out?"—"Why can't men have babies?"—"Will I have a baby too?"—"How does a baby get inside the mother?"—"When do you and daddy make babies?"—and countless others. At a later stage, there are other questions which preoccupy teenagers, as shown by the questions asked at sex education meetings: "Should teenagers go steady?"—"Should teenagers neck or pet?"—"How far should I go?"—"What about premarital intercourse?"—"What is birth control?"—"Is it wrong to masturbate?"—"What are venereal diseases?"

Dr. W. B. Pomeroy, author of *Boys and Sex*, says that in the course of interviewing more than 7,000 adults and children, he was impressed by the anguish, unhappiness and disappointment caused by widespread misinformation, misconceptions, myths, fears and inhibitions about sex. The sentiments expressed to him time and time again were, "If only I had been given more information about these things when I was young I wouldn't have made such a mess of my life."

Withholding Information

An important issue raised by the psychologist Derek Wright concerns the nature of the emotions we judge appropriate to sexual arousal. Among the emotions that are currently associated with sex in magazines, films and advertisements are desire for social status and success, aggression and cruelty, self-contempt, fear and guilt.

Wright suggests that if sex is to be fully human and personal, then it ought to be linked as early in life as possible with affection, tenderness and awareness of the feelings of others. He believes that this is the outcome of a warmly affectionate and reasonably permissive upbringing. "Rather than lament the fact that sexual appetite is now being encouraged," he argues, "we might more profitably spend our time trying to ensure that the emotions that are integrated with it are the ones we approve of. To condition sexual arousal to moral feelings of guilt and obligation may destroy the ties with affection as effectively as conditioning it to cruelty or disgust." This is what makes the issues of sexual development, curiosity and sex education so important. Knowledge has usually been thought the best antidote to the forces of ignorance and darkness. Yet it is precisely in the field of sex that knowledge is considered dangerous by those who recommend withholding information from children.

Sex play, masturbation, interest in the how, where and when of childbirth are common and early manifestations; they are to be welcomed as part of normal development and curiosity about the world. Those who deny any sex life to the infant commonly do so because they are conscious only of adult sex experiences and consequently imagine, when it is suggested that the infant or very small child is affected by sex, that it must have a comparable feeling. If the

adult has guilty feelings about sexual arousal and thinks it degrading, then it is not surprising that he should reject with indignation the proposition that the "innocent child" should show an interest in sex.

So much depends on the adult's attitude to sex. For some it is the logical, inevitable conclusion to a feeling of love, reverence and warmth for another human being. The making of love in sexual union, for such people, is the physical manifestation of an emotional bond—a form of bodily conversation in which two people meet and become part of each other in both a psychological and physical sense. If sex is regarded as a thing separate from the rest of the personality of the individual, it may come to represent the sorts of things which the advertisements tell us we need as necessities of life. If this is the way we feel, then the attitudes we inculcate in our children about sex and the examples that are set them will associate sexual arousal with guilt and shame.

In the opinion of many psychologists and educators, sex education is not simply a narrow teaching of the "facts of life" concerning the human sex instinct, reproduction, menstruation and the physical changes of puberty. However excellent the teaching about sex—formal and informal—at home and at school, the most important aspect of sex education, in its broadest aspect, is the parents' example. Through the kind of family life they live, youngsters can learn that love and sex are based on respect for other human beings—a respect they can feel only if they first have it for themselves. Such an atmosphere is likely to foster an individual who is relaxed and happy in his sexual relationships rather than fearful, anxious or aggressive. The sociologist Michael Schofield found in a survey that two-thirds of the boys and a quarter of the girls in his sample had learned nothing about sex from their parents. Half the boys and 14 percent of the girls did not receive any sex education at school. And nearly half the boys and girls felt they should have been told more about sex at school.

Different Backgrounds

The variety in the questions young people ask highlights a fundamental difficulty in sex education—particularly in schools where the children are from different home backgrounds, with differing religious, ethical, and moral training. Some of their questions can be answered "scientifically," as matters of biological information.

Others involve moral and personal values. Should a teacher (or, for that matter, a parent) go further and explain not only the biological elements of sex but also the whole complex of love life to which they are inextricably bound? While books on sex, films, special talks and expert lecturers can be very helpful in the educational process, only the parent who knows the child very well is able to answer the supplementary questions that almost always follow, sometimes much later when the information is digested. Only the parent can fit the biological facts into the system of values.

Dread of Learning

A common question parents ask is, "When should you start sex education?" This question provokes the counterquestion, "Why should sex education be different from other training given to the child?" It would seem that difficulties are sure to arise when sex is treated as something quite apart from normal everyday activities, something to be discussed in hushed tones (if at all). Sex education starts in intangible ways almost at the beginning of a child's life: the parent is providing sex education simply by being there. Psychologists claim that it is not what parents *say* so much as what they *do* that educates the young child in the home. It is at two or three, when the child is talking and is taking an interest in his own body and those of people around him, that he begins to ask specific questions.

The humorist James Thurber says in a piece entitled "What should children tell their parents?" that parents hesitate to discuss things calmly and intelligently with their children for two reasons: either they feel a kind of dread of learning something they don't want to know, or, if they must learn anything at all, they would like to be spared the humiliation of learning it from their offspring. Just what children are capable of grasping depends on the development of their "sex awareness," a vague and dimly felt sensation of what certain facts and actions really mean. Before this stage is reached, educational efforts are wasted: the children are impregnable to sexual instruction from outside.

Here, of course, lies the difficulty of classroom sex education; certain information simply passes the child by if he is not ready to assimilate it. Most experts seem to agree that the right age to inform a child about sexual matters is when he asks questions. Whether he feels able to go to his parents with these questions depends upon the atmosphere surrounding such "intimate" matters, which he "tunes into" in everyday life at home.

Most parents give reasonable and truthful answers to the questions a child asks about the world around him —so why teach him lies and distortions about sex? Whenever the mother betrays confusion or shame over a child's question, she is conveying more to him by the form of her answers (the faltering speech, euphemisms, facetious comments, and circumlocutions) than by the content of what she says. And what she is communicating is that there is something odd and sinister about sex. Sex education, whatever the words used, should be expressed in as simple a manner as possible.

Playing Doctors

When a child asks about intercourse or reproduction, *that* is the time to answer him; but what if the child never asks questions? A marriage, pregnancy or a birth in the family or neighborhood are all quite natural events which can be brought up casually as starting points for a talk. If the child cannot open up, it may well be something in the parents' attitude that hinders his approach. If he discovers that his parents can speak freely, he becomes less fearful of his curiosity and can vent his feelings.

A child is curious by nature. Sex play with other children often takes the form of undressing or exploring a friend's body while playing doctors or mummies and daddies. Sexual interest and behavior in these immature youngsters is intermittent, casual, and in fact rather indifferent. But it is quite common by the age of four and even more so in nursery school. In a survey of heterosexual play in boys it was found that the incidence rises from nearly 5 percent at five years to a third of the boys at eight years. As many as two-thirds had indulged in sex play by the age of thirteen. The rates of sexual activity in girls are lower than in boys but also show an increase with age. Homosexual play—boys playing with boys—also rises in incidence as youngsters get older. It usually takes the form of handling each other's genitals and occurs in 30 percent of 13-year-old boys. The figures for girls are not very different.

The adults who reported their sexual behavior in the Kinsey studies were brought up in a far less sexually permissive atmosphere than exists today. Even the "Victorian" repression of their childhood sexuality was singularly unsuccessful in its aim. Half of the men and women had sexual contacts with their peers before adolescence. It has been argued that the only effect of extreme efforts at suppression is to drive the behavior underground and to permeate it with a sense of shame and an aura of furtive excitement. The repression of sexuality in girls during childhood and adolescence is one of the major factors in adult frigidity.

The direction of the individual's sexual interests (the choice of a sexual role) and his identity as a psychological male or female (gender identity) are very rarely explained by chromosomal or hormonal anomalies. The die is pretty well cast as to whether a person *feels* like boy or girl by about age six. Early life experiences seem to play a part in many cases of homosexual inclination. Poor relationships with parents—particularly the parent of the same sex—are thought to contribute to this, though when we consider how many strongly *heterosexual* individuals have had poor relationships like this, the theory is robbed of most of its value. There remains, nevertheless, strong evidence that early family relationships are in some way involved in this and other deviations, but the precise "hows" and "whys" remain a mystery.

Source of Pleasure

Most children masturbate at one time or another, something that causes parents a great deal of unnecessary concern. Late in the first year of life it is already possible to see the infant's increasing awareness of his own body: he explores his mother's facial features and then turns to explore his own; inevitably he discovers and then fiddles with his own genitals. The psychologists John and Elizabeth Newson found that 36 percent of the mothers of one-year-olds in their research group reported that their children play with their genitals, boys more often than girls. The child becomes vaguely aware of pleasurable sensations when his mother bathes him. His personal discovery comes when he is not so wrapped up in diapers, and it tends to come earlier in boys than in girls—probably because the boy can see his penis. It is quite common for babies to masturbate occasionally, especially at bedtime, though infants who are given playthings and reasonable attention do not focus so intensely on this source of pleasure.

By late infancy genital play seems not only to produce pleasure, it sometimes results in orgasm. Orgasm has been observed in children as young as 5 months, but it usually occurs somewhat later, and, of course, ejaculation does not occur before puberty. Preschool children—between two and five years—show increasing interest in their genitals; according to one investigation, 55 percent of the boys and 16 percent of the girls of this age were found to masturbate. A major function of masturbation (like thumbsucking) at bedtime seems to be to close off contact with the outside world in preparation for sleep. About 80 percent of boys masturbate by their thirteenth year, and at this stage it probably leads to ejaculation and may be accompanied by fantasies.

Stunt Your Growth

A study of parental attitudes to masturbation showed that there is considerable emotional reaction from mothers. Although most modern mothers have heard, read, or know for themselves that masturbation is harmless—that it does not stunt growth, cause insanity, sterility or impotence —they feel anxious when their children masturbate. Fewer than one-fifth of the mothers interviewed felt that a certain amount of playing was to be expected; one-half considered it wrong or harmful. Some said masturbation might not have any bad effects if it happened just once, but they would not like it to happen just the same. However, they did not back up their strong opinions with strong action, since 54 percent of them used very mild correction, or none at all, against masturbation, and only 5 percent used severe pressure.

Most Western cultures train children not to masturbate—a training which almost universally breaks down at adolescence and even before then, particularly among boys. *Elaborate* measures to curb infantile masturbation are thought by most experts to be inappropriate.

Parents' own knowledge of the physical and psychological problems of growing up can help to give them tolerance and compassionate insight into this difficult period of adjustment. Sex education at school can be particularly helpful at this stage because so many teenagers feel too shy to approach their parents about sexual problems and anxieties. Attaining sexual maturity has a profound effect upon an adolescent's image of himself and his status among those of his own age. Immense physical changes happen at puberty with the maturing of the sex glands, accompanied by even more important emotional and

social developments—which have been taking place since childhood.

One writer has spoken of the "tensions and indefinable longings of puberty" aroused by the awakening sex drive—"the mysterious force that drives men and women together in the sex act." The average age of sexual maturity for boys is about two years behind girls, as is their social development; it happens at 14 for most boys, but may not appear until 18 or even later. In both boys and girls the average age has steadily lowered over the last century and precocious sexual maturity is quite frequent. The first ejaculation was found to occur either before the eleventh or after the sixteenth year in 10 percent of boys in the Kinsey survey, which means that, in normal boys, the age at which puberty occurs ranges over five years. The early-maturing boy is more likely to become a leader and to participate widely in school clubs and activities, whereas the late-maturing boy usually suffers from acute feelings of inferiority.

In girls puberty can occur anywhere from 10 to 16½ years. A girl who shows the signs of precocious sexual development may be self-conscious about her body image and the fact of her menstruation. But these are *social* adjustments; premature sexual devel-

"Sugar and spice and all things nice" encounters "frogs and snails and puppy dog's tails" for the first time.

opment seldom means premature sexual outlets of an adult kind. In general, premature puberty leads to an increase in sexual arousal, but psychosexual behavior tends to remain roughly in line with the child's actual age and social experience.

The First Time

The qualities that boys and girls look for in a partner are surprisingly in keeping with what their parents see as desirable in a date and potential mate: mental and physical fitness, dependability, pride in manners and appearance, clean speech and action, a pleasant disposition, a sense of humor, consideration, and "acting your age." Dating can lead to feelings of insecurity, not only for many young people, but also for their parents—who worry particularly about their offspring's sexual feelings.

Given the widespread beliefs about sexual permissiveness in young people, their own attitudes to sex before marriage are somewhat surprising. Michael Schofield's research among 1,873 British teenagers did not show as great a degree of permissiveness as might have been expected. He

estimated that at the age of 18, 34 percent of the boys and 17 percent of the girls were sexually experienced, and that sexual intercourse before 14 or 15 was rare. By 16, only 14 percent of the boys and 5 percent of the girls had had sexual intercourse, their first experience usually with someone who was already experienced. The first partner was often older and, in the case of the girls, was quite often an adult; the partner was usually a friend and, more often than not, intercourse took place in the parental home.

Pressures to Conform

The first experience was often unpremeditated and unplanned, and a majority said they did not enjoy it: shame and fear were common reactions experienced by girls, and disappointment the predominant reaction of boys. Schofield believes these results show that premarital sexual relations are a long way from universal among teenagers, as over two-thirds of the boys and three-quarters of the girls in his sample had never had sexual intercourse. On the other hand, it is equally clear that teenage premarital intercourse is not something to be dismissed as a minority problem confined to a few deviates: it is common enough to be one manifestation of teenage conformity.

Despite the physical urges and social pressures to conform, many manage to resist the temptation of sexual intercourse. There *are* several differences—according to Schofield —between those who do and those who do not have premarital relations.

It is important to remember in connection with the "who, what and when" of guiding youngsters to sexual maturity that there are no absolute rules which can be applied rigidly to all children by all parents! Children, family situations, and the religious and moral aspects of sex—the sexual value system—vary from home to home. This means once again that guidelines can only be suggested. And even these must be interpreted flexibly. There are many "experts" on sex education and books on the subject, but the views they express (and these often differ) are only opinions— even though they may be informed opinions, based on experience of educating many children. Dogmatic statements about right or wrong ways of teaching all children are not possible. The real expert about a particular child is his mother—if she is a woman of reasonable sensitivity—and she knows best how to adapt general principles to her offspring.

ENCYCLOPEDIA OF HUMAN BEHAVIOR

PERVERSION
Any pattern of behavior, particularly sexual, which is prohibited by a law or considered to be offensive to society. The term is a relative one and its interpretation varies from society to society.

PETIT MAL
A relatively minor epileptic fit in which consciousness is probably not lost. Symptoms are confined to strange sensations or a feeling of detachment or uncertainty.

PEYOTE
The hallucinogenic drug produced from a cactus.

PHAGOCYTE
A white blood cell which attacks bacteria and other alien microorganisms within the body.

PHAGOMANIA
An abnormal desire to eat.

PHALLIC CHARACTER
A term drawn from psychoanalysis which refers to an individual unusually preoccupied with sexual prowess and characterized by boastfulness, vanity, and a somewhat aggressive approach to women.

PHALLIC STAGE
The third basic stage in sexual development according to Freud, which follows on the *oral* and *anal*, and should normally be reached by about the fifth year. At this point the child first consciously appreciates the pleasure that can be obtained by stimulation of the genital organs.

PHALLIC SYMBOL
Any long or pointed object, from a pencil to a church steeple, which, according to psychoanalytic theory, is taken as a symbol or a kind of "disguise" for the penis. The phallic symbol is particularly important as a key to dream interpretation.

PHALLUS
The erect penis, the subject of near-religious worship in ancient Greece.

PHANTASM
A striking and apparently real vision of a person which either cannot be witnessed by other people or disappears on closer inspection. Most reports of phantasms are probably hallucinations, but they are occasionally attributed to ghosts or disembodied spirits. No one has successfully photographed a phantasm, so the evidence that they exist only "in the mind's eye" seems strong.

PHANTOM LIMB
A vivid and unpleasantly durable illusion, suffered by patients who have had a leg or arm amputated, that the missing limb is still present. Not only do they sense apparent muscle contractions in the limb, but they can also feel pain, which sometimes persists even when the stump has been given a local anesthetic. Phantom limbs may persist for the whole of the person's natural life.

PHARYNX
The passage which leads from the mouth and nose to the larynx and esophagus.

PHENGOPHOBIA
An abnormal fear of the day or daylight.

PHENOBARBITAL
A barbiturate drug used to relieve anxiety and promote sleep. It is habit-forming.

PHENOMENALISM
A philosophy, advanced notably by Kant, that we can never know reality, only the appearance of it.

PHENOMENOLOGY
The study of mental processes and the way in which the brain interprets and understands sensations from the external world.

PHENOTYPE
The visible appearance of something as opposed to its basic genetic structure.

PHENYLKETONURIA
A once common genetic disorder which produced mentally retarded children. The basis of the retardation was a failure in the body's metabolism of amino acids.

PHI PHENOMENON
An illusion more commonly known as *apparent movement*. It is the basis of most moving electrical advertising signs.

PHILOSOPHY
The study of the nature of existence and knowledge.

PHOBIA
A strong and persistent fear of something which seems to be out of proportion to any real threat of danger to the sufferer, and which no amount of reasoning or common sense can eliminate. No completely satisfactory theory as to how phobias arise has been put forward, but psychoanalysts believe that the phobias are disguises for other fears which the individual is unwilling to admit.

PHOBOPHOBIA
An abnormal fear of being afraid.

PHONATION
The production of speech sounds.

PHONETICS
The study of the sounds of speech.

PHONOPHOBIA
An abnormal fear of sounds, but particularly of hearing your own voice.

PHOSPHENE
A faint illusion of light seen in total darkness if the eye is moved. It is caused by mild stimulation of the retinal cells by the fluid inside the eyeball.

PHOTIC DRIVING
The way in which the electrical rhythms of the brain can be synchronized with light flickering at certain frequencies. The alpha rhythm, recorded from the back of the brain and normally beating at about 10 cycles per second, is particularly susceptible to being induced by this effect. The brain state which accompanies the alpha rhythm is most notably characterized by inattention to external stimuli. Photic driving is sometimes assumed to be responsible for some of the fainting fits brought on by brightly flickering lights.

PHOTISM
Any kind of hallucination of light.

PHOTOPHOBIA
An abnormal fear of light.

PHOTOPIC VISION
Daylight vision. The eye has one set of cells sensitive to bright light and another which comes into action only when illumination is low and deals with dark or nighttime vision.

PHOTOTROPISM
The automatic movement of any living thing towards light.

PHRENOLOGY
A primitive approach to psychology which held that various faculties—memory, strength of mind, or industry—were located in certain parts of the brain and that differences in individual skull shape indicated which faculties were strong.

PHYLOGENESIS
The evolution and development of a living species.

PHYLUM
One of the major units of classification of living things. The phylum of man, for example, is the vertebrates.

PHYSIOGNOMY
The study of facial characteristics in an attempt to determine mental or intellectual qualities.

PHYSIOLOGY
The study of the structure and function of living organisms.

PHYSIOTHERAPY
The approach to medicine which employs physical forms of treatment such as massage, exercise, and cold baths.

PIAGET, JEAN (1896-   )
The Swiss psychologist whose greatest contribution has been the study of the intellectual development of children.

PICTOGRAM
A pictorial representation of an object, idea or word. The earliest forms of writing were pictographic.

PICTURE-COMPLETION TEST
A test used for very young children or the mentally retarded. The subject is shown a simple picture with an important part missing and is asked to "fill in the gap."

PIGMENT
A substance which absorbs light and is present in the sensitive cells in the retina of the eye.

PILOMOTOR RESPONSE
An automatic reaction to fear or cold in which the hairs on the body surface become erect. It is commonly known as "goose pimples."

PILTDOWN MAN
Fossil remains of what was once thought to be a creature halfway between ape and man (the "missing link"), found near the village of Piltdown in England. Given the scientific name Eoanthropus (dawn man), the remains were later found to have been a clever hoax.

PINEAL GLAND
A tiny glandular body in the brain, whose function is not properly understood. It is possibly the evolutionary remnants of a heat-sensitive "third eye," and was believed by the philosopher Descartes to be the point at which mind and body interacted.

PINEL, PHILIPPE (1745-1826)
A French doctor who was the first man to free lunatics from their chains, and is acknowledged as the father of psychiatry.

PITCH
That aspect of sound, generally described as varying from high to low, which is determined by the frequency of sound waves. Humans can perceive pitch in the range from about 20 to 20,000 cycles per second.

PITHECANTHROPUS ERECTUS
An extinct species of apelike man, sometimes called Java man. He was one of the first of our ancestors to have a completely upright posture and so is also known scientifically as Homo erectus.

PITUITARY GLAND
A tiny gland at the base of the brain which produces important hormones which themselves tend to monitor the hormone output of other glands. It has an important function in the control of growth.

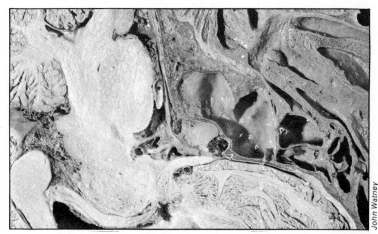
John Watney

Median section of the pituitary gland.

PLACEBO
Something without any medical quality which has no direct effect on the body, but which is given to patients because they believe it to be effective. Placebos are used on many hysterical and neurotic patients who might otherwise become drug-dependent; they are also used as controls in testing the efficiency of genuine drugs.

PLACENTA
The organ by which the fetus is attached to the uterus and through which food and oxygen pass from mother to child.

PLANARIA
A tiny flatworm, important in psychology because of some controversial experiments in which it has featured. Planaria which had been taught a simple problem were killed and portions of their remains injected into other living planaria, who it was then found had acquired some knowledge of the problem taught the original animals. Many scientists dispute the results of the "transfer of training" controversy.

PLANCHETTE
A heart-shaped board on wheels with a pencil attached to it, used supposedly to reveal messages from the spirit world. If you place your hands on the board it will move easily and may sometimes write words or phrases. The material is probably drawn from the unconscious mind, but spiritualists believe that it represents communications from the dead.

PLANTAR REFLEX
The instinctive curling of the toes when the sole of the foot is tickled.

PLASMA
The liquid part of the blood in which the oxygen and nutrients float.

PLASTICITY
The ability to change or, in the case of the nervous system, to adapt to circumstances.

PLATO (427-347 B.C.)
The archetypal Green philosopher who was one of the first men to produce a theory of the soul and emotions.

PLATONIC LOVE
Love which contains no erotic or sexual overtones.

PLAY THERAPY
Allowing inhibited or disturbed children the opportunity to express themselves through play, relieve concealed aggressions, and perhaps even give the therapist some clues about the origins of their disturbance.

PLEASURE CENTER
A relatively small and not precisely defined area of the brain in animals which when stimulated electrically gives a sensation of pleasure. The discovery of this center goes back to the 1950s, when scientists at McGill University in Montreal found that rats with electrodes implanted in a particular part of their brain would, if given the opportunity, endlessly stimulate this area electrically by pressing a lever.

PLEASURE-PAIN PRINCIPLE
The psychoanalytic doctrine which holds that man's two primary goals are the search for pleasure and the avoidance of pain.

PLEXUS
A network of nerves, veins or other channels.

PLURALISM
A belief that reality consists of a large number of totally different elements. It contrasts with *monism* (that the universe is essentially only one thing) and *dualism* (that it consists of two things, mind and matter).

POGGDENDORFF ILLUSION
The apparently jagged appearance of a straight line when it passes "behind" two sets of parallel lines.

POLARIZATION
The process of inducing light waves coming from a number of different sources to become parallel.

POLIOMYELITIS
A disease bringing on muscle paralysis caused by a viral infection of the protective myeline coating of the spinal cord.

POLTERGEIST
A supposedly disembodied spirit of a mischievous nature, causing objects to move and unusual sounds to occur. Poltergeist phenomena tend to be associated with young children and most psychologists believe that the children cause them in a normal way when adults are not looking.

POLYANDRY
A social system where it is considered to be legally and morally reasonable for a woman to have several husbands at the same time.

POLYDACTYLISM
A mutant condition in which the individual has more than five fingers or toes.

POLYGAMY
A social system in which it is legally and morally acceptable to have more than one wife at the same time.

POLYGRAPH
A technical name for the device used by police departments as a lie detector. It measures heart rate, blood pressure and skin resistance.

POLYMORPHISM
Relates to an animal which passes through several stages in its life cycle.

The pupal stage of the magpie moth.

POLYURIA
An abnormal need to urinate.

PORNOGRAPHOMANIA
A compulsive desire to write obscene letters.

PORTEUS MAZES
A series of maze drawings, ranging from very simple to very complex, which can be used as intelligence tests for children and adults from the age of four upwards.

POSITIVE AFTERIMAGE
A brief but definite visual experience of something after the

initial stimulus has been removed. The positive afterimage is the same color and brightness as the original stimulus and needs to be discriminated from the negative afterimage, which has the same size and shape but is less bright and of a different color, and yet persists longer.

POSITIVE FEEDBACK
A spiraling effect which leads an organism or machine to increase its output with increasing input. A vivid example is a cat running on ice, when the more its feet slip the faster it runs.

POSITIVISM
An approach to philosophy which says that knowledge can never go beyond personal experience and that true reality, in cluding all metaphysical questions, can never really be discovered by science.

POSTHYPNOTIC SUGGESTION
A suggestion given to someone in a hypnotic state which they will unconsciously carry out at a later time.

Hypnosis allows a shy girl to throw off her inhibitions.

POSTPARTUM PSYCHOSIS
A severe, though often temporary disturbance of mood and personality which occasionally occurs in mothers after giving birth. Its most common symptom is an unbearable depression, and it is now believed that it is a reaction to the major biochemical changes which take place in the body as the result of pregnancy.

POSTROTATIONAL NYSTAGMUS
Uncontrolled flicking movements of the eyes which occur after a person has been spun around a number of times.

POSTURAL REFLEX
An automatic muscle response which maintains the balance or position of the body.

POTENCY
Literally power, but the term has come to refer to the ability of the male to perform the sex act satisfactorily.

POTENTIAL
The power to do something. In physiology, it refers to the peak strength of a nervous impulse.

POTLATCH
An anthropological term referring to the ritual conspicuous destruction of valuable property practiced by the Indians of the northwest coast of America. An individual achieves status in his society in proportion to the amount of property and goods which he can afford to destroy publicly.

PRACTICE LIMIT
The upper limit of achievement or mastery of a skill that can be reached by practice.

PRAGMATISM
A philosophy that the ultimate meaning of an action or activity of any kind lies in its consequences.

PRÄGNANZ
One of the laws of perception put forward by the Gestalt school of psychologists. It states that the brain attempts to mold a perception into the "best" form possible under the circumstances. A slightly wiggly circle shown for a brief period of time will be seen as a completely round figure.

PRECOCITY
Rapid or early development of any biological or intellectual function.

PRECOGNITION
A term used in parapsychology to refer to the alleged ability of some individuals to predict future events.

PRECONSCIOUS
A psychoanalytic term referring to that part of the unconscious mind which, while not always available to consciousness, can yet be reached. We do not, for example, have immediate access to all the names of all our friends, but most of these can be recalled with some effort.

PREDICATION
Associating one concept with another.

PREDICTIVE VALIDITY
The power of a psychological test to predict or measure what it sets out to do.

PREDISPOSITION
A tendency, particularly an inherited one, to behave in a certain way or be subject to particular influences such as disease.

PREFRONTAL AREA
The most forward part of the frontal lobe of the brain.

PREGENITAL PHASE
A psychoanalytic term for the period of infantile sexuality, the so-called oral and anal stages, when sexual pleasure is derived from stimulation of the mouth and anus. From this there should be a natural evolution to the genital phase, which is supposed to be dominant in adults.

PREGNANCY
The state of the female from the moment of conception until the birth of the child.

PREHENSILE
Having the ability to grasp hold of something.

PREMENSTRUAL TENSION
Relatively minor changes of mood, notably irritability, which

occur in some women before the onset of menstruation.

PREMONITION
A feeling, often accompanied by anxiety, that one has received a glimpse of a future event.

PRENATAL INFLUENCE
Anything that affects the fetus before birth. For example, drug addiction in the mother can lead to innate addiction in the child.

PREPARATION
A term used in physiology to refer to an animal that has been treated to allow an experiment to be performed on it.

PREPOTENT RESPONSE
Any response, generally automatic or instinctive, which takes precedence over or overrules another response.

PREPSYCHOTIC BEHAVIOR
An activity or personality change which indicates the approach of a psychosis.

PRESBYOPHRENIA
A psychosis common among old people in which memory is seriously disturbed but the individual otherwise appears sharp and alert.

PRESBYOPIA
Blurring of close vision, common in middle age due to a hardening of the lens of the eye.

PRESSURE SPOT
An area of the skin particularly sensitive to pressure.

PRIAPISM
A state in which the penis is constantly erect and does not subside with orgasm.

PRIMACY LAW
The principle that the first act learned in a series will be the one that is remembered best.

PRIMAL ANXIETY
A psychoanalytic term referring to the intense anxiety assumed to be associated with the separation of the infant from the mother at birth.

PRIMAL TRAUMA
In psychoanalytic theory, an event experienced in infancy which has a permanently damaging effect on the individual.

PRIMARY COLORS
In layman's terms, the basic pigments red, yellow, and blue, which are used to mix other colors. In scientific terms, however, the primary colors are red, green, and blue. These are light frequencies in the visual spectrum which when mixed in the proper proportion give any other color.

PRIMARY MENTAL ABILITIES
The basic factors which, when combined, are supposed to make up intelligence. There is no definite agreement as to how many there are, but they are often listed as being verbal and numerical ability, memory, and perceptual and reasoning factors.

PRIMARY NEED
A basic biological need which does not have to be learned.

Hunger, thirst and sex are obvious and immediate examples.

PRIMATE
An important order or zoological classification of mammals. It includes all apes, monkeys and man himself.

PRIME NUMBER
Any number which can be divided only by itself and by one.

PRIMITIVE SOCIETY
In anthropology, a social group which is largely illiterate and has no written history.

PRIMITIVIZATION
Returning, generally under stress, to levels of behavior or attitudes which were more suitable at a younger age.

PRIMORDIAL IMAGE
A Jungian term to refer to a memory lying in the unconscious which was not actually experienced by the individual, but is in fact part of the "collective unconscious."

PRINCIPLE
A basic law of nature which can be relied on in making assumptions in experimental science.

PRISM
A wedge-shaped lens which breaks up white light into the basic colors of the spectrum.

PRIVILEGE
Something which is gained as the result of power or social status.

PROACTIVE INHIBITION
The interfering of previously learned material with the memory of more recently learned matter.

PROBABILISM
An attempt to predict future events scientifically as the result of a careful study of the present.

PROBABILITY
The likelihood of an event taking place in a particular way. Mathematicians use a sliding scale from 0 to 1. At 0 it is counted as being certain that an event will *not* take place, at 1 it is counted as being certain that it *will*. A probability of .5 would be equivalent to the popular "a 50/50 chance."

PROBABILITY THEORY
The branch of mathematics which attempts to deal in a logical way with such elusive concepts as chance, significance and predictability.

PROBATION
A legal term referring to a condition where an individual is not sent to prison because of some violation, but has some basic restrictions put on his freedom.

PROBLEM BOX
A container in which a creature is placed and has to perform a task or series of tasks in order to escape.

PROCESSING ERROR
A data error which occurs in collecting or analyzing it.

PROCESSOMANIA
An obsessional interest in legal action.

Ron Embleton

Green-eyed monster

Jealousy hath a human face—say the Songs of Experience. Could it ever be yours?

There is a particularly painful emotion which affects all of us at one time or another. It is that variety of "psychic toothache" we call jealousy.

Jealousy can arise in many situations and if taken to extremes can prove a highly destructive force. Mrs. Jackson crossexamines her husband in a rather unsubtle way about his business trip. He becomes resentful and interrogates her again about *that time* when she returned so late from her friend's home and was given a lift by a man she met there. Four-year-old Sonya is angry and upset at the fuss the visitors make over her new sister and says that mummy loves the baby more than her. Teenage Joseph gets furious with his girlfriend for the smiles and attention she gives a handsome stranger at the dance. He sulks and shows interest in another girl.

All four of them are experiencing

that poignant, hurtful (and yet, at times, oddly enjoyable) blend of hostility, anxiety, envy and resentment which makes up jealousy. Anxiety and envy arise from the belief that your position in another's affection or esteem is being undermined, or from a feeling that someone is getting more than his fair share of available resources. The hostility and resentment come from the attempt to maintain a certain status. They make for a corrosive mixture. Yet jealousy, after all, is a motive which lies at the core of man's life as a social creature, though no society has ever tried to make a virtue of envy. It is an emotion or drive which occurs as soon as two individuals become capable of mutual comparison.

Jealousy (within certain limits) is a normal by-product of growing up. All children are susceptible to this emo-

tion and, despite parental efforts, it is impossible to banish it altogether. Its roots go so deep that certain forms of animal behavior can be viewed as envy-like activity: take the farmyard pecking order.

Brotherly Hate

The earliest jealousies, and perhaps the most agonizing ones, occur within the family. Jealousy between brothers and sisters—sibling rivalry—is almost inevitable: the Bible is a source of many case histories, the best known being the story of Cain and Abel. Although not many boys go so far as killing their brothers, the actions of Cain appear in the fantasies of many, and feelings similar to his can often be unraveled during psychotherapeutic sessions with children. Then there was Joseph, the favored son of Jacob, whom God had blessed with a dream of greatness. He was envied by his brothers. "And they conspired against him to slay him . . . and they took him, and cast him into a pit."

The Austrian sociologist Professor Helmut Schoeck, author of *Envy: A Theory of Social Behavior*, believes that child psychology, drawing on its studies of sibling jealousy, may help to explain why envy arises over small differences rather than big ones. We are more likely to feel really jealous of a neighbor who has a better car than ours than of the millionaire with a collection of Rolls-Royces, yachts and palatial homes. In so far as the disposition to envy is acquired mainly through suffering sibling rivalry, what is involved is almost a conditioned reflex towards the perception of small inequalities. Within a family group the coveted possession is generally similar to one already possessed (often it is, indeed, exactly the same and it is only in the resentful child's imagination that it appears bigger, better, newer or more expensive). Unconsciously the jealous individual almost *expects* that his emotion will be aroused by minimal differences between himself and another, just as it was during his childhood and adolescence.

Latent Envy

Dr. Benjamin Spock, in his book *Dr. Spock Talks with Mothers*, has this to say about the force of jealousy: "Of all the factors that make for ordinary quarreling between children, I think that jealousy is by far the most potent. The strongest attachment in childhood is of course the one between the child and his parents. To some degree he wants the parents' love for himself alone, and fears that the affection which goes out to brothers and sisters will be subtracted from his share. This makes him suspicious and resentful of them. We have to realize that this possessive, jealous element in love is not simply an unfortunate flaw in the character of man. It is part of the essence of our humanness. It's part of what makes us tick together as husband and wife, as families, and as other groups. Otherwise our relationships would be as casual as the relationships of insects."

This point is an interesting one. Professor Schoeck states that without envy there could be no social group of any size. The mutual and spontaneous supervision exercised by human beings over each other—in other words, social control—owes its effectiveness to the envy latent in all of us. If we were quite incapable of envy and, more important, if we were also convinced that our behavior would not be envied by anyone, that mutual exploration of the threshold of social tolerance—a constant social process upon which the predictability of social life depends—would never occur.

Sigmund Freud came to the conclusion that jealousy is an entirely normal phenomenon, a universal stage in the early development of personality. An older child may feel an intense jealousy towards a new baby. This does not always appear immediately; sometimes it comes when the baby begins to sit up and become more recognizably a "personality" to the older brother or sister. But certainly, the advent of a new member of the family is an alarming event. The near-monopoly position of the up-to-now "youngest one" (especially in the case of the firstborn) is broken. Often the baby demands so much time and care that the elder child really is deprived of even his fair share of attention. His fears are confirmed.

Cold Shoulder

In the excitement and bustle of bringing a new baby home, the other child is likely to feel left out and resentful. It may help if he is taken out for the day and comes home when all is calm and his mother has time to welcome him, preferably not with the baby in her arms. If certain changes have to be made around the house—if, for instance, he has to move into another room—it is important for him not to feel that he is being pushed out. It may be an idea to make whatever changes are necessary a few months before the baby is due. The youngster must be told that the baby is going to arrive, and the way the news is broken

PAF International

Only when she's sure her mother has enough love to go around will she accept the demanding intruder.

PAF International

to him will help determine his attitude.

The first few weeks after the baby's arrival are important because the older child can easily form the impression that the household now revolves around the baby. His mother is forever busy with diapers and bottles and may seem to have no time for him. Visitors who used to make a fuss of him now immediately go to look at the baby instead. It does not have to be like this. Visitors can be tactfully discouraged from showing too much (or sole) interest in the baby. In any event babies sleep most of the time in the first few months and do not require constant attention, and they can often be fed and cared for while the older child is engrossed in a game and does not want attention.

If he is very young the child may make no secret of his rage and jealousy. He may show his hostility by making the infant cry or by saying uncomplimentary things about it. He may express resentment by being disobedient, rough, or babyish with his mother. In some instances, he may regress to an earlier phase, refusing food or wetting and soiling himself in an attempt to regain his parents' attention. Or he may be aggressive to the baby and seek an opportunity to harm him. If the parents fail to make allowances for this and are shocked by their elder child's bad behavior, or punish him for it, he may repress his jealousy. Older children are even more likely to feel guilty about their jealousy and hostility, repressing their feelings to such an extent that their parents

Once a pattern of rivalry is set up, the smallest slight ends in a row.

remain totally unaware of the conflict.

The best way to deal with jealousy is to accept it for what it is—a need for affection and reassurance, resulting from a sudden feeling of insecurity—and to give the child these things, within reasonable limits. At the same time he can be encouraged to be "grown-up." If he is reassured of his parents' affection, he will soon revert to his normal behavior. Some children adopt a parental attitude to the baby, wanting to help look after him. This may still be, in part, a way of dealing with jealous feelings by denying them. In taking a parental role, the child is saying that the baby's arrival does not threaten him. He will express the warmest affection to the baby and seem anxious to help nurse him. But if allowed to do so unsupervised, he may allow some accident to occur.

By learning to restrain—not merely repress—his jealous inclinations, a child takes a vital step towards maturity. This is why the feelings he has should not be suppressed by authoritarian, punitive methods, but be allowed to surface and work themselves out. Preoccupation with some unexpressed conflict may be evident from the way he talks about the baby much more than would be expected. The parent can try to give the child opportunities to talk about his feelings: it helps if the child can admit to himself that he feels jealous.

On the other hand, jealous acts have

to be kept in check in the general interest of the safety of the helpless baby and the peaceful atmosphere of the home. There has to be, in other words, a balance. There are dangers in either extreme—unbridled expression of jealousy and complete denial or inhibition of the emotion. Unless the child's feelings of insecurity and anger are brought into the open and coped with successfully, they can persist throughout childhood and affect his ability to deal with other jealousy-provoking situations he will meet later.

In dealing with open jealousy the mother has to do two things: make it quite clear that the child will not be allowed to hurt the baby, and at the same time reassure him that he is loved as much as ever and his jealous feelings are unfounded. In reassuring the child that he is loved the mother should not in any way apologize for the baby's presence—the child must realize that the baby has a right to be in the house. If parents react strongly to demonstrations of jealousy, this may increase the child's fear of rejection and may also cause him to conceal his jealousy in the future, which is not at all the same thing as controlling it. Such concealment merely increases a child's bitterness and makes it less likely that he will be able to control himself when he is finally left alone with the baby and can express his hostility.

Jealousy can lead to emotional disturbance in some circumstances. For an eleven-year-old girl named Pearl, a highly strung and emotional child, it resulted in nightmares and a refusal to go to school, where she was usually in trouble. When he was five, her little brother, of whom she had apparently been extraordinarily jealous, had fallen into a canal and been drowned. Pearl was not at home at the time but had taken his death very badly, and her parents dated her behavior difficulties from that time.

Pearl developed the habit of telling people—at every opportunity—about her brother's death, but the story she told was quite inaccurate. She would describe coming home from school, seeing her brother at the edge of the canal, and calling out to him—in this way she assumed actual responsibility for the accident because of the harmful wishes she secretly harbored against him. Her refusal to go to school and her flagrant misbehavior there were apparently punishment-seeking devices.

Jealous rivalry between older children has its roots in insecurity. Children are naturally competitive and they vie for parental favor. If they believe they are receiving less than other children, they feel threatened and may fight desperately for the affection they think they are missing. It is not whether a child has cause to be jealous that matters, but whether he *believes* he has. Children place great importance on matters of which adults are mostly quite unaware—who is going out with dad, who had the biggest helping.

A young child who feels that he is taking second place to another member of the family will usually make some attempt to win the attention which he believes is given to his rival. Jealous children often become excessively naughty to gain attention. Others become excessively good. However, a child may express his disturbance in a more indirect way, such as refusing to go to school, or he may become quiet and withdrawn.

Having learned that open jealousy of other members of the family is frowned on, he may suppress it but give vent to his feelings by expressing resentment of other children at school. Jealousy is almost self-fulfilling: it is such an ugly attribute that an openly jealous child is not particularly lovable. Rejecting a child by punishing him for being jealous is the most self-defeating approach. His fears must be allayed, not reinforced.

Jealousy is not restricted to children; competition for the children's love is one source of jealousy between husband and wife. Immature parents may vie with one another to win the love and preference of their offspring. This is likely to cause emotional conflict in the child, which becomes particularly oppressive and tragic when there is a separation or divorce.

Forgotten Fathers
A parent may feel envious of his or her child. The birth of the first child may sometimes arouse jealousy in the father, who feels he is being excluded from his wife's attention. An aging mother may feel a pang of jealousy when her husband spoils their teenage daughter, especially when she gets her way by being flirtatious.

It is obvious that the situations which provoke jealousy in adults are numerous. An older woman working with young girls may become jealous of the attention they receive from male colleagues. In heightened emotional settings like a hospital ward, one patient may excite jealous reactions if he seems to be getting more than his fair share of attention. Parents may resent those who take over the

care of their children. Women who are childless are often jealous of their fertile friends. The later months of pregnancy are often associated with fits of jealousy.

Insatiable Appetite
The most fertile ground for jealousy to grow and prosper in is marriage. Jealousy between husband and wife can reach a state of such bitterness that the marriage can be undermined and the family fragmented. First, and most obvious, is sexual jealousy. Whether men and women—or whether women but not men—are by nature monogamous and endowed with a capacity for life-long fidelity is something which has long been argued, and the debate will no doubt continue. What is certain, however, is that a very large number of married men and women are unfaithful at some time or another, and this can cause a feeling of such intolerable jealousy in the other that forgiveness is very difficult, especially if one partner is more attractive than the other.

The major difficulty in coping with a jealous mate is that jealousy, unlike any of the other emotions which affect relationships, has an enormous, insatiable appetite. It can feed on *anything.* A husband's glance at a pretty girl in the street is fuel for his wife's jealousy. But his studied effort *not* to glance at a pretty girl can be taken in the same way.

If there are no real events on which it can feed, jealousy will find fuel in the imagination. Jealous people are prone to "come across" letters, photos, significant bills and receipts in which they can find a hidden meaning. In truth, they look for them. Similarly, they are extraordinarily receptive to "suspicious" looks.

Given that jealousy is part of normal life, both inside and outside the family, when is it abnormal? One means of evaluating it is to determine if there is a just cause and to ask, even if the provocation is real, whether the response is out of proportion to the cause. Is the person amenable to argument, or is every available piece of evidence, however tenuous, brought in to support the jealous accusations?

A husband may see in every word or glance which his wife directs towards another man a secret and seductive invitation. Because of his violent anger and jealousy, his wife, not unnaturally, may reject him sexually. If she does, he may think she has a lover and in his rage accuse her of infidelity. He may make wild accusations that she has men in the house

while he is out, that she has to rush to the bathroom as soon as he comes in to rearrange her clothes. Any new clothes which she has are thought to be presents from lovers. Money which she earns or borrows is thought to be obtained immorally. In extreme cases, the husband may beat his wife to extract a confession from her or to punish her for the supposed crimes. When jealousy is irrational, when it has no foundation in reality, an obsessively jealous mate will, somehow and somewhere, find a reason in fantasy if not in fact.

Crime of Passion
When the causes of jealousy are founded on fact, and a person does behave in such a way that his partner feels threatened and humiliated as a direct result, the appropriate course of action is relatively simple. The partner who, without regard for the feeling of his mate, makes sexual conquests outside the relationship, or who is a compulsive flirt, is behaving in an irresponsible way. In a healthy relationship this should not happen. A mature person does not intentionally hurt someone he loves for selfish reasons. Frank and open discussion of the problem should reveal the cause of the unhappiness, and appropriate steps can be taken—if only one is creative enough to try.

Because jealousy may be experienced in countless circumstances and at different levels of intensity, there are a variety of ways in which it may be expressed, apart from voicing it. Sulking or withdrawing are both methods of showing how severe the reaction has been. In extreme cases, it may result in striking the rival, or in earlier times offering to fight a duel. The anger and tension which jealousy releases may be so great that the unfortunate recipient is killed. In fact, French law recognizes a lowered degree of responsibility in "crimes of passion." The rage, however, may damage only the one who is jealous.

Jealousy can have a constructive face, if we are willing to learn from it. It can stimulate people into new attitudes and fresh endeavors. It may teach us not to take our partners and children for granted. It may help us, when we see others achieving successes which we thought impossible, to recognize that there are potentialities of action which we, too, might reach. But it will do this only if the jealousy is restrained and kept within limits, so that it does not corrupt and destroy the best qualities of our humanity.

Trial and error

Every "wonder drug" has to pass controlled clinical trials before appearing on the market.

Medicine was once synonymous with magic. The cures and potions of the witchdoctor were mysterious, closely guarded secrets, his power to cure was regarded as a supernatural gift.

In fact, the magic of the ancient seer was an acquired skill, a combination of trial and error and experience handed down from the past. In a modern context, these are still the basic ingredients of all medical research, and yet we still speak of successful results as "wonder drugs."

A cure for cancer, a drug to conquer arthritis, to annihilate multiple sclerosis—glimmerings of hope for all afflicted with these and many other vicious diseases—make up the life's work of many scientists and doctors. There is nothing magical about their continuing struggle: the work is technical, factual, repetitive to the point of boredom, and careful in the extreme. To be struck by inspiration is not enough—it is only the beginning of weeks of tests, carried out with perhaps thousands of patients under every conceivable set of conditions. What may cure one sufferer may have no effect at all on others, or worse, it may even do damage, as the worldwide thalidomide tragedy and its aftereffects have taught us.

Side Effects

Throughout the history of medicine, more and more meticulous safeguards and controls have been imposed on experiments with drugs and treatments devised to eliminate just such disasters. A system of controlled clinical trials has been evolved which, though laborious, is now regarded as the most exhaustive method of forestalling harmful side effects and predicting the value of any new drug.

In the past, new drugs and treatments went through a characteristic cycle of approval and disapproval. They were either rejected by the "skeptics" or accepted enthusiastically by the "believers," who initially were very few. Slowly the drug would become accepted, but then as side effects and drawbacks appeared, there was an inevitable swing back in the other direction.

Finally, the new treatment took up a stable position: it was found to be useful in *certain* diseases, and in

Marshall Cavendish

certain doses. Its side effects were listed and their frequency taken into account. The new drug (or treatment) had then "arrived" and could occupy its place in medical textbooks. Until, of course, it was ousted by something better. Today, procedure is different, largely due to controlled clinical trials.

Assume that a new painkilling drug has been discovered. At first sight it may seem a simple matter to perform a clinical trial. All that would seem

necessary is that some patients be given the drug and its effects noted. That seems to be a commonsense procedure and indeed it was normal until about 1950. The trouble was that this simple method was not "controlled." It did not allow for the effects of any number of important variables.

Only in the last three decades have controlled trials come into prominence. But the principles were known as early as 1747, when James Lind performed the trial which was later described in his classic book, *A Treatise on the Scurvy.*

Lind, a Scottish physician, served with the Royal Navy. Naturally, he was concerned with scurvy, scourge of the sea in those days. We now know that scurvy is caused by the lack of vitamin C (which comes from fruits like lemons, limes and oranges). On long sea voyages at that time, sailors were fed on a monotonous diet, very low in foods containing vitamin C.

Lind wanted to find out whether scurvy could be prevented and carried out the first recorded controlled clinical trial. He selected twelve patients, all severely ill with scurvy, and divided them into six groups of two patients. All were then put on the same diet.

Ahead of His Time

Lind gave one group two oranges and one lemon each day. Now comes the vital step. He also gave something in their place to each of the five other groups. One group was given a quart of cider daily, another half a pint of seawater daily, another two spoonfuls of vinegar, and so on.

From the ensuing observations came the conclusion that citrus fruits were effective in the treatment of scurvy, a conclusion later confirmed. So effective was the citrus fruit diet that limes became standard issue on British ships, and earned for the English sailors in America (and subsequently for all Englishmen) the widespread nickname "Limey."

Lind's "control" groups are at the heart of today's controlled clinical trials, combined with three other elements that have long been common in medical practice: experiment, the "double-blind," and the use of statistics. Each of these elements has played a vital role in the history of medicine: each can be traced from its earliest beginnings until the present day when together they form one of the very strongest branches of scientific medicine.

Certain figures stand out in history as men born before their time and, in medical history, we can point above all to William Harvey, who lived from 1578 to 1657. Harvey was the first physician to employ experiment, the scientific method. What is routine to doctors nowadays was, for him, a notable innovation, for in his day the

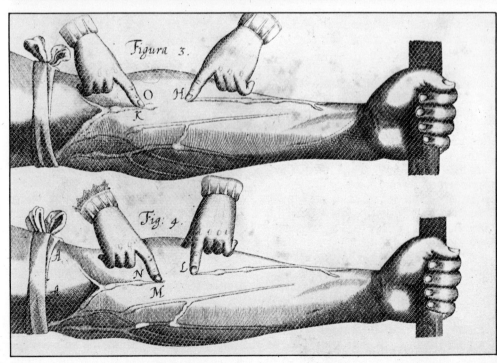

Physician William Harvey (top) used experiment and the scientific method to discover the function of valves in the veins of the forearm (right), which he meticulously illustrated.

use of observation, hypothesis and experiment was not a routine at all.

In his book *On the Movement of the Heart*, published in 1628, he demonstrates the function of valves inside the veins of the forearm. He shows a detailed picture of a forearm, with a pair of tiny hands (wearing elegant seventeenth century lace cuffs) pointing to the valves in the veins. Step-by-step he shows how to prove that the valves are one-way structures: if you stroke a vein in one direction, away from the heart, the vein bulges up to the valve but not beyond it; if you stroke a vein the other way, towards the heart, the blood passes easily through the valve.

Harvey's experiments share an important feature that we nowadays recognize as essential to the scientific method: they are objective, and they may be repeated at any time by any experimenter. What is more, the way to do the experiments, the set of experimental procedures, is made quite clear and explicit.

Rigorous Requirements

Those elegant hands from Harvey's book point to us over three centuries and carry our eyes down to our own forearms. We can repeat Harvey's experiments exactly, because he tells us exactly what to do. Science has been called "organized common sense" and, when applied to Harvey's experiments, this description is very apt. Once they have been shown to us, his results seem "obvious," but they were by no means obvious at the time he did them.

William Harvey's work demonstrates the principles of the scientific method. First, it is a procedure which can be repeated again and again by anyone who follows the experimental procedures as they are described; secondly, it neither requires any special qualities on the part of the experimenter nor allows for any special subjective methods of evaluating the results.

These are the rigorous requirements of science and, when fulfilled systematically, they have proved spectacularly successful. Chemistry has never looked back since its first faltering steps were turned into a confident stride by men like Lavoisier, Priestley and Dalton. Since Newton, physics has forged ahead. And in medicine, Harvey laid down the first principles of experiment. But it was not until two centuries later that these principles were amplified—until the development of controlled experiments.

An experiment is said to be "con-

Mary Evans

trolled" when important variables, other than the factor under observation, are kept constant. William Withering, a country doctor who flourished (in Shropshire, England) during the eighteenth century, in his book on the treatment of "the dropsy," describes an early example of the use of controls. He had come across a folk medicine of undoubted power, a mixture of many different herbs which had long been given to patients suffering from "the dropsy"—swelling of the ankles and elsewhere, which accompanies certain diseases, especially heart failure.

Withering identified the many ingredients of the medicine and then tried them out separately on his patients. In the process he discovered the active ingredient to be a wild flower called foxglove. Even if Withering had already known that the foxglove was an active ingredient he would still have had to try out all the others individually, to be sure that the power of the mixture was due to the

Harvey charted the circulation of the blood and demonstrated the phenomenon to King Charles I.

foxglove *alone*. All the other ingredients, however improbable their curative effect, had to be eliminated before Withering could prove his conclusion. And in testing each of the herbs and potions separately, he set up a system of control experiments, variables by which to measure the potency of the foxglove cure. This kind of "proof by comparison" was what Lind also used to verify the effect of citrus fruit in the treatment of scurvy.

But even after sifting all the individual ingredients in a new drug, even when strict control experiments have been set up to contrast with the treatment under survey, scientists have yet another variable to contend with: the susceptibility of the human mind. The human element—the attitude of the patient and of the doctor to the treatment—can have an enormous effect on results. If the patient learns

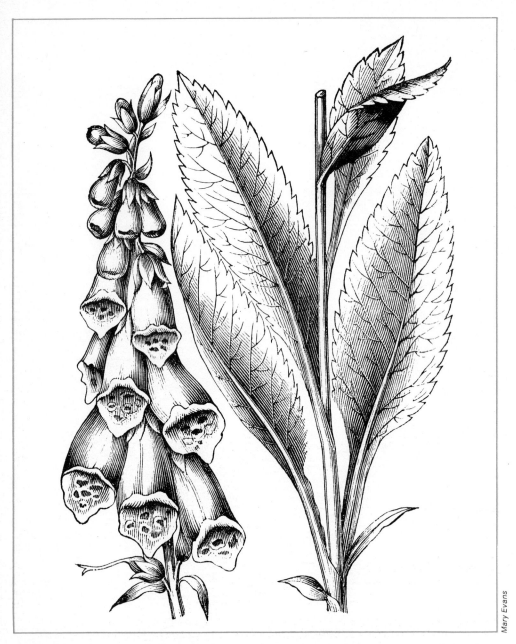

An early controlled clinical trial revealed foxglove as the active ingredient in a remedy for dropsy.

Mary Evans

that he is testing a new drug, he may well be influenced, and feel better for it. His morale may mount higher and higher. Conversely, if he knows he is not taking the active drug but is merely acting as a control, his expectations will be lower.

The doctor, too, may be psychologically affected by the test. If he knows which patients are on the drug he may tend to assess them more favorably than the rest, even though there is no real difference.

To maintain a strict scientific method, even this most ephemeral human element must be eliminated like all the other variables. And to do this, medical science has evolved the system called the "double-blind."

The patients, both the controls and those being given the drug, all appear to be getting the same medicine but, unknown to them, two medicines are being used: one an active drug and the other a pharmacologically inert substance like sugar.

Both the drug and the "dummy" will look alike and will be presented in the same way. Both groups will be given the same amount of encouragement, as will the doctors who make observations on their progress. Only those who designed the test will know the truth.

In theory this seems a simple, effective idea, but in practice the patients themselves can sometimes detect which drug they are on. The drug may have a prominent side effect—like drowsiness—and if the patients once detect such differences then the trial is no longer truly "blind." And since they will tell the doctors of their symptoms, the doctors too will be influenced by the knowledge.

Another problem of the control group, and with the double-blind system, is that some patients respond favorably to any treatment at all, even to the dummy medicines used in tests. Even when a patient does not need any drug or when there is no drug available which would help him, he still needs to feel that the doctor is concerned to help him. Doctors have long been in the habit of giving these patients a dummy medicine—a *placebo* (literally "I will please him") —to calm or encourage him, to put him in the frame of mind to get better.

Before setting up a clinical trial, someone must decide how many patients will be needed to prove the efficacy of a certain drug, and how many controls. And they must decide how patients and controls are selected, with regard to age, sex, and other variables. This is the point where the medical statistician is brought in. He decides on the number of patients to receive the active drug and how many the dummy, and when the trial is over he examines the results to see if the new drug has lived up to expectations.

Recently a rather new kind of trial has been developed, called a "sequential trial," where the statistician and the doctor decide upon what degree of superiority the active drug must show over the dummy before the trial can be stopped. Its advantage is that when a drug reaches the criterion of success the trial can be stopped at once, and this is sometimes a matter of life and death for control patients on inferior treatment.

The widespread use of controlled clinical trials has raised a question of medical ethics which every doctor who designs such a trial must answer. The question is: To what extent is he justified in withholding a drug that he believes to be helpful from some of his patients while giving it to others?

In practice this question is seldom so awkward as it sounds. Sometimes in crucial diseases it is too risky to deprive the control patients of any treatment whatever, and while the new drug is given to the test group a tried and trusted drug—that is already in wide use—goes to the controls. Both groups are then getting some treatment, and only a careful analysis of the results will show which one is the best. But the most obvious answer is that, since the doctor is performing a trial in the first place, he cannot be sure about the value of the drug. The trial may show it to be valueless but, should it turn out to be useful, then it can be confidently administered to all his patients, not to mention others all over the world.

Son and lover

D. H. Lawrence's tragedy was that his disregard for conventional morality interested the public more than his writing. Even today it is his Oedipus complex which attracts attention.

D. H. Lawrence shocked his contemporaries and is still shocking those who today continue to misunderstand his attitudes to sex. He has been called bestial, depraved, decadent, a genius and a messiah. The quality of his writing has been praised and the sensuality of its content condemned. His books have been regarded by some as revelations; they have also been publicly banned.

Today he stands as one of the acknowledged great figures of English literature and yet, almost half a century after his death, critics and public alike still quibble about the morality of his message.

Finger on the Pulse

To many people, Lawrence is known only as the author of *Lady Chatterley's Lover*, and the public exposure of bigotry and false argument that surrounded the famous trial of the book at the beginning of the 1960s in Britain first brought Lawrence's name to their notice. More recently he has become known as the author of the book of the film *Women in Love*. Once again, the public and the critics have seized on the chance to air their inhibitions and set them for comparison against the values of the working-class son of a miner, who so accurately put his finger on the pulse and the moral disorder of his generation and in consequence brought down on himself their righteous indignation.

Lawrence was primarily concerned with the relationships between men and women. "I'll do my life work," he wrote in a letter to a friend, Sally Hopkin, in 1912, "sticking up for the love between man and woman." A year later, when his novel *Sons and Lovers* was published and when he was beginning to write *Women in Love*, he wrote in another letter, "I can only write what I feel pretty strongly about: and that at present is the relation between men and women. After all," he continued, perhaps a little melodramatically, "it is *the* problem today, the establishment of a new relation,

or the readjustment of the old one, between men and women."

Because of the depth of Lawrence's sensitivity and perception of the malaise that beset his generation— and has since followed us through

several generations—it was not easy at the time (and still may not be) to understand exactly what he was trying to say, what he was condemning, and what he was trying to establish in its place. It is, unfortunately, only *too*

Far from the soot and grime of Nottingham, Lawrence eventually found peace of mind in New Mexico.

easy to interpret what he has to say in oversimplified terms; these over-simplifications have given rise to the misunderstandings of his attitudes.

For instance—and the example is central to Lawrence's thinking and the opposition to him—it was assumed by many of his contemporaries that Lawrence rejected the intellect in favor of the senses: a meeting of minds was nothing, they interpreted him as saying; the meeting of bodies was what mattered, pure and simple. It was difficult to find much objectionable, physical contact in *The Rainbow*, one of his earliest books, but nonetheless it was suppressed.

Drags It Down

The eminent author John Galsworthy read *The Rainbow* and found it "aesthetically detestable. As to the sexual aspect," he wrote, "the writer forgets—as no great artist does—that by dwelling on the sexual side of life so lovingly he falsifies all the values of his work—for this reason if for no other: the sexual instinct is so strong in all of us that any emphasis upon it drags the whole being of the reader away from seeing life steadily, truly and whole; drags it away from the rest of the book, stultifies the writer's own efforts at the presentation of human life and character."

When *Sons and Lovers* appeared, Galsworthy acknowledged that there was genius in the book but once again resented the intrusion, as he put it, of the sexual passages. "The body's never worthwhile," he wrote in a letter, "and the sooner Lawrence recognizes that, the better. . . ." Lawrence disagreed entirely. It was just this dry intellectualism that repelled him, the idea that the real values of life excluded the body.

To Lawrence, morality was a reverence for a naturalistic life; sex seemed essential to fulfill life and human relationships. Not only was a relationship without sex barren, but a relationship that did not openly acknowledge the value of sex as a component part of any relationship was equally barren.

Lawrence's contemporaries missed the point. What they heard was "Take sex for a bit of pleasure"—a disruptive, morally undermining attitude that was far from Lawrence's preaching. He himself condemned "sex for sheer pleasure." Those of his characters who indulged in sex as their only means of communication, or solely

for satisfaction, he does not approve.

Gudrun and Gerald, who use sex as the last resort to keep them together in *Women in Love*, do not achieve happiness. In *Lady Chatterley's Lover*, the relationship between Lady Chatterley and the artist Michaelis is also doomed, because both are seeking little more than temporary satisfaction.

Lawrence spurned love for the sake of having someone to love just as much as he rejected sex for the sake of sex; love and sex as the be-all and

end-all of existence was not, as many seemed to believe, the morality he was preaching. Love and sex were not, to him, merely the means to the end of security; they were not the "means" to anything, except insofar as Lawrence set his characters, as sexual beings, against the dehumanization and artificiality of the industrial world, which he hated and feared as the source of all moral evil.

Love and sex were part of life, without which life was meaningless. To

The house Lawrence was born in. Prior to his birth his mother kept a shop in the front room.

Lawrence, sex itself, and the relationship between two people, was a process of reunification with nature, a harmonizing process that was spontaneous and liberating for the individual and the couple.

It was no good. Explanations of this kind sounded false to the critics and the public; they picked on the purple passages. They did not wish to be called hollow, dead, unloving, without tenderness, themselves immoral. To them, the philosophy that Lawrence expounded was the voice of the libertine. Everything he said sounded like a good excuse to indulge in sensuality. When *Women in Love* appeared, the critics had a field day. "A frenzy of sexual awareness," wrote J. M. Murry, "bestial, a thing that our forefathers had rejected when they began to rise from the slime."

One of the most infamous reviews of the book was by W. Charles Pilley, in *John Bull* magazine, and carried the banner headline "A Book the Police Should Ban: loathsome study of sex and depravity—misleading youth to unspeakable disaster." The author of the article did not claim to be a literary critic but, he wrote, "I know dirt when I smell it and here it is in heaps—festering, putrid heaps which smell to high heaven."

Today, a review like this would ensure any book a place in the best-seller lists. "In real life we should not be troubled with Mr. Lawrence's characters—they would be safely under lock and key. For instance, there is the idiot who undresses and wallows in wet grass, delighting to have his back scratched with thistles and his skin lacerated with the sharp points of fir cones. Doctors have a name for this sort of thing which at the moment I do not recall. Then there is the female degenerate who half kills her lover in a fit of frenzy and, as she strikes the blow, feels a 'delirium of pleasure' because, as she tells herself, she is going at last to her consummation of voluptuous ecstasy.

Sheer Filth

"We know well enough where this sort of thing leads to in real life. Criminal lawyers know all about it. It is precisely the mania that keeps the jails full and the hangman busy. . . . The book reeks of Bedlam horrors, . . . an epic of vice. . . . The chapter headed 'Gladiatorial' (in which the two men wrestle nude together) is sheer filth from beginning to end. . . . This is the sort of book which, in the hands of a boy in his teens, might pave the way to unspeakable moral disaster."

Contrast this with Lawrence's own comment in his foreword to the book: "Lewdness is hateful because it impairs our integrity and our proud being." Obviously, this misunderstanding between himself and his detractors was an unbridgeable gulf. That gulf has never been narrowed.

The points of difference between Lawrence and his contemporaries arose from more than his novels. It did not help that the subject he chose to write about was still largely regarded as taboo by so-called civilized society. It helped even less that the man who so dogmatically wrote about the subject came from the working classes and was therefore considered by many of the literate public to be naturally incapable of appreciating the finer and higher points of love: it was no wonder that "sensitive"

Lydia Lawrence, the writer's mother, exerted a powerful influence on her son until her death in 1910.

readers saw in his elevation of sensual experience nothing more than an indulgence in the fundamental sexual animalism that could only be expected of the lower classes.

Lawrence wrote at a time when class distinctions in Britain were still very strong. He was regarded with suspicion by those who could not understand how he could possibly *be* a genius with his background—and with incomprehension by those who recognized the work of a genius but viewed his message with apprehension.

Lawrence did not try to make his way easier. Just as he believed—as was apparent in the treatment his books received—that England had rejected him, so he rejected England. He spent ten years of his most fruitful writing period outside the country.

Born in Eastwood, Nottinghamshire, in September, 1885, Lawrence was the fourth of five children. Eastwood was a small mining village and Lawrence's father worked in the local colliery. The class conflicts that run so fiercely through Lawrence's novels began early in his life, for though his father was rooted in the working classes, his mother had once been a schoolteacher and came from a relatively prosperous family. His parents' marriage was not very happy; they quarreled continually about the manner and the extent of their children's education, Lawrence's mother always wanting more for them than their father thought proper or necessary.

It was inevitable that the intelligent and inquiring Lawrence should become devoted to his mother and reject his father and a great deal of what he stood for. His close relationship with his mother was reflected in *Sons and Lovers,* a largely autobiographical novel, in which the son is torn between love for his mother and a girl.

The girl, in real life, was Jessie Chambers, the daughter of a neighboring family and a powerful influence on Lawrence as he grew up. Jessie encouraged his writing and received in turn repeated assurance that everything he wrote was done for her. After the novel was published, Jessie was so upset at the treatment she received in the story that she never communicated with Lawrence again.

Sudden Elopement

He left school in 1901, worked briefly for a surgical appliance manufacturer, fell ill with pneumonia, and then became a pupil-teacher in Eastwood and subsequently at Ilkeston. After coming out top in the whole of England and Wales in a King's Scholarship examination in 1904, he went to Nottingham University College, which he left in 1908. His mother died two years later, an event that shattered what remaining links he had with his background village and brought, in consequence, the resentment of his working class contemporaries, who believed that he was betraying them and misusing his education.

But an even more dramatic and far-reaching event occurred in 1912, when Lawrence met the German wife of his former professor of French at Nottingham University, Ernest Weekley, and fell in love. Her name was Frieda, the daughter of Friedrich von Richthofen and cousin to the "Red Baron." Within only a few weeks of their meeting, Frieda and Lawrence went off to Germany. They married two years later, when her divorce was made final.

It was just the sort of thing that Lawrence's detractors might have expected from him. For a young man to go off with an older, married woman was a far more shocking event than we can possibly imagine today. Many critics implied that it was just another

Frieda von Richthofen became the new female influence in Lawrence's life after their first meeting in 1912.

K. Werner

gesture of defiance. This was unfair. Through happy and difficult times, the couple stayed together until Lawrence's death in 1930.

Their marriage marked another rupture with Lawrence's past, emphasized by the publication of *Sons and Lovers* in 1913, and by Lawrence's attitude to World War I, which broke out the following year. He utterly condemned the war, though he was lucky enough not to have to argue his case in court as his physical condition anyway made him unfit for service. In *The Rainbow*, he referred to "wooden soldiers," and it may have been this reference as much as the sexual scenes that brought about the banning of the book.

The couple spent some time traveling in Italy and Germany and finally left England completely in 1919. The rest of Lawrence's life was spent in a search for fresh roots, which he came nearest to finding in New Mexico, after visiting first Ceylon and then Australia. After three years in New Mexico, he returned to Europe. He died in March, 1930, in Venice.

The public outrage over Lawrence continued long after his death. Half the trouble was that he did not care whom he offended. He wished to stir

people out of their complacency, their soulless relationships; he scorned those who could not take his writing.

In 1917 he wrote to the American poet Amy Lowell, "Nobody will publish *Women in Love*—my best bit of work. The publishers say that it is too strong for an English public. Poor darling English public, when will it go in for a little spiritual athletics?"

Trial of Taboos

And when his paintings were exhibited in London in 1929, the year after the publication of *Lady Chatterley's Lover,* and received an outcry of indignation because the nudes possessed sexual organs and pubic hair, Lawrence wrote a collection of poems called "Gross, Coarse, Hideous (Police Description of My Pictures)", one of which had a verse:

Lately *I* saw a sight most quaint:
London's lily-like policemen faint
in virgin outrage as they viewed
the nudity of a Lawrence nude.

But it was *Lady Chatterley's Lover* that aroused the greatest debate of all Lawrence's work. When the unexpurgated edition of the book was put on trial in the early 1960s, it was not just Lawrence that was in the

Flight Back into Paradise: **like his writing, Lawrence's painting was bold and explicit.**

dock: it was the moral attitudes of the whole of society, more than thirty years after Lawrence himself had attempted to readjust them. The central theme of the story—the relationship between Lady Chatterley and the gamekeeper was known to everyone.

The arguments in favor and against the book ranged between literary merit and moral degeneration—as they always had. No one cared much about the values of life expressed in the book; the case was a test of public morals, a trial of permissiveness, a trial of taboos. After the trial, when the bookshops were stacked with copies, there were record-breaking lines in the streets.

When Lawrence became legal tender, he was not understood any better. The license to sex that the trial ostensibly granted was not a moral value of any worth, certainly not one Lawrence himself expounded. It was bereft of tenderness; it did not occur as a natural development in a relationship; it was as artificial in its way as the values he had deplored.

A dirty business

"They've paved paradise and put up a parking lot." Cars take precedence over trees in the consumer society, and in the pursuit of happiness we have polluted our air and water and turned our cities into garbage dumps. But it's not only ugly . . . it's lethal.

Every time you go out in your car you are contributing to a sequence of atmospheric changes which may cause the polar ice caps to melt and eventually to flood the very road you are driving along. Each time you throw away a carton, a bottle, or a can, you may be signing the death warrant of thousands of fish or water plants in a neighboring river or estuary. With each mouthful of a breakfast cereal, you may be condoning the killing of birds, animals, insects, plants, organisms and microorganisms, which you depend on for next year's breakfasts.

The connecting link between these commonplace occurrences and their astonishing consequences is pollution. At the point of consumption you finish off a process of pollution which began with the gathering of the raw material and continued in the stages of production, packaging and distribution, through which any article you buy must go. Then in discarding its wrapping, its residue, and ultimately the product itself, you start off another.

The rapid rise in the world's population has been accompanied by an even greater increase in the demands which man has made on the earth's natural resources. Using technology, both in industry and agriculture, he has aimed to secure for himself not only an adequate supply of the necessities of life—food and shelter—but also the additional advantages of power, mobility, leisure, security, longevity and all the luxuries which make for a high standard of living.

Tampering with Nature

To achieve these goals he has devised ingenious ways of maximizing the earth's resources and of converting them to his needs by industrial processes. But in so doing he has compelled nature to do two things which it is not necessarily obliged to do: he forces the environment to produce more than its usual quota of resources, and to take back unprecedented quantities of waste products when man and his technology have done with them. It is when nature fails to come up to these expectations that pollution occurs.

The word "pollution" means "contamination"; the word "contamination" means "defiling by touching and mixing." By touching the environment with advanced technology, tampering with nature's time-tested self-renewing systems, and introducing "foreign bodies" in the form of synthetic compounds and chemicals, we have injected a virus to which our planet is not immune, and from which it might never recover.

Death Warrant

The signs of this contamination are everywhere. The casualties are fish destroyed and washed up on ocean shores into which industrial plants have disgorged their poisons; sea birds with their wings gummed up by jettisoned oil from a leaking supertanker; feathered or furred creatures whose life-support systems in woodlands and hedgerows have been obliterated by man's ambitious construction programs; benevolent insects which found themselves in the firing line of pesticide sprays intended for their malicious neighbors; trees, flowers, and plants choked into oblivion by exhaust fumes from roadways and air corridors. Already the death toll is huge, and these casualties constitute the thin end of a very thick wedge.

Supposedly, these misfortunes are all for the benefit of man. But man himself has not escaped the consequences. People have died from mercury poisoning after eating contaminated tuna fish, others from eating the meat of pigs accidentally fed seeds coated with poison intended for crop-destroying insects. Excess lead content in water supplies has permanently blighted some lives—causing nausea, nervousness, and insanity—while others have been foreshortened by the constant intake of polluted air which leads to heart disease, bronchitis, emphysema, and cancer. In terms of output, the case for advanced technology in industry and agriculture has been proved; but we have to be sure that the sacrifice of animal, plant, and human life has not been in vain and that the overall benefit is lasting.

That case is still before the open court.

First and foremost, people require food. The widespread starvation and undernourishment in the contemporary world shows that agricultural technology has fallen far short of its goals. To achieve them it needs heavy machinery to take on the back-breaking labor of plowing, sowing, and harvesting; fertilizers to add nutrients to the soil; and pesticides to ensure that the farmer gets to his crop before nature's predators. But each of these introduces elements into the farming process which have no established links with the traditional and natural production system. The weight of heavy machinery which discharges oil fumes close to the ground may be slowly destroying the texture of the earth beyond self-repair. Impregnation of chemical fertilizers, intended to boost the growth and to compensate the land for previous overexertion, may be gradually undermining the natural goodness of the soil and irrevocably reducing a crop's ability to reproduce in its own good time. Furthermore they seep into waterways to infect aquatic life there.

Pests That Protect

Pesticides—DDT and other chlorinated hydrocarbons like Dieldrin and Endrin—are sprayed over vast acreages of arable land and shoot much wider than their mark. Along with pests—flies and insects carrying disease to livestock or destroying crops—perish creatures and plants which far from doing the crops harm actually make a positive contribution to their growth. The same goes for herbicides, which if indiscriminately used destroy vegetation that is either beneficial in itself or protects the soil from erosion.

Nature is an integrated whole. Its regenerative cycle depends on a chain of events in which every living organism participates, each reproducing itself, but also in life and death contributing to the survival of the next in line in the natural hierarchy. An insect which lives on plants is devoured by another creature which in turn becomes the victim of a larger predator, whose waste products and ultimately his own body are consumed by microbes which feed the soil where the plants grow, and so on. The survival of life depends on the natural cycle being followed through, so that every creature gives back to nature what he has taken out. But man has interfered with this system.

By destroying whole populations of pests he removes from the natural cycle something which was there before; and in doing so with chemical and synthetic substances he introduces something which was *not* there before. That new element is a killer, a contamination which far from dying with its victim is passed from one organism to another, and will subsequently find its way into the soil, into the waterways, or into the air.

Bring Back the Cats

All pollution, to a greater or lesser degree, has its impact not just on a part of the natural cycle but on the whole system. By wiping out one species you also starve into extinction another which preyed upon it. You also have on your hands a population explosion of some creature whose numbers the pest you have destroyed kept down, which may be even more damaging to crops. A graphic illustration of such a sequence of events was experienced in a Bolivian town, where DDT was sprayed to control malaria-carrying mosquitoes. It also killed most of the local cats, whose absence was exploited by rats who invaded the town carrying black typhus, which killed several hundred people before the cats were restored.

In this case it was easy to relate cause and effect and to see how the balance of nature had been disturbed. Not so easy to see, though, are similar disruptions occurring at the level of microorganisms, but there is no doubt that any pollution or contamination introduced higher up the scale will filter down to them. And it is there that the most damage might be done.

Once you have unleashed a poison into the environment it is bound to reappear sooner or later. If sooner, the results are obvious—like the ten to fifteen million fish killed by the pesticide Endrin leaking into the Mississippi River in the 1960s. If later, it is not always clear where the damage has been done or what caused it. For instance, species which are most exposed to some chemical may build up an immunity to it, so that it does not kill until it has passed through the food chain to a less resistant creature.

If it does not destroy it, the substance may affect it in some other way. For instance, it is known that some birds, as a result of chemical intake, lay eggs with shells so thin that they crack when laid. It may be years before the full impact of that reduced bird population is felt.

Chemicals are sometimes long-lived. Malathion—an insecticide used on fruits—has survived eight months in cold storage without losing any of its potency. Some chemicals are given not only to longevity, but also to wanderlust—and turn up in the most unlikely places miles away from their starting point. For example, DDT has been found in penguins living thousands of miles from where it was used.

So, in order to appreciate the full effect of pollution, we have to look far beyond immediate horizons. This is why it is causing such alarm among environmentalists and public-spirited citizens. It can be assumed that the damage it is doing on the surface is not as severe as the contamination which, unseen and unbeknown to us, is infecting the very foundations of our life-support system. Since this deeper penetration into the environment takes time, we can be sure that some of the most serious repercussions of pollution which occurred long ago have yet to be felt.

Nobody denies that insecticides and fertilizers have a perfectly legitimate function, but what we must be on our guard against is indiscriminate and careless overuse. We must also heed the warning—first sounded by Rachel Carson in her pioneering book *Silent Spring*, which was mainly concerned with deleterious side effects of pesticides—that more research and more knowledge is needed before we can be sure that scientific exploitation of resources is of long-term value.

Pollution Power

Far harder to justify, though, is injecting the waste products of industry into the environment. Next to food, the most pressing demand of technological man is for power and energy to drive his factories and machines. Power plants are the greatest contributors to the pollution of the atmosphere: most of the world's energy supplies come from the combustion of coal and other fossil fuels which give off sulphur dioxide, oxides of nitrogen, and soot and ash into the air.

These combine to cause disease, get people and property dirty, absorb sunlight, and reduce visibility on the ground. Add the carbon monoxide from oil-burning plants and from that arch polluter, the motor car, to the accumulation of toxic gases in the atmosphere, and the consequences are infinitely more far-reaching. Every ton of wood coal burned releases *several* tons of carbon dioxide into the atmosphere. Its effect is to allow sunlight to reach the earth but to limit the reradiation of the generated heat back into space. The temperature of the earth therefore rises, and it might in the not too distant future be enough to melt the polar ice cap, raising the sea level by 400 feet.

Radioactive Rain

As coal and oil resources are being depleted, scientists are having to look for alternative means of power. Some, like tidal barrages, thermal power, or solar energy will be low on pollution, but nuclear power could turn out to be the most dangerous source of energy yet devised. Fallout from nuclear tests contaminates every part of the earth's surface and all living things upon it. Strontium 90 is just one of the radioactive isotopes rained down from the stratosphere to the earth, penetrating the soil and passing through plants to animals, and eventually to man, causing genetic damage or cancer.

Arctic Eskimos, found to have high levels of fallout radioactivity in their bodies, show how this dangerous substance passes through the food chain. Lichens, which grow on rocks, draw their nutrients from the air absorbing the fallout. They in turn are eaten in large quantities by caribous, which provide the Eskimos' diet.

The generation of nuclear power for industrial purposes presents two hazards. The first is from thermal pollution, the discharge of hot water from cooling processes into oceans and rivers: fish and other aquatic life are particularly susceptible to sudden changes in temperature. The other danger is that some radioactive elements in gases and effluent might seep into the atmosphere. The amount may be small, and every effort is made to contain all the radioactivity given off in nuclear power generation. Some elements are short-lived, but others have a lifetime of thousands of years, and there is always the danger of some major breakdown when the safeguards may prove inadequate.

Top right: When herbivorous animals find their food source depleted, the fine balance of nature is disturbed and a chain reaction leads to soil erosion. Right: Public Enemy No. 1—wanted for air pollution and noise. Far right: A breathtaking view.

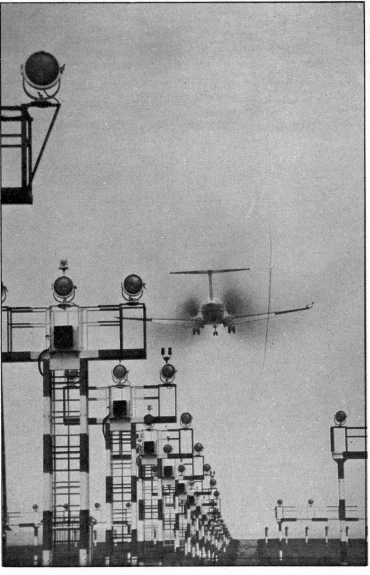

The very same land and waterways which are required to dispose of increasing amounts of industrial wastes also serve the cities which house the industrial labor force. Large concentrations of people demand more power, more food, and more goods, and the greater quantities of effluent, sewage, and detergents are often more than the natural disposal systems can cope with. Dissolved oxygen is the main agent of natural decomposition in water, and bacteria which break down waste matter depend on it; so does all aquatic life. But it is not in unlimited supply, and nothing can

survive once all the oxygen has been used up, except certain bacteria which effuse repulsive gases.

But the job of decomposition is still not done. Having destroyed all life which might eventually have broken it down, waste matter just accumulates, turning the waterways into lifeless, stagnant sewers. Also choking them up are the inorganic materials which cannot be decomposed.

The growth of industry and the cities has led to a geographical separation of the consumer from his supplies of food and materials. This makes further demands which technology must

fulfill: transportation, distribution, and packaging. The motor car—apart from being a hazard to life and limb —is a great polluter of the air, particularly in the cities where the atmosphere is already overloaded with toxic emissions from industrial and domestic chimney stacks. Vast stretches of good productive agricultural land must be torn up to build roads and to clear sites for their ancillary services, exposing the neighboring land and its wild life to the exhaust fumes of vehicles and the waste products of a mobile people.

Throwaway Needs

The packaging industry makes a very substantial contribution to the pollution of the environment. As a heavy industry, some is caused at the production stage when bottles, cartons, tin cans, and other containers are made. In 1970, the United States produced 60 million tons of packaging materials, but it is the fact that over 90 percent of that output will be discarded after a very short life which sets the packaging industry apart.

Estimates vary as to how much garbage we throw away, but most people agree it is excessive. In the United States, the total is more than one billion pounds of solid waste a day, or one ton per head of population in a year. A typical breakdown shows that this waste is composed of 7 million cars, 100 million tires, 30 million tons of paper, 4 million tons of plastics, 48 billion cans, 26 billion bottles, and hundreds of thousands of obsolete domestic appliances.

The obvious question is: Where does it all go? The answer is equally obvious: Into the environment. But few of these materials go "back to nature" in a form which is beneficial to the natural cycle. Some are burned, contaminating the air; some are buried, polluting the land; some are poured into overburdened waterways.

To breathe clean air, to drink pure water, to eat uncontaminated food, and to enjoy natural beauty have always been inalienable human rights. The rights to possess material goods, to move about at speed, to produce and consume, and to strive towards greater wealth and leisure are all perfectly legitimate, but only insofar as they do not conflict with our priorities. The right to pollute the environment in pursuit of these goals cannot be guaranteed—or justified.

One drop of oil from a leaking tanker is enough to gum up a sea bird's wings.

Friends of the Earth

John Watney

Mother knows best

The way our parents shape us is the crucial factor in determining how well we fit into society.

Adaptation is a concept which is central to Charles Darwin's theory of evolution. Over countless thousands of years, new species appeared and flourished because genetic mutations allowed some forms of life to *adapt* better than others.

Even in the psychological realm the slogan might be "Adapt or perish." Those whose adjustive mechanisms are defective (for example, the severely subnormal or the mentally ill) have to be taken care of in special institutions because they cannot survive in the outside world. There are many individuals who cannot make the necessary adjustments to life and opt out of it by committing suicide. And there are countless others who survive, but whose survival is so marginal that they are barely existing. Feeling as they do—alienated, un-

loved, unreal and aimless—they cannot be said to be living life to the full.

Each person discovers and evolves his own set of strategies to cope with life. But no two approaches are the same and there are great difficulties in defining effective adjustment. *How* an individual behaves depends upon both the situation he finds himself in and the adjustive strategies he brings to that situation, which consist of various attitudes, skills, abilities.

In a survey of 275 American families, nearly all the mothers reported a number of undesirable forms of behavior in their children. Problem behavior tends to be very annoying, but this does not necessarily mean that all behaviors which annoy and create problems are to be equated with maladjustment. Parents vary in what they can tolerate in the way of "bad"

behavior. The eminent child psychiatrist Leo Kanner observed that "the high annoyance threshold of many fond and fondly resourceful parents keeps away from clinics . . . a multitude of early breath-holders, nail-biters, nose-pickers and casual masturbators who, largely because of this kind of parental attitude, develop into reasonably happy and well-adjusted adults." It has been found that the reason behind referring a child to a guidance clinic is as closely related to the reactions of his *parents* (that is, whether they are anxious, easily upset and lacking in ability to cope with children) as to whether *he* actually has a problem.

Margaret Mead's work among the South Sea Islanders showed how different styles of upbringing create variations in patterns of adjustment.

The Arapesh of New Guinea are quiet, gentle, peace-loving people, among whom self-assertion is so rare as to be regarded as abnormal. For their periodic celebrations, they have to force some of their members, much against their will, into the role of organizers. Passivity and selflessness form an essential part of the nurture and education of each individual. From birth, the child observes these traits in those about him and, during the course of his development, integrates them into his own personality.

Code of Behavior

In complete contrast, another island group, the Mundugumor, fosters aggression from infancy. If a suckling baby does not take a firm grip on his mother's breast, she will pull the nipple away and the infant will go hungry. As a child grows up his early experience is reinforced by training in warlike pursuits. In other tribes, women were found to assume the dominant role and do the important work; men were submissive and responsible only for domestic tasks.

A stable home and the presence of both a mother and a father are generally thought to be necessary influences for healthy development of the child's personality. Notions of right and wrong, a code of behavior, a set of attitudes and values, the ability to see the other person's point of view — all these basic qualities which mold an individual into a socialized personality flow in the first instance from the family setting.

The psychologist Gordon Allport describes two aspects of the developing self-image: the way the individual sees his present abilities, status and roles; and what he would like to become, his aspirations for himself — in other words, his idealized self-image. Research studies consistently indicate that personal happiness and satisfaction in life depend on a reasonable agreement between the present and the idealized self-concept. Marked discrepancies arouse anxiety; they are a feature of neurotic personalities and occur commonly in the psychological crises of middle age.

An individual's self-esteem is also shaped by his ability to perceive how other people see him and to compare his image of himself with what he believes others expect of him. The individual's perception of the way he appears to a particular group of other people or one significant other person, has been termed his "subjective public identity." One person may have as many such identities as there are

groups of significant people he believes perceive him in a distinctive way.

There is a marked variation in the degree of permanence and stability with which the self is organized. Some individuals have a very loosely organized pattern of different selves, with only a small core of common elements to all. Such a chameleonlike person is described as "poorly integrated." His self consists of the various roles he characteristically plays.

Parental love and affection during early life and their unfolding attitudes toward the child as he copes with his impulses and failures are of import-

Fathers are especially useful when you're too tired to go it alone.

ance in the more and more sophisticated evolution of his self-image. The expressed attitudes and behavior of everyone in the family provide him with information about his mastery, goodness and worth. Living up to parental expectations (or always failing to do so in the case of overcritical or hostile parents) becomes part of his self-concept.

Dr. P. M. Symonds, an American psychologist, published a comprehensive review of findings in the

2238

1930s, based on many years of experimental and observational research, concerning parent-child relationships. Two major dimensions—acceptance-rejection and dominance-submission—emerged from this work. Children of submissive parents appeared to be more aggressive, stubborn and disorderly, although more self-confident than the offspring of dominating parents. Dominating parents tended to produce children who were more sensitive, submissive, orderly and polite, better socialized but more dependent. Children who were accepted seemed to manifest characteristics which are generally thought desirable, while those who were rejected were reported to be more neurotic, rebellious and delinquent.

Ideal Mother

More recent studies of parent-child relations have concentrated on the same themes but are made more precise by the application of special psychological instruments; computer techniques have also been used to reduce the rich variety of childhood and parental behaviors to a few main dimensions. Two main underlying components of parental attitudes and behaviors still emerge from many of the studies: firstly, attitudes which are "warm" (or loving) at one extreme, and "rejecting" (or hostile) at the other; secondly, attitudes which are restrictive (controlling) at one extreme, and permissive (encouraging autonomy) at the other.

Dr. Earl Schaefer, a development psychologist, describes parental behavior in terms of the interactions of the two main attributes, thus a "democratic" mother is one who is both loving and permissive; an "antagonistic" mother combines hostility and restrictiveness; a "protective" mother is both loving and restrictive, and so on.

According to the researches of psychologist Dr. Diana Baumrind, a "permissive" mother is one who attempts to behave in a nonpunitive, accepting, and affirmative manner toward her child's impulses, desires, and actions. She consults with him about policy decisions and gives explanations for family rules, making few demands for household responsibility and orderly behavior. She presents herself to the child as someone to call upon for help and company as he wishes, not simply as an active agent responsible only for shaping or altering his ongoing or future be-

Practical skills like cooking are best taught informally at home.

havior. The "permissive" mother allows the child to regulate his own activities as much as possible, avoids the excessive exercise of control, and does not encourage him to obey absolute, externally defined standards. She attempts to use reason instead of overt power to accomplish her ends.

This empirical analysis is very different from the popular usage of the word "permissiveness," which tends to be reserved for the extreme end of the dimension with its connotations of lax discipline, unbridled license, and only too often indifference.

According to Dr. Baumrind the "restrictive" or "authoritarian" mother (as she emerges from detailed investigations) is one who attempts to shape, control, and assess the behavior and attitudes of her child according to a set standard of conduct, usually an absolute standard, motivated by theological considerations and formulated by a higher authority. She values obedience as a virtue and favors punitive, forceful measures to curb self-will at those points where the child's actions or beliefs conflict with her idea of proper conduct. She believes in indoctrinating the child with such values as respect for authority, respect for work, and respect for the preservation of traditional order. She does not encourage verbal give-and-take, believing that the child should accept her word for what is right.

Reviews of research into child-rearing techniques suggest that there is a happy medium and that the extremes of permissiveness and restrictiveness entail risks. A blend of permissiveness and a warm, encouraging, and accepting attitude fits the recommendations of child-rearing specialists who are concerned with fostering the sort of children who are socially outgoing, friendly, creative, and reasonably independent and self-assertive. Warm, loving, and consistent discipline, in which (when the child can understand them) reasons are given, is thought to produce a rational sort of obedience rather than a blind and emotionally dependent following of orders.

Recognition of Rights

The balance is perhaps best illustrated in the philosophy of what Baumrind calls the "authoritative parent." This kind of mother attempts to direct her child's activities in a rational manner determined by the issues involved in any particular disciplinary situation. She encourages verbal give-and-take and shares with the child the reasoning behind her policy. She values both the child's self-expression and his so-called "instrumental attributes" (respect for authority, work, and so on); she appreciates both independent self-will and disciplined conformity. Therefore, she exerts firm control at points where she and the child diverge in viewpoint, but does not hem in the child with restrictions. She recognizes her own special rights as an adult, but also the child's individual interests

and special ways personal to himself.

The "authoritative parent" affirms the child's present qualities, but also sets standards for future conduct. She uses reason as well as power to achieve her objectives. She does not base her decisions solely on the consensus of the group or the individual child's desires; but she also does not regard herself as infallible or divinely inspired. Baumrind found that authoritative parents are most likely to facilitate the development of competence and self-reliance in young children by enhancing responsible, purposive, and independent behavior.

Tinker, Tailor . . .

In the wake of thinkers like Pavlov, almost exclusive emphasis has been placed on environmental influences in the development of behavior. And parents, being the major feature of the child's early environment, received all the blame when things went wrong. But possessing certain combinations of temperamental qualities can make a child exceedingly "difficult" no matter how skilled the parents are.

John B. Watson, a psychologist at Johns Hopkins University during the first decades of the century, believed that planned habit training could mold the child in any desired direction. This is how he expressed it: "Give me a dozen healthy infants, well-formed, and my own specified world to bring them up in, and I'll guarantee to take any one at random and train him to become any type of specialist I might select—doctor, lawyer, artist, merchant-chief, and yes, even beggarman and thief, regardless of his talents, penchants, tendencies, abilities, vocations, and race of his ancestors." He discounted the influence of differences in children's individual capacities and their reactions to their environment. Environment *is* vital in determining individual differences, but it should not be forgotten that inborn attributes are also significant.

Bearing these inborn limitations and tendencies in mind, it still is undoubtedly possible for parents to instill certain qualities in their offspring. Most parents wish their children to grow up unselfish. British psychologist Derek Wright lists the main family influences that promote this crucial aspect of humane and compassionate behavior. "First, there must be a warm and affectionate relationship between parents and child. This provides the setting in which empathic responsiveness is most effectively learned and gives the first major incentive for altruistic action in the child's life. Secondly, the parents must themselves be sympathetic, both to the child and to others, and set a good example of altruistic action. The child can then learn through imitation a full repertoire of altruistic patterns of behavior. Thirdly, as the child grows older, his parents need to provide him with a rationale for altruistic tendencies to people outside his immediate circle of family and friends."

Outlet for Aggression

Parents also wish their children to grow up to be morally aware. Dr. M. L. Hoffman, a developmental theorist, believes that all disciplinary encounters have a great deal in common, regardless of the specific technique used. They all have three components, one or the other of which may predominate: power assertion, love withdrawal, and induction. Hoffman contends that the most reliable finding in parent-child research is the negative relationship between power assertion and moral behavior. Punitive techniques are self-defeating.

Parental disapproval and the child's subsequent anxiety about losing their love are the major contributing factors to the child's internalization of parental values. There is evidence that this love withdrawal may contribute to the inhibition of anger, for it produces anxiety which leads to the renunciation of hostile and possibly other impulses. However, although Hoffman recognizes the contribution of love withdrawal in making the child more susceptible to adult influence, he maintains that this does not necessarily affect moral development.

Induction is the type of discipline Hoffman finds most conducive to moral development. It involves pointing out the effects of the child's behavior, giving reasons and explanations. To be effective the disciplinary technique must enlist already existing emotional and motivational tendencies within the child. In other words, a basis of affection must fuel the child's need for approval and hence his readiness to attend to and heed what is being conveyed to him. All three of these disciplinary techniques communicate some negative evaluation by the parent and are thus likely to elicit the child's need for approval.

Like riding a bicycle, bringing up children is a question of balance.

Love's labors lost

Rechanneling your sex drive is fine as long as there's a light at the end of the tunnel.

The standards of Western culture simply will not allow us to give vent to all our sexual urges whenever we please. Unfortunately, the laws of nature are not so easily contravened by the dictates of society, and there is trouble ahead if this tremendous instinctual energy does not somehow find an acceptable outlet.

Sexual sublimation is the unconscious process by which repressed energy of sexual impulses is diverted towards new aims and activities. Most of us have experienced it at some time in our lives—unless we have given full rein to every sexual desire from our childhood onwards.

An adolescent in our culture is unlikely to be able to satisfy his newfound sexual appetite through the usual channels available to adults, such as intercourse or other more sophisticated means of sexual gratification. He may not even masturbate, either because he does not know how or because the atmosphere he has been raised in is hostile or repressive towards this quite normal activity.

The Boy Scout movement, for example, while encouraging boys to acquire various skills and exhorting them to exemplify the ideals of Christian behavior, positively discouraged its members from either thinking about or expressing their sexuality. Boys were told to· stifle their "unnatural desires" and to take cold showers instead—advice which many modern psychiatrists would view as positively harmful to the boy's psyche, since guilt and repression at this age may have a permanent effect on future attitudes to sex.

This is not to say that it would be desirable to encourage teenagers to indulge their sexual desires to the full, even though there is evidence to suggest that the age when they first have sexual intercourse is nonetheless getting steadily lower over the years. But to deny the existence of a strong sexual urge at and immediately after puberty is equally wrong.

Possibly the most obvious exponents of the art of sublimation exist in those religious orders where the members have chosen or been compelled to accept chastity as a way of life.

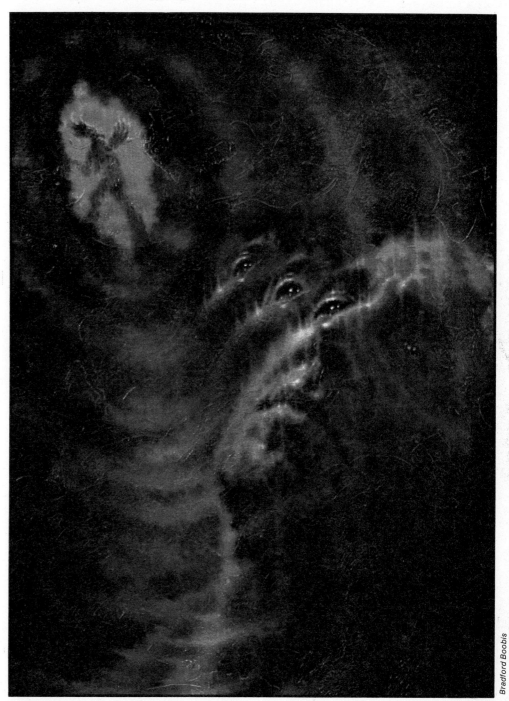

Bradford Boobis

An ordained Roman Catholic priest, for example, has to forego any sexual relationships with women, as does a nun with men. Whether or not homosexuality or autostimulation occurs among these celibates can only be a matter of conjecture, but sexual contact with a member of the opposite sex, if discovered, would be enough to result in excommunication.

In spite of revolutionary moves within the Catholic church to modify the celibacy laws, many priests still believe that chastity is preferable. Father McIntyre explained why he felt this way: "One of the traditional arguments is that if a priest has a wife and family of his own to care for, he cannot devote his entire life to God and his parishioners, and I think there is a good deal of truth in this. I have been asked by several people how a priest copes with sexual desire. This is difficult to explain unless you understand the entire reasoning behind the law of celibacy, and anyway it varies from man to man. Fundamentally, I believe it is a question of faith—in God and in your duty as a priest to be 'available' to all men and women, which necessarily precludes any involvement or obsession with one in particular.

Unhealthy Obsession

"I have seen people 'thinking aloud,' wondering whether I notice that a particular girl is attractive. Of course I notice, but this does not mean I desire to take her to bed. Certainly sublimation is involved, and I believe this has led to an incredible number of good things, from the creation of beautiful art—painting, music, singing—to the greater awareness and understanding of life at all levels. You might say that a man is not fulfilled unless he has contact with a woman, but who is to say that such contact is worth more—to himself, God, and the world—than a life completely devoted to some greater cause?"

One reason we find it so hard to accept the idea of sublimation is that we are more aware of sex today than we have ever been before. It is undeniable that an increased understanding of the nature and mechanics of sex, leading to greater personal satisfaction, is a good thing. But with this increased awareness has come a preoccupation, some would say an unhealthy obsession, with sex as the cause of and answer to most of our problems.

Nevertheless, many of us practice sublimation, even if we are not always aware of doing so. The sex drive varies enormously from person to person, and men and women who are very highly sexed may through force of circumstance be unable to gratify their sexual urges all the time. When a sexual drive exists, but cannot be satisfied, it is more than likely that the person involved will "attack" some other kind of activity with unusually powerful vigor.

John, a young photographer of 28, admits that he feels sexually aroused very easily, and frequently. "Obviously I can't lay all the women I fancy. I mean I see at least half a dozen women a day I'd like to make love to, some of them very beautiful models indeed, but apart from the fact that few of them would be willing, I'd never get any work done that way!

I think that wanting them but not being able to have them definitely makes me a better photographer. Taking pictures is like painting them: if you have a beautiful, desirable subject, you are obsessed by 'capturing' it—for the painter on canvas, for me in a photograph.

Neat as a Pin

"All your energies are directed to preserving the beauty you see at a particular moment and, far from spoiling your concentration or skill, feeling sexually excited lends an extra sensitivity and impetus to your performance. I definitely work better, get better results, if I desire a woman, and if I feel she is attracted to me that's even better. This sort of suppressed desire on both sides brings out the best in the model and the photographer, so I believe strongly in sublimation as a way of achieving a better standard of work."

On a more mundane level, Goldie, a young housewife, claims that she can get around the house in half the time and with much better results if she is feeling in a sexy mood. "When we haven't had time to make love in

If model and photographer find each other attractive, the result is often a picture with "sparkle."

the morning, but have wanted to badly, I usually throw myself into all the chores that normally I would spend hours over. Being turned on gives me a lot more energy and I seem to zip through work like lightning. Mind you, if I had to do without for days on end I think the reverse would happen, and the house would go to pieces, but once in a while it's a great help! We even joke about it because my husband knows that if we haven't had time to make love before he leaves the house, he'll come back to find it neat as a pin. He says we will never need a cleaning woman; all he has to do is oversleep twice a week!"

Physiologically it is easy to explain why the enforced suppression of sexual fulfillment can lead to an increase in energy, which can be diverted to other forms of activity. In an excited sexual state, the body is geared to a highly energetic performance. If sexual intercourse or some other form of sexual gratification follows, and is satisfactory, the normal result is that the body becomes quiescent and completely relaxed.

If on the other hand there is no sexual outlet, the energy remains, however temporarily, and needs to be used up. Hence the superb photograph, or the shiny house, neither of which would have happened in quite the same way if the photographer or housewife had been able to slake their sexual appetites immediately.

Sublimation can sometimes have unhappy repercussions, however. Where it becomes a way of life, where the sex drive is constantly rechanneled in order to achieve a better performance in another field, the natural expression of sexuality can be thwarted—or may even become impossible altogether.

Mary was engaged to Ian for two years before she finally decided to break it off, "not because I didn't love him any more but because I could not accept his attitude to our sex life. He rowed for a famous club and was very good, I know, but the rigorous training—at least that's what he maintained—meant that we went without sex for nights on end, weeks sometimes when he was preparing for a very important event. He reckoned that having sex reduced his performance the following day and that he needed every ounce of strength and energy to give his best efforts. It wasn't for lack of interest—he was a very passionate man—and when we did have sex it was usually marvelous, but it just wasn't often enough.

Difficult Choice

"Sometimes in the rowing season I used to go nearly out of my mind. He was loving and friendly, but shied off any real sexual contact as though I were diseased. Some of his friends held similar views, but not all. At least one boy, who also rowed, told Ian that he would lose me if he didn't pay more attention to me. I suppose my frustration must have been showing pretty badly at the time. The awful thing is that I never wanted him to give up rowing—I knew he loved everything about it and was good—but in the end I had to make him choose between me and rowing. He wouldn't make a decision, saying he could keep both. He made me feel like a sex maniac because I said this enforced celibacy was driving me crazy. He was very upset when I broke off the engagement, but he's still rowing like mad, though I know he hasn't had a regular girlfriend since."

Ian's sublimation was a conscious process in some ways, since he be-

lieved that withholding and rechanneling his sex drive would actually improve his performance as an oarsman, and his coach and many colleagues concurred with him. Inasmuch as he *was* aware of the redirection of his desire, it could be argued that he was not practicing sublimation, but some psychologists believe that the process does not have to be entirely an unconscious one, but may be in part pragmatic.

True sublimation, however, has, by definition, to be an unconscious process. It could be argued, in fact many art historians and music critics have substantiated the theory, that some of the greatest paintings and musical compositions are the indirect results of sublimation, with the vital component of genius, of course. If all the great masters had had comfortable lives with "normal," fulfilling sex lives, the world's artistic heritage would probably have been greatly diminished. The Brontë sisters, for example, created not only as a result of sensitivity, imagination, and talent, but also because they were sexually frustrated. *Jane Eyre* is a classic example of sublimation, of one girl's hopes and desires of the real world transmuted into a superb work of fiction. Tchaikovsky also, who had a tortured sexual

nature which included both incestuous and homosexual leanings, practiced sublimation, creating beautiful, agonized music from his genius and his troubled, unfulfilled sexuality.

In modern life a number of apparently normal activities bear the stigma of sublimation. Driving a powerful sports car, for instance, especially if done by a man whose sex life is disappointing, could be classed as sublimation, as a doctor specializing in behavioral problems observed. "Not all men who drive big, fast cars are sublimating; to say that would be ridiculous. But for the man with sexual difficulties, driving such a car could be a way of using up the sexual energy which has no satisfactory outlet. Aggression is a vital component of sex, and a man or woman who is sexually frustrated will most probably have a good deal of aggression to cope with.

"Football even, which would seem a perfectly innocuous sport, can be the vehicle for sublimation. Rita, a football player's wife who came to see me, swore that her sex life would

The film *The Music Lovers* showed how Tchaikovsky sublimated his incestuous and homosexual feelings into creating beautiful music.

be better 'if all my husband's skill and energies were directed at me and not at that awful ball.' And though the average football enthusiast would throw up his hands in horror at the suggestion, I believe that there is more to the hugging and back-slapping that happens after scoring than simply straightforward pleasure at the achievement.

All Work and No Play

"Even the violence of some football fans, particularly the young ones, can be seen as a kind of sublimation; I suspect that if many of the young hooligans who wreck trains and stadiums and who regularly get involved in physical brawling had satisfactory outlets for their sexual desires, they would on the whole be less inclined to this kind of violence. It is only a theory, and of course many other personal and social factors are involved; but it is a theory which a number of psychologists and sociologists are investigating."

"All work and no play makes Jack a dull boy" is a well-known cliché. But the person who is unable to stop working may not just be dull; he may also, in fact, very probably, be forced to sublimate his sexual desires. It is not uncommon for people who have unhappy or frustrating sex lives to spend more and more time at work, not because they want to but because in so doing they avoid confrontation with their sexuality.

Hilary, whose marriage has been rocky for three years now, explained that it was her fault that her husband was hardly ever at home, although she felt powerless to rectify the situation. "Three years ago he discovered that I was having an affair with his boss. His immediate reaction was to leave me, which he did for two weeks. Then he came back and said it would be stupid to wreck our home and the children's lives because of this one incident. I knew he was terribly broken up about it, but I hoped that in time he would forget.

"He started to stay at work for a couple of hours in the evening, then he began to go in early in the mornings, and now he often spends all day and all night there. At first I thought it must be another woman, so I checked on him—I used to phone up at odd hours, and even dropped in on him. He was always alone, working, and even his colleagues told me to stop him from working so hard or he would have a nervous breakdown. On the contrary, he has had four promotions in the past three years and is now number three in the firm. We have made love only six or seven times in the last three years; it isn't that he doesn't still want to, I know, but my affair seems to have dealt him a blow he can't recover from.

"Working the way he does is total sublimation. He has had some brilliant successes, done things which three years ago he wouldn't even have dreamed of, and I'm convinced that it's because all his energies and desires are channeled into one thing—his work. He is a stranger to the children now, and I know he regrets this, but it's as though he's possessed by a demon and just can't stop."

When sublimation is as total as this, it is doubtful whether the person concerned will be able to return to a life of normal sexual activity unless some outside circumstance powerful enough to change his way of life occurs, or unless he becomes aware of what he is doing and has a genuine desire to change the pattern. The interesting, though on a personal level tragic, aspect of his sublimation is that it reinforces the belief that a rechanneled sex drive can produce excellence in the occupation to which all energy has been diverted, be it writing a symphony or designing a house. It is normally assumed that it is only the happy, whole man who is capable of producing his best work, but there is more than enough evidence to suggest that the thwarted man may also manage to achieve excellent results.

Mixed Feelings

Sublimation does not have to be total, nor permanent. It may even be "used" to enhance a situation. One well-known novelist, who writes, and publishes, one best-selling novel every year, uses sublimation as a positive force from the moment he first sits down at his typewriter until his book is finished, which may take anything from three weeks to three months. "There is usually a slow buildup before I start writing the book, and during this period I may be morose, retiring, or downright aggressive. Then the moment occurs when I have to begin to write. After this *all* my energies center on the book, and only the book.

"My wife says she both dreads and welcomes this moment: dreads it because it is the end of real communication, whether emotional or sexual, until I've finished, and welcomes it because I've been behaving in an outlandish way for weeks beforehand and she wants 'to get the show

Writers may use sublimation as a positive force, directing their sexual energy into creative work to bring a chapter to life.

on the road.' When I've started the book there is literally no time or energy for anything else. If I have to describe a sex scene, for example, I can only do it when I'm keyed up myself, feeling positively horny as I write the chapter. Otherwise I can't write convincingly.

"If I were to do the obvious thing and go and make love to my wife, that section of the book would die, because in trying to capture the desire on paper, without actually living it, I can express sexuality, but if I'd just fulfilled it, there would be no impetus. That's sublimation as far as I'm concerned: getting all my thoughts, needs and desires down on paper rather than acting them out."

For this writer sublimation is a tool, not a way of life. His rechanneling results in a keener awareness, an enhanced performance. But at the point where this performance becomes the only reason for his existence, where sublimation occurs at all levels, it threatens the quality of his life, no matter what heights his diverted drives have helped him achieve, and he becomes a victim of external pressures which stifle the development of his full capacities.

ENCYCLOPEDIA OF HUMAN BEHAVIOR

PROCREATION
The act of reproducing the species.

PRODIGY
Someone who shows exceptional ability in any sphere, particularly in childhood.

PRODROME
A symptom which acts as an ''early warning'' for oncoming disease.

PROFESSION
An occupation which requires a sustained period of high-level education beyond the normal school years.

PROFICIENCY
Any skill which has been developed to a very high degree.

PROGESTERONE
The hormone produced by the ovaries which prepares the uterus for pregnancy.

PROGNATHISM
A condition in which the jawbones, upper and lower, project in front of the line of the forehead. It is characteristic of the apes and primitive man.

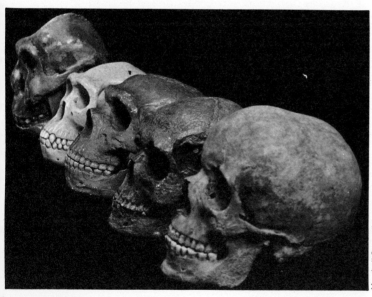

Marshall Cavendish

PROGNOSIS
An attempt to predict the end course of a disease.

PROGRAM
A set of instructions fed to a machine or computer which determines its future course of action.

PROGRAMED LEARNING
An early approach to automated instruction in which so-called teaching machines were given the capacity to interact with humans through simple lessons. Programed texts are special books which, while far less effective, nevertheless have a self-tutorial function.

PROJECTION
In psychoanalysis, one of the defense mechanisms by which the ego rejects its own unpleasant motives by attributing them to other people.

PROJECTION FIBERS
Nerve cells which conduct impulses into or away from the sensory areas of the brain.

PROJECTION TESTS
Psychological tests which rely on providing the patient with a rather vague or ambiguous stimulus—a picture is the most common example—and inviting him to interpret or elaborate on it in some way. The theory behind such tests is that in the course of his elaboration the patient will reveal, unconsciously, some feature of the problem, anxiety or sense of guilt which is affecting him. The two best known, and in many ways the most effective, projection tests are called the Rorschach and the TAT respectively. The Rorschach consists of an inkblot on a sheet of paper, which is then folded and smudged to produce a bilaterally symmetrical pattern, itself more or less formless but capable of any type of interpretation. Anxious patients see monsters or frightening shapes, repressed individuals often reveal aggression, and so on. The TAT (thematic apperception test) provides more definite stimulus in the form of drawings of people in vague, uncertain situations. The kind of story the patient feels often turns out to be a fantasy about his own life situation. Projection tests are by no means an infallible method, and they do rely on skilled interpretation and insight. At the very least they can often work wonders by getting withdrawn patients to talk and thus open communication lines.

PROMISCUITY
Indiscriminate sexual intercourse.

PROOF
Evidence which convincingly and—ideally—conclusively supports a belief.

PROPAGANDA
Statements or actions made by one group with the deliberate aim of changing the beliefs of another.

PROPHYLAXIS
Any systematic attempt at avoiding a disease.

PROPRIOCEPTOR
A nerve cell which responds to movement within the body and also indicates to the brain the position of various parts of the body.

PROSTHESIS
A device which takes the place of a missing part of the body, such as an artificial limb.

PROTANOPIA
A type of red-green color blindness.

PROTEIN
A chemical substance comprised largely of nitrogen which is an important constituent of all living matter.

PROTOPLASM
The fluid which makes up the bulk of living cells.

PROTOZOA
Single-celled organisms which are among the simplest living creatures.

PROVERB TEST
A test for children and people suspected of being mentally retarded, in which the subject is asked to explain the meaning of a simple proverb.

PSEUDESTHESIA
Any kind of false or illusory sensation.

PSEUDOSCOPE
A device shaped like a cumbersome pair of spectacles that transfers images which should have gone to the right eye into the left eye and vice versa. It is used in studies of perceptual learning. A pseudo*phone* swaps *sounds* from right to left ears and vice versa.

PSI
A word used by parapsychologists to denote any form of extrasensory perception.

PSILOCYBIN
The hallucinogenic drug taken from a Mexican mushroom.

PSYCHALGIA
Feeling pain when there is no organic cause.

PSYCHASTHENIA
An obsolete term for all neuroses involving anxieties, phobias and obsessions.

PSYCHE
The mind, soul or self.

PSYCHEDELIC DRUG
A drug which acts directly on personality or self-concept to produce dramatic changes in mood and sometimes hallucinations.

PSYCHIATRIC SOCIAL WORKER
Someone, not necessarily medically or psychologically qualified but nevertheless specially trained, who helps to deal with mentally disturbed individuals.

PSYCHIATRIST
A medically qualified doctor who has also taken a post-graduate course in abnormal psychology. His primary role is in the treatment of mental disorder.

PSYCHIATRY
The practice of the diagnosis and treatment of mental disorders.

PSYCHIC BLINDNESS
Failure of vision for which there is no organic cause and which is related to a personality disturbance of some kind. It is also known as *hysterical blindness.*

PSYCHIC DETERMINISM
The belief that for every mental process—including such things as dreams, slips of tongue, and lapses of memory—there is a conscious or unconscious cause.

PSYCHIC ENERGY
Mental or intellectual drive. This term is also used in psychical research to refer to paranormal power of the mind.

PSYCHICAL RESEARCH
The study of unusual phenomena, including such things as telepathy, ghosts, dreams about the future, and so on, for which there is no natural explanation.

PSYCHOACOUSTICS
The study of the mental and physiological processes involved in hearing.

PSYCHOANALYSIS
The approach to understanding the human personality and treating its disorders first developed by Sigmund Freud. The essence of psychoanalysis is the belief that the mind has at least two aspects to it: the conscious, which is what we normally experience, and the unconscious. The unconscious in fact plays an enormous part in controlling behavior, but because it is unconscious we tend not to be aware of it and even to doubt its existence. The problem is that unconscious and conscious motives may clash, producing an overall disturbance in personality which leads to neurotic conditions and general psychological suffering. Psychoanalysis itself is a technique for approaching the unconscious and attempting to discover the forces which control us without our conscious knowledge. Its principal aid is the study of dreams, which Freud believed allowed messages from the hidden mechanisms of our mind to filter through, even if in disguised form. Many psychoanalytic theories were considered outrageous and shocking when they were first advanced, and even today its principles are by no means fully accepted in scientific terms. Furthermore, evidence that psychoanalysis is a really effective form of therapy for severe mental illness is hard to come by. However, one of its principal arguments as advanced by Freud—that man is controlled by powerful unconscious forces—is only too obviously true. For many people this is the single achievement of psychoanalytic theory.

PSYCHOANALYST
Someone who practices the techniques of psychoanalysis. He need not be medically qualified but must have had a training in psychoanalytic methods.

PSYCHODRAMA
A feature of group psychotherapy in which patients as individuals or as a group try to act out their emotional problems. Through this technique they hope not only to give free expression to inhibited ideas, but also to get insight into their condition from the comments of others.

PSYCHOGALVANIC RESPONSE
A change in the electrical resistance of the skin brought on by a fluctuation in emotional state. It is also known as the *galvanic skin response*. Devices to measure it form part of the polygraph or lie detector.

PSYCHOGENIC DISORDER
An illness which has no obvious physical origin and is therefore assumed to be due to some mental conflict.

PSYCHOKINESIS (PK)
A technical term used by parapsychologists to refer to the alleged power of the mind alone to move or affect objects.

PSYCHOLINGUISTICS
The study of the mental processes involved in the origins, learning and use of language.

PSYCHOLOGICAL WARFARE
Attempts to attack or weaken an enemy based on a knowledge of his psychological mechanisms. At the individual level, this would include brainwashing; at the mass level, carefully designed propaganda.

PSYCHOLOGIST
Someone trained in the functioning of the mind and brain who attempts to use his knowledge to understand his fellow men, diagnose and where possible treat their illnesses, and apply this knowledge to the ultimate improvement of society in general. In the course of this work, psychologists may study animals, human beings as individuals or in groups, or specific aspects of the brain and its physiology.

PSYCHOLOGY
The scientific study of the mind and behavior. The field embraces not only experimental psychology, but also some aspects of psychiatry and psychoanalysis.

PSYCHOMETRY
The measurement and assessment of differences in mental abilities and behavior. It has a special meaning in psychical research to refer to the alleged capacity of mediums to gather impressions about the history of an object simply by holding it.

PSYCHOMOTOR TESTS
Tests which measure human abilities, particularly those between the brain and physical movement.

PSYCHONEUROSIS
An alternative term for *neurosis*, a relatively mild and generally curable mental disorder.

PSYCHOPATH
Someone whose personality is characterized by a significant lack of concern about the consequences of his actions and an apparent indifference to the future. The term is rapidly becoming obsolete.

PSYCHOPATHOLOGY
The study of mental disorders, in particular their origins.

PSYCHOPHARMACOLOGY
The study of the effect of drugs on the brain and central nervous system.

PSYCHOPHYSICS
The investigation of the capacity of the human senses.

PSYCHOSEXUAL
Relates to the study of human sexuality, in particular the interaction between mental life and sexual behavior.

PSYCHOSIS
A severe mental disorder generally with some organic cause, which may be biochemical or pathological in the form of brain damage. Psychoses characteristically disrupt the personality to the extent that hospitalization and prolonged periods of treatment may be necessary. Unlike the neuroses they tend to be long-term, seriously disabling, and not always easy to cure.

PSYCHOSOMATICS
The study of the interaction between mental and physical processes. It is also the study of physical disorders which are thought to have a mental or psychological origin.

PSYCHOSURGERY
The attempt to treat very severe psychological disorders by surgical destruction of parts of the brain. It tends to be a "last-ditch" approach and is falling out of favor in modern psychiatry.

PSYCHOTHERAPY
Any attempt at alleviating psychological disorders when conducted by someone qualified in psychological methods.

PSYCHOTOMIMETIC DRUGS
Drugs which produce in the normal person a state similar to a psychosis.

PUBERTY
The period of growth when the reproductive organs reach maturity. It generally ends at the age of 13 or 14.

PUDENDA
The external genital organs, especially of a woman.

PUERILISM
A tendency to act in a childish way.

PUERPERAL
Relating to the process of childbirth.

PUPIL
The opening on the iris at the front of the eye which widens or narrows to let in more or less light.

PURITIS
Itching caused by nervous irritation or anxiety.

PURKINJE AFTERIMAGE
A visual sensation, also known as *Bidwell's ghost*, which occurs after a bright light has been briefly fixated upon. It is generally in the color complementary to the original stimulus.

PYKNIC TYPE
A physique which tends to be fat and short, once believed to be characteristic of people suffering from manic-depressive psychoses.

PYROMANIA
An abnormal interest in watching or creating fires.

PYROPHOBIA
An abnormal fear of fire.

QUADRIPLEGIA
Paralysis of the four limbs.

QUALITATIVE DIFFERENCE
A difference in kind or nature rather than degree.

QUANTITATIVE DIFFERENCE
A difference in degree rather than in kind.

QUANTUM
A basic or individual unit of something.

RNA
A biochemical substance which plays a significant role in the mechanisms of genetics and inheritance.

RACE
One of the major subdivisions of the species *Homo sapiens*. Racial boundaries are not so clear-cut as those between species, but individuals are said to be from the same race when they have a common ancestry and a certain number of significant physical features in common. As far as the various human races are concerned, there is no scientific evidence for significant intellectual differences.

RACIAL MEMORY
A controversial concept which proposes that humans have, in addition to personal memories stretching into infancy, access to a pool of "collective memories" which go back into the distant past of man. The evidence for such memories is almost negligible, and the closest that we might get to them is in instincts, when a behavior pattern established possibly millions of years ago recurs in every member of a species. The notion of racial memory is important in Jungian psychology, where the roughly equivalent term *collective unconscious* is also used.

RACISM
An attitude of mind or collection of beliefs about racial difference, and the relative superiority of certain races. It has more political than scientific significance.

RADIONICS
A pseudoscience largely concerned with the study of waves or "vibrations" not detectable by orthodox scientific equipment, but allegedly measurable by eccentric devices like pendulums or dials. A small but thriving field of fringe medicine is based on radionics ideas and equipment.

RAMUS
The branch of a nerve or vein.

RANDOMNESS
An elusive concept, important in psychology, statistics and most fields of science. A set of numbers is said to be random when it is impossible by looking at any series of them to predict with any degree of confidence the one that follows. It also has the more general meaning "occurring by chance."

RANDOM SAMPLING
Picking items or numbers from a group in such a way that it would have been impossible to have predicted beforehand which items would be chosen.

RAPID EYE MOVEMENTS (REMS)
Jerky movements of the eyes made during sleep which have been shown to be associated with dreaming. If people are woken during REM sleep they will generally report a dream, whereas they will not if woken at other times.

RAPPORT
A close, intense relationship between people.

RATIONAL BEHAVIOR
Activity which is guided by reasoning and has describable origins and goals.

RATIONALISM
Plato's basic philosophy that truth can be acquired only through the use of reason.

RATIONALIZATION
The process by which people seek a reason or justification for any act or thought. In neurotic or psychotic behavior, sound reasons are rarely easy to come by and patients make bizarre explanations of their eccentric behavior.

RAT-MAN
The name given by Freud to disguise the identity of one of his patients who had been crippled by phobias and obsessive behavior. Freud's year-long psychoanalysis of the "rat-man" was the first successful treatment of this kind for a major obsessive-compulsive neurosis.

RAUWOLFIA
Plant from which the antipsychotic drug *reserpine* is derived.

REACTION
The response of a living thing to any stimulation.

REACTION FORMATION
One of the basic mechanisms, according to Freud, by which the ego or self defends itself from unwanted or unpleasant ideas or thoughts. The process involves counterattacking the particular thought by subconsciously disguising it with one which is opposite to it. At its simplest level, you might express great friendliness towards someone whom you disliked intensely because you did not wish to admit this dislike to yourself.

REACTION TIME
The time lag between the onset of a stimulus and the appropriate response by the organism.

REACTIVE PSYCHOSIS
A psychosis brought on by overwhelming problems in the environment.

REACTIVE SCHIZOPHRENIA
Schizophrenic behavior which has a sudden onset and often appears to be due to some identifiable problems or pressures. It is frequently of short duration.

READING SPAN
The number of words or figures which a person can understand when given a brief look at them—as, say, when they are flashed onto a screen for less than half a second.

REALISM
The philosophy which holds that the universe exists, and will exist, whether any person knows about it or is aware of it. In other words, matter can exist independently of mind.

REALITY PRINCIPLE
An important Freudian concept which says that the ego or conscious self realizes that it cannot have immediate gratification of all the desires and needs of the body, and therefore makes appropriate compromises and adjustments. That part of the unconscious mind known as the id, on the other hand, is always seeking constant satisfaction and therefore has no "sense of reality."

REBIRTH FANTASY
A dream or fantasy often experienced in the course of psychoanalysis in which the individual believes that he has some memory of his own birth. In dream symbolism this often occurs as a figure emerging from the sea.

RECAPITULATION THEORY
The theory that in the development of the embryo and fetus, every organism passes through the evolutionary stages resembling the series of ancestral types from which it is descended—fish, reptile, and so on.

RECEPTOR
A highly specialized cell whose function is to receive sensory stimuli, such as light or sound waves, and convert these into a nervous impulse which then passes to the brain. There are four main types of receptors: those responsive to light, to touch (including sound), to chemicals and to heat or cold.

RECIDIVISM
Recurrence of a mental disorder after it appears to have cleared up. It is also used for recurring criminal behavior.

RECIPROCAL INNERVATION
A balancing neural mechanism of some kind. The most common example is the way one pair of muscles, when tense, automatically causes relaxation in the opposing pair.

RECOGNITION TEST
A test of memory in which the subject is presented with a number of alternatives and asked which of them he has seen before. Recognition is a simpler approach to memory than recall, in which the subject is expected to remember the items without any aids.

RECONSTRUCTION
One of the main tools of psychoanalysis, in which the therapist attempts to interpret the patient's symptoms, dreams, and so on in an effort to establish the origins of his conflicts. Freud likened it to "mental archaeology."

RECOVERY TIME
The period after a response has been made or a nerve has been fired, during which no stimulus can bring on the response. This blank period is assumed to be related to a kind of "rest period."

RECRUITMENT
A term used in physiology to refer to the way in which a constant stimulus at a particular point in the nervous system will cause a steady increase in the number of active cells in the area of the stimulus.

RED
The color perceived by the brain when the retina is stimulated with light whose wavelength is 650-750 millimicrons.

RED-GREEN BLINDNESS
The most common form of color blindness in which reds and greens are confused. Almost 10 percent of males suffer it to some degree, but it is much rarer (less than 1 percent) in females.

REDINTEGRATION
The evoking of a complete memory when only part of the associated stimuli is present. A fragment of a tune will often allow us to recognize or remember the whole of it.

REDUCTIONISM
An approach to science which states that the best way to understand a phenomenon is to break it down into its component parts. The argument carries little weight among psychologists, few of whom feel that the mind is best understood by examining all the individual cells in the brain.

REDUNDANCY
A term used in information theory and cybernetics, and relevant to psychology, to refer to any excess of information or duplication of items in a message. Redundancy is important in human speech because it allows occasional mishearings or errors to be made without breaking up the sense of the whole message.

REFERENCE GROUP
In sociology, any collection of people with whom an individual feels able to identify.

REFERRED PAIN
Pain felt in one area of the body which actually originates in another. Most people come across this at the dentist when drilling in one tooth will often produce sensations in another part of the mouth or jaw.

REFLEX
An automatic response to a particular stimulus which is generally supposed to be unlearned or inherited.

REFLEXOLOGY
The approach to psychology which attempts to explain all brain and mental operations in terms of conditioned reflexes.

REFRACTION
The bending of a light wave when it passes from one medium (like air) into another (like glass).

REFRACTION ERRORS
An imperfect image on the retina produced by some irregularity or distortion in the eye's refracting media.

REFRACTORY PERIOD
The period of time after a nerve has been stimulated before it will respond to a second stimulation. It is sometimes known as the *recovery period*.

REGENERATION
The regrowth of a missing part of the body. This tends to be a capability of lower forms of animal life.

Lessons in love

It's supposed to come naturally, but enjoying sex is something some of us have to work at.

Sex is only one part of a full relationship. A man and a woman in love and sharing their life together, whether married or not, enjoy each other's company and support in many ways. Many of the rewards of marriage have little direct connection with a couple's love-making—establishing a home together, raising children, building up a network of friends and relatives, helping each other through emotional or work crises and carrying through the long-term involvements of marriage.

Stresses and Strains

Love-making, however, can set the whole tone of the relationship. The couple who get on well in bed are communicating happily on at least one level and this has a happy effect on everything they do together. Problems may still exist but at least the partners will not lose touch with each other. But when the couple's sexual involvement is plagued with troubles, the resulting tensions and misunderstandings can affect every aspect of their relationship. A marriage can survive despite these problems—they settle for other rewards—but there is always a danger that it will fall apart. In this situation sexual therapy offers a couple the hope of finding sexual fulfillment and of reestablishing their marriage on a firm basis.

The first stage is recognizing that there is a source of conflict within the relationship—and that help from outsiders can be useful. One difficulty is that the couple themselves may not realize that their sexual disharmony is disturbing other areas of their life. And they may not know where to turn for help and advice.

Where the sexual failures are closely interlinked with the general strains of marriage, then friends, relatives and even colleagues at work may ease the burden almost without knowing they have become involved. One common situation comes when a young couple have a baby. The husband may still be working long hours to establish himself in a job; the wife, lacking any real guidance, expends vast amounts

Even minor sexual difficulties often seem insurmountable to a young and inexperienced person.

of energy on attempting to keep the house tidy and cope with the baby. Exhaustion sets in, love-making suffers and possibly ceases. Sexual frustration stretches the couple's nerves and begins to turn minor upsets into major quarrels.

Because the signs of strain are so obvious to outsiders, advice and help may be proffered unasked for. Colleagues may suggest to the husband that he shed some of his work load; one of the grandmothers may offer to take care of the baby for two weeks to give the couple the chance to take a vacation and reestablish the sexual side of their relationship. A break such as this—so long as the couple take the opportunity to assess what is happening to them—may be all that is needed to banish any sexual troubles since these are a symptom, rather than a cause, of difficulties.

Situations where problems revolve more directly around sexual conflicts may still respond to simple advice from easily accessible professional contacts such as the family doctor, the staff of a birth control clinic, or a marriage guidance counselor. Where misconceptions and anxiety are all that lie behind sexual difficulties then reassurance and straightforward instruction may be all that are needed.

Straight Talking

Many young couples have little direct knowledge of sexual matters and, especially during the early period of adjustment to each other, may become confused about just how they should approach love-making and what they should expect from it. Dissipating this confusion requires straight talking by someone knowledgeable about sexual matters rather than the half-embarrassed mumbles of acquaintances.

Several colleges in the United States and elsewhere have established centers where advice about sexual problems is readily available—backing this up with pamphlets such as *Elephants and Butterflies* from the University of North Carolina and *Sex is Never an Emergency* from the University of Pennsylvania. No one functions well in any sphere—physical, intellectual, social, or emotional—

when troubled by sexual anxieties, and these counseling centers, together with others open to non-students, can be of great help. Much of their activity revolves around providing contraceptive advice and assuaging young people's feelings of guilt about masturbation or sexual intercourse itself. But they go far further with help for young men complaining of impotence or premature ejaculation or young women who fear they might be frigid.

Friction or Feeling

Once again, advice and reassurance may be all that is necessary. Early sexual contacts can be fraught with anxiety. Commenting on just how common some experience of impotence or premature ejaculation is can stop a young man thinking that he alone among his fellows is sexually abnormal; explaining the nature of female sexual responses helps a young woman understand why she has not yet reached orgasm with her boyfriend; contraceptive advice takes away the inhibiting fear of pregnancy. And above all, the detached outsider can point out the difference between friction and feeling: under the frenetic conditions of one-night stands, of searching for a personal identity amid shifting concepts of what a rewarding relationship might be, sex is not as fulfilling as it might be in a more stable and secure situation.

When the problems are more deeply engrained, then more specialized professional help may be needed. Talk and advice can go only so far. The doctor, counselor, religious advisor or even lawyer who first sees one of the partners—the woman alone makes the initial move in the majority of cases; only about one in ten times do the couple appear together—may, for example, suggest psychiatric care. Where one or both partners is suffering from depression, anxiety or some other mental illness, love-making can become perfunctory and this further upsets the couple. Drug treatment or other forms of psychotherapy which alleviate the psychological disturbance ultimately may restore normal sexual functioning as part of a general return to mental well-being.

Therapy which aims directly at relieving symptoms of sexual failure is, however, becoming increasingly common. The reasons for this have much to do with the recommendations of Dr. William H. Masters and Virginia E. Johnson which resulted from their researches into human sexuality. Over a decade of research at the Reproductive Biology Foundation, St. Louis, Missouri, provided the material for their book *Human Sexual Response*, published in 1966. *Human Sexual Inadequacy*, which followed in 1970, describes their innovative clinical work and defines their attitude towards sexual dysfunction. Masters and Johnson have themselves trained therapeutic teams, others follow their guidelines, and many therapists subscribe to their basic viewpoint.

Sexual functioning, they believe, is so important to the well-being of the personality that restoring it is of prime importance. Treating sexual dysfunction directly—instead of as an adjunct to a general therapeutic program—sidesteps the psychological problems that sexual difficulties themselves produce. But they stress the importance of treating sexual dysfunction within the context of a couple's relationship and life-style. Additional therapy and counseling programs aimed at dealing with other aspects of the couple's psychological and social problems may well be necessary, but Masters and Johnson suggest that in many cases the restoration of a full and rewarding sex life can be so beneficial that the couple find they are emotionally strong enough to cope themselves with problems that previously appeared insurmountable. Masters and Johnson estimate that as many as 50 percent of married couples are afflicted by sexual problems and that many of these could be helped by some form of therapeutic program.

Rocky Relationship

Masters and Johnson telescope their therapeutic program into two weeks of night and day activity at their clinic facilities; other programs may be spread over weeks or months with visits to the therapist interspersed with controlled sexual expression and satisfaction, while another group of therapists supplements guided sexual exploration with drugs or hypnosis.

Masters and Johnson, pioneers in the field of sex therapy, use wooden dolls in counseling sessions to show couples how to stimulate and explore each other sexually.

But virtually all sex therapy programs have a common underlying structure.

The early stages involve an exploration of the psychiatric, social, and medical background of the person or couple seeking treatment. Any program aimed directly at overcoming sexual dysfunction requires the backing of counseling sessions aimed at reducing psychological and marital stresses that are involved with sexual failure, together with a medical examination to make sure that physical factors such as undiagnosed diabetes are not involved.

Exploration of specifically sexual problems follows. In the vast majority of cases these fall into the areas of male impotence and premature ejaculation and female lack of sexual response and difficulty in attaining orgasm. Talking about the individual's problems in a calm and sympathetic way sets the tone for the treatment that follows. Often this is the first time that the sufferer has been able to discuss sexual matters openly and in an adult fashion.

The therapist will be careful to avoid apportioning blame or hinting at personal inadequacy: one of the aims of therapy is to stop the kind of self-defeating recrimination that can plague a rocky relationship. Masters and Johnson's program uses a team of therapists, one male and the other female. At this stage the male therapist talks to the husband, the female to the wife, followed later by four-sided discussions. This arrangement avoids the problems that can arise if one partner feels a single therapist is siding with the other partner. The two therapists continue to supervise and offer guidance and analysis throughout the program.

With the problem areas now fully identified, some therapists will take the sufferer on a "trip into the past." By searching out and revealing the

Half of all married couples have sexual problems: therapy could help in the majority of cases.

fears, anxieties, and earlier sexual failures that have contributed to the present dysfunction, the therapist hopes to give the sufferer insight into his condition and to pave the way for a more fulfilling sexual relationship.

In one mode of therapy, particularly when the sufferer is single or is undertaking therapy separately from his partner, the therapist will give relaxant drugs or use hypnosis to produce an equivalent relaxed state, and then talk the patient through an imaginary version of the disquieting sexual act. Over several sessions of "imaginary love-making" the sufferer hopefully comes to terms with his or her anxieties and, with the help of the therapist, can transfer this newfound confidence to a real sexual encounter.

Surrogate Partners

Many therapists prefer to consult with both partners in a relationship. They believe the object is to restore full sexual functioning to both partners within the context of their ongoing involvement. Where therapists are following the Masters and Johnson

guidelines, they will attempt to alleviate the couple's sexual dysfunction by leading them through a guided program of shared sexual exploration and stimulation, aimed at destroying the ingrained reflexes that prevent full sexual functioning, and substituting responses that lead to fulfillment.

Sometimes when a single person is being treated the therapists may arrange for a surrogate partner (as Masters and Johnson have done), a volunteer whose sexuality is firmly based and who leads the sufferer through sexual exercises that ultimately lead to full intercourse.

Some therapists will even have sexual relations with certain people they treat to demonstrate to the patients that their physical sexual functioning is normal, but this can have explosive results if the patients invest their emotional energy in the therapist instead of seeking to strengthen an ordinary relationship.

The main aim of these "sensate focusing" programs is to instill sexual habits and attitudes towards love-making that will build into a

continuing fulfilling sexual life. One of the most important aspects is educating the partners in what Masters and Johnson call the "give-to-get" principle. When a couple encounter sexual failure they are liable to withdraw into their own personalities, to become critical spectators of their love-making rather than participants. Teaching each partner to give pleasure to the other begins to restore their emotional participation, and the stimulation they in turn get from the partner's increased pleasure completes the process.

Source of Pleasure

Sharing the responsibilities and enjoyments of sexual stimulation is another aspect of love-making the therapist stresses. In treating a man's premature ejaculation, his partner is shown a simple technique in which, by pressing on his erect penis around the ridge of the penile glans, she can delay his urge to ejaculate. As the man nears orgasm during foreplay he tells his partner, she squeezes, and they continue foreplay until he nears orgasm again. The man realizes it is possible to postpone his orgasmic reflex with his partner's aid and eventually learns to control his ejaculation himself. As his partner finds that she, too, has a measure of control over his reactions they begin to look upon the man's erection as *theirs,* a source of pleasure for both, rather than a focus of sexual failure for him alone.

Mapping out a route that leads the partners to full and satisfying mutual physical stimulation is the final component of the therapeutic program.

More clinical forms of sexual therapy are available to people whose problems appear more directly debilitating than lack of sexual fulfillment in an otherwise rewarding relationship. A homosexual, for example, unhappily unable to come to terms with his diverse sexual inclinations, may find a behaviorist-influenced therapist prepared to help him shift his sexual focus from males to females. An unassuming sexual deviant such as a voyeur or exhibitionist may be helped towards a maturer expression of his sexuality. And in research projects among more serious sexual criminals convicted of rape or molesting young children, scientists are investigating the effects of treatments such as hormone injections in the hope that they will enable these people to control their unacceptable sexual urges.

But the greatest contribution of

Marshall Cavendish

sexual therapy comes in aiding the vast number of ordinary relationships in which some improvement in sexual functioning pays off over and over again. The happiness of newlyweds enabled to consummate their marriage after months of frustration, the extra lease on life their renewed discovery of sexual enjoyment can give a middle-aged couple, the greatly

Some couples feel embarrassed about discussing private matters with a stranger. When they can, the battle is half won.

increased effectiveness, in all aspects of life, of the young man or woman who is freed from sexual anxiety—these are the real justifications and rewards of sexual therapy.

Trevor Sutton

Cloisterphobia

Life at college is a whole new ball game: neither in school nor out, neither adolescent nor mature, not yet independent but with no one but yourself to depend on. All this . . . and studying too?

The life of a student—though in many ways a privileged one—is also, for a variety of reasons, very stressful.

Firstly, it is usually during the late adolescent years that students arrive at college—a period that is inherently difficult for all young people. Establishing an adult identity and learning to form relationships with the opposite sex make heavy demands on their time and emotional energies, often accentuated by the fact that for the first time they are living away from home. This is the time when they may be learning to cater for themselves, to cook and eat a balanced diet, to budget and manage on a small allowance, to cope with being ill or unhappy, without the cushioning comfort of their families. And on top of this, they must evolve their own way of working now that they no longer have the regimentation of school to fall back on.

Then there are the particular problems that may preoccupy the student in a new environment. He may be a foreigner, or for the first time find himself living alongside foreigners in his own country. He may be black in a predominantly white college; *she* may be a woman in a predominantly male college, or a ''mature student'' who feels conspicuous among the younger majority. Whatever his worries, the student cannot afford to be ''thrown'' by them: for all the time the pressure is on him to do well.

One of the shocks that hits most students, once they have actually managed to reach that vaunted goal, the university, is the sheer amount of work that is demanded of them.

First they are given their timetables of daily events—lectures, seminars and tutorials, and laboratory work for the science student—and then they are confronted with a formidable list of recommended books from each of their teachers. To be presented with a whole term's reading at once is intimidating to some; to others it constitutes such an insurmountable problem that they are inclined to give up before they even begin.

But if the student is not yet daunted by the whole prospect, he may also take a look at past examination papers —to see what questions all this learning will equip him to answer—and this is the point that an attack of panic is most likely to set in.

Big Fishes

At this stage, the anxious student can get little help from his new classmates. The other students all appear to him to be terrifying, a group of sophisticated scholars who are far better read—and harder working—than himself. Before long, the camaraderie of anxiety will be established, and these paragons will reveal themselves to be as worried as he is . . . but as yet they still have their defenses up, just as he does.

Only when the student begins to own up to his apprehension can he begin to take a realistic view of his own abilities compared to the rest of his classmates. And this may come as something of a shock. At high school, the child who finally reached university standard was often the "big fish in the small pool." He was among the few who aspired to further education, and as well as walking off with most of the class prizes and accolades, he probably also received a great deal more interest and enthusiasm from his teachers than the rest of his year. Whether or not he took any particular pride in it, he was—of necessity—one of an intellectual elite.

University can come as a healthy shock to the youngster who has never yet had to stretch himself intellectually: most of the students there have reached his standard of education, are as bright, if not brighter. And he will have to readjust his view of himself, to realize that he is at the bottom of this new ladder, not the top, and must begin all over again the process of heaving himself up. There are some—those, perhaps, who have in fact reached the summit of their potential at school but who have been encouraged to struggle on to greater things—who will be daunted by this new competition, exhausted by the

idea of the steep academic climb. But to most, it acts as a challenge, a stimulus that wards off boredom.

On the other hand there are students who have never been confident of themselves, who have approached the idea of college with great trepidation, and who will gradually realize that they are more or less of the same standard as their peers and have at least a fighting chance.

During his first year at college the student's most pressing task is learning how to organize—both himself and his periods of work and relaxation. At school, the organization of the pupil's timetable is in the hands of the teachers. All he can do is try to establish disciplined habits of work, realistic levels of expectation.

Once at university, however, the student is on his own, and the amount of time and work he has to organize can be alarming. He must avoid the temptation to get away with as little studying as possible—and the (surprisingly) more common fault of spending *too much* time studying. And he must take care to cover every aspect of his course, and not to ignore the compulsory subjects that do not interest him as much as the rest.

Many colleges offer "packet" courses, combining what seem to be irrelevant subjects with the topics which the student has chosen to do. This often causes fury and frustration among students of literature, for example, who are forced to make fools of themselves in math classes, or scientists who tend to yawn their way through art history lectures.

Dreaded Chores

The philosophy of education that aims to develop the complete man, the broadly based mind, is sometimes responsible for spawning the militant activist who kicks against these imposed values. But unless he can succeed in making sensible changes to the syllabus, the student must decide to make the best of it: he has opted to do the full course when he chose the college, and, although it may seem crazy to him, bad grades in literature could kill his chances as a research chemist. Part of the process of learning to organize must be to apply himself to the dreaded chores as much as he does to the subjects he enjoys.

Tutors, if they understand the problems of the reluctant student lurking at the back of class, can help him by recommending interesting textbooks that take the drudge out of his least favorite topics, and, with luck, may even bring him to enjoy them.

Very few students ever come to enjoy the examinations, however. The specter of the final assessment, whatever shape it takes, can turn an otherwise competent, even a brilliant, student into a pathetic, shaking, incapable nervous wreck.

This is not true for all, of course: exams are hurdles that clever schoolchildren have obviously already taken in their stride. But the more urgent pressure to do well at college and the high hopes of family and friends back home can weigh on some students heavier than ever before. Most survive, but there are a few who go under. And it is vital that these few are carefully handled: the greatest intellect in the world will be of little use to a boy or girl—either at college or in the working world—if it buckles under strain. The student must learn, like everyone else, to cope with challenges and emergencies.

Stiff Upper Lip

Every student is fearful of the exam room and its implications. Most benefit by overcoming that fear for themselves, but some just cannot do so without help, perhaps even medical help. These are the people for whom the natural dread has become severe enough to warrant the title "phobia" —an irrational fear. The rearguard, stiff-upper-lip brigade of academics find it hard to reconcile themselves to the idea of psychological help, kidglove treatment, for students who suffer like this. Often they fail to recognize that there is anything peculiar about a student who has worked himself up to a fever pitch of fear. But psychological care has reached a long arm into the universities, and is now often available to such students, once they have been identified.

Treatment for exam phobia—as with other phobias—is a process of "systematic desensitization," developed from the work of the psychiatrist Joseph Wolpe. He devised a two-part method of desensitization: first, the patient is taught how to get into a very pleasant state of relaxation; then the therapist presents to him a series of stimuli related to his phobia—either the stimuli are actually present or the patient is told to visualize them in his mind's eye. These stimuli are arranged in order of severity and only a few are presented at one session, so that over a period of time the patient builds up endurance and finds that he can stand the most terrifying of the stimuli without becoming anxious.

Applied to exam phobia, this method succeeds if a series of stimuli are

Ron Embleton

worked out beforehand with the patient's help. One stimulus might be to imagine the scene in the examination hall; another might be to write an actual exam paper.

Examination Phobia

This method often brings results, but if it is not effective—or if no such treatment has been available—there is another alternative for the student who suffers from exam phobia. If all else fails he may in special circumstances be allowed to escape the terrifying, charged atmosphere of the exam room itself, and write all his papers in a room set up by his student health service—under supervision of course, but with psychological and medical help available if he needs it.

Whether it is because of an actual phobia, or because of lack of application or talent, or even because of sheer laziness, there are always students who fail completely—or fail in their own or their parents' eyes. Looking ahead to the expected quality of their degree, some students may, quite realistically, predict that they will be on the borderline between passing with distinction and just scraping through. The choice is then to decide whether to push themselves across that borderline or to give up the struggle. And even those who decide to make the effort—helped by their tutors, who are always more willing to help the hard workers—may eventually fail to reach their targets.

In the closed society of the college this can be a totally demoralizing and heartrending experience. All the anxiety, nervous energy, and long hours of studying for the exams, if it is followed by a huge disappointment, can bring about a complete emotional

If he's anxious about how he shapes up in class, he is doubly worried about how he looks to other students.

collapse, from which it may take months to recover. But the best way to recover is to become, as quickly as possible, a part of the world outside the university, where a completely different set of criteria applies. Outside college, the all-important matter of how exalted your degree was means little or nothing. The fact of having been to a university—and of having learned to apply your mind—means much more. Getting on with life and finding a job and a new frame of reference brings another, more pressing, sense of reality.

The hothouse atmosphere of the college is, without doubt, responsible for a great deal of neurosis among students. Many will come into the care of the university's health service suffering from the whole gamut of neurotic illness: anxiety, depression, phobia and obsessive-compulsive reaction. As in the outside world, some students are inherently more prone to neurosis than others, and for some it is not their studies that bring about their extreme anxiety but the other, equally exhausting, processes of becoming an adult.

Love School

Even for the most fortunate of students—with a secure background, a stable personality, a good brain—these years are years of difficulty. For he is seeking his role in life, building his image of himself, learning a sense of personal identity. What is more, the image he constructs depends, to a large extent, on how he thinks other people are seeing him. And the most crucial person in this respect will, to a large extent, be his lover.

Realizing that he is actually an object of love gives the student great self-confidence and increased vitality across a whole range of activities. But this crucial relationship—with someone whom he values and who values him in turn—is just where many of his problems begin.

Perhaps they should not be called problems at all: perhaps it is more realistic to allow that life *is* difficult at times, and that it is precisely in overcoming these difficulties that people grow to be adults. It is, of course a matter of degree, and it is when the problem gets too big to handle himself that the student calls out for help. There are endless love difficulties which the student may come to think of as "blighting his life," or as symptoms of all-around failure that might even drive him to think of suicide, let alone ruin his studies—the reason for his being there at all.

He may be unable to find a partner, particularly as some colleges have a distinct minority of women. (Girl students may have the opposite problem seeming to be at the center of terrible rivalry and turmoil.) He may collapse after the end of a relationship—whether he or his partner finishes the affair. He may be consumed with jealousy, or overcome with shyness. He may feel he is a complete flop with the opposite sex.

A relationship at college is apt to become intense in the extreme, perhaps because it may be the first true sexual love affair. There will be anxieties about contraception, embarrassment at lack of sexual expertise, fears about impotence, or frigidity. And there may be the trauma of an unwanted pregnancy to go through. Some students will need a great deal of counseling, for this is the time when many underlying problems will begin to emerge for the first time—hang-ups and misconceptions left over from childhood which are only now coming to the surface.

An astonishing number of young people go to the university completely unequipped to cope with the problems that the first serious love affair will bring. In the opinion of one British student health doctor, sex education at present is "hopeless, and arouses contempt": students go to college badly prepared, if prepared at all, for one of the most important facets of life there. All the more reason to use college as an opportunity for this broader form of student education, as "institutions of higher education are ideal for proper love/sex education because of the age group they serve and because their students will be future molders of opinion."

Sex Education

What are the consequences of this lack of sex knowledge which students bring to the university? Since most universities do not offer sex education the students take it upon themselves to organize, for example, lectures by "controversial" speakers—thus often causing an immediate outcry from some quarters and the condemnation of such activities as immoral and obscene.

Otherwise, there are various people who pick up the pieces, including the university health service doctors and the chaplains of the different religions. There are also organizations like the Samaritans and "Contact" who will lend an ear to a desperate voice on the other end of the telephone.

Tutors and other members of staff get a few cries for help. One very

PAF International

Not every student has problems: college can give the expanding intellect room and time to develop.

important job that they can do is to spot the fact that a student is ill: he may have drifted imperceptibly into a mild depression and nobody has noticed it. Someone who sees a student at regular intervals, such as at weekly tutorials, may be able to detect small changes that indicate trouble.

Drug Problems

If students do develop more severe psychological illnesses, such as schizophrenia or manic depression, they may just disappear inside their lodgings, or their home, without trace. It is most important to spot these illnesses and to ensure that the student is seen by the university doctor in case they need hospital treatment.

Only too often student problems are compounded by drugs. With the vigorous action of the police in recent years, the illegal use of drugs among students has probably been reduced, but the problem is always there, lurking in the background, and it is one which can severely disturb a student's career, even his whole life.

The drugs in question are mainly cannabis and LSD, but amphetamines

and opiates such as morphine and heroin are also sometimes involved. An important feature of the drug taker's world is that he is given the opportunity to join the drug "subculture" a group of fellow drug takers who may provide the student with a sense of belonging, a group of people who are, in some sense, superior to the earthbound culture outside. This superiority may rest on a quasi-mystical experience of a deeper reality with which the drug taker feels he is in contact.

Objectively, little of positive value appears to come out of the drug subculture. Moreover, any contact with even the milder drugs may be very dangerous for the impressionable student, since it opens up the possibility of moving from the innocuous cannabis to the dangerous LSD, the very dangerous amphetamines and the deadly opiates—morphine and heroin.

According to Anthony Ryle, in his book *Student Casualties*, about 30 percent of all students have at least one experience of drug taking, but only about 10 percent take any drug regularly—and often it is no more

Much of the education that goes on at college — learning to form the first mature relationships with both lovers and friends — happens outside the classroom.

dangerous than cannabis or hash.

However, a small number of students go downhill and become addicted to the opiates. They are then likely to fail academically and to run into troubles with the police. The treatment of patients such as these is extremely difficult and their outlook is very depressing indeed.

The benefits other students have at college are enormous—but so are their needs. They are exposed to very many stresses and can easily make a series of well-recognized errors. At one time or another most students will need a helping hand—someone who really understands their problems. University student health services have collected a great deal of valuable information about the various hazards and pitfalls of the student life: by plowing back all their experience they will be able to contribute a great deal to the happiness of students.

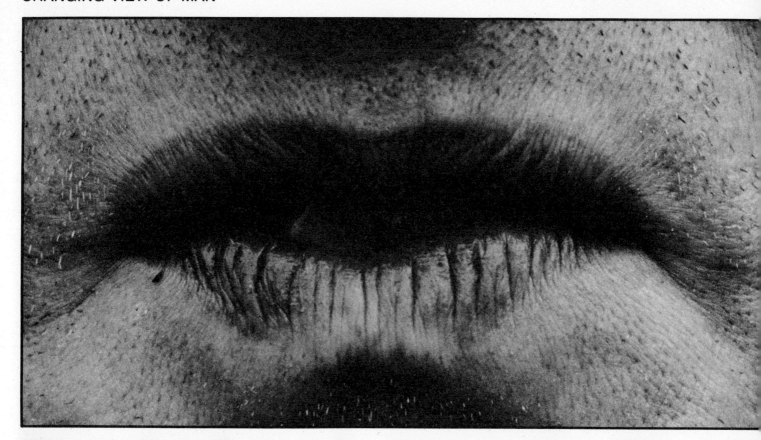

Deleted expletive

The decline and virtual fall of the naughty word has been one of the many side effects of the permissive society. The naughtiest words of previous decades are widely established in our daily vocabulary with the result that their naughtiness is nullified.

Historically speaking, there were three separate elements comprising the value of the naughty word. It was risqué, it could shock, and it provided a useful safety valve: a verbal outburst was often more practical than a physical one.

Swear Box

The risk of using obscene language or swearing reached a peak in Scotland in 1645, when the Scottish Parliament made cursing a crime punishable by death. The British Profane Oaths Act of 1745 contented itself with fines that varied according to the offender's social standing. Laborers, soldiers or sailors were fined a shilling, anyone who was beneath the rank of gentleman, two shillings, and those above it, five shillings. Insolvent offenders were awarded ten days hard labor instead. The potential financial disadvantage was increased by the fact that a man who went in for a succession of oaths paid for each one separately. Presumably to avoid this penalty, the crafty cursers evolved a cunning system of composites, such as "Deviltakethefathersonand holyghost." For some reason, the act did not apply to women, who were probably considered to be above such base forms of expression.

Times have changed. In Britain in the autumn of 1965, the literary director of the National Theatre, Kenneth Tynan, dared to use a four-letter word on a BBC television program. There was an instant and outraged uproar. A motion was even proposed in the House of Commons asking for Tynan's dismissal. At this point, the outcry was exposed to ridicule when a more liberal MP suggested that Tynan should not be dismissed until the Minister of Defense had discharged from the armed forces all soldiers, sailors, and airmen who had used the forbidden four-letter word during the previous five years.

Nowadays, the risk of a private individual being prosecuted for the use of obscene or blasphemous language is negligible. The danger element in the use of naughty words may be extinct, but the shock and safety qualities are still with us. There is widespread agreement on the psychological benefits of swearing. Coleridge referred to it as "so much superfluous steam that would endanger the vessel if it were retained," while Tristram Shandy's father informs us, "I swear on until I find myself easy."

Vengeful Verbosity

Swearing of this sort is very closely allied to verbal threat, and one of its intriguing characteristics is that we swear or threaten far more than it would be practical to fulfill. "I'd like to tear him limb from limb" is a threat which would require greater strength than most of us are endowed with, and would be messily unpleasant anyway. The heights of vengeful verbal destructiveness that we reach so easily tend to exceed the degree of damage we are really prepared to do.

Although letting off steam by swearing may alleviate the strain on a nation's hospital services, the shock-

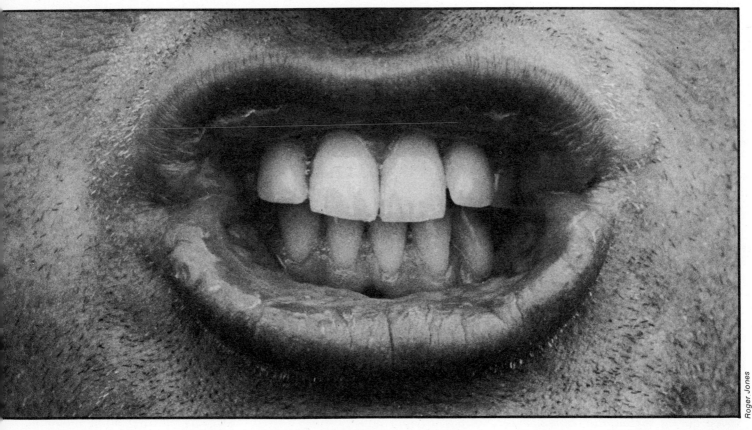
Roger Jones

ng aspects of naughty words fulfill an equally important personal function. If some insensitive human being irritates us, we may be too cowardly or too frightened of the terrible results of our own strength to resort to physical violence. So we rely on swearing, which relieves our own tensions and, hopefully, upsets the opposition.

Term of Endearment

Our aggressive verbal currency is at the moment sadly devalued. Of the two principal kinds of swearing, the religious is dead and the secular is difficult. The religious type is defunct because the majority of people today are utterly unimpressed by Father, Son, Holy Ghost, and the whole host of saints who once provided such varied inspiration for swearing. The secular form is difficult because it is almost impossible, except for someone blessed with a diseased or completely depraved imagination to conjure up anything that will remotely shock anyone any more. Swearing is inevitably subject to social considerations: to succeed in being supremely abusive, a swearer needs detailed knowledge of his opponent's views.

"Bastard" used to be an unforgivable term of abuse among the lower classes, for whom illegitimacy constituted a serious sin. In the aristocracy, however, there was far greater tolerance of bastards, who often had noble or even royal blood in their veins. Under the title of "natural

sons and daughters," they often enjoyed more privileges than their kin born on the right side of the blanket.

On the other hand, "bugger" was a pointless insult among the lower classes, who were less prone to homosexual practices. Dr. Johnson even defined the word as "a term of endearment among sailors." But among the upper classes, who were more conscious of the stigma of sexual deviation, the accusation was an outrage. If Oscar Wilde had merely been called a bastard, no one would have minded.

There was also an extremely strong taboo on mentioning the private parts of the body. This could reach ludicrous extremes, as in the case of a wounded soldier who, when asked by a visitor where he had been shot, could only reply, "I'm so sorry, ma'am, I don't know; I never learned Latin."

Equally strong was the lavatory taboo. This is not particularly surprising in itself, since not even the most permissive campaigner can claim great aesthetic qualities for defecation. What is difficult to understand is the extraordinary amount of territory this unnatural modesty obscured. Not only was it considered obscene for a man to show a woman the way to the lavatory, but even man to man, or woman to woman, an evasive phrase had to be used, "Would you care to wash your hands?" or "Have you seen the geography of the house?" were suitable substitutes. Intimate friends would not even consent

to notice each other if one of them was emerging from the lavatory or entering it and, if this was the first meeting of the day, would greet each other half a minute later on untaboo ground with every pretense of novelty and surprise.

The readiness with which the term "shit" is bandied about in the permissive society is indicative of the erosion of this traditional area of reserve. The same is true of the more sexual terms of abuse. Indeed, because previous values have been turned upside down, the more excessive the accusation of sexual deviation, the more flattering it is to be accused. "Son of a bitch" has been common usage for several decades as the tale of an American tourist, Mrs. Beech, who was staying in Paris after the war, related. An elderly Frenchman who was introduced to her greeted her cordially, "Ah, Misses Beech, you are one of ze noble muzzaires who gave so many sons to ze war."

Mentally Ill

Possibly the only area where taboos remain strong enough to provide valuable ammunition for obscene swearing is that of incest: hence the popular epithet which accuses a man of having sexual intercourse with his mother. The principal problem faced by swearing in a society overwhelmed by frankness is whether it should attempt to go even further or whether it should take a different course. For instance, a most effective insult could be to call someone a virgin!

Apart from its use in aggressive swearing, obscene language is also prevalent among the mentally ill. Some emotionally disturbed cases tend persistently to utter obscenities. This is associated with their lack of respect for other people, which is in turn bound up with their own loss of self-respect. Freud, with his characteristic determination, if not accuracy, decided that obscene words represented attempts to force the hearer to picture the content of the word. Thus obscenity, in the presence of a woman, may be a form of verbal rape.

According to some sources, there are men who insist that their women indulge in obscene language before or during sexual intercourse. As one lady put it, "I not only have to do it, but say it as well." There are also some men who enjoy talking to their partners in obscene language. This is presumably a kind of decadent antithesis to the men and women who like to be told how much they are loved during sexual intercourse.

Naughty verbal obscenities are not confined to swearing and sexual stimulation—they can also be entertaining. Evidence of our delight in naughty words is provided by the enduring popularity of the entire tradition of bawdy literature and dirty jokes. The father of English literature, Chaucer himself, knew how to turn a smutty line or two. In *The Merchant's Tale,* we find an interesting and highly gymnastic passage (modern translation):

> . . . and with a spring she thence
> —Ladies, I beg you not to take offense
> I can't embellish, I'm a simple man—
> Went up into the tree, and Damian
> Pulled up her smock at once and in he thrust.

Likewise in *The Miller's Tale:*

> Now Nicholas had risen for a piss
> And thought he could improve upon the jape
> And make him kiss his arse ere he escape,
> And opening the window with a jerk,
> Stuck out his arse, a handsome piece of work,
> Buttocks and all, as far as to the haunch.
> Said Absalom, all set to make a launch,
> "Speak, pretty bird, I know not where thou art!"

> This Nicholas at once let fly a fart
> As loud as if it were a thunderclap.
> He was near blinded by the blast, poor chap,
> But his hot iron was ready; with a thump
> He smote him in the middle of the rump.

The Elizabethans were particularly fond of naughty puns and Shakespeare was no exception. Hamlet's wordplay on "country matters" is typical, as is his play on "nunnery" with its Old English meaning of whorehouse.

Bawdy Books

What was considered acceptable in literature has, like everything else, varied with the age. The process seems to be one of extremes, pivoting from an age in which excessive sanctity prevails to one where nothing is sacred. Bawdy literature did not do too well under the puritans but the succeeding age, as exemplified by Fielding in *Tom Jones*, took a delight in every kind of naughty situation.

To shock others some people rely very heavily on four-letter words.

The Victorian age went, once again, to the other extreme, and novelists like Thomas Hardy were forced to remain so entirely inexplicit on anything even faintly sexual that some passages became awkwardly muddled as a result. The Victorians were, however, responsible for the popularity of one of the greatest devices in the history of naughty verse, the limerick.

There was a young girl of East
    Anglia
Whose loins were a tangle of ganglia
    Her mind was a webbing
    of Freud and Krafft-Ebing
And all sorts of other new-fanglia.

Much more recently we have been presented with obscene language in cinemas and theaters. Its function is not necessarily to amuse, but often to provide so-called realism. The desire to shock the audience can also form part of the motive. And usually it works. The power of words was demonstrated by the furor over the Marlon Brando film *Last Tango in Paris*. The visually explicit scenes of sexual intercourse did not arouse nearly so much indignation as the stream of gratuitous obscenities pouring from Brando's mouth.

However, what some four-letter pundits fail to realize is that shock is not a long-lasting reaction and audiences eventually become immune to even the foulest language when they are constantly bombarded with it. In stage shows like *Hair* and *Oh! Calcutta!*, the shock value of the previously banned four-letter expletives tended to become devalued.

The Art of Innuendo

In terms of naughty words, the cinema has advanced a long way since the early days of sound. The movies have always had more to contend with in terms of censorship than the theater because of their undeniable status as a popular—as opposed to privileged—entertainment medium. There was bound to be a slight discrepancy between what the educated patrons of the theater felt was suitable and tasteful for their own cultural diet and what they considered safe fodder for the uneducated masses. The production code concocted by Hollywood's Hays Office reflected this principle exactly.

The code outlawed a total of 28 words which were entirely unacceptable whatever the situation or circumstances. They included "hot," when applied to women, and "gawd." Certain less iniquitous words were allowed "where essential and required for portrayal in proper historical con-

text." One of these was "damn," though the Hays Office still caused an impressive uproar over Clark Gable's "Frankly, my dear, I don't give a damn" in *Gone With the Wind*.

The Office even went so far as to emulate an eminent Victorian called Bowdler, who compiled a "family" edition of Shakespeare minus the naughty passages, by raising objections to the use of "bastard" by Laurence Olivier in his 1945 production of *Henry V*. There the code's provision that some words could be allowed "for the presentation in proper context" (meaning for the sake of realism) did not seem to help him much.

The perennial problem of word censorship is typified by one of the scourges of the Hays Office, Mae West. No matter how many laws the moral watchdogs of the spoken word may choose to formulate, they can never entirely smother the obscene innuendo. Mae West put it in a nutshell when she said, "It isn't what I do, but how I do it. It isn't what I say, but how I say it. And how I look when I do it and say it."

Lines like "Is that a gun you're wearing or are you just pleased to see me?" are a censor's nightmare. There are no rude words involved at all but the sentiment is blatantly sexual. In the thirties, Mae West proved too hot to handle, and the howls of puritanical outrage secured the bowdlerization (he added his name to the language to make up for all the words he removed) of her scripts and her eventual demise at the box office.

Better to vent your aggression on a wall than on another person.

But *double entendres* are the exception rather than the rule of the modern cinema with its more open-minded attitude to sexual reference and description. To succeed in shocking, a contemporary movie soundtrack must be something a little special, like Brando "talking dirty" in *Last Tango*. The same is true of the stage, and where the novel is concerned the front line of defense against obscene language was breached long ago by *Lady Chatterley's Lover*. In the wake of the lusty gamekeeper there have followed homosexuals, lesbians and even enthusiastic masturbators, all of whose various activities have been graphically described.

The general rule of thumb, where naughty words in the arts are concerned, seems to be that, as long as an incident can qualify as an integral part of the main story, anything goes. As long as the inventive things that Portnoy gets up to can be seen as crucially central to our essential understanding of his character, then it is acceptable to describe them.

The arts have always been subject to more stringent standards than private conversations, which is hardly surprising when we consider the impact they have on us. The permissive society has removed most of our personal taboos on swearing and obscenity, and the arts have followed suit. But who really started the ball rolling is a subtle point.

ENCYCLOPEDIA OF HUMAN BEHAVIOR

REGRESSION

Literally, any kind of movement backwards. In psycho-analysis, it refers to a tendency on the part of the individual to return, when faced with a conflict situation, to some behavior pattern which was "successful" in similar situations at an earlier time in his life. Thumb sucking, nail biting or even smoking under stress are classic examples of this. Another good example is the child in the cartoon strip "Peanuts" who regresses to his blanket at difficult times.

Marshall Cavendish

REGRESSION TIME

In a test of reading the amount of time devoted to rereading words already passed.

REHABILITATION

The various techniques employed to bring a person back to his normal level of functioning following a mental disorder. Its main features are retraining and controlled reassurance.

REICH, WILHELM (1892-1957)

The remarkable, if highly eccentric, German psychiatrist and former star pupil of Freud's who emigrated to the United States and formed his own approach to psychology. Initially this was just a rather extreme variation of psycho-analysis, but later it embraced theories not only of the mind but also of life and universe. He thought that he had discovered the essential life substance, which he named "orgone," and he believed it was properly distributed in the body following orgasm. He also invented gadgets of various kinds to catch and release orgone in human beings.

REIFICATION

Taking an abstract idea or concept and treating it as though it were real.

REINCARNATION

The ancient belief that man's soul passes on to a new body after the death of the old one.

REINFORCEMENT

Used in psychology and physiology with roughly the same meaning as *reward*. Its specialized use has arisen from Pavlov's studies and theories of the conditioned reflex. Something is learned, according to Pavlovian and other similar theories, because the conditioned reflex has been reinforced: if an animal in an experimental situation has the opportunity to choose between a black door and a white door and finds, on his first go, that food exists behind the black door, he will be more likely to choose the black door on the next occasion. If over a large series of trials the animal consistently finds food behind the black door and never behind the white door, the conditioned reflex is said to be even more strongly reinforced. The more strongly a reflex is reinforced, the longer it will be before it dies away when *unreinforced.* If food is now suddenly taken away from the black door, the animal will continue to choose it on a large number of occasions before it begins to investigate the white door again.

REJECTION

A psychoanalytic term for one of the mechanisms by which the ego or conscious self defends itself against unwanted or threatening ideas. An enormously common strategy, it consists merely of a refusal to gratify unconscious urges by "giving in to them," and yet acknowledges their reality in the conscious mind.

REJUVENATION

Literally, making youthful again. No known mechanism for rejuvenating body cells exists, but many life situations are known to produce psychological rejuvenation—a change to a more congenial job, a new partner in love or involvement in some political idea.

RELAPSE

The return of symptoms of an illness after a period of apparent cure.

RELATIVISM

The theory that behavioral and even mental disorders are not necessarily symptoms of something at fault within the individual, but may merely be inappropriate to that particular person's society. In other words, "mental illness" can be judged only against a cultural background—what may be disturbed behavior in one culture could be perfectly normal in another.

RELAXANTS

Drugs which promote muscle relaxation and by doing so help to relieve anxiety.

RELAXATION THERAPY

An approach to psychotherapy in which the main goal is teaching the individual to relax, on the assumption that his troubles are essentially the product of tension.

RELEASE THERAPY

An approach to child psychotherapy which attempts to eliminate traumatic incidents, or the memory of them, before they have an opportunity to get established and build up a long-term neurosis. The child is encouraged to play and by doing so release the "psychic energy" bottled up by the original trauma.

RELEASER

A stimulus which may be of a simple or a complex kind and yet triggers off a highly specific pattern of behavior. Releasers are very important in the study of animal behavior, where a silhouette of a bird of prey produces specific startled and protective behavior patterns in other birds.

RELIABILITY
In psychology, the extent to which results are consistent when an experiment is repeated.

RELIGION
A system of belief which allows human beings to understand and relate themselves to the universe. In the last century or so, and in Western societies in particular, it tends to refer to those aspects of the universe not otherwise covered or "explained" by science. Most religions have at least three prime functions: first, they attempt to explain the origins and purpose of the universe; second, they attempt to explain the nature of man and what happens to him after death; and third, they offer up some kind of yardstick for assessing good and evil.

RELIGIOUS MANIA
Overzealous enthusiasm for religious matters carried to such an extent that it seriously interferes with an individual's working and social life. In some paranoid states, people may believe they are in direct communication with gods, angels, and so on.

REM SLEEP
Rapid eye movement sleep, known to be associated with the process of dreaming.

REMEDIAL INSTRUCTION
Psychological techniques employed in the training and education of children with learning difficulties.

REMINISCENCE
Taking a particular memory or set of memories and considering them at length in one's mind. This term is sometimes used to refer to circular thinking (covering the same ground over and over again) which is often a feature of anxiety states.

REMISSION
A relief of symptoms.

RENAL
Relating to the kidneys and their functions.

RENIFLEUR
Someone who gains sexual excitement from a particular smell or smells.

REPETITION COMPULSION
An overpowering desire to repeat a particular act or series of acts. This is a common feature of many severe neuroses and psychotic behaviors. The reason for such bizarre behavior is very uncertain, but psychoanalysts believe that the sufferer resorts to constant repetition during times of great anxiety or stress and uses it as a device to steer his thoughts away from the true nature of his problem.

REPRESSION
A major tactic by which the conscious mind or ego attempts to ward off from consciousness conflicts and anxieties of various kinds. Psychoanalysts in fact believe this to be the main psychological defense mechanism, which consists of a deliberate removal of unpleasant thoughts from the conscious into the unconscious mind. While this may prevent them from bothering the patient at a conscious level, the repressed ideas are by no means eliminated and can produce an underlying sense of anxiety which is all the more unpleasant because the individual cannot explain its origins.

RESERPINE
The trade name for the drug extracted from the plant rauwolfia. The drug has a powerful antipsychotic effect, but some side effects include sleepiness and an increase in heart rate. The interesting thing about the drug, which was one of the first antipsychotics to be discovered in medical science, is that the plant from which it comes has been traditionally chewed by many primitive people for its supposed effects on mental illness.

RESISTANCE
The term used to refer to a particular phase which occurs in the course of psychoanalytic treatment when the patient begins to erect blocks, of varying degrees of subtlety, to his own progress. Typically he may suddenly announce that he feels totally cured and wishes to conclude the analysis, or alternatively he may begin to complain about the slow progress that is being made and use this as an opportunity to break the treatment off. Freud argued that the real reason was that the patient's unconscious mind was becoming exceedingly sensitive to the psychoanalyst's probings and was anxiously defending its repressions from the cold light of day. The phase of resistance therefore is considered to be of great significance for it suggests that the analysis is reaching a critical phase.

RESOLVING POWER
The ability of the eye to discriminate very fine detail.

RESONANCE
Vibrations in an object induced by sound.

RESPONSIBILITY AGE
A legal term which refers to the age at which a person is assumed to be not only able to control his own actions but aware of whether they are legally acceptable or not.

RETARDATION
Slowing down of physical or mental development.

RETENTION
A physiological term for the inability or disinclination to empty the bladder or bowels.

RETICULAR ACTIVATING SYSTEM (RAS)
An important collection of nerve fibers situated at the tip of the spinal cord whose main function seems to be to control levels of attention, awareness and general activity.

RETIFISM
Sexual abnormality in which the individual gets gratification through fondling or masturbating with the shoe or foot of another person.

RETINA
The sensitive layer of cells at the back of the eye which convert light into electrical energy and send appropriate signals to the brain. The retina is composed of two basic sets of cells, the cones which handle bright lights and colors, and the rods, which come into action during low illumination.

RETINAL RIVALRY
The alternation of images which takes place when one eye

fixates on one pattern or color and the other on a totally different one.

RETROGRADE AMNESIA
Loss of memory for events which took place before the accident or event which caused the amnesia.

RETROSPECTION
Systematically going over recent events in one's mind.

RETURN SWEEP
The jump backwards which the eyes make after completing the reading of a line of text.

REVERBERATORY CIRCUIT
A system of cells in the brain which for some reason continues its activity after the originating stimulus has ceased. Thought processes are believed to be formed by circuits.

REVERIE
A dreamlike state in which thinking is under partial conscious control.

REVERSIBLE FIGURE
A simple pattern which can be seen in either of two possible states and which appears to change rapidly from one configuration to the other.

REWARD
Something given to an animal or some change in an animal's environment which, at the end of a sequence of behavior, will increase the probability that it will perform that particular sequence again: if an animal is given sugar for performing a trick, this serves as a reward to induce it to do the trick again.

RHEUMATOID ARTHRITIS
A disease of the joints which causes them to seize up and to be painful to move.

RHINE, JOSEPH BANKS (1895-   )
The biologist who formed the first university department of parapsychology, the scientific investigation of extrasensory perception and other supposed paranormal faculties of the mind. The Parapsychology Laboratory at Duke University functioned from 1927 to 1964, when it closed on Rhine's retirement from the university.

RHINENCEPHALON
The part of the brain which handles the sense of smell.

RHODOPSINE
A pigment known as *visual purple* which exists in the retinal cells known as rods. It bleaches in bright light and recovers in darkness.

RIGHTING REFLEX
An automatic response which causes an animal to return to an upright position after it has been thrown off balance. Cats are known for this ability to "land on their feet."

RIGIDITY
A psychoanalytic term for a type of personality which is particularly inflexible and resistant to change.

RODS
Sensitive cells in the retina of the eye which are concerned with vision in poor illumination.

ROGERS, CARL (1902-   )
The American psychologist who developed the so-called "client-centered" approach to psychotherapy. In this kind of treatment, the patient's symptoms are not explained to him and he is not "told what to do." The therapy relies on creating an atmosphere of support and tolerance, hopefully allowing the patient to regain the psychological strength to handle his own problems.

RORSCHACH TEST
The most famous of the projection tests used in psychology to diagnose neurotic and psychotic behavior. The individual is shown an inkblot and asked what images or thoughts it triggers in his mind. Depressed patients produce depressive images, frustrated patients aggressive ones and so on.

ROTE LEARNING
A relatively inefficient approach to learning in which the individual simply memorizes words or facts without considering their meaning or the relationship between them. This contrasts with *ideational learning*.

RUFFINI CORPUSCLE
A tiny receptor cell found in the skin which is believed to deal with the sensation of warmth.

SACCADIC MOVEMENT
The jump that the eye makes when it changes fixation from one point to another.

SACRUM
The triangular bone at the base of the spinal column.

SADISM
Sexual perversion in which pleasure is gained only by inflicting pain on another person.

SADOMASOCHISM
Sexual perversion in which gratification is associated with pain in general. *Sadism* relates to the enjoyment of giving pain to others; *masochism* relates to having pain inflicted on oneself. Sadomasochists find both situations enjoyable.

SAGGITAL FISSURE
The gap or chasm that separates the two cerebral hemispheres and runs from the front to the back of the skull.

SAINT VITUS'S DANCE
A disease of the central nervous system which leads to extreme agitation and restlessness.

SALIVARY REFLEX
The automatic and instinctive reaction which causes the mouth to water when a person is hungry and food is near.

SALPETRIERE
The famous French lunatic asylum where the physiologist Charcot conducted experiments on treating the insane through hypnosis. Freud was a pupil there for a short period.

SALPINGECTOMY
Surgical removal of the fallopian tubes as a contraceptive measure.

SAMPLE
A small group, ideally selected at random, which is taken as being representative of the larger group from which it is drawn, usually for some kind of testing purposes.

SANGUINITY
A state of mind or personality characterized by optimism, enthusiasm and freedom from anxiety.

SANITY
A state of mind which is relatively free from disorders, anxieties or mental conflicts of any kind.

SAPPHISM
Female homosexuality, also known as *lesbianism*.

SATIATION
A state of total gratification of any drive.

SATURATION
Depth, strength, fullness or "richness" of color.

SATYRIASIS
An abnormally strong and dominating sexual drive in males. The condition, which is roughly akin to nymphomania in females, most frequently has a psychological cause. An abnormal preoccupation with sex is often an indication of underlying anxieties in the individual's personality.

SCALAR TYMPANI
A spiral tube of the cochlea, a minute but important organ in the inner ear. The tube is shaped like a snail and is filled with a fluid sensitive to sound vibrations.

SCAPEGOATING
The process of transferring the aggressions and anxieties of a group onto one individual in an attempt to absolve the rest of the group from guilt.

SCANNING SPEECH
Drawn out, slurred or halting speech.

SCATOLOGICAL SPEECH
Speech which contains many obscene expressions or involves constant references to excrement, and so on. It is common, in an extreme form, in schizophrenia.

SCHEDULED REINFORCEMENT
An experimental situation in which an animal is rewarded for performing a task according to a preselected pattern. Instead of receiving a pellet of food every time it presses a bar, it might receive one only every third time, or only when it presses a bar after a light has flashed on three times.

SCHIZOID PERSONALITY
Someone with a tendency to suffer from one or another variant of the psychosis known as schizophrenia. In particular, it refers to those forms which produce a highly depressed or withdrawn personality.

SCHIZOPHASIA
Scrambled, nosensical speech, characteristic of many schizophrenic states. It is also known as *word salad*.

SCHIZOPHRENIA
The group name for a variety of severe psychoses in which the principal symptoms are disruptions of the sense of reality, a collapse of the ability to form concepts and perceive logical relationships, and marked disturbances in behavior and intellectual activity. Schizophrenia is not easy to treat and there is often a steady advance of the illness. The word was once employed to refer to multiple or "split" personality, a condition which is in fact only one aspect of the psychosis as it is known today. It was also at one time known as *dementia praecox*. The origins of schizophrenia are now assumed to be due to a physical disorder of some kind, possibly biochemical in origin. Claims that schizophrenics have been cured by psychoanalysis are viewed with skepticism by most psychologists, and treatment today, which almost always involves hospitalization, relies on the new antipsychotic drugs and psychosurgery.

SCHIZOTHYMIA
A condition in which some schizophrenic symptoms are present, although the individual appears normal in most respects.

SCHOOLS OF PSYCHOLOGY
The various attempts to provide a theoretical background to psychology which have appeared from time to time since the subject began as an experimental science just over a hundred years ago. The most important schools in the twentieth century have been the *behaviorists*, based on Pavlov's ideas and largely concerned with learning; the *Gestalt school,* based on the theories of Wolfgang Köhler and his colleagues and largely concerned with perception; and finally the *psychoanalytic schools*, springing from the work of Freud and mainly concerned with personality. A rather diffuse school based on ideas drawn from cybernetics and computing science is also beginning to emerge.

SCHOPENHAUER, ARTHUR (1788-1860)
German philosopher who anticipated Freud by suggesting that mental illness might have its origins in the unconscious mind.

SCIENCE
A systematic attempt to study the universe and gain enough information about it to be able to change it at will, and predict with confidence the outcome of such changes.

Waste not, want not

Until recently man took his environment for granted—let's hope it's not too late to save it.

It is all very well to rail against industrialists who allow their filth to foul the air, against agriculturalists who destroy wild life with their potent chemicals, against distributors whose vehicles shatter our calm with their noise, and against wholesalers and retailers whose wares leave us with so much garbage to dispose of. But are they really to blame for the pollution which is threatening the quality of life in this technological age?

Perhaps we should blame ourselves, for it is our demands which they are trying to meet, although it could be argued that it is the marketeers who have heightened our expectations and encouraged our excessive consumption habits. But it is too late for recriminations, and no purpose will be served by looking for culprits and bringing the guilty to account, when the pressing question facing us is "What should be done about it?"

Pollution is not a subject we can brush under the carpet or leave for someone else to sort out. Finding a solution is something which involves

Above: Industrial waste has turned a country stream into an eyesore.

us all because even if we are not contributors to this menace (which is supremely unlikely) we are certainly its victims. While some—the manufacturer and the motorist—cause more pollution than others—the craftsman or the cyclist—the cost is shared by us all in equal measure.

The full cost of pollution cannot be assessed in monetary terms and will never appear on the balance sheet of an industrial company. Expenditure on equipment installed to reduce pollution may be entered up, but the cost incurred in other ways is "invisible," incalculable, and far more considerable. Now, in the end, it is that company which pays the bill; the expense becomes an additional production cost which is passed onto the consumer in higher prices. Similarly if a government takes steps to control pollution which involve huge public expenditure it is the taxpayer who has to fork out.

Among the greatest assets of any industry, even if not so tangible as financial or capital investment, are the health and welfare of its work force, a high degree of productivity and co-operation, good working conditions, a low rate of absenteeism, an agreeable environment, and a pleasant community life for its workers and their families. Pollution can eliminate all these advantages at a stroke.

The story of the community rising up against its industrial overlords for destroying the valley to which they once promised prosperity is as old as the hills they have scarred and blackened. Their chimney stacks belch forth smoke, soot, corrosive acids, toxic fumes, and grime which rain down over a much wider area sullying people, their clothes, their homes, their gardens, their property. Meanwhile the surrounding countryside becomes pockmarked with dumping sites for industrial waste, and the rivers and streams which once flowed through the playgrounds of the local community become conveyor belts for rotting refuse and stinking effluent.

The workers fall prey to industrial diseases from the lifelong intake of contaminated air and water, or they become psychologically demoralized. They either cannot work or do so without enthusiasm. The people and the industry they serve, which in turn serves them by providing employment, become sworn enemies. If all this could be totted up and seen in terms of a financial liability to be entered on a company balance sheet as losses, pollution would be seen for what it is.

Safe Limit

The Council of Environmental Quality estimates that lost working days take $6 billion a year out of the economy of the United States. The loss to industry is one thing, but the cost to the individual absentee is proportionally greater. There are his lost earnings to be considered as well as his having to meet doctors' or hospital bills. Even where he is taken care of by the state, or compensated or reimbursed by some other enterprise, it does not mean that his health will necessarily be reinstated.

Sadly, pollution is here to stay. We have accepted not only that it is inevitable, but that a certain amount is permissible. We, and other living things on this planet, are sufficiently resilient and adaptable to resist small doses of contamination without suffering undue harm. But where do we draw the line? We can fix limits to the amount of pollution acceptable—the safe limit of the nitrate content of water set by the World Health Organization at 100 parts per million.

But establishing such thresholds is fraught with complications. The susceptibility to contamination of any sort varies from person to person. And while we are simultaneously exposed to a variety of forms of pollution—in the air from toxic gasses and radiation, in our water supplies, and in the food we eat—our bodies may be able to cope with a certain amount of one or another kind of poison but may not be able to overcome the cumulative

Our beaches are now tarred and feathered as well as littered.

Camera Press

effect. The same goes for the resistance of the natural environment to waste matter. Moreover, we never know precisely when and where the agents of contamination are present and in what concentrations.

The only way to be absolutely sure of effectively protecting ourselves and our environment is to set the limit of pollution permissible as low as possible—that is to say, none at all. But this means no industry, no technology, no modern techniques in agriculture; it means outlawing the motor car and all forms of speedy transport; it means evacuating the cities and dispersing their populations in the hills from which they came.

Although some people would say that these would be the most "progressive" steps man could take, they are clearly impracticable, and even the most stentorian cry of "Stop the World!" is unlikely to be heeded. Backtracking is far more difficult than forging ahead. So we have to find ways of scaling down pollution which our existing industrial and domestic systems create, reorganize our economic arrangements so that unnecessary pollution can be eliminated, devise new methods of disposing of solid, liquid, and gaseous wastes, or else rely on science to come up with new sources of power and means of production which do not have pollutant by-products.

Heavy Penalties

These aims are being vigorously pursued, but meanwhile we have to deal with the present emergency. This has arisen because up until recently the natural environment has been regarded as a free repository for human and industrial waste. Large-scale polluters have not always been impressed by the argument that he who makes the mess should clear it up, for to do so would be, in economic terms, a waste of money, manpower, time, and energy. Although, as we have seen, the effects of pollution rebound directly onto the industries which perpetrate it, even that has not proved sufficient incentive to prompt countermeasures. Moral obligation has therefore to be reinforced by law.

But legislation is always behind the times, often enacted long after the damage has been done. With pollution the damage often takes years to make itself felt, and the law might take even longer to catch up. Even now companies can pollute the environment in any number of ways, imposing intolerable discomfort and hardship on the neighboring community and its

wildlife, and still be operating within the letter of the law. Legal enforcement always involves public expenditure which falls upon the taxpaying citizen, who also has to pay in higher prices for any measures the polluter is himself constrained to take.

Among the most successful anti-pollution laws was Britain's 1956 Clean Air Act, which established smokeless zones in which it is now forbidden to burn untreated coal. This significantly reduced the amount of sulphur dioxide being released into the air in the cities. There have been other such statutes, but governments and municipal authorities can exercise further control of airborne pollution by setting limits on the amount of this and other gases like oxides of nitrogen passing into the atmosphere, and of solid and liquid effluent passing into waterways. Enforced by roving inspectors who ensure that the thresholds are not exceeded, such laws would carry heavy penalties in the form of bans and prohibitive fines, so that polluters are regarded not just as antisocial but as lawless. The penal system must be harsh so that it is in the long run

Nonreturnable bottles are returned to an offending manufacturer.

cheaper to refrain from polluting.

Because pollution is not just a local matter, affecting the immediate environs, but enters air and waterways, finding its way far afield, there is increasing demand for international legislation to minimize its effects. This is particularly urgent in the case of oil pollution of coastal and ocean waters. The *Torrey Canyon* disaster, which wrought havoc on the beaches of Britain, has underlined the need for this. Britain herself, with the Prevention of Oil Pollution Act, has set the maximum penalty for oil pollution at £50,000 and in 1973 won 43 cases.

So legal sanctions against polluters, while imperative, are not as effective as they might be. Even imposing charges on polluting industries for the privilege of discharging wastes into the environment—thereby shattering the illusion that dumping is free—does not strike at the heart of the problem. Like legislation, such charges would reduce the amount of indiscriminate pollution and cause potential despoilers to tread warily.

Yet they do nothing to change the industrial, domestic, or agricultural processes where it originates, nor do they impose any restraints on the demands of the consumer. In this respect action is required from the industries themselves and from the professional bodies which regulate their activities. For instance, the Soap and Detergent Association sets standards for the chemical content of all brands under its aegis to minimize the dispersal of phosphates and nitrates into domestic disposal systems and water supplies, while overseeing research into less harmful ingredients.

Alternative Energy

Science and technology have been examining thermal, tidal, and solar power as alternative sources of energy. It will be a long time before they can be tapped for industrial use or domestic consumption, or adapted for transport. If and when this happens, many of our pollution worries will be over, but they will eliminate only the power generation stage of the pollution process. That still leaves us with the emissions and waste materials of the production processes themselves and the aftermath of consumption. While it is easy to conceive of other means of power and disposal, it is harder to envisage alternative sources of food. Assuming we shall continue to eat what we have always eaten, the land will have to produce more than ever to feed the swelling populations of the world, which implies increasing reliance on chemicals.

The nonpolluting alternative to chemical treatment of the land is biological control. Nobody is suggesting that chemicals should be banned altogether, considering particularly that in parts of Asia 25 percent of a harvest goes to feed predators rather than people. But there have been spectacular failures of pest control which have cast doubt on the validity of chemical methods. Perhaps the most notable of these was the attempt to eradicate the fire ant from the south eastern states of America. Twenty million acres were sprayed with heptachlor, which, so it was later found, was transformed into a toxic derivative which turned up in meat and milk. Not only was wild life destroyed as a result of this scorched earth program, the fire ant still flourished and spread to other states. Contrast this fiasco with the successful assault on the screwworm fly, a pest harmful to livestock, which has been annihilated without a drop of chemical being sprayed. A massive program was launched to sterilize the

male of the species. As the female mates only once, the rate of reproduction could be abated by releasing the sterile males into infested areas. It worked, and the pest was eventually exterminated. This kind of biological control, as opposed to chemical control, calls for far greater ingenuity and imagination and takes longer to show results, but in the long run it may prove safer than the pesticide sprays that have been in use.

Introducing predators or viruses to attack specific pests is another form of biological control. This demands a comprehensive working knowledge of the cycle of nature. Like pesticides, such action introduces something new into the natural system, and, by wiping out a whole species, removes a link from the food chain. But unlike chemicals, there is no residue of poison destroying other life in its wake, impregnating the land, and seeping out into waterways—and all that inevitably ensues. The fail-safe method of biological control, however, is to develop strains of crops and livestock resistant to pests, disease, and contamination.

Financial Incentive

But how can we deal with the increasing rate of waste disposal? In the absence of nonpolluting methods, the answer seems to be to throw away less. As long as producers find it cheaper and more efficient to use new materials rather than reuse old ones, the rate of disposal will continue to rise, the amount of discarded matter will just go on accumulating, and there will be no financial incentive for anyone to reverse the trend. The incentive will eventually be sheer survival, for the rapid depletion of world resources and the sudden shortage of materials will force us to adopt "waste not, want not" philosophies.

The word "recycling" is very much in vogue and is being bandied about in the highest government quarters. Recycling is particularly pertinent to the packaging industry, which produces billions of tons of containers which once emptied are useless and contribute significantly to domestic pollution that is even now overwhelming municipal refuse disposal authorities. Metal, glass, plastic, paper and countless other natural or synthetic materials are all reusable if returned to the appropriate processing plant. As it is, the bulk of these materials is dumped, burned, buried, or submerged, in most cases both needlessly and destructively.

If we even reach the point where all

serviceable material is recycled, we will have succeeded in reproducing in our technosphere a "natural cycle" similar to the one which already successfully operates in the biosphere—despite our worst efforts to disrupt it. The two worlds will then work in harmony so that technology can forge ahead without prevailing upon the environment to pick up the pieces.

Another specter—more nebulous, yet more haunting—casts a shadow over the future: even if we *could* reduce pollution by using new approved materials and disposal techniques to supplement our natural absorption and decomposition processes, the combined defense mechanism would be no guarantee against some drastic imbalance of nature occurring or some catastrophic breakdown or accident befalling our technology. What if a nuclear power station were unwittingly to release vast quantities of radioactivity into the environment? What if some unforeseen chemical reaction proves too powerful for industrial safety precautions? The safeguards we introduce to cover such eventualities—and the atomic energy industry is more safety conscious than most conventional undertakings—may prove inadequate. As we press on with our technological development, taking chances and ignoring the warnings of environmentalists, we will maximize production by overusing, overloading, and overexerting the system beyond its capacity.

In between the indiscriminate polluter and the fanatic "ecofreak" there is room for more people with scientific and technical skills coupled with good sense and compassion, whose efforts would give us some confidence that the pollution menace is facing strong opposition. The ecological and conservationist lobby is becoming more and more boisterous, and is more often drawn into consultations, while the preservation of the environment is rising higher in the scale of priorities considered by politicians, legislators, and administrators.

Technology is much more powerful than man himself, and certainly more so than the environment in its natural state. So long as it remains under man's push-button control, it can be used either to preserve and protect or to desecrate and destroy.

The human element is still the decisive factor, and the survival of life on this planet depends on whether man, its senior species, exercises the wisdom and reason with which he has been endowed or displays the abysmal folly of which he is supremely capable.

What happens now?

Nothing is as sure as death, yet when a loved one dies it still leaves us in a state of shock.

The specter of the death of a loved one—a member of the family—plays a central role in the life of every individual. We have all known, or will know, death, grief and mourning.

Avoiding the Subject

The writer Suzanne Ramos describes how a friend of hers died, leaving her husband and a five-year-old son, Mark. After several weeks Mark became very depressed. He grew more and more silent. He would sit for hours just staring out of the window. He picked at his food. And then he began to refuse to go to school. His father consulted the family doctor, who referred him to Gilbert Kliman, an American child psychiatrist who speci-

alizes in helping children cope with such traumatic experiences as death, serious illness, and other crises that shake families from time to time. He was able to reassure Mark's father that the boy's reaction was not particularly unusual. The father was given concrete guidance on how to help Mark mourn the death of his mother and thus come to terms with his loss.

A recurring problem is the understandable tendency for parents to avoid the unpleasant subject of death. They say, "There's plenty of time to worry about that later." But all children who lose a parent, a brother or sister, a beloved relative, or a playmate can be spared unnecessary serious emotional repercussions

Above: Time is a great healer but it can take a long while to get used to his not being around any more.

later if they have had their eyes opened to the reality of death and if it occurs, are encouraged to express their feelings at the time. If they are helped to mourn the loss they can eventually come to accept the death, although this does not always work, even with adults!

John Smith was 47 when his wife died unexpectedly after a short illness, leaving him with two children of school age. No one was concerned at first when he appeared desperately unhappy and withdrawn. In fact, people left him alone with his sorrow.

Marshall Cavendish

Marshall Cavendish

However, as time went by he remained persistently depressed and unable to work. He was referred for psychiatric help by his family doctor. It was clear that the main difficulties causing his failure to adjust to his wife's death lay in his personality. He had always been a quiet, shy man, whose only close emotional links had been with his wife—"We did everything together." He had become isolated from his family and had no friends, no one to turn to when he needed help. Consequently he had to take on the role of his dead wife—he was doing all the household chores and could not go to work because there was no one to care for the children when they came home from school. With the support of a social worker, he was gradually able to make contact with neighbors, who, as it happened, had been anxious to help but too shy to make an approach. He arranged for a young couple with children to take lodgings in his house, and he was eventually able to overcome his grief and return to work. He had lacked the practical and emotional support of friends and neighbors.

Grief, as it is used in everyday conversation, usually refers to extreme sorrow associated with loss or separation. We grieve the departure of a dear friend to another country; the child grieves when his mother leaves him in the hospital; we feel grief when we lose a loved one's affection or when we lose our illusions about him. According to the psychoanalyst George Pollock, normal grief seems to pass through three stages. First, there is a short period of intense shock when the bereaved person feels numb and unable to give full vent to his distress. This results from the disruption of the individual's psychological equilibrium—a sudden awareness that the loved one no longer exists in time and space. Luckily, this period, which may last for a few hours or even a few days, is usually a very busy time when members of the family gather around the bereaved and give him a great deal of help and support with the many purely practical problems which have to be dealt with after a death. The overwhelming task of coming to terms with the shock may not be dealt with successfully and may then result in panic; shrieking, wailing or moaning may follow, or there may be complete collapse.

The reactions in this initial phase vary in intensity according to the

Reflecting on the good times is a bittersweet sensation for the bereaved, but preserving their memory keeps the dead alive.

suddenness of the death and the amount of preparation the bereaved had beforehand. Death following chronic and prolonged illness is responded to differently from an unexpected loss. In certain predisposed individuals, Dr. Pollock reports, the shock can be great enough to precipitate a serious physical disorder. Where long anticipated, mourning reactions may occur prior to death.

Feeling of Impotence

The second stage postulated by Dr. Pollock is the "grief reaction." In *The Expression of the Emotions in Man and Animals*, Charles Darwin described the physical aspects of grief. In the early stage it is characterized by muscular hyperactivity, like hand wringing, aimless wild walking, pulling of hair and clothes. Darwin believed that this behavior indicated the impotence felt by the mourner—the feeling that he was unable to reverse the death which had occurred. These restless, frantic movements subside when he realizes and accepts that nothing can be done. Then deep despair and sorrow take over: the sufferer becomes very quiet, sits motionless or gently rocks to-and-fro, sighs deeply and becomes muscularly flaccid. All the facial features are lengthened, giving the characteristic appearance of grief. Fatigue, exhaustion, and anorexia are often part of this acute phase of grief.

As the shock phase merges into the grief stage, so numbness turns into pain. Dr. Pollock says, "The suffering ache is initially of much greater intensity than what subsequently follows in the later chronic grief phase. Accompanying this psychic pain may be the sudden screaming, yelling and other nonverbal but vocal manifestations of this grief reaction. The acute initial response later becomes the more characteristic depression. The spasmodic crying changes to tearful lamentations, and gradually verbal communications become more frequent though still accompanied by much sobbing."

Transfer of Bonds

In the stage of acute grief the bereaved may suffer from acute feelings of guilt. Could he have made the last days of the dead person more pleasant? If he had been taken to the hospital earlier, would his life have been saved? The bereaved may even go so far as to accuse himself of contributing actively to the death by neglect.

The final phase is one of slow recovery, both physical and emotional, in which the grief is slowly dissipated by renewed contact with the external world. All the shared emotional bonds are gradually transferred to other people and activities as the bereaved person rebuilds a new pattern of life. It is only when new emotional bonds are established in place of the old that a person has come to terms with his grief and "filled the gap."

Freud, in his monograph "Mourning and Melancholia" (1917), compared the normal emotion of grief and its expression in mourning with the psychosis melancholia. He based this comparison upon the general picture of the two conditions as well as upon the external precipitating causes, which were the same in both cases.

According to the argument, the loss of a loved object gives rise to behavior and feelings collectively referred to as mourning; these psychological processes are always set in train by the disruption of a precious attachment. If mourning takes its normal course, the person gets over the tragedy and is capable of making a new attachment. But it might also (in people of a pathological disposition) give rise to a deep-seated depression or melancholia.

In melancholia, the symptoms are: painful dejection; loss of interest in the external world; inhibition of activity; loss of capacity to love; loss of self-esteem and hence self-reproach and delusional expectations of punishment. These are the same symptoms as in mourning, with the exception of loss of self-esteem and the expectation of punishment.

In both mourning and melancholia —according to Freud—the precipitating cause is the same: the loss of a loved object. It need not involve another human being; it may concern something which has taken the place of the loved object such as a person's freedom, his fatherland, or some ideal. Both mourning and melancholia are marked by departures from normal behavior. However, the grief of mourning is not regarded as a pathological condition: no one thinks of sending the mourner to a psychiatrist.

It is anticipated that time will cure grief, and usually people think that grief should be left alone to take its course. However, according to the eminent British researcher Dr. John Bowlby, infants and children may, in certain circumstances, react to separation from their mothers by mourning processes which predispose them to psychiatric illness in later life.

Essential Mourning

The normal processes of mourning bring about a withdrawal of emotional concern from the lost person and commonly prepare the ground for making new relationships. Psychoanalysts have emphasized that the identification of the bereaved person with the deceased is the main process involved in mourning—part of himself, an extension of his ego, has died. This theory makes it plain why working through the mourning process is essential to self-recovery.

Bowlby formulates a theory of mourning which, like Pollock's, distinguishes three main phases but has more to do with personality changes. During the first phase, the individual's attachments are still focused on the lost object, but for obvious reasons they cannot be resolved. As a result, the bereaved experiences repeated disappointment, the anxiety of persistent separation, and, insofar as he accepts reality, grief. So long as the affections and dependencies are focused on the deceased, there are strenuous and often angry efforts to recover him. The widow may strive in actuality or in her mind to retrieve her husband. She may attend spiritualist seances to get in touch; she cries for him and calls out his name. There may be outbursts of anger when she reproaches him for deserting her.

The futility of such efforts is obvious to others and sometimes to the bereaved herself, yet the efforts may continue. Dr. Bowlby believes that the seeds of much mental illness are sown in this phase. When the mourning process proceeds healthily, however, the various needs of the individual cease to focus on the dead, and the efforts to recover him stop.

Emotional Detachment

In the second stage, before the final resolution, there is a disorganization of the personality accompanied by pain and despair. In the first two stages, feelings fluctuate, often between angrily demanding and pitifully expecting the loved one to return, between a despair expressed in subdued pining and total lack of any expression. Though hope and despair may alternate for a long time, there evolves, at last, a degree of emotional detachment from the deceased.

During the third stage, the function of mourning is complete, and a new and different state has come about: a reorganization of attitudes and feelings, partly in relation to the image of the lost person, partly in connection with a new object or objects. Children show this pattern of mourning when separated early in life from their mothers. The consequences, if adequate substitute care is not provided, can be serious.

The psychiatrist Dr. Spitz made a study of 123 unselected children at a nursery for the babies of women offenders. The infants stayed in the nursery from their fourteenth day of life until the end of their first year and in a few cases until the end of their eighteenth month. All shared the same environment, care and food. When the infants were somewhere between their sixth and eighth months, their mothers were kept almost totally from them, seeing them at best once a week, whereas before the separation they had had full care of their babies and spent more time with them than is probably usual for an ordinary mother in an ordinary home.

A striking syndrome was afterwards observed in the babies. The principal symptoms were not all necessarily present at the same time, but all of them were noticeable at one point or another in the clinical picture. They were: apprehension, sadness, weeping; lack of contact, rejection of environment, withdrawal; retardation of development and reaction to stimuli, and slowness of movement; dejection, stupor, frozen immobility; loss of appetite, refusal to eat, loss of weight; and insomnia.

Added to these, they showed a facial expression which Spitz found difficult to describe, but which in an adult would indicate depression. This syndrome developed in the course of four to six weeks following the mother's removal. None of the children whose mothers had not been removed developed the syndrome.

The depression syndrome occurred only in those children who were deprived of their love object for an appreciable period during the first year of their life, although, on the other hand, not all the children whose mothers were removed developed the same syndrome. Hence, Spitz suggests, maternal separation is a necessary—but not a sufficient—cause for the development of this "anaclitic depression" syndrome.

Animal Parallel

Mourning the death of a loved one is not exclusively human behavior. Dr. Bowlby claims that the evidence, fragmentary though it is, makes it fairly certain that each of the main behavioral features alleged to be characteristic of human mourning is essentially shared with other animals. Animals also protest at the loss of a loved object and do everything in their power to seek and recover it. Frequently they become hostile and withdrawn, rejecting a potential new object; apathy and restlessness are the rule. Yet, given time and opportunity, they eventually find a new object of affection and recover.

Dr. Bowlby's theory has received support from the zoologist Konrad Lorenz in his studies of jackdaws, geese, dogs, orangutans, and chimpanzees. A greylag goose which had lost its mate at first began a frantic searching and calling. Then followed the phase of depression: the bird lacked energy, its movements were slow, its eyes seemed smaller, its feathers were loose and slightly fluffed, its head and neck were less erect, and it was noticeably less keen to fly. These bereaved geese also exhibit a disinclination for social contacts. They are generally ignored by other geese, Lorenz maintains, and "grief-stricken widows of this type are hardly ever courted by males, even if a quite considerable shortage

of females prevails in the goose society. . . . The general picture of grief is just as clearly marked in a widowed goose as it is in a dog."

A chimpanzee reacting to the death of his mate made repeated efforts to arouse her; he yelled with rage and expressed his anger by snatching at the short hairs of his head, and then gave way to crying and moaning. Later he became more attached to his keeper than he had been and would become angry if the keeper left him.

Sequence of Behavior

On many levels, animal and human mourning are similar. But there are features of mourning specific to humans—uniquely human responses. Perhaps the most significant of these is the intimate relationship between grief and the intense emotional anxiety caused by separation.

Dr. Spitz's work suggests that when the infant or young child loses his mother he habitually shows responses comparable to pathological mourning in the adult. This observation is also based on studies of healthy children undergoing limited separation in residential nurseries or hospital wards. The predictable three-stage sequence of behavior appears in the separated child. At first, with tears and anger, the child demands the return of his mother and seems hopeful he will succeed in getting her. This phase of *protest* may last days.

In the subsequent periods of *despair* he becomes quieter, but it is clear that he remains preoccupied with his absent mother and still yearns for her return; his hopes, nonetheless, have faded. Often the first two phases alternate: hope turns to despair and despair to renewed hope.

Eventually, however, a greater change occurs. He seems to forget his mother and, when she does come back to him, he is curiously uninterested in her, perhaps not even recognizing her. This is the phase of *detachment.* In each of these phases the child is prone to tantrums and episodes of destructive behavior, often of a disquietingly violent kind. Bowlby believes that there is good reason to believe that this sequence of responses—protest, despair, and detachment—is, in one variant or another, characteristic of all forms of mourning.

When a child loses a mother or father, brother or sister, the psychological effects in the short term are always profound. In many instances a type of personality may develop which either breaks down in later life or is

more vulnerable to breakdown. If the loss of a loved one happens in early childhood, decisive changes in the personality structure often follow. What is critical is the way the matter of the death is handled and whether loving and continuous substitute care is at hand. The emotional scars from such traumatic occurrences appear to be more profound the younger the age of the bereaved.

In Mark's case, for instance, his father and the aunt who took care of him had not realized how important it was that the five-year-old should be encouraged to talk about his mother's death. If Mark had been able to put his fears into words, they would have discovered that he was harboring all sorts of fantasies that he could not cope with, including the fear that he was responsible for his mother's death.

The child often suffers severe guilt if he has had feelings of hostility, even death wishes, against the deceased. If, for example, a brother died, the fantasies of childhood may lead the surviving child to believe that he is responsible. One researcher investigating attitudes of the young towards death quotes two reports by mothers concerning their children's expressions of guilt. "I should have given Tim my tricycle. He wanted it, Mummy. Then he wouldn't have died, would he?" said a six-year-old. "Is it my fault that granny died?" asked an eight-year-old girl. "I didn't carry her bag up the steps."

If an adult finds death difficult to deal with, what might it be for a child who does not comprehend its irreversible consequences and who has such a limited conception both of time and the meaning of separation? Dr. Kliman believes that children should learn about death before it touches their own lives closely.

Buried Pets

A small dose of painful experience, he maintains, "can be mastered by even a very small child. The death of a pet, or even the discovery of a dead bird in the park or the backyard, might provide the first learning experience. Some parents, who have not come to terms with the idea of death themselves, don't—possibly can't—take advantage of such opportunities." As he put it, "Recently I heard a mother shriek, 'Get that thing out of my sight!' when her little girl toddled up to her carrying a dead mouse. Unknowingly, this mother missed a chance to help her daughter absorb the concept of death."

When a pet dies, parents can help

the child cope with his sadness and sense of loss—just by accepting it. Dr. Kliman suggests that parents encourage a child to mourn the pet. A little marker showing where the pet was buried, for instance, will help a child remember the sadness he felt. Simple as this is, it will increase the child's ability to face death and to express his feelings about it.

When someone dies whom the child knew only slightly—a playmate's grandfather, for instance—he should be told about it. He will experience some sadness and he will little by little come to understand some of what his friend feels. When a child loses someone who had been very close—his brother or sister, or worst of all, his mother or father—then the emotional impact is tremendous. This is a critical time. And the way his immediate family reacts, both to the death and to the child, is vitally important.

Most children are not as severely shaken by a death in the family as Mark, but many are. And often the trauma could have been lessened if the parents had prepared the child. Explaining death to children and help-

ing them cope with an actual loss is difficult. But it should not be avoided. If it is handled correctly, the child's emotional development is less liable to suffer. If it is handled incorrectly severe problems may result.

Adults also need help in coping with death. The mourning ritual followed by Orthodox Jews provides a very good example of how this can be done. The period of intensive mourning lasts seven days—corresponding well with the period of intense grief—during which time the mourners, who are supposed to move and do as little as possible, are visited frequently by friends who talk among themselves about the merits of the dead person. The silent, listening mourners find this helps them to concentrate their grief into a short period of time.

After the seven days' intensive mourning the men continue to go to the synagogue twice a day to say a special prayer for the dead for 11 months before the period of mourning is over. This ritual provides the support and reassurance needed, allows grief to be expressed, and imposes a time limit which corresponds with the natural course of grief. Only too often

Grief takes many forms: the first reaction is often numbing shock, followed by wailing and shrieking. The help and support of family and friends is invaluable at this time.

in other communities a bereaved person is put into a kind of purdah—a state of lonely isolation. Wrongly (in most cases) people think mourners wish to be left alone for a long period after their loss.

While grief itself cannot be considered an illness unless it is unduly prolonged or severe, it is undoubtedly associated with a tendency towards illness and death. Studies have shown that recently widowed people fall ill much more often and have a greater mortality rate than groups of single or married people of the same age.

There are many factors which enable people to cope with grief: disturbance of any one of these may mean that the period of mourning is prolonged and intensified to the point of abnormality. And although we can identify many of these factors by observing both animal and human bereavement in general, some are hidden deep within the individual.

Asking the right questions

Interviewing can mean anything from going around a shopping plaza with a clipboard finding out what brands people buy, to asking awkward questions of a celebrity on a TV show. But some of the same aptitudes are involved in all kinds of interview.

Can You Talk to People?

There are "born" interviewers, and others who can learn a lot from special training. Some personalities, however, are unlikely to make good interviewers. To see if you have the necessary personality traits, answer the questionnaire.

1. Do you find that strangers open up and talk to you easily?
a. often
b. sometimes
c. rarely
2. Once someone starts talking to you, can you get him to stop?
a. with great difficulty
b. not without hurting his feelings
c. pretty smoothly, as a rule
3. In conversations, do you talk
a. as much as everyone else?
b. more than everyone else?
c. less than everyone else?
4. Do you watch other people as they talk to you, interpreting their expressions and understanding what they feel?
a. often
b. sometimes
c. rarely
5. Are you soft-hearted?
a. very
b. sometimes
c. not particularly
6. Can you tell if someone is not telling the truth?
a. yes
b. sometimes
c. rarely
7. In a discussion, do you find it hard to stick to the point?
a. rarely
b. sometimes
c. often
8. Have you ever asked a tactless question at the wrong time?
a. seldom
b. not recently
c. frequently
9. Have you been mistaken in your opinion of people?
a. rarely
b. occasionally
c. often
10. Can you assess a person's qualities, setting aside your own feelings about him?
a. usually
b. you hope so, but fear that your judgment may be colored by your feelings
c. it is almost impossible for you to switch off your feelings and give a neutral assessment

How Good is Your Approach?

The art of asking questions is basic to the process of interviewing. Test yourself out on your approach.

1. You are part of a research team investigating child-rearing practices. What you want to know is how much physical discipline is used. Which question(s) would you use?
a. Do you ever spank your little boy?
b. What do you do when your little boy is being really difficult?
c. When did you last spank your child?
d. What sorts of thing would make you spank your little boy?
2. You are interviewing a temperamental actress on a television show. She has recently had a spectacular bust-up with her husband, and no one quite knows what happened. Which question(s) would you use?
a. Is it true that you have split with your husband?
b. Would you like to tell us what really happened with you and your husband?
c. We all know that your husband has left you. Have you anything to say to other women in the same situation?
d. How do you like being free again?
3. You are interviewing a student for admission to a course which involves a lot of close study and difficult reading. He needs to have an interest in books and a critical awareness. Which question(s) would you use?
a. Can you tell us about a book you have read?
b. What are you reading now?
c. Do you enjoy reading?
d. Which book that you have recently read did you most dislike?

Question d. is a kinder, more face-saving way to approach the problem.

Scores—a.0, b.1, c.3, d.2.

3. Questions a. and c. will give you practically none of the information that you want; a. invites a prepared response, and c. is too general. Question b. is more likely to get at the truth, but d. is easily the best.

Scores—a.0, b.2, c.1, d.2.

Total your scores. The maximum possible is 16. If you scored 10 or more, you know a good question when you see one. If you can use the right one at the right time, you may have a talent for interviewing.

How Do You Rate with People?

Personal Warmth
1. a.3, b.2, c.1.
2. a.3, b.2, c.1.
3. a.3, b.2, c.1.
4. a.3, b.2, c.1.
5. a.3, b.2, c.1.

If you have less than 10, your manner may be too distant or shy for you to make the necessary quick rapport demanded by interviewing. On the other hand, if you score more than 12, your warmth could be a handicap: you need to direct the flow of talk in the desired direction.

Judgment
6. a.3, b.2, c.1.
7. a.3, b.2, c.1.
8. a.3, b.2, c.1.
9. a.3, b.2, c.1.
10. a.2, b.3, c.1.

To be really good at interviewing, you should have scored highly on both Warmth and Judgment. A total of 23-29 indicates a high level of the necessary personality attributes. More than that means that you have not answered quite honestly! A score of 15-22 is average; if this score was equally balanced between the two parts of the questionnaire, you might just make an interviewer. Less than 15 indicates little aptitude for the job.

Rate Your Approach
1. You are dealing with a delicate situation. Mothers are reluctant to divulge that they do something disapproved of. If you ask question a, you are likely to be told "never," whether or not it is true. Question b, is better; it is open-ended and suggests some sympathy for the position of the mother. You could well get at the truth, though you may have to listen to a lot of irrelevant material. Question c. is of the classic type used in the Kinsey Report. The subject is caught off guard, so she may be tricked into answering. Question d. makes the same assumptions, but in a less abrupt way, and it could yield up more information.

Scores—a.0, b.1, c. and d.2.

2. Here your function is a little different. You are concerned with what would make good television, rather than with getting at the truth. Question a. could easily lead to a boring answer. If you ask question b. you also risk a "no comment" response. Using question c. could make you very unpopular, but it would be much more likely to call forth a spirited reply.

Be a better husband

In some societies, marriage is an economic and dynastic arrangement: romantic love is something quite separate. We expect marriage to fulfill both functions—small wonder that we are often disappointed.

Yet our ideal of marriage is attractive. Pair-bonding may be a part of our instinctive nature, so the feeling of coming to rest with one special partner runs very deep.

Are you Satisfied?

Only the lucky or undemanding couples are likely to be completely satisfied with their present marriage. Most of us experience some areas of difficulty, and so it is important to know where the problems lie to make constructive changes. The questionnaire will help you rate your degree of satisfaction, and locate the sources of dissatisfaction. How true are these statements for you?

1. I can talk easily to my wife about the things that are important to me.
a. very true
b. partly true
c. mostly untrue
2. My wife confides in me the things that are important to her.
a. very true
b. partly true
c. mostly untrue
3. When we have a problem, we sit down and talk it over together.
a. nearly always
b. sometimes
c. rarely
4. I like to spend a lot of my leisure time with my wife.
a. very true
b. partly true
c. mostly untrue
5. I can put up with my wife's habits quite happily.
a. usually
b. sometimes
c. with great difficulty
6. My wife puts up with my habits quite happily.
a. usually
b. sometimes
c. with great difficulty
7. Our sex life is very enjoyable.
a. usually
b. sometimes
c. not at all
8. I feel that I "belong" when I'm with my wife.
a. usually
b. sometimes
c. on the contrary, I feel restless and unhappy
9. I rarely get bored when I am with my wife.

a. very true
b. sometimes true
c. untrue
10. I feel reasonably free within my marriage.
a. true
b. sometimes true
c. untrue

Sources of Disharmony

Check off the areas of tension or difficulty in your marriage.

Communication. This is the most important central problem. If honest and clear communication is not taking place, all other difficulties will be magnified. When did you last tell your wife your real thoughts and feelings? You may feel that she is the one who blocks communication between you, but one of you has to make the initial effort if things are to improve. Counseling can help sort out the tangled lines.

Money. This is often symptomatic of personal problems. You may quarrel about money, but what are you really saying to each other? Do you complain about extravagance when you actually resent the fact that your wife stays at home while you work, or that her father makes more than you do? Or when your wife says you don't give her a big enough allowance, is she saying that you don't give her enough appreciation? The feeling of being undervalued is often disguised. You don't have to bring home flowers every day, but try thanking your wife for some of the things she does; notice when she makes an effort; praise her rather than carp at her failures.

Children. They can make or break a marriage. If you quarrel a lot about the children, ask yourself if, in some ways, you resent them. This is a very common feeling. Both wives and husbands can use their children to get at each other. In our society, men usually have less to do with young children and may well feel isolated from them. Talk it out with your wife.

Freedom. However close two people are, they are two people and need to feel that they are individuals as well as part of a couple. Modern marriage demands a degree of freedom for both partners. This can be a real dilemma, because when you love someone, you don't want her to be too free. Freedom does not necessarily mean freedom to have extramarital affairs (though it could mean that) but simply the opportunity to be your own person some of the time. Securing personal freedom has traditionally been more of a problem for women. Are you

guilty of tying your wife down? Or does she cling to you in a claustrophobic way? Reluctance to give or take freedom often springs from insecurity. Help her to feel secure; encourage her to be herself. If your insecurity is the trouble, try to get a fresh perspective on yourself.

Sex. What are your expectations of sex? Are they unrealistically high? Are you dogged by puritanical fears? Sex problems in marriage can spring from other problems—it is difficult to become warmly responsive to someone you resent. In general, sex problems are of two kinds: the sexual appetites of the couple can differ, or boredom can set in. Frankness and genuine caring for the other can help in either case. Men and women differ in their needs, but when you can bring out your needs to each other, half the problem has gone. Medical help is also available for every kind of problem, so no situation is hopeless unless you believe it is.

Boredom. One of the reasons for the continued popularity of marriage is that it can be restful, but there is a fine dividing line between peacefulness and boredom. It is natural for people to settle down together; it is also natural for people to seek stimulus. If you both function as individuals, there is less chance of becoming bored, and you each have something to bring back into the marriage. Don't expect to find all your satisfactions from one person. A wife is more likely to give up her friends and career to devote herself to her husband, and so she may narrow her horizons and stagnate. But some husbands make excessive demands of their wives. If you have settled into a dull routine with your wife, it is easy to change it. Surprise her once in a while; go somewhere you've never been before. She will probably follow your example and make life more interesting for you. Boredom is the easiest problem to tackle, for you never really get to the end of a person.

How Do You Rate?

Score 2 for every a. answer; 1 for every b. answer; 0 for every c. answer.

15–20—congratulations! You have a happy marriage.

9–14—you are not too dissatisfied, but there is room for a good deal of improvement in your marriage.

0–8—at present, you are not at all happy about your marriage. Before you resign yourself to it or cut loose, consider how you could improve it.

Be a better wife

You have often been told how to make a better marriage. Get a New Hairstyle. Cook a Different Dish. Pamper the Brute. If that sort of advice works for you, fine. If not you probably want more out of marriage.

Are You Too Romantic?

When a marriage is less than happy, it is often because of faulty, unrealistic expectations. Women are perhaps more likely to suffer from these because our society cherishes the myth that women are longing to get married, while men avoid it until they are "caught." Rate yourself on the questionnaire—you may be more of a romantic than you realize!

1. Do you look at your wedding photographs
a. often?
b. occasionally?
c. you don't even have any?
2. When your husband is preoccupied and fails to notice that you have made a special effort to look good, do you
a. feel hurt, maybe even cry?
b. accept it philosophically?
c. not mind, because you did it for yourself anyway?
3. If you are in the mood to make love, do you
a. act seductive?
b. show affection?
c. invite your husband in a straightforward way?
4. If it becomes clear that you and your husband differ about a political or social issue, would you
a. come around to his point of view?
b. try persuading him to agree with you?
c. go your way and let him go his?
5. Do you find that marriage is
a. much less fun than you thought it would be?
b. pretty much as you expected?
c. more fun than you expected?
6. If your husband were ever unfaithful to you, would you
a. feel totally betrayed and hurt?
b. feel wounded but not mortally, and, anyway, it would depend on the exact circumstances?
c. feel curious about it?
7. Do you wish that your husband would make some effort to be attractive to you?
a. often
b. sometimes
c. rarely
8. If you imagine having an affair with someone, would it be because
a. you want to make your husband jealous?
b. you feel like a change?
c. just because you want to?

Old-fashioned Girls

Traditional marriage leaves only three possible roles for women—the Romantic Wife, the Child Bride, and the Earth Mother. If you are reacting against them, first ask who put you into a stereotype? It wasn't your husband—he thought he was marrying a nice, sexy, companionable human being. It may have been your mother, but you are grown up now.

You are confining yourself. Not consciously, of course. But you carry about in your head a heap of assumptions about what it is to be a wife. You set up a pattern, and you may have regretted it.

Whatever your husband is like, you need to get back to being your own person, and that starts in your head.

Are You Overdependent?

The overdependent wife puts an enormous strain on her husband and children. She lives through them, drinking their vitality, curbing their initiative. Even if they stay, they are likely to feel great resentment and frustration because they cannot be themselves. Still, it is difficult to be loving and protective, yet at the same time not make impossible demands for gratitude and a sense of purpose. Check your dependence rating.

1. When your husband is late coming back from work, and he has not called you up, do you
a. get very anxious and think of all the terrible things that can happen?
b. feel angry with him?
c. stay calm, knowing he must have some reason, and get on with your own activities?
2. You have been invited to a party while your husband is away on business. Do you
a. refuse instantly?
b. go if you know your hosts very well, but feel odd without him?
c. accept and have a good time?
3. You have been offered a job that you would love, but it involves some evening work and your husband would have to get his own supper. Would you
a. turn it down?
b. tentatively talk to your husband about it, and arrange to make it very easy for him if he agrees to your taking the job?
c. take it and expect your husband to share your happiness?
4. Do you call your husband at work about trivial things?
a. often
b. rarely
c. never
5. Do you suggest interesting things to do and places to go?
a. rarely
b. occasionally
c. often
6. Who pays the bills and makes most of the major household decisions?
a. your husband
b. both of you
c. you
7. Your husband has the chance of a sporting holiday and asks if you would mind being left alone for a couple of weeks. Would you
a. feel frightened at the thought?
b. tell him that you'll be fine and send him off?
c. agree, provided that you can have a similar chance?
8. When you get together in the evening, do you
a. expect him to tell you everything that happened to him, since nothing ever happens to you?
b. exchange news, but feel that his is more exciting?
c. exchange news, feeling that your accounts are equally interesting?

How Romantic Are You?

The more as you have, the more romantic you are. More than 5 shows it could be holding you back from making the best of the situation you have. The b scores show a more realistic approach: you reject romanticism, perhaps without knowing what to put in its place. A high c score indicates an antiromantic attitude. Make sure you do not get too hard and suppress your emotions.

Your Dependence Rating

Mainly as (5 or more)—you seem to be too reliant on your husband. Perhaps you think that a wife should live through her husband. Are you convinced that he welcomes your dependence? You will probably find that a little more self-sufficiency and initiative gives him a boost.

Mainly bs (5 or more)—you are breaking out of excessive dependence, although the stereotypes in your head are still there. If you meet resistance from your husband, don't give in or quarrel with him right away. He too needs time to adjust.

Mainly cs (5 or more)—could you be too independent? It could sometimes look like indifference, and your husband may feel rejected. Developing a more democratic relationship would improve your marriage. If you want to be entirely free, why get married?

It makes sense for every wife to be a human being in her own right; that way, she does not make draining demands (or accept them) and she can bring more into the relationship, avoiding the twin traps of resentment and boredom.

Appreciating poetry

Why are we afraid of poetry? It is something we often find embarrassing to admit; we "ought to" enjoy it, but if we are honest we know we do not. There are many reasons for this.

A lot of poetry is difficult to understand, and perhaps it seems unrealistic and irrelevant in the modern world. When you were a student, it may not have been worth the trouble wading through poetry when prose could express the same thoughts more clearly. You were probably bored by it because you felt then that it gave you no information, not even the suspense and excitement of your favorite comics—so why bother?

In fact poems can give you all this and more. Some of them tell our most cherished stories, like this one by Walt Whitman on the death of President Lincoln.

When lilacs last in the dooryard
    bloom'd
And the great star early droop'd
    in the western sky in the night,
I mourn'd, and yet shall mourn with
    ever-returning spring.

It is a basic human need to celebrate great events; if Whitman had said simply, "The spring will always remind me of my grief at Lincoln's death," we would find that only a fraction of our feelings had been expressed.

Reread those lines and you will see just how much more Whitman is saying. The lilacs and the evening star are, in an everyday sense, quite irrelevant to the "story" that the poem is telling, but how essential they are in another sense! They fix the actual moment of grief and so involve you, the reader, in it. More, they suggest that the natural world of flowers and stars is mourning for Lincoln, too. Looked at rationally, this is an absurd idea, yet it gives vent to strong emotions, which are often accompanied by bizarre memories.

Yoking incongruous elements is an important poetic device, and it is a valid concept. Test this for yourself. Think back to a similar important moment: the death of President Kennedy, for instance. You will remember vividly "irrelevant" details charged, like Whitman's lilacs, with chilling significance.

Precious Gift

Poetry is power—it can tap potent feelings we may not even know that we have. In ancient times, this power inherent in words seemed magical. Language was a precious gift and a valuable tool, more complex and useful than any possessed by other living creatures. Words could communicate, impress, control, and skill in combining words effectively was highly prized.

Old spells and magical riddles still retain something of that primitive strength:

In marble halls as white as milk,
Lined with a skin as soft as silk,
Within a fountain crystal clear
A golden apple doth appear.
No doors there are to this
    stronghold,
Yet thieves break in and steal the
    gold.

Words like these could guard secrets, revealed only to those who could understand. The answer to this riddle is—an egg! Poetry still echoes this sense of keeping a secret, another reason why you may have found it difficult at school. But now you can appreciate its subtlety and find pleasure in experiences that are not obvious or banal.

Word of Mouth

You are ready to explore what makes poetry uniquely powerful. First, poetry is durable because rhyme and meter make it easy to remember. Before written records, poets were those who preserved significant events for the whole community, by enshrining them in a memorable pattern of words. Poems—especially the long narrative tales of kings and princes going to war, like the Greek *Iliad* or the Norse sagas—were handed down by word of mouth. They were the community's history, giving it a sense of security and continuity with the past. We all need our experience to be interpreted and reflected by others before we can fully grasp it for ourselves. Poetry is one of the most direct ways of doing this.

The great modern poet T. S. Eliot wrote that it was just as difficult to be precise about feeling as it was about rational thought. If we are not used to confronting our feelings in all their ambivalence, poetry can be threatening. A good poem is good because it is ruthlessly honest and will not let poet or reader off the hook; and a poem is bad not because it is technically incompetent, but because it sentimentalizes, makes difficult things too easy, or gives us only what we expect to hear. That is why the rhymes in greeting cards, for instance, are not poetry.

This does not, of course, mean that good poetry has to be complicated or difficult to understand. The simplicity of these anonymous lines actually makes the feelings expressed all the more poignant:

O Western wind, when wilt thou
    blow
That the small rain down may rain?
Christ! that my love were in my arms,
And I in my bed again.

Being in love is a heightened state of emotion and poetry can express that "special" quality by involving the powerful forces of nature—the wind and the rain—in the personal experience of falling in love. Although we know rationally that our longings do not affect the world around us, feeling that they do is one of the most exciting parts of the experience of love. And that is what the poem brings out for us.

John Donne found that poetry could calm disturbed feelings, too:

Grief brought to numbers cannot
    be so fierce,
For he tames it, that fetters it in
    verse.

Missing Links

By now you will realize that emotional, not rational, order is the aim of poetry. Do not look for cause and effect or logical argument as in prose, but be alert to the emotional resonance of words. Connecting links are often left out, and this can cause problems if the reader is unable to break away from formal patterns of thought.

This old verse works on a "non-logical" basis:

A man of words and not of deeds,
Is like a garden full of weeds;
And when the weeds begin to grow,
It's like a garden full of snow;
And when the snow begins to fall,
It's like a bird upon the wall;
And when the bird away does fly,
It's like an eagle in the sky;
And when the sky begins to crack,
It's like a stick across your back;
And when your back begins to
    smart,
It's like a penknife in your heart;
And when your heart begins to
    bleed,
You're dead and dead and dead
    indeed.

It does not tell an obvious story, but the images develop and become more menacing, leading up to the repeated "dead" in the last line.

Literally, of course, it does not make sense, but emotionally it does. Rational methods and thought processes help us to understand the laws that structure the universe; but poetry gives us the vital psychological sense that we can relate to it in peace and harmony.

DISCOVERING ANTIQUES

THE STORY OF WORLD ANTIQUES

GREYSTONE PRESS/NEW YORK · TORONTO · LONDON

This superb full-color work is brought to you in its entirety from the original publisher, The British Publishing Corporation. Only the arrangement has been slightly altered. In fact, rather than disturb the text in any way, you will find the English monetary system used throughout the set. Here is a handy conversion table showing the value of a Pound (£) in terms of U.S. dollars.

DATES	U.S. Dollars equal to one Pound (£)
1939	$3.92 to 4.68
1940 to Sept. 1949	4.03
Sept. 1949 to Nov. 1967	2.80
Nov. 1967 to Aug. 1971	2.40
Aug. 1971 to June 1972	2.60
June 1972 to present	2.45 (floating rate)

20 shillings = one Pound (£)
21 shillings = one guinea

In February, 1971, the guinea was taken out of circulation.

TITLE PAGE PHOTO CREDIT: *Face of a bracket clock,* probably by John Martin, c. 1700. (Victoria and Albert Museum, London.)

Contents

Grinling Gibbons, Master Carver to Royalty

David Green

Fig. 1 (Frontispiece) *Cosimo III panel by Grinling Gibbons (1648-1721). Limewood, 60 x 48 ins.*
In 1682 Charles II sent this panel as a gift to Cosimo III de' Medici, Grand Duke of Tuscany. (Museo Nazionale, Florence.)

Of all the woodcarvers England has ever known (and there have been some good ones) one and one only — Grinling Gibbons — has come down to posterity as a household name

Grinling Gibbons was not only skilled, he was lucky; lucky to be born in the Netherlands in 1648, when a family of master-carvers and sculptors called Quellin were busy in Antwerp and Amsterdam; lucky to be discovered at Deptford in 1671 by John Evelyn, who introduced him to Wren and to Charles II. Charles, while in exile, had acquired a liking for Flemish carving, a taste never more characteristically reflected than in Gibbons' marble font and limewood reredos in the church of St. James's, Piccadilly, or in the King's Eating Room at Windsor Castle, enriched by Gibbons with fish and game in limewood.

Born of an English father in Rotterdam, Gibbons is believed to have been apprenticed to the Quellins, then carving in marble at the Stadthuys in Amsterdam. For anyone conversant with the carvings of Gibbons, whether in wood, marble or stone these Quellin carvings at Amsterdam must stand out as an important source of his inspiration. His shell-festoons are there (as in the reredos of St. James's, Piccadilly) and so are his trophies of musical instruments (as at Petworth), and his doves.

A. F. Kersting

Fig. 2 **The Carved Room,**
Petworth House, Sussex. Most
of the carved work is by Gibbons,
1689-1692.
Horace Walpole considered this
room to be the 'most superb
monument of Gibbons' skill'.

Fig. 3 **Portrait of Grinling
Gibbons** engraved by J. Smith
after a painting by Sir Godfrey
Kneller (1646/49-1723).
(Victoria and Albert Museum,
London.)

Fig. 4 **Truss** by Gibbons in the
Waterloo Chamber, Windsor
Castle.
The naturalistic treatment of
flowers, leaves and fruit, in
which the details are delicately
undercut, illustrates the skill
of Gibbons and his school.

But in the shaping of Gibbons' style and repertoire, there were other influences, notably the devotional paintings of Flemish masters such as Jan Phillips van Thielen and Daniel Seghers. He must surely too have been familiar with Rubens' *Garland Madonna* (the flowers by Brueghel the Younger) and with the flower-baskets of Jean Baptiste Monnoyer. It has been said that the originality we ask of the artist is originality of treatment, not of subject, and that his calibre may be gauged from the use he makes of what he annexes. Certainly Gibbons was quick to annex everything that would gracefully yield to his chisel, and that meant not only fruit and flowers but birds, fishes, shells, angels and cherubs, crowns and medals, swords, palms, musical instruments . . . and to these he added inventions of

his own such as the whorled acanthus-scroll which none but a virtuoso would dream of attempting.

At the same time he was fastidious. He resisted old-master tricks with butterflies and peeled lemons. Indeed, he seldom introduced the clumsier fruits – oranges, lemons, pomegranates – at all. His flowers are flowers, not buds; his designs, seemingly casual, so calculated as to allow every leaf some elbow-room and at the same time to afford answering trusses symmetry without repetition. In an overmantel or a reredos by Gibbons you will find opposing drops balancing while they differ in content. Even when a panel is as packed with symbolic emblems as is that sent by Charles II to Cosimo III of Tuscany (it is still in Florence) each is given its say, whether it be crown, cravat, dove or walnut. Nothing has been forgotten, not even the carver's signature, nor the quill with which he is supposed to have written it.

The most elaborate work undertaken by Gibbons for James II was not in wood but in marble. This, executed in partnership with Arnold Quellin, was the altarpiece for the Roman Catholic chapel Wren added to the palace at Whitehall. Fragments of it survive in the church of St. Andrew at Burnham in Somerset. More heartening is the survival, again in St. James's, Piccadilly, of Gibbons' organ-case, which was carved in wood for that same short-lived chapel, destroyed by fire in 1698. The trumpeting angels and the *putti* who literally crown it, are all gilt and show no trace of their rugged and round-about journey from Whitehall.

With the accession of William and Mary, Gibbons' luck still held. His Dutch background was distinctly an asset. Moreover, Mary decided that Gibbons' overmantels were exactly right for setting off her vast collection of Delft and of Chinese porcelain. His designs for her galleries at Kensington and at Hampton Court are in the Sir John Soane Museum. For Hampton Court alone, the quantity and variety of Gibbons' commissions for woodcarving were fantastic. His immense frames still to be seen in the state-rooms are *tours de force*; but, in addition to these, room after room was enriched in Queen Mary's Water Gallery. Everywhere they went, William and Mary passed through Gibbons doorcases and were surrounded by Gibbons cornices, these last carved with tulips, with curling acanthus or, as in the frieze of the King's Bedchamber, with birds, wheat and flowers. Not surprisingly, in 1693 William appointed Gibbons Master Carver.

And then came calamity. In 1694 Queen Mary died of smallpox (Gibbons carved the inscription on her coffin) and every project she had cherished died with her; William had no heart for them. Nothing short of the fire, which four years later destroyed Whitehall Palace, could have made him take up the reins again at Hampton Court. In 1698 work was feverishly renewed. On the north, Wren devised a state entrance worthy of an emperor, (except for the avenue, it was never even begun) while on the south, he was commanded to demolish the Water Gallery and to use some of its materials to enrich the small banqueting-house William envisaged beside the Thames. No king is known to have used it; yet there it stands, looking modest enough but stuffed with mouldings – for doorcases, cornices and looking-glasses – carved by Gibbons at his inimitable best.

In the interval, while Hampton Court was

Grinling Gibbons

Fig. 5 **Choir,** *St. Paul's Cathedral, London. The Bishop's throne was carved by Gibbons.*

Fig. 6 **Design for an overmantel at Hampton Court** *by Gibbons illustrating his drawing style and the way in which he worked out his elaborate designs. (Sir John Soane's Museum, London.)*

Fig. 7 **Organ-case,** *St. James's, Piccadilly, originally carved by Gibbons for James II's Chapel at Whitehall Palace.*

quiescent, Gibbons and his assistants laboured at St. Paul's Cathedral. This last was, of course, a gigantic commission. Standing in the choir today, one is staggered that such a volume of superlatively fine work could ever have been contemplated, let alone 'determined, dared and done' in little more than two years.

Gibbons had been carving at Hampton Court not only in wood but in stone, and it was in stone – those symbolic panels of the virtues (Prudence, Justice and the rest) beneath the lower windows – that he carved at St. Paul's before the choir was ready for his chisel in 1696. The work there, in every way his greatest, amounted to carving the whole interior of a collegiate chapel, even to the communion table. There were the choir-stalls, with thrones for bishop, dean and lord mayor, and there were the galleries above them, supported by boy-atlantes; dividing nave from chancel there was Wren's organ-case: a screen of towers and pipes and trumpeting angels of the utmost beauty, ingenuity and elaboration.

The whole frame, borne on cherubic wings, seems to float above the altar

Near-perfection is precarious, a lure for vandals. Early in the nineteenth century the organ-case was taken down, part of it being forced back into the sides of the choir. Nothing short of a conflagration (or Cromwell) could, acoustically and aesthetically, have done more damage. However, the rest of the choir is unharmed. Indeed the bishop's throne alone, its oak columns damascened with lilies and tuberoses, oak leaves and acorns, as though swathed in embroidered brocade, is worth going far to see. This is not Gibbons at his most exuberant; Petworth is the place for that. It is Gibbons controlled by Wren, and the carving is in oak, not lime. Wren's endeavours, so wrote his grandson, were to build for eternity; and with that in mind, he chose seasoned oak for the choir, both within and without. For Gibbons this meant limited undercutting and projection for, whereas with lime he could laminate to what depth he chose, oak took less kindly to lamination and, rather than risk warping, with few exceptions he restricted projection to not more than two inches from the surface of the single board used for each panel. In the ambulatory outside the choir, where grills by Tijou are flanked with oak wreaths by Gibbons, this noble severity is most marked.

And where else should one go for the best examples of Gibbons' woodcarving? Most certainly to Petworth House, Sussex. In the Carved Room you have Gibbons' full repertoire, from 'Monnoyer' baskets of flowers (crown-imperial, double poppy, turk-cap lily) and trophies of musical instruments (he is known to have been musical), to birds and palms and cornucopiae and convolutions of whorled scrolls, for all the world as though he had been challenged to do the impossible and had smoothly accomplished it again and yet again.

His patron there was Charles Seymour, the proud Duke of Somerset, painted by most historians as a pompous clown. But the creator of Petworth must have been more than that. He was in fact Chancellor of Cambridge University and there, in the library of Trinity College, he caused

Country Life

Author's Photo

Gibbons to enrich the bookcases with ciphers and with coats of arms. And as though in answer to this, we have in the chapel of Trinity College, Oxford, a lime and pearwood reredos of unexcelled craftsmanship. Gibbons never did anything finer. At the head a great chalice of grapes, wheat and flowers between whorled scrolls, is supported by winged cherubs who, singly and in pairs, help to balance and punctuate the long drops below. These drops, which flank a parquetry panel, consist of trusses of fruit and flowers with light ropes of entwined stalks and stems, crossing and recrossing to bind the design, as though in a knot-garden. Such is its artistry that the whole frame, borne on cherubic wings, seems to float above the altar.

The fashion for carved wood was catching but not lasting. At the turn of the century companies of skilled carvers, sometimes with Gibbons, sometimes without, moved from one great house to another – from Belton to Burghley, from Chatsworth to Sudbury, from Hackwood to Kentchurch – leaving apartments enriched with elaborate frames

Fig. 8 **Wreath** *carved by Gibbons for St. Paul's Cathedral. It is now in St. Paul's, Covent Garden, where Gibbons is buried.*

Fig. 9 **Garland Madonna** *by Sir Peter Paul Rubens (1577-1640), the flowers by Jan Brueghel (1568-1625). Gibbons was acquainted with the work of many artists and it is reasonable to suppose that this type of painting had some influence on him. (Alte Pinakothek, Munich.)*

Fig. 10 **Detail of the Modena Panel** *by Gibbons showing a medallion with an inscribed self-portrait. (Museo e Medaglirve Estense, Modena.)*

and mouldings, and the halls with carved staircases. For some of these houses, such as Ramsbury in Wiltshire, Gibbons carved but one limewood frame. For others, such as Dalkeith and Drumlanrig, he carved overmantels in marble as well as in wood. And then fashion changed. For Queen Anne it was enough that her Dutch brother-in-law had liked carving, for her to dislike it. She suffered Gibbons to carve, for Wren, a limewood reredos in the chapel at Hampton Court, but thenceforward such commissions, royal or private, would be few. Blenheim Palace, in fact, is encrusted with Gibbons' stone-carving, but that was not Anne's doing, nor was it to the taste of her Groom of the Stole, Sarah Duchess of Marlborough. 'I will have no one thing carved,' she declared of another of her houses, 'my taste haveing always been to have things plain and clean, from a piece of wainscot to a lady's face.' It can hardly have pleased her that Blenheim bristled with Gibbons' stone trophies, urns, finials, chimney-pieces and coats of arms. For the Saloon she managed to veto his walls of niched statues, but his

marble door-cases remain in princely splendour.

Gibbons' church monuments are, for the most part, handsome without ranking as masterpieces. The best examples are at Exton in Rutland, at Badminton and in Westminster Abbey. Most of his statues leave one in doubt as to his mastery of the sculpting of the human form. In the casting of one outstanding exception, the bronze of James II, now outside the National Gallery, he is said to have had assistance from two Flemish sculptors.

Gibbons' woodcarving has since been much imitated, at times so cleverly that, without bills or other written evidence, it is next to impossible to tell genuine from counterfeit. Fragments of his carving from demolished houses may yet be stumbled on. Not long ago, such a fragment – a wreath discarded from the organ-case in St. Paul's – was given by the Cathedral to its brother church, St. Paul's Covent Garden, as a memorial to Gibbons, who is buried there. His house was close by, in Bow Street, his workshop at the foot of Ludgate Hill. He died, leaving daughters but no sons, in 1721.

ARTHUR NEGUS COLLECTORS' ITEM

WINE COASTERS

It was customary in Georgian and early Victorian homes to remove the used tablecloth before dessert was served. The servants were then dismissed and the host and his guests could relax over what remained of their meal. There was, therefore, no-one left to serve the wine and bottles or decanters were slid or 'coasted' over the polished table in wine-coasters, which were useful also in protecting the surface of the table from ring marks. Coasting (particularly if the diners had already been well wined) became a kind of game as the decanters were spun dizzily around the table with great skill and expertise, and from about 1760 no well-appointed table was without its coasters.

Coasters generally have a wooden base with a baize-mounted panel on the bottom. The silver gallery could be decorated with embossing, engraved work or intricate piercing. The earliest examples were made completely of silver and had concave bases, but these did not prove very satisfactory. They did not coast well because they were too light and the kick — the

indentation in the bottom of the bottle — created a vacuum, causing the bottle and coaster to stick together when lifted.

By the mid 1770s this type had been almost completely abandoned in favour of one with a hardwood base with shallow rings cut around the centre to allow air to reach the kick. In this way the bottle lifted easily from the stand. A further advantage of this development was that the wooden base added weight so that they coasted excellently.

Collecting Hints

Dating presents no problem if the silver is hallmarked, and Sheffield plate marks can also be helpful. Unfortunately many are unmarked and in these cases decoration can indicate age. It must always be borne in mind, however, that designs, particularly from the eighteenth century, are copied frequently, even today.

The decoration is usually concentrated around the gallery. Pierced galleries are for the most part eighteenth-century, the designs being mainly either geometrical, or sometimes a band of rosettes and vine leaves. One of the most common patterns, popular because it was cheap and easy to produce, was of four horizontal rows of oblong holes alternating with circular ones. In the 1790s the gallery was sometimes fluted and embossed and the lower part pierced, but after 1800 this format was usually reversed and the piercing appears at the top. Total embossing with suitably bacchanalian motifs such as figures

intermingled with flowers and vines came into vogue at the beginning of the nineteenth century and by 1820 an abundance of decoration was being cast in relief. After the 1830s decoration became lighter again and old patterns were often modified.

Look out for 'wine waggons', which are double coasters on wheels, and single coasters in sets which can be linked together to form a waggon. Some double coasters are also shaped like boats and can be either coasted or mounted on wheels.

Prices

Remember that the finest silversmiths made sets of wine coasters and examples bearing the marks of Storr or Bateman will be well beyond the means of most collectors. But very attractive coasters can be found at quite reasonable prices. Coasters of Sheffield plate are of course the least expensive, probably fetching between £12 and £15 a pair. Nineteenth-century silver coasters can be bought for between £20 and £30 a pair, depending on whether they are early or late examples, and good eighteenth-century examples are at least £100 a pair. A single coaster will normally cost less than half the price of an equivalent pair.

Where To Buy

Silver dealers and silver auctions are obvious sources, but wine coasters can sometimes be bought in non-specialist shops which carry odd pieces of silver.

Top left **One of a pair of silver coasters,** London, 1807. Silver coasters are relatively rare. This pair is worth about £250.
Top centre **One of a pair of Sheffield plate coasters,** c.1800. Of quite common design, these would cost about £25.
Top right **One of a pair of Sheffield plate coasters,** c.1800. Similar to those above, these are crested, and also worth about £25.
Bottom left **Pair of Sheffield plate coasters,** c.1820. These are of a more popular, ornate design, and are therefore worth about £28.
Opposite: **One of a pair of plated coasters,** mid-Victorian. Of extremely unusual and attractive design, these would cost £30.

1

A Revolution in Glass Making

Peter Lazarus

With the invention of lead glass by George Ravenscroft in 1676, England became the leading glass producer in Europe, turning out wares of unrivalled durability and sophistication of design

George Ravenscroft was born in 1618, but we know very little of his early life, the side he favoured in the Civil War and what occupation he followed as a young man; there is no doubt, however, that the production of crystal glass became Ravenscroft's sole interest in the latter years of his life.

Ravenscroft was of gentle birth, described in all contemporary writings as 'Gent.' or 'Esq.'. His family were the Squires of Shalton in the parish of Hawarden in Flintshire. His elder brother John looked after the family estates, while his younger brother Thomas rose to be a member of the Privy Council. He himself became a shipping merchant who carried on considerable trade with Venice. It is here that one likes to think that his interest in glass was first aroused, and it is interesting to note that the most important name in English glass only began this career at the age of fifty-six, when he opened his glass-house at the Savoy in 1673.

Ravenscroft was awarded a seal or mark – a raven's head

Although highly professional in his dealing with the Glass Sellers' Company, Ravenscroft's greatest interest in glass was academic and scientific rather than professional. From the foundation of his glass-house until his actual invention of lead glass in 1676, he experimented mainly with the production of various types rather than shapes, of glass.

Up until his invention of lead glass, all glasses had been of brittle 'façon de Venise' (in the Venetian style), easily shattered, extremely difficult to work and not suitable for engraved designs. Ravenscroft's experiments with the introduction of lead oxide were not without their failures; the quantity of lead added to the mixture varied and the glass became infected with 'glass sickness or crizzling'. By June 1676, his teething troubles had been eliminated and he had produced a superb quality glass similar to rock crystal, with a fine ringing tone. The Glass Sellers' Company issued him with a document to certify that this was so and he was also awarded a 'seal or mark' which was a raven's head.

Naturally these early Ravenscroft glasses are exceptionally rare but it is from this beginning that the supremacy of English glass really made itself felt and for more than a hundred years the English glass trade maintained its reputation for producing the highest quality glass in the world. It was not until 1781 that the French were able to break the secret of English lead glass.

In 1677 Ravenscroft renewed his agreement with the Glass Sellers' Company for a further three years but it is interesting to note that he actually terminated this agreement at the end of February 1678. Even so, Ravenscroft's patent was still in

Fig. 1 (previous page) *Wineglass*, Newcastle, 1745. Height 6¾ ins. Engraved with a royal coat of arms, this beautiful glass has a ball knop with a tear in the stem. (Private Collection.)

Fig. 2 (left) *Wineglass*, Anglo-Venetian, 1685. Height 5½ ins. The propeller stem with pincered bowl is exceptionally rare. (right) *Mead glass* with gadrooned bowl and hollow baluster stem, 1690. Height 6½ ins. (Author's Collection.)

Fig. 3 (from left to right) *Baluster goblet* with cone knop and flared bowl, 1715. Height 8⅝ ins. *Baluster wineglass* with perfect mushroom knop and central tear, 1710. Height 5⅜ ins. *Baluster wineglass* with bell bowl and triple annular knop, 1720. Height 6½ ins. (Author's Collection.)

Fig. 4 (from left to right) *Baluster wineglass*, extremely rare, with cylinder knop, 1710. Height 6⅛ ins. *Baluster wineglass*, the rarest of all baluster types, with tyre knop and flat tear, 1710. Height 5⅜ ins. *Baluster wineglass* with thistle bowl and acorn knop, 1715. Height 6½ ins. (Author's Collection.)

Fig. 5 (from left to right) *Fine baluster glass* with bell bowl and true cone knop, 1710. Height 5⅞ ins. *Baluster wineglass* with triple annular knop, 1720. Height 6¼ ins. *Large baluster glass* with very fine true baluster stem, 1715. Height 7 ins. *Baluster wineglass* with slightly flared bucket bowl and annular knop, 1710. Height 5½ ins. (Author's Collection.)

Fig. 6 (from left to right) *Light baluster wineglass* of the 'kit-kat' variety, 1715. Height 6¼ ins. *Light baluster sweetmeat glass* with a small-lipped ogee bowl, possibly Newcastle, 1715. Height 5⅜ ins. *'Kit-kat' glass* with flared trumpet bowl and columnar stem with air tear above a fine base knop, 1715. Height 6½ ins. (Author's Collection.)

English Glasses
from the Ravenscroft period

Derek Balmer

Fig. 9 (left) ***Baluster glass,***
Newcastle, 1730. Height $7\frac{1}{2}$ *ins.*
The extremely fine round funnel
bowl is engraved with branches
of flowers around a drinking scene.
Two men are seated at a table
with a 'shaft and globe' bottle;
they hold their glasses by the
foot instead of the stem. The
bowl is set on a Newcastle stem
with ball knops and an inverted
baluster, with folded foot.
(right) ***Baluster glass,***
Newcastle, 1730. Engraved with
vines, swags, birds and a Latin
inscription. Folded foot.
Height $6\frac{3}{4}$ *ins.*
(Author's Collection.)

Derek Balmer

Derek Balmer

Fig. 7 (from left to right)
Small baluster wineglass with drawn bowl above a light pure baluster, 1720. Height 5¼ ins.
Large wineglass with a flattened ball knop above a central ball knop, possibly Newcastle, 1730. Height 6¼ ins.
Small wineglass with an annular knop above a ball knop and large air tear throughout the stem, 1740. Height 5¾ ins.
Early wineglass with flared bucket bowl set on a cushion knop over a columnar stem on a small base knop, 1730. Height 6¾ ins.
Triple series light baluster wineglass, with drawn funnel bowl set on a double collar on domed foot, 1730. Height 6¼ ins. (Author's Collection.)

Fig. 8 (from left to right)
Wineglass engraved with a continuous band of flowers and a cross chequered pattern, Newcastle, 1750. Height 7 ins.
Massive goblet, Newcastle, 1730. Height 9½ ins. The deep funnel bowl is engraved with a very fine scene of five men sitting around a table with their five goblets. The motto reads 'Peace Good Neighbor Hood and Property (sic) to this Society'. The central swollen knop has been blown with many air tears.
Glass, Newcastle, 1750. Height 8 ins. The tall funnel bowl is engraved with an old French motto around two figures. The central knop of the stem has five small air tears.
Wineglass, Newcastle, 1750. Height 7¼ ins. The round funnel bowl is finely engraved with a continuous band of foliage and birds and set on a multi-knopped stem. (Author's Collection.)

Fig. 10 (left) *Armorial wineglass with air beaded knop, 1745. Height 7⅞ ins. The funnel bowl was engraved in Holland with the arms of William IV. There are two royal mottoes in French: 'Honi Soit Qui Mal Y Pense' of England and 'Il Maintien Drai' of Holland.*
(right) *Wineglass, Newcastle, 1750. Height 7 ins. The round funnel bowl is decorated with a bird perched upon an open cage, surrounded by fine swagging and a motto. The stem is a light baluster with a beaded knop over a plain section. (Author's Collection.)*

existence until 1681. He in fact died at the beginning of May of that year and was buried just one week before his patent expired.

There are still quite a few glasses in existence of the 'Ravenscroft period', which is to say that the glass, although still influenced very strongly by the Venetian designs and styles is a 'glass of lead'. In the remaining years of the century many glass-houses sprang up around the City of London. By 1696 there were nine flint glass-houses working in London itself, five at Bristol, two at Stourbridge and two at Newcastle-upon-Tyne.

After Ravenscroft's death, the Savoy glass-house passed to another great glass-maker, Hawley Bishopp, and there is no doubt that he carried on the traditions and the ideas of Ravenscroft, probably using his seal, although this has never been proved.

Glass presents problems in dating as it bears no mark

Of all English antiques, glass is the hardest of all to date definitely; there are no maker's marks as in silver or porcelain to indicate the factory, and those glasses which have been engraved with a definite date were more than likely made in the earlier decade or so. English antique glass is dated not so much by the shape of the bowls of the various glasses but by the stem and overall formation of the glass. The entire eighteenth century can be roughly broken into five groups, and in each case there is no clear-cut date-line between one group and the next. They are: baluster stems, including balustroids (1685–1735); moulded pedestal and plain stems (1715–50); air-twist stems, including composite stems (1740–65); opaque-twist stems, including incised, mixed and colour-twist stems (1755–85); and faceted stems (1770–1810).

Strength, clarity and brilliance together with pleasing and simple designs

When trying to simplify the grouping system of eighteenth-century glasses there are many sub-groups, such as Newcastle balusters, excise stems, composite stems, incised-twist stems, mixed-twist and colour-twist stems. The earliest lead glasses of the period prior to 1700 still showed signs of Venetian influence; gadrooning on the bowls, pincerwork on the stems, flammiform, or flame-shaped, work and hollow blown knops, are all common to this period, but it is the arrival of the true baluster which is most important at this stage of the development of the English drinking-glass.

Until the last quarter of the seventeenth century almost every glass made in Europe was Venetian in concept, influence and design, but as the great glass-houses throughout Europe developed national characteristics in style and method, the supremacy of English glass was established.

With the rapid and successful development of English lead glass the glass-makers could for the first time produce a glass that combined the qualities of strength, clarity and brilliance with the extremely pleasing, but very simple, designs of the

period. No longer did the glasses fracture and break at the slightest mishap or with the somewhat rough handling that they were bound to receive at the hands of the gentry who drank from them, or the servants who had to wash and store them.

Among other features of glass of this period was the folded foot and, in some very rare cases, the folded rim. This first style was achieved by the enlargement of the foot during the manufacture of the glass which was then folded under to give a double thickness; in early times the fold was very narrow but later it could be as wide as a quarter to three eighths of an inch. The folded foot was designed to add strength to the base of the glass and save it from being chipped by everyday use. Indeed, to find a glass with a folded foot which is damaged in any way is extremely rare but, even so, by the year 1750 the folded foot has almost disappeared.

A tax of 'one penny per pound weight' on all the ingredients of glass

In 1745–46 the Government passed the first Glass Excise Act which taxed all glass-masters 'one penny per pound weight for all ingredients that went into the making of the glass'. Very naturally, this caused considerable consternation in the trade; economies had to be made, the most important of which was to abandon the folded foot. This not only saved glass, now taxed severely; it also lightened the glass considerably and after a short time benefited the glass industry as glasses with plain feet broke or were damaged more easily than those with the fold.

The baluster-stem glasses spring from the architectural designs of this period and had been popular on the Continent since the middle of the seventeenth century, but it is the inverted and true baluster which is typically English and it is from this one type of stem that all other stem formations were developed. Probably the greatest importance of the now very rare baluster glass is that it is the basis of any antique glass collection.

Glasses were in demand from all levels of society

The glass-makers of the period were not very ambitious with regard to the designs of their bowls. The two basic styles were 'round funnel' and 'conical' with variations, but it is in the stems themselves that the craftsmanship of the early eighteenth century becomes apparent. The fine balance and design of each glass is a work of art in itself and in many cases some of the stems have more than one variation of knop. (This refers to the actual shape of the stem formation.) Some are extremely rare and are highly prized by collectors throughout the world. There are approximately twelve basic variations of knops and the following list is in order of rarity: tyre knop, egg knop, cylinder knop, acorn knop, mushroom knop, cone knop, drop knop, cushion knop, angular or annular knop, ball knop, flattened knop, and shoulder or base knop.

Where there are one or more knops in the stem, it is usually the ball or flattened knop which is in combination with other knops. Probably the greatest attraction of this type of glass is a combina-

Fig. 11 *The Ravenscroft seal,*
which was granted to Ravenscroft
personally by the Glass Sellers'
Company in 1676, and is now
extremely rare.
(Victoria and Albert Museum.)

11

12

13

Fig. 12 *Gadrooned bowl bearing*
the Ravenscroft seal, c.1676.
Diameter 8⅞ ins.
Ravenscroft's seal was probably
used by his successor, but all
pieces bearing it are rare.
(Cecil Higgins Art Gallery,
Bedford. By permission of the
Trustees.)

Fig. 13 *Helmet-shaped jug,*
bearing the Ravenscroft seal on
the base of the handle, c.1676.
Height 9 ins.
Ravenscroft produced a great
deal of very fine lead glass, but in
some of his earliest experiments
he used so much alkali that the
glass became 'crizzled' or cloudy
as in this example.
(Cecil Higgins Art Gallery.)

tion of simplicity of form and true balance. On many occasions where the bowl and stem appear to be a trifle short they are enhanced by the doming of the foot in order to give the glass correct architectural proportions; this, in itself, is an accolade to the craftsmen of the period.

With very few exceptions the diameter of the bowl of these glasses is usually less than the diameter of the foot; this gave grace to the style and added to the general stability of the glass. In light baluster or balustroid glasses made between about 1715 and 1735, the prevalence of extremely wide feet diminished although the same basic shapes were maintained; the glasses became lighter in style, with bowls of slightly smaller capacity. These series of glasses which retained folded feet, are far more common than the heavy baluster. It is in this series that for the first time we come across 'ginette' and 'dram' glasses, used for drinking the rough corn spirit so popular at the time.

Certainly one of the main reasons for the decline in the vogue for heavy balusters was the fact that glasses were no longer confined to the noble and to the rich but were in demand for all levels of society from those frequenting the lowest ale house to royal tables. In consequence, very heavy glasses which cost quite a considerable amount as, at the time, glass was purchased by weight as well as quantity, gave way to the lighter and smaller glasses, the price of which suited every pocket.

Superb portraits, landscapes, coats of arms and commemorative glasses were commissioned

A feature of all glasses in the eighteenth century, with the exception of the late faceted stem glasses made from 1780 onwards, is that of the pontil or punty mark. This was the scar left when the punty rod, which held the glass during its manufacture, was broken away from the finished glass. It tends to be rough, sometimes even sharp, and is found on the centre underside of the foot of the glass. The main reason that glasses of this period had such a high conical and sometimes domed foot was that if the glass were to be as flat as are our modern day glasses, the pontil mark would surely scratch the table when the glass was placed upon it. Another indication of this age of craftsmanship is the very fine lines sometimes found vertically marking the bowls, and called 'spring tool marks'. These were made when the glass was held in a pair of small calipers called the 'spring tool', an instrument which looked like miniature sheep shears. The glass was held for only a few moments while the punty rod was broken off, but in those few moments the spring tool frequently left almost imperceptible vertical lines from the rim of the bowl downwards; often when an eighteenth century glass is held to the light and turned slowly, these marks become apparent to the naked eye.

Possibly the greatest commercial successes of the eighteenth century were the Newcastle glasshouses; as far as we know, these were originally founded in the seventeenth century by a Bristol family named Dagnia and it is from these glasshouses that the most advanced forms of decoration and style emanated. By 1730 there was a vigorous export trade from Newcastle to the Low Countries

and it was from Newcastle that all types of engraving, stipple, wheel and polish work were carried out. Superb portraits, landscapes, coats of arms and commemorative glasses were commissioned; the Dutch and German artists, engravers such as Jacob Sang, Franz Greenwood, and David Wolff, were as much sought after to decorate these Newcastle glasses as was a fashionable portrait painter to paint the head of the household.

Extremely fine stems with varied ornament

In general, nearly all Newcastle glasses had plain conical feet and only the earliest examples were folded. The metal of the glass was very light and thin, and in nearly all cases the bowls tended to be tapering 'round funnel'. Again, however, it is the stems which are so interesting; these were extremely fine and had many and varied small knops, inverted balusters, ball and annular; some were plain, but more often than not they had small air beads inserted into each knop. The surface and quality of the glass was very fine and thus suited the varied tastes of the engravers. It is interesting to note that the famous David Wolff was still importing Newcastle glass in the last decade of the eighteenth century.

Newcastle became so famous that in the 1750s a qualified glass-master, James Keith, was sent to Norway to start a glass-works at Nøstetangen where he worked for some thirty-five years. His glass was of such fine quality that even today glasses from this factory cannot be definitely attributed either to Norway or to England.

The steady transition from the solid and simple baluster to the lighter but still simple balustroid is an obvious one while the grace and beauty of the light, many-knopped Newcastle glasses seem strangely out of place. From their inception in the very early years of the eighteenth century they remained far in advance in the designs and patterns of all other styles of glasses and in consequence held their popularity throughout most of the eighteenth century.

MUSEUMS AND COLLECTIONS
Baluster glasses may be seen at the following:
Belfast: Ulster Museum
Bristol: City Art Gallery
Harvey's Wine Museum
Cambridge: Fitzwilliam Museum
London: Victoria and Albert Museum
Manchester: City Art Gallery
Oxford: Ashmolean Museum
St. Helens,
Lancashire The Pilkington Museum
U.S.A.
New York: Corning Museum of Glass

FURTHER READING
Old Glass by O. N. Wilkinson, London, 1968.
English and Irish Antique Glass by Derek Davis, London, 1964.
The Collectors' Dictionary of Glass by E. M. Elville, London, 1961, 1965.
English, Scottish and Irish Table Glass by Bernard Hughes, London, 1956.
Glass Through the Ages by E. Barrington Haynes, Harmondsworth, 1948, 1959.
A History of English and Irish Glass by W. A. Thorpe, London, 1929, 1969.

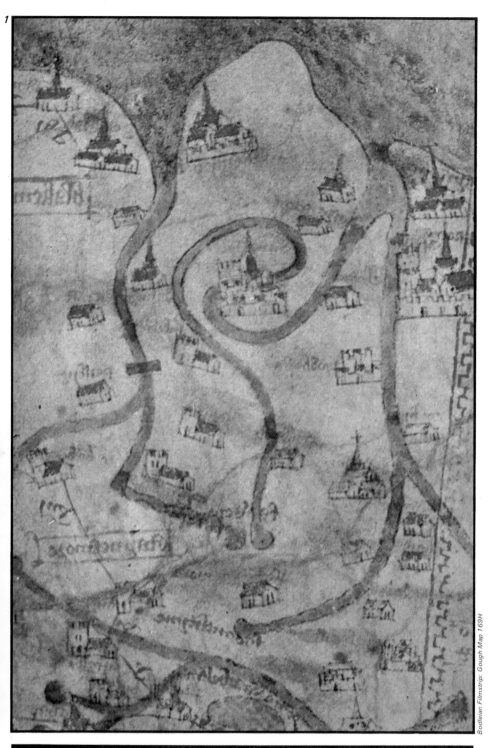

€arly €nglish maps

P. J. Radford

Although few maps of England existed before the early sixteenth century, the proliferation of maps and charts in the sixteenth and seventeenth centuries produced some objects of surprising accuracy and great visual beauty

It is difficult to imagine what it must be like not to have any notion of the shape or appearance of one's country, county or the immediate area in which one lives and works. In the British Isles in the early sixteenth century, the lower and middle classes probably had no idea of this and few of the nobility would have had a much better idea unless they had travelled or had access to learned works or libraries. Such a library was that formerly at Battle Abbey, where the Anglo-Saxon *Map of the World* was kept (now in the British Museum) which, although compressed into a solid rectangle, depicts a recognisable British Isles in one corner. Hereford Cathedral has the thirteenth-century manuscript *Mappa Mundi* and at the Bodleian Library, Oxford, there is Gough's fourteenth-century *Map of England and Wales* (Fig. 1).

The earliest recognisable printed map of the British Isles

Atlases based on Claudius Ptolemy's views and study of geography were being printed in Italy from 1477 and in Germany from 1482. Many old centres of learning had their own collections of manuscript draughts and surveys.

The earliest recognisable printed map of the British Isles is the one that is attributed to George Lily and was first printed at Rome in 1546 (Fig. 3). It was printed from a copper-plate and one version was engraved and printed in London by Thomas Gemini, who came from the Low Countries. Another map of great importance, only three copies of which are known to exist today, was that of Gerard Mercator, which depicted the British Isles on a scale of fourteen and a half miles to the inch. It is dated 1564 and was engraved on about eight copper-plates. Mercator's sources for this map are not known.

Probably the most important cartographic event relating to this country was the great survey by Christopher Saxton that resulted in the first set of accurate printed maps of the counties of England and Wales (Fig. 2). Saxton, a Yorkshireman born in the West Riding in about 1542, eventually came to London and went into the employ of Sir Thomas Seckford. To Seckford we owe much, as it was due to his encouragement that Saxton considered the vast undertaking and it was certainly due to his financial backing that the project was carried out so efficiently and with such regard for quality. The attention of Queen Elizabeth was gained and her permission obtained for Saxton to make and sell his maps in the succeeding decade. With this authority he could gain access to any high building or other vantage point from which he could map the

Fig. 1 (previous page) *Hartlepool and surrounding area* from the *Gough Map, c.1335. Manuscript. The detailed symbols on this map did not appear on printed maps until three centuries later. (Bodleian Library, Oxford.)*

Fig. 2 *Hertfordshire* by Christopher Saxton, 1577. *Engraved by Nicolas Reynolds of London. The arms are those of Sir Thomas Seckford. (British Museum, London.)*

area, using a form of the triangulation method that is still practised today. This survey commenced in about 1570 and the first maps were completed in 1574.

The maps would almost certainly have been sold separately, as issued, until the survey was complete and the final engraving had been finished. They were bound into atlas form and offered for sale as a set in 1579. Some were sold plain, but most appear to have been highly coloured. A magnificent frontispiece to the atlas depicts Queen Elizabeth enthroned with symbolic figures on both sides of her (Fig. 5). Although it is thought that she disapproved of this representation, in that alterations were effected to simplify her jewellery, change her forearms and re-arrange the folds of her dress to hang more naturally, she rewarded Saxton by granting him both land and armorial bearings.

The maps themselves are of magnificent quality, beautifully engraved with place names superbly executed. The trees, hills and towns are shown in elevation, a practice that was to be followed for the next two centuries. Each map is richly ornamented, as befits this colourful period, and bears the

5

arms of Seckford, Saxton's patron and, as a tribute to his Queen, the royal arms. To the collector this monumental series is the focal point of any collection dealing with the British Isles.

The next great name in British cartography in the age of Elizabeth I is that of John Norden, an able and painstaking map-maker, who carried out surveys and made maps of the counties of Surrey, Sussex, Middlesex, Hampshire and Hertfordshire. These were engraved, but early copies are exceedingly rare. He also surveyed Essex, Cornwall and Northamptonshire and possibly Warwickshire and Kent, but only the first two have been engraved and printed – Cornwall in 1720, and Essex as late as

1840. He had also travelled to the Isle of Wight and the Channel Isles by 1595.

Norden, born in the West Country in 1518, had a brilliant and original mind, for he was the first map-maker in this country to show roads on his maps; he also invented the triangular distance-table that is still used in motoring handbooks.

Although he also obtained the Queen's authority, and was presumably esteemed at Court, he failed to find a financial backer. A last personal appeal to the Queen seems to have elicited no response. Thus a figure who could well have been a very great influence on the cartography of this country was eclipsed all too soon by lack of funds.

Other, single maps were made, often of remarkable quality, such as the large map of Kent by Philip Symonson issued in two sheets. No complete copy of the first issue is known, but a single sheet bearing the date 1596 is extant. Symonson also was a pioneer in showing roads upon his map.

Superb engravings after the defeat of the Armada

There are a number of rare engraved items, any one of which would constitute the *pièce de résistance* of a collection. After the Armada had been vanquished, Robert Adams produced a series of charts depicting the engagements along the Channel which were superbly engraved by Augustine Ryther, one of the engravers of Saxton's maps.

The first English sea charts were the result of a translation by Anthony Ashley of Lucas Jansz Waghenaer's *Spieghel der Zeervaert*, which was translated as the *Mariner's Mirrour* and published in 1588 (Fig. 6). They are extremely decorative and, although any one of the forty-five charts is of great interest, those dealing with the British Isles are naturally the ones most sought after in Great Britain.

Maps ornamented with heraldry, portraits, coins, views and town plans

A rare English map of the world was engraved for *Hakluyt's Voyages* in 1600. It is by Edward Wright (1558-1615), a writer on mathematical and nautical matters, who laid the foundations for vast and revolutionary changes in navigation, and his draughts were used (without acknowledgment) for Mercator's *Map of the World*.

In 1627 was published *The Prospect of the Most Famous Parts of the World* by John Speed. This was an important atlas, usually bound with the collection of Speed's county maps, and it was the first completely English world atlas. It was re-issued in 1631, 1662 and 1676. This last issue is of particular importance as it was expanded to include maps of New York and New England, Virginia and Maryland, Carolina, Jamaica and Barbados, the East Indies, Russia and Palestine. With the American ones in particular, the description in English upon the reverse of each map is of great interest. As with the county maps, all the maps in the *Prospect* were reflected in the miniature atlases published by William Humble.

Fig. 3 *The British Isles* by George Lily, Rome, 1546. Very rare. Lily was a Catholic refugee. (British Museum.)

Fig. 4 *Isle of Man* by John Speed, first issue of 1611 with original colouring. (Author's Collection.)

Fig. 5 *Frontispiece* from Christopher Saxton's atlas, published in 1579. Two versions extant. British Museum.)

Fig. 6 **Brittany** *from the* Mariner's Mirrour *by Anthony Ashley, 1588. Translated from* Spieghel der Zeervaert *by Lucas Jansz Waghenaer, 1584.*
This highly decorative chart is one of the forty-five by Ashley which were the earliest series of printed English sea charts. As was common practice, the maps have been taken from a Dutch source.
(British Museum.)

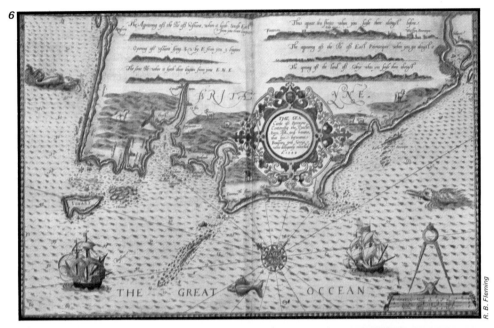

Fig. 7 **County Slego** *from* Hiberniae Delineatio *by Sir William Petty, 1685. Engraving. This set of maps was the first complete survey of Ireland to be made. It was completed in 1685, but many of the maps date from as early as 1636. The crudeness of the engraving is surprising, as it was executed in Amsterdam, long a centre for fine graphic work. (British Museum.)*

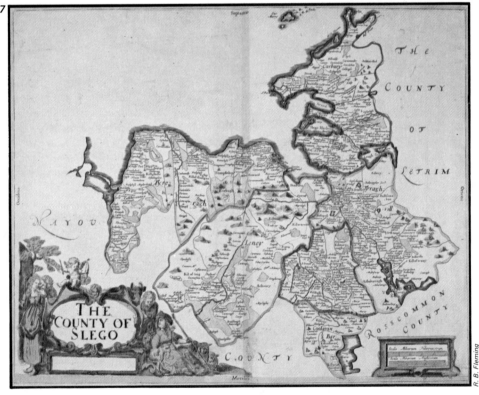

Maps of the counties of England and Wales published in this country include the fine series, mostly after Christopher Saxton and John Norden, which was engraved by William Hole and William Kip for William Camden's topographical history of Great Britain, *Britannia*. This set of maps is of very high quality, the whole spirit and style being, as with much Jacobean work, Elizabethan in character; this is hardly surprising as the Queen had, after all, died only four years earlier. The 1607 edition was published in Latin, but English editions were published in 1610 and 1637.

John Speed's atlas of county maps, *The Theatre of the Empire of Great Britain*, was issued in 1611–12 (Fig. 4), although many of the maps are dated 1610. These achieved a deserved popularity which was shown by the number of increasingly large issues during the subsequent century and a half. It was an indispensable part of every gentleman's library, and is mentioned by Samuel Pepys in his diary. Speed drew upon many sources in order to compile and ornament his maps, including heraldry, portraits, coins, views and town plans. The last are among the most important, as a number of these are the earliest known printed plans of some of our cities, and about fifty of them are believed to be the result of Speed's own surveys.

In the field of nautical atlases, one of the most important productions from the point of view of accuracy was by an ex-patriate Englishman residing in Florence, Sir Robert Dudley. He was a man of the sea and a mathematician and so was ideally suited to perform the task of compiling a set of accurate sea charts. They were clearly and beautifully engraved by Antonio Francesco Lucini, who took some eight years to do the work. The atlas was published in 1646 (Fig. 8). The character of the charts is of great interest, as, with decoration kept to a minimum, it achieves a beauty of appearance that is due wholly to the fastidious elegance of the design and the quality of Lucini's engraving. A second edition appeared in 1661.

The most accurate surveys of the British coast yet published

The nautical charts that John Seller published from 1671 under the title *The English Pilot* were very decorative, but the venture proved too much for Seller's means and, instead of continuing to engrave original charts, he was forced to buy out-of-date Dutch plates which he altered, often substituting his own cartouches.

Meanwhile a fine set of charts of the coast of the British Isles was in preparation. Captain Greenvile Collins was appointed in 1679 to survey the coast of the British Isles in two vessels, first the *Merlin* and later in the *Monmouth*. This he did from 1681 to 1688 and the complete set of charts was first published in 1693 under the title *Great Britain's Coasting Pilot*. They are decorative and were the most accurate surveys of the British coast that had been produced to date. The chart of Harwich bears a dedication to Samuel Pepys, and the chart of the Torbay area of South Devon is embellished with a view of the landing there of King William III in 1688, in a decorative setting flanked by two figures. These charts were frequently re-issued throughout the eighteenth century.

At last the English mile was standardised

In 1681 Richard Blome's small county maps were published. They were re-issued in various forms until the last, much-altered issues of 1715, published by Thomas Taylor, and 1750, by Thomas Bakewell.

The larger county maps by Blome, issued in 1673 in his *Britannia* had the same crudely attractive appearance, and each map also had the dedication with the armorial bearing of the subscriber to

Fig. 8 *Asia* from Del Arcano del Mare *by Sir Robert Dudley, Florence, 1646–7. Engraved by Antonio Francesco Lucini. (British Museum.)*

Fig. 9 *Monmouth to Llanbeder by John Ogilby, 1675. From a series of a hundred road maps; to be read from the lower left corner. (Francis Edwards Ltd., London.)*

Fig. 10 *Dedication and arms on a map of the East Riding of Yorkshire from* Britannia *by Richard Blome, 1673. (Francis Edwards Ltd.)*

At this period, however, two most important cartographical publications were produced. First was the set of one hundred carefully surveyed road maps by John Ogilby, issued in 1675 (Fig. 9), and later in 1698. They were ingenious and carefully thought out, as well as being of interest, as they show details near the road such as an inn, a notable hill, a tree or country seat, a beacon, or sometimes gallows. One reason for their importance is that they finally standardised the English mile, which had previously had local variants.

Secondly, the publication in 1685 of Sir William Petty's *Hiberniae Delineatio* (Fig. 7) was a milestone, as previously there had been no detailed survey of Ireland and, although Petty was commissioned to undertake only a partial survey within narrow political limits, he took the opportunity the task offered and compiled a set of detailed surveys. They date from as early as 1636, but the complete set was not published until 1685, even though the engraving appears to have been completed several years earlier. A surprising feature is the crudeness of this engraving, the more so as it was executed in Amsterdam, the centre from which the finest work had emanated for so many years.

The well-known county maps of Robert Morden are well engraved but not always laid out to satisfy the eye. They were issued fairly frequently from 1695, the last issue being published in 1772. The maps appeared in William Camden's *Britannia*, a new edition that had been edited and newly translated from Camden's original Latin by Dr. Edmond Gibson of Oxford.

In about 1694, a set of miniature county maps by John Seller was published, which were also reissued in various forms during the next century. The early issues are attractive and scarce.

This brief survey covers only maps produced by British map-makers. The subject is vast, and it is hoped that it will be seen what a very rich field there is for the student, the scholar, the collector and the ever-increasing number of enthusiasts who are interested in the maps and map-makers of the past.

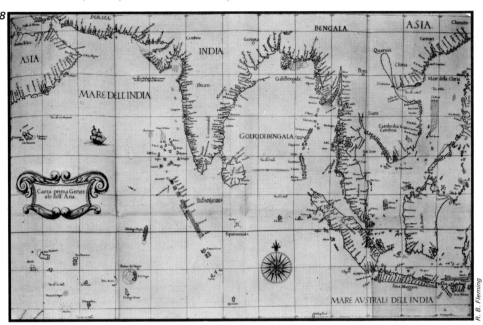

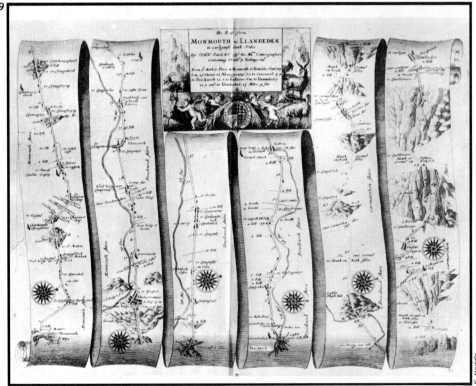

whom Blome applied prior to publication in order to obtain funds (Fig. 10). The arms and dedication upon each map are thus at once the visible reward to the subscriber and a gratification of his vanity.

Moses Pitt conceived an English version of the large folio atlas in a number of volumes similar to those of the Dutch cartographers, Blaeu and Jansson, but only three volumes were issued between 1681 and 1683. The maps are, in the main, re-worked Jansson plates. As with earlier map-makers such as Blome, Seller and Norden, the projected publication of a set of fine works was not realised because of insufficient funds.

MUSEUMS AND COLLECTIONS

The only large collection of English maps is in the Map Room of the British Museum, London. There is usually a display of early maps inside the rear entrance to the Museum.

There are also small local collections throughout Great Britain, mostly with maps of the area in which they are situated. These include the Birmingham Public Library, the Kingston-upon-Thames Record Office, and the Essex Record Office.

FURTHER READING

Antique Maps by P. J. Radford, London, 1971.
Antique Maps and their Cartographers by Raymond Lister, London, 1970.
Investing in Maps by R. Baynton-Williams, London, 1969.
How to Identify Old Maps and Globes by Raymond Lister, London, 1965.
Printed Maps of London c.1553–1850 by Ida Darlington and James Howgego, London, 1964.
Explorers' Maps by R. A. Skelton, London, 1958.
Maps and Mapmakers by R. V. Tooley, London, reprinted 1970.

Fig. 1 **Dial** *from one of a pair of clocks made for John Flamsteed, the first Astronomer Royal, by Thomas Tompion, 1676. (British Museum, London.)*

Fig. 2 **Hanging wall clock** *by Joseph Knibb, London, c.1690. This alarm clock has only one hand, which serves to mark the hours. (Private Collection.)*

Fig. 3 **Carillon clock** *by Nicholas Vallin (1565?–1603), c.1598. This is one of the earliest known English domestic clocks. It has thirteen bells. (British Museum, Ilbert Collection.)*

Fig. 4 **Travelling clock** *by Thomas Tompion, c.1700. By the most famous of English clockmakers, this example is in a highly decorative case. (Mrs M. L. Giffard. On loan to the Science Museum, London.)*

Fig. 5 **Striking lantern clock,** *signed 'Jeffrey Baylie at ye turn-style in Holburn fecit', seventeenth century. Brass case, converted from a foliot escapement to pendulum. (Clockmakers' Company Collection, Guildhall, London.)*

The history of English clocks begins as early as the fourteenth century. The quaint mechanisms of early lantern, bracket and pendulum clocks were housed in cases of great beauty and increasing elegance

As soon as man began to organise himself into social communities, he felt the need for some public means of timekeeping. For many centuries, the shadow dial around a large obelisk, such as Cleopatra's Needle, was supplemented by artificial timekeepers that depended on dripping water, running sand, or slow-burning powder and wick. The biggest single step in time measurement was the invention of the mechanical clock in Europe, perhaps in Burgundy, some time before the last quarter of the thirteenth century.

The 'art and mystery' (meaning the knowledge and working method) of clockmaking spread to England. The earliest record is a manuscript by Richard of Wallingford, Abbot of St. Albans, dated 1330, about a complicated astronomical clock he had made. The clock unfortunately no longer exists.

It is possible that clockmaking as a trade began in England in 1368, when King Edward III invited three Dutch clockmakers to work in England for a year. The Salisbury Cathedral clock, the oldest functioning clock in the world, is reliably dated 1386 and was probably made by them. It has no dial but correctly strikes each hour.

Clocks of this kind were very large and magnificently wrought in iron by blacksmiths. Other grand clocks include the Cassiobury turret clock that may have belonged to Richard of Wallingford, now in the British Museum (Fig. 9), the clock in Rye Church, Sussex, that has a pendulum so long that it swings in the church below (it has just been re-dated to about 1390), and the Wells Cathedral clock dated 1392, now in the Science Museum, London. Exeter Cathedral and East Hendred church, Berkshire, also have grand clocks.

The first truly indigenous designs of great clocks (now called tower or turret clocks) were produced by blacksmiths between 1490 and 1500. They have vertical iron or wooden frames. At least ten still exist, most of them in the West Country. Those at Cothele House, Cornwall (National Trust), Ottery St. Mary church, Devon, and Sydling St. Nicholas church, Dorset, are still in working order.

The Science Museum has a clock from Dover Castle, one of few surviving complete, which has generated a certain amount of mystery over its date. It could have been made between 1490 and 1500, although it is usually dated much later, because at least five similar clocks have in recent years been identified in churches in Kent and about eight more in other southern counties. It is possible that these lesser iron clocks, and undoubtedly others still awaiting discovery, were imported (perhaps from Holland or Belgium) during the late fifteenth and early sixteenth centuries.

England is by far the richest country in medieval clocks.

All the clocks so far mentioned were made for public use. The domestic clock was introduced from the Continent, at first as a very expensive novelty for the rich. It was a scaled-down version of the great clocks and was also made of iron. Some more sophisticated clocks, powered by springs instead of weights, were imported from about 1500 onwards.

In the middle of the sixteenth century, brass, known as latten, came quickly into use for various mechanical devices. At that time, most clockmakers in London were of foreign origin and used designs which they had brought with them. Perhaps the first to introduce a truly English design was Nicholas Vallin who, in 1598, made a remarkable carillon clock (Fig. 3). Most iron clocks were open, but Vallin boxed in the mechanism with brass plates and applied architectural principles to the exterior design, in the renaissance style. However, he was before his time, since the style that became typical of the first English clocks was the brass or latten clock, now called the lantern clock, that had four brass corner posts inside which the iron movement was fixed and to which enclosing brass plates were fastened (Fig. 5). The lantern clock had a single hour hand and struck the hours on a bell at the top. A cut-out brass fret decoration above the open dial represented crossed dolphins or a heraldic device.

Lantern clocks continued to be a main product of English makers throughout the seventeenth century. During the second half of the century another hand to show minutes was added and the balance wheel controller under the bell was superseded by the pendulum hanging on the outside at the back. Clocks remained weight-driven, however, and had to be hung on the wall or mounted on a pedestal.

From about the middle of the seventeenth century some makers enclosed the clock in a separate wooden hood and stood it on a wall bracket, to create what is now called a hanging wall clock (Fig. 2). The weights still hung below. The spring-driven clock did not offer much challenge to the more accurate and cheaper weight clock at this time, although a few London makers offered versions of continental spring-driven table clocks for their wealthier customers.

Clockmaking was entirely transformed by the introduction of the pendulum to control clocks. This replaced the early oscillating bar balance and wheel balances without balance springs. It had long been known that a pendulum would provide a better timekeeper; astronomers used a swinging weight on a string for making accurately timed observations. The problem, however, was in applying it to a clock; a problem that was eventually solved by the Dutch mathematician and astronomer Christiaan Huygens, who acquired a patent for his invention in 1657 and published a book about it in 1658. Working in London at the same time was a family of Dutch clockmakers called Fromanteel. The head of the family, Ahasuerus, must have heard of the grant of the patent soon after it was made, for only eleven weeks later one of the younger Fromanteels, John, while still an apprentice, was sent over to The Hague to work for Salomon Coster, to whom

From Lantern to Long-case

Eric Bruton

Early English Clocks

Fig. 6 (left) **Ebonised bracket clock** by Jonathan Lowndes, c.1695. This ornate clock case has what is called a basket top. (right) **Ebonised bracket clock** by Daniel Quare (1647–1724), c.1700. (Messrs. Garrard and Co., London.)

Fig. 7 **Long-case clock** by Fromanteel and Clarke, late seventeenth century. Finely figured mulberry wood with alarm, the movement by Fromanteel, 'Clarke' added later. (Private Collection.)

Fig. 8 **Long-case clock** by Ahasuerus Fromanteel, c.1660. Ebony. (British Museum, Ilbert Collection.)

Fig. 9 **The Cassiobury turret clock**, made by blacksmith-clockmakers, perhaps in the fourteenth century, but possibly later. It may have belonged to Richard, Abbot of Wallingford, and tells the time exclusively by striking. (British Museum.)

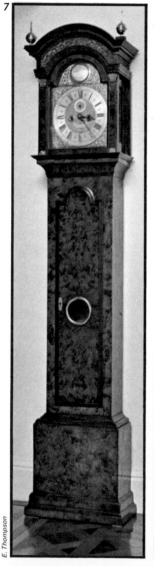
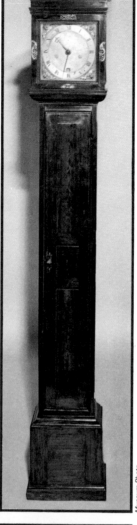

Fig. 10 **Long-case clock** signed by John Knibb, Hanslope, Bucks., c.1711. Marquetry case. (Messrs. Garrard and Co.)

Fig. 11 **Astronomical clock,** the only one ever made by Thomas Tompion, London, c.1677. (Fitzwilliam Museum, Cambridge.)

Fig. 12 **Eight-day table clock** by Samuel Knibb, seventeenth century. The dial 9¾ ins. square. (Clockmakers' Company Collection, Guildhall.)

Fig. 13 **Long-case clock** by Edward East (born c.1610), London, c.1675. Eight-day clock in marquetry case. (Clockmakers' Company Collection, Guildhall.)

Huygens had assigned the first right to make pendulum clocks.

As early as October 1658, Ahasuerus Fromanteel was able to advertise in England clocks that kept 'equaller time than any now made without this Regulator (examined and proved before His Highness the Lord Protector . . .)'. The Regulator was the pendulum and the Lord Protector was Cromwell, who encouraged new inventions and activities.

Pendulums were soon applied by other makers to wall clocks and to bracket (table) clocks. They became so popular so quickly that large numbers of lantern clocks were converted (Fig. 5) and new ones were made incorporating pendulums. It was an amazingly rapid transition at a time when it normally took twenty or even fifty years for ideas to spread within a single country.

The pendulum brought with it another fundamental change. The continental spring-driven table clock was made with plates top and bottom, held apart by four posts, one at each corner. Huygens turned this frame on its side for his weight clock, so that the plates were front and back. The pendulum was then hung from the back plate. The construction became standard for all clocks, spring- or weight-driven.

The London makers' first major contribution to the evolution of design was to enclose the weights of the clock in a wooden trunk, which stood on the floor, thus creating the long-case clock, subsequently called the grandfather clock (Fig. 8). The

10
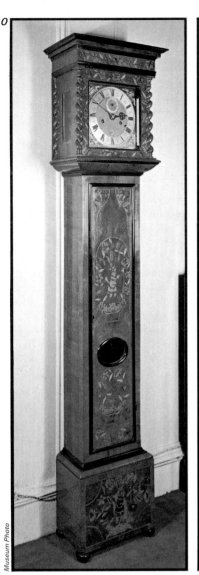

11
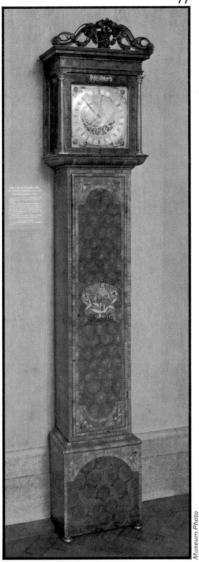

12

13

14

Fig. 14 *Long-case clock by Joseph Knibb (1640–1711), 1690. Ebony.*
Made by the most celebrated member of a clockmaking family, Joseph Knibb, this handsome clock has the Roman striking skeleton dial which Knibb introduced into England. (Fitzwilliam Museum.)

Fig. 15 *Dials from the Bath equation clock by Thomas Tompion, London, c.1706. This sophisticated clock was presented by Tompion to the City of Bath after he took a cure there in 1709. The top dial indicates the difference between sundial and clock time. (Grand Pump Room, Bath.)*

15

earliest ones, now rare, stood only six feet six inches, or less. The case was narrow, with a long narrow door, and was made of veneered ebony. The hood at the top was based on classical architecture, after Vallin's lead, having a ridged top with pillars at the corners. A short pendulum hung on the back of the clock movement. The first pendulum was about ten inches or shorter in length, with a pear-shaped brass bob at the bottom.

The first spring clocks with wooden cases made in London were almost identical with the top or hood of the long-case clock of the period, and also architectural in style, a fashion that lasted only about ten years. Almost as early as the architectural style for both types of clock, was a flat top with spiral Jacobean pillars at the corners. This style persisted until about 1700, after which the plain pillars of the very first clocks returned to almost universal use.

Eventually London clockmakers established themselves as leaders in the field

Despite its immediate popularity, the short pendulum was not without faults. It was applied to the clock with the original form of escapement known as the crown wheel and verge, recognisable by the wheel that looks like a royal crown. It was discovered that a much longer pendulum would control the clock more efficiently and the first to make an escapement through which a long pendulum could control the descending weight of a clock was probably William Clement, advised perhaps by the brilliant and irascible experimenter Dr. Robert Hooke. Clement used a device that looked like a miniature ship's anchor and became known as the anchor escapement.

This was what London clockmakers had been awaiting. They increased the width of their long cases to accommodate the swinging pendulum, and the heights grew to seven feet and more. The dial became bigger in proportion and the hour- and the minute-hands were joined by a third, the small second-hand with its own circle of second marks. The second-hand proceeded in a series of half-second jumps, one at each tick, or swing of the pendulum. A second weight hanging in the trunk operated an hour-striking mechanism.

Although the long-case clock introduced an entirely new shape in furniture, its greatest influence was in the accuracy of its timekeeping. It would keep time accurately to within about ten seconds a day, against the quarter of an hour or so of earlier clocks. There was no universal standard of timekeeping for the whole country, and each community kept more or less to local time as shown by the sundial. To set a clock to time, therefore, a sundial was necessary, and one was usually supplied by the clockmaker with his finest clocks. A sundial alone was not sufficient, however, because of the varying lengths of sundial hours, so the clockmaker would supply also a table of figures, known as the Equation of Time, showing how fast or slow the clock should be set against the sundial. They were first published by John Smith in 1668.

Thomas Tompion, the most celebrated clockmaker of the eighteenth century, invented a mechanism that could be incorporated in the clock itself to show how fast or slow the clock was in relation to the sundial. A famous long-case equation clock by Tompion stands in the pump room at Bath (Fig. 15).

While the novelty and excellence of the long-case clock may seem to have overshadowed the bracket or table clock, production of bracket clocks was expanding rapidly in London, which had become the centre of the craft. Its prominence was reinforced after the Worshipful Company of Clockmakers was incorporated by charter in 1631 to regulate the trade.

The spring-driven bracket clock made up in convenience for what it lacked in accuracy. It could be carried from room to room and could also be taken away and set up elsewhere on extended visits.

A strong form of conservatism in design for some reason restrained makers, and a basic square shape became established, without side pillars and veneered in ebony. The top was domed, with a carrying handle on its summit (Fig. 6). After 1700, case design hardly changed for half a century, except for the introduction of the break-arch dial which became almost universal after about 1725.

Makers supplied matching wall brackets for their better bracket clocks to stand on. Nearly all bracket clocks struck the hours, and after 1700 many were made with quarter repeating work. These could be made to strike the last hour and quarter at any time by pulling a cord at the side of the clock. It was a valuable feature when the only means of seeing at night was to use flint and tinder.

By the first quarter of the eighteenth century, London makers had established themselves as the dominant clockmakers of the world. The period that followed was one of high production and precision, and also of novelty.

MUSEUMS AND COLLECTIONS

Early English clocks may be seen at the following:
GREAT BRITAIN
Bury
St. Edmunds: Gershom-Parkington Collection
London: British Museum, Ilbert Collection
Guildhall, Clockmakers' Company Collection
Science Museum
Victoria and Albert Museum
U.S.A.
Washington,
D.C.: Smithsonian Institution

FURTHER READING

Clocks in the British Museum by H. Tait, London, 1968.
Clocks and Watches, 1400–1900 by E. Bruton, London, 1967.
The Longcase Clock by E. Bruton, London, 1964.
The Knibb Family, Clockmakers by R. A. Lee, Byfleet, 1964.
Old Clocks by H. A. Lloyd, London, 3rd edit. 1964.
Thomas Tompion. His Life and Work by R. W. Symonds, London, 1951.
Old Clocks and Watches and their Makers by F. J. Britten, London, 4th edit. 1919.
Watchmakers and Clockmakers of the World by G. H. Baillie (A general list of makers who were working up to 1825), London, several editions.

1

Museum Photo

Early Looking-Glasses

Edward Pinto

Of rather crude construction when production began, English looking-glasses progressed to become works of art in their own right, with frames of great complexity and beauty

In Act IV of Shakespeare's *Richard II*, set in 1399, the King sends for a looking-glass, which he dashes to the ground, where it is 'cracked in a hundred shivers'. This is almost certainly an anachronism. Shakespeare was writing some two hundred years later, when looking-glasses, although not commonplace, were well-known but expensive novelties, imported in small numbers for the wealthy.

Mirrors of the early Middle Ages were usually polished gold, silver or bronze plates; in the fifteenth and early sixteenth centuries steel was added to the range of reflecting metal surfaces. Although there had been earlier experiments with metal-backed glass, the results were so dark, spotted and distorted that looking-glasses were not serious rivals to polished metal plates until after the establishment of the specialized Italian glasshouses at Murano, early in the sixteenth century. Not until the nineteenth century did the term 'mirror' oust 'looking-glass' or 'glass' in common parlance.

Early glasses were usually small toilet mirrors

Inventories of Henry VIII's possessions show that he owned several small, imported 'glasses to look in', but in some instances there is a contradiction, because the 'glasses' are specifically described as being made of steel. Until the manufacture of English looking-glasses commenced in the seventeenth century, the majority of those who could afford mirrors of any kind still used small plates of polished metal.

Early in the reign of James I, one of the King's favourites, Sir Robert Mansell, obtained a patent for making looking-glasses, and brought over 'many expert strangers from foreign parts beyond the seas to instruct the natives of this Kingdom in the making of looking-glass plates'. In 1620, the importation of foreign glass was prohibited. When Mansell's patent was renewed in 1623, he was able to state that at his manufactory in Southwark he provided employment for five hundred people in the 'making, grinding and foyling of looking-glasses'. Although the ban on imported mirrors was lifted in 1624 it did not prevent Mansell from expanding his manufacture to other glass-houses in provincial towns in England, Wales and Scotland.

None of these early glasses appears to have survived, but as they were of blown glass and of poor reflective quality, due to lack of skill in grinding and polishing, they would have distorted the image. Moreover, as they were mostly small toilet mirrors, they were doubtless scrapped when plate glass became available. This was after 1663, when Charles II granted a patent to George Villiers, second Duke of Buckingham, to set up his glass-

524

> *Early English
> Looking-Glasses*

Fig. 1 *(Previous page)* **Looking-
glass** *c.1707. Carved wood
cresting and verre eglomisé
frame with gold ornament on
a blue ground. The verre eglomisé
technique was introduced from
France around 1690.
(Victoria and Albert Museum,
London.)*

Fig. 2 **Looking-glass,** *1730–40.
This piece suggests the manner
of Benjamin Goodison, carver to
George II. Carved and gilt wood.
(Sotheby's, London.)*

2

Fig. 3 **Looking-glass in silver
frame,** *engraved with the cipher
of William III, c.1697.
(Windsor Castle. By kind
permission of H.M. the Queen.)*

3

house at Vauxhall.

In 1664, imported mirrors were once more banned and the Worshipful Company of Glass-Sellers and Looking-Glass Makers was incorporated. Thence mirrors, although remaining valuable, expanded their usage from the realm of toilet requisites into that of luxury furnishing and interior decoration. On 19 September, 1676, John Evelyn, visiting Vauxhall, wrote in his diary that they made 'looking-glasses far larger and better than any that come from Venice'. Although this was doubtless true, Vauxhall plates seldom exceeded three feet in length, and examples sometimes less than two feet long were described in inventories as 'great glasses'.

Variety in colour and rich elaboration were much to the fore

To make these expensive luxuries more important, it was usual to enhance them by wide and elaborate frames, further increased in height by crestings. Two rarities (Figs. 6 and 7), both dating from the 1670s, would probably have ranked as great glasses, although the frames enclose glasses less than three feet in height. The example in Fig. 7 has the frame covered with fabric embroidered with Stuart stump-work (relief needlework), which displays the usual naïve lack of proportion between human figures, birds, beasts, insects, fruit and flowers common to textile work of the period. What makes it possibly unique is the pristine freshness of its colouring, due to its still being in the original oak outer case and enclosed by a pair of doors with pierced brass hinges and mounts. Some wide frames of this period, covered in flat needlework or stump-work, were additionally ornamented with scalloped outlines (Fig. 8). This example is even rarer than stitchery, being an early example of straw-work decoration, on a grey silk ground.

The range of wooden mirror-frames available in the last quarter of the seventeenth century was vast, both in covering materials and in finishing techniques; in accordance with the fashion, naturalism in the depiction of motifs, variety in colour and rich elaboration were much to the fore, irrespective of the medium chosen.

In a period of great liking for high-relief, naturalistic carving, the presiding genius was Grinling Gibbons, who executed beautiful work within the orderly framework of Sir Christopher Wren's decorative architectural schemes. In domestic furniture, such as mirror-frames, Gibbons' technically brilliant compositions are often too large in scale, and they tend to overpower the small plates enclosed within the complex of delicately carved fruit and flowers, or shells and seaweed, accompanied by chubby *amorini*. A frame which incorporates many of the usual motifs employed by Gibbons, but treated in a more formal manner, is shown in Fig. 6. This frame, the wood finished with burnished silvering, incorporates in the cresting the arms of Gough of Perry Hall, Staffordshire, granted in 1664. It exemplifies how a plate only about thirty-four inches high was doubled in height by framing and cresting.

Charles I collected Old Masters; his son's

predilection for young mistresses with extravagant tastes engendered a demand not only for silvered furniture but also for furniture covered in repoussé and engraved silver plate. Nell Gwynn possessed not only silver framed 'great looking-glasses' but also an ornamentally embossed silver bedstead. Furthermore, she vied with the Duchess of Portsmouth in the ostentatious extravagance of a mirror-panelled room. John Evelyn was most indignant: in September 1675 he recorded: 'I was casually shewed the Dutchesse of Portsmouth's splendid appartment at White-hall, luxuriously furnished, and with ten times the richnesse and glory beyond the Queene's; such massy pieces of plate, whole tables, & stands of incredible value'. The description probably refers to a type of dressing-suite consisting of a wall mirror above a table flanked by a pair of *guéridons* or *torchères* – tall, floor-standing candlesticks; such suites were made in all the fashionable finishes, but in the course of time the four matching pieces have usually become separated.

A somewhat larger table was also used, on which could be arranged the silver toilet set, which included among its many pieces a pair of candlesticks and a strutted mirror. The majority of these sets were repoussé with or without chasing, but a few, such as the toilet mirror in Fig. 10, dating from about 1680, were quieter in taste, being chased only with *chinoiserie* decoration. The somewhat hybrid motifs are derived from contemporary pictures of the Far East, supplemented by the inclusion of European plants and foliage. The set, of which this mirror is the centrepiece, is said to have been given by Charles II to the Strickland family of Sizergh Castle, Westmorland.

At Windsor Castle there is a silver-framed mirror of the architecturally controlled style of the William and Mary period (Fig. 3). Dating from about 1697, the frame, with its pediment bearing the royal arms and cipher of William III, brings the total height to seven feet, six inches. It was presented to the King by the Corporation of London.

Other frames in vogue towards the end of the seventeenth and in the early eighteenth centuries were of japanned wood, of framing overlaid with strips of bevelled silver plate and, probably most popular of all, the convex or 'cushion' types, which were frequently veneered with walnut, olivewood, ebony or laburnum; they were usually surmounted by a fretted cresting. Additionally, many frames were decorated with floral marquetry, following the general fashion in furniture. First came formal isolated marquetry panels. These were followed by continuous and more naturalistic floral marquetry, sometimes including ivory jasmine flowers and stained green foliage. Finally, at the end of the century, came the much quieter arabesque marquetry.

With the opening of Queen Anne's reign, several comparatively fresh trends were apparent. Mirrors were now considered necessary decorative features in all important rooms and their valuable contribution to reflecting both daylight and candlelight was given due consideration in positioning. The regularity of eighteenth-century domestic architecture and the usual proportions of windows and width of pier walls between them brought about considerable standardisation in the placing of furniture, particularly in rooms used for formal

Fig. 4 **Mirrored cabinet,**
probably by John Channon,
London, c.1735. Mahogany
with gilt-brass mounts.
This is a fine example of the
mirrored furniture which
reflected day or candlelight.
(Victoria and Albert Museum.)

Fig. 5 **Looking-glass,** second
quarter of the eighteenth
century. Walnut veneer with
parcel-gilt carved ornament.
Becoming gradually heavier in
their detailing, and using
mahogany veneer, architectural
mirrors of this sort were made
until the middle of the century.
(Sotheby's.)

Fig. 6 **Looking-glass,** 1670–80.
Carved and silvered wood.
This rare and elaborately carved
frame displays to perfection
the late seventeenth-century
love of ornate furniture.
(Victoria and Albert Museum.)

Fig. 7 **Looking-glass,** 1670–80.
The frame of stump-work.
Being still in the original oak
outer case, the coloured silks of
this charming piece have
retained their original freshness.
(Private Collection, formerly in
the Fred Scull Collection.)

Fig. 8 **Looking-glass,** 1670–80.
The frame of straw-work.
Although many people think that
straw-work was done only by
French prisoners of war in the
Napoleonic period, it was in fact
a craft hobby of amateurs much
earlier. The pieces of straw were
cut out and attached to the
wooden base like elaborate
marquetry.
(Victoria and Albert Museum.)

Fig. 9 *Overmantel in the Queen Anne style. The mirror is jointed because of limitations in the size of sheet glass.* (Christie's.)

Fig. 10 *Toilet service with mirror, c.1680. Silver chased with chinoiserie decoration.* (Victoria and Albert Museum.)

9

Christie's Photo

10

Museum Photo

11

A. C. Cooper

Fig. 11 *Overmantel, style of 1730–35. A way of making overmantels more important was to include a painting above the glass. This example shows Wren's ideas for Westminster Abbey.* (Christie's.)

entertainment. In a room with two windows there were three pier walls, and in a room with three windows there were four.

Pier walls were dark, not only because of their position, but also because of heavy window draperies. It became customary, therefore, to hang long and decoratively framed mirrors on pier walls, frequently with matching console-tables below. To reflect more light, matching mirrors might be provided on the wall opposite. If the chimney-piece came opposite the window, it would probably have a mirrored overmantel; if at the end of the room, it might be matched by a large console-mirror opposite. In a sitting-room with two or four windows, the central pier was often occupied by one of the fashionable bureau-bookcases with mirrored doors and candle slides below, so that the candles were reflected in the mirrors.

As large glasses were now the vogue, but mirror sizes were still limited, it became normal practice to joint them. This might be accomplished by butt-jointing the shallow bevelled plates, or by covering joints with an ornamented, gilt or carved metal or wood strip, or by means of a strip of bevelled, silvered glass. This last is seen in Fig. 9, a six foot wide Queen Anne overmantel mirror with silvered glass framing, cresting and joint covers; the framing and engraved cresting have the terminals of the joints covered by gilt leaf-engraved clasps.

Another variant of the frame itself was *verre eglomisé* (Fig. 1). This came into fashion about 1690 and continued for some twenty-five years. Intricate arabesque and other designs in gold or silver were worked on the backs of glass border strips, on grounds of black or coloured enamel. In 1691, soon after the introduction of the fashion from France, a Mr. Winches of Bread Street was advertising his mastery of the craft. The handsome mirror with gold on blue ground border in Fig. 1 has the border jointed by gilt metal cover strips.

Around 1727, when George II came to the throne, some handsome, pedimented, walnut-veneered frames with parcel-gilt carved ornament were made in the architectural fashion of the day (Fig. 5). Becoming gradually heavier in their detailing and substituting mahogany for walnut, they continued to be made until the mid-eighteenth century.

By far the most popular framing for mirrors from the end of Queen Anne's reign to the end of the eighteenth century was carved and gilt wood. During the early part of George II's reign, when Palladian architecture and complementary decoration and furnishing were the height of fashion, carved gilt mirror frames often show the somewhat overpowering architectural influence and crowded detailing associated with William Kent's designs. Benjamin Goodison was a great cabinet-maker who made some of the finest furniture for the royal family during George II's reign. His designs, of which Fig. 2 may be one, are light and original in composition.

Fine examples of eighteenth-century mirror-faced furniture

Reference has been made earlier to eighteenth-century mirror-faced furniture; Fig. 4 must be as fine an English example as exists. It dates from about 1735, is of mahogany, inlaid with engraved brass and with gilt brass mounts. It is attributed by the Victoria and Albert Museum to John Channon of St. Martin's Lane. As yet, little is known of the Channon family, but such work of theirs as has come to light in recent years suggests that they were in the first rank of their trade.

In the first half of the eighteenth century, instead of jointing up silvered plates to make overmantels more important, landscape, seascape or architectural paintings were placed above plates, in the same frame. Sometimes the two are not contemporary, the looking-glass being cut and framed to suit an existing picture. The example in Fig. 11 probably all dates from the 1730–35 period. The painting of Westminster Abbey, with central spire and western towers, shows the design as envisaged by Sir Christopher Wren; the spire was never built and the towers were completed by Hawksmoor. 🙰

MUSEUMS AND COLLECTIONS

English looking-glasses may be seen at the following:

Birmingham:	Aston Hall
Leeds:	Temple Newsam House
London:	Ham House
	Hampton Court Palace
	Victoria and Albert Museum
Sevenoaks:	Knole
Stamford:	Burghley House
Near	
Tonbridge:	Penshurst Place
Windsor:	Windsor Castle

FURTHER READING

English Looking Glasses by Geoffrey Wills, London, 1965.
Shorter Dictionary of English Furniture by Ralph Edwards, Vol. II, London, 2nd edit. 1969.
Furniture Making in Seventeenth and Eighteenth Century England by R. W. Symonds, London, 1955.
A Short Dictionary of Furniture by John Gloag, London, 2nd edit. 1969.

Fig. 1 *Easton Neston*, *Northamptonshire by Nicholas Hawksmoor (1661–1736).* Fig. 2 *Castle Howard*, *Yorkshire by Sir John Vanbrugh (1664–1726).*

A
Reign of unpretentious Elegance

David Green

England in the Reign of Queen Anne	

Queen Anne
Born 1665
Acceded 1702
Died 1714

Fig. 3 *Blenheim Palace, the Bow Window Room by Vanbrugh, begun 1705.*
Fig. 4 *Queen Anne by Sir Godfrey Kneller (1646–1723). (Blenheim Palace, Oxfordshire. By courtesy of His Grace the Duke of Marlborough.)*

The reign of Queen Anne was a time of paradox in England. The strict etiquette of the Court combined with the simplicity of the Queen's tastes to create a national style of spontaneous style and elegance

For moving a chair from its place against the wall at Versailles, Madame de Maintenon was reproved by Louis XIV. By so doing, he told her, she spoiled the architecture. This, of course, was ridiculous; yet it was typical of an age when, in England as well as in France, etiquette meant so much.

To Queen Anne, though at war with France for most of her reign, it mattered enormously that a courtier should be wearing the right clothes and the right wig, and that Court mourning, even to the blackening of silver sconces and nails on coaches, should be fully observed. As Princess Anne she had meticulously conformed to these rules. On one occasion, when she found herself seated too near the Queen (her sister Mary) she had the stool moved; and when Mary was in Holland, she wrote to ask Anne whether she should kiss lords' daughters or suffer them to sit in the royal presence. In her reply Anne owned that she kissed them all, but sitting was a different matter. Ever since the death of Charles II, she added, she had sat in his gallery in the Chapel Royal, 'and there the great chair stands just as if the King were to come hither, and I sit on a stool on the left hand of the chair and . . . no ladies sit there but just my own'.

3

Thomas, Oxford

4

Thomas, Oxford

5

Gordon Coates

Fig. 5 *Low Middleton Hall, County Durham. A smaller country residence of the Queen Anne period.*

Fig. 6 *Princess Anne of Denmark by an unknown French artist, (Detail). Engraving.*
This charming portrait depicts Anne after her marriage to George, Prince of Denmark, in 1683 and before her accession to the throne of England in 1702.

Fig. 7 *Design for the Bow Window Room at Blenheim Palace by Vanbrugh. This detailed plan has been endorsed by Sarah, Duchess of Marlborough, probably for the benefit of James Moore. (Blenheim Palace. By courtesy of His Grace the Duke of Marlborough.)*

Author's Photo

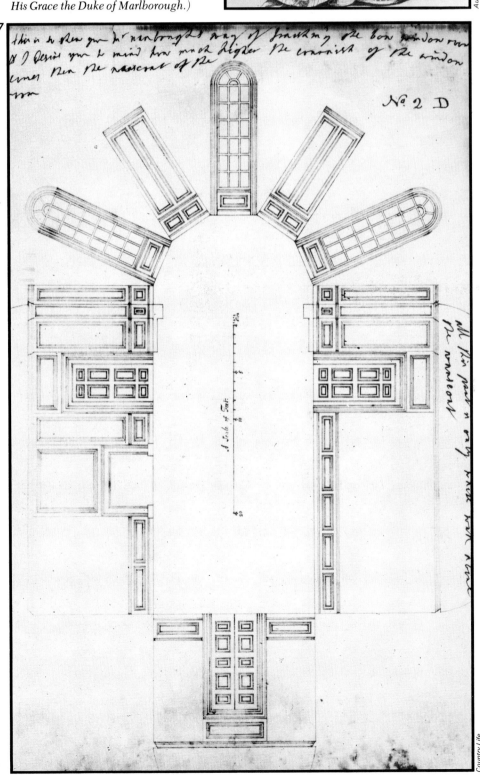

Country Life

Comfort had low priority. A French engraving of Anne, again as princess, shows her seated on a straight-backed sofa of an exacting type (Fig. 6). Behind her in the area of the picture not illustrated here, brackets support such pots as her sister Mary and her followers collected, 'piling their china', as Daniel Defoe says, 'upon the tops of cabinets, scrutores and every chimney-piece, to the tops of the ceilings, and even setting up shelves for their china-ware, where they wanted such places'. As she sits on her sofa, herself in satin to the ground and with a wired lace head-dress (the *tour*, or *cornette*) a foot high, fixed to a cap covering all but the front of her fair-auburn curls, Anne wears large pearls and holds a closed fan to her mouth.

And how much of all this, when in 1702 she became Queen, would be retained? The high head-dress stayed until 1708; curls hung down over one shoulder (she at times wore a wig), while the dress would become a 'manto' (*manteau*), so cut as to set off a richly embroidered petticoat (Fig. 4). Anne had little fondness for jewels, but the fan would be necessary in stuffy closets. It would be found useful too, quickly held to the mouth as her signal for silence. But the clutter of shelves and chimney-pieces piled high with china would have to go. In the royal apartments, as elsewhere, there would be an orderliness and a symmetry which, as at Versailles, gave every high-backed chair its place, permitting ladies with trains and layers of petticoats to curtsey without risk of collision with the furniture.

Anne's preference for small rooms was curious. Ambassadors were shocked at the unpretentiousness of the closets they were received in at Kensington and St. James's; while at Windsor, Anne stayed whenever she could at her Little House rather than in the Castle, where gout, as she called it, made it impossible for her to negotiate state-rooms or to mount the stairs.

As patron of the arts Anne cannot be said to have shone. She lacked the taste of her grandfather and the enthusiasm of her sister, Mary, who had all but overwhelmed Grinling Gibbons with commissions for elaborate wood-carvings. In Anne's day carved overmantels and frames were already regarded by the sophisticated as out of fashion; and the same could be said of tapestry. Yet Marlborough was to line his staterooms with new tapestries at Blenheim (begun in 1705) and Gibbons, too, did much carving there, but his work was almost entirely in marble or in stone.

'A clean sweet house and garden though ever so small'

Anne's reign is packed with paradox. Hers is not the Age of Elegance, yet what could be more elegant than a Tompion clock? In architecture there could hardly be a greater contrast than that between Blenheim Palace (Fig. 9) and Marlborough House (Fig. 10); yet they were built in the same reign and for the same family. The difference is deliberate. Sir Christopher Wren, Marlborough's Duchess explained, was given the commission on condition that the house should be 'strong, plain and convenient, and', she added, 'he must give me his word that this building should not have the least resemblance of any thing in that called Blenheim,

8

Country Life

which I had never liked but could not prevail against Sir John [Vanbrugh]'. She longed for 'a clean, sweet house and garden though ever so small'. Blenheim could not claim to be that, but could Marlborough House? It cost, she owned, £50,000, but it was 'the best and strongest house that ever was built', and its staircase walls were covered by Laguerre with frescoes of Marlborough's victories. In Wren's well mannered, no-nonsense style no doubt it was 'strong, plain and convenient'. At Blenheim, on the other hand, as at his first great house, Castle Howard, Vanbrugh's expressed aim was for state, beauty and convenience, in that order.

Castle Howard (Fig. 2), the 'top seat and garden of England' in Yorkshire, begun in 1699 for the Earl of Carlisle, was in comparison with Blenheim a straightforward country mansion; Blenheim needed to be a monument as well as a dwelling. In both cases, however, protocol had to be observed. There had to be grandeur, there had to be rooms of state, there had to be what Vanbrugh called 'noble rooms of parade'. The entrance halls were immense, stairs were hidden behind walls, and corridors stretched to infinity. The Saloon at Blenheim, with frescoes by Laguerre, was fit for a royal banquet, and in the Gallery, running the length of the west wing, half the Court might comfortably dance a minuet.

A visit from the Queen and her 'mob' was dreaded and yet angled for

As in Elizabeth I's time, so in Anne's: a visit from the Queen and her 'mob', as Anne once called it, was dreaded and yet angled for, if only for prestige. At Blenheim the state-rooms – two self-contained suites of antechamber, drawing-room and bedchamber – flank the Saloon, which forms the centre of the south front. All these rooms are intercommunicating and at the same time have boltholes: doors hidden behind tapestry, and 'my Lady Duchess's backstairs'. In the east wing, which was the private wing and so built first, Vanbrugh provided on the main floor a tower room for the Duke on the south, and on the north another for the Duchess, which she split up into closets. Between those towers lay the bedrooms and sitting-rooms; Sarah's favourite was, by tradition, the Bow Window Room where their two suites met; for there she could sit in the window-alcove and watch the world (Fig. 3). She would, she promised herself, fill the attic storey with her friends. That is difficult to imagine. There was, however, that short but mellow time when Marlborough was just well enough to enjoy Dryden's *All For Love*, acted by his grandchildren and their friends in this very alcove. For their dressing-up no children ever had richer materials; these were the velvets and silk damasks which the Duke of Manchester had sent from Genoa to enrich Blenheim's furniture and walls, and Mark Antony wore Marlborough's diamond sword.

9

BLENHEIM HOUSE:
Built at the Expence of the Public and settled on the
DUKE of MARLBOROUGH, & His POSTERITY.

K. Hoddle

A stately setting for magnificent ceremonial occasions

In the state apartments the scene, with Marlborough's battle-tapestries in their places, was set with magnificence, even though no queen was to sleep in the state bed. From Vanbrugh's plans, as Professor Webb has explained, it is clear that the internal arrangements were adapted to 'a special type of daily life quite as carefully as the most up-to-date modern villa residence is modelled on the requirements of the social and intimate life of the middle-class household that will inhabit it. Vanbrugh's patrons', he points out, 'required something quite different; in the first place a stately setting for magnificent ceremonial occasions, and secondly, and more importantly, an arrangement suited to the ritual of their daily lives, a ritual devised to protect the great man from the importunities of his clients and to increase his dignity by elaborating the processes whereby he could be approached' All this Vanbrugh provided, even though, thanks to Sarah, he had to leave Blenheim long before it was finished.

Sarah then sent for the man she called her oracle, James Moore the cabinet-maker, with whom she had had dealings at Marlborough House. There

10

The South-West Prospect of his Grace ye Duke of Marlboroughs House in St James Park.

Author's Photo

Fig. 8 *Detail of a window in the Duke's study at Blenheim Palace. The carving is by Sir Charles Hopson and his son John.*

Fig. 9 *Blenheim Palace, the north or entrance front, by Vanbrugh, early eighteenth century. Engraving. Vanbrugh's aim in designing this palace was for state, beauty and convenience, in that order.*

Fig. 10 *Marlborough House, the south front, by Sir Christopher Wren (1632–1723), early eighteenth century. Engraving. The Duchess specified to Wren 'that this building should not have the least resemblance to any thing in that called Blenheim.'*

could be no doubt that, as a maker of pier-glasses and of tables, whether in lacquer or in gilt gesso, he was a master-craftsman, but Sarah found him 'understanding in many trades besides his own' and employed him as an architect. It took time to show her that she would have to recall Vanbrugh's partner, Nicholas Hawksmoor, to finish the Gallery. In the meantime Moore continued to make the pier-glasses which Marlborough had long since stipulated that Blenheim would need to reflect the fine paintings he would be bringing from Flanders. There they remain, those in the Bow Window Room, with the tables beneath them, being among the finest Moore ever produced. It is amusing to note that even on Vanbrugh's plan for that room Sarah, perhaps for Moore's benefit, scribbled her endorsements; but then she could never resist endorsing anything (Fig. 7). Here she scrawls: 'This is to shew you Mr Vanbrugh's way of finishing the bow window room & I desire you to mind how much higher the cornish (*sic*) of the window comes than the wainscot of the room'. Grinling

'very fine Scotch plaid given the Duchess by the Duke of Athol'.

One wonders what it looked like when all was done. The tapestries were magnificent; so were the pictures and the glasses that reflected them, but what of the rest? Horace Walpole, visiting Blenheim in 1760 (Sarah had died in 1744), saw 'all the old flock chairs, wainscot tables and gowns and petticoats of Queen Anne that old Sarah could crowd among blocks of marble'. 'It looks', he said, 'like the palace of an auctioneer who has been chosen King of Poland and furnished his apartments with obsolete trophies, rubbish that nobody bid for and a dozen pictures that he had stolen from the inventories of different families.'

Not many years after Anne's death the style of architecture known as English Baroque, of which Vanbrugh and Hawksmoor, Archer and Gibbs were the chief exponents, was decried by the Palladians and abandoned; while by the reign of George III men of taste were looking back to the beginning of the eighteenth century as to an age of barbarism.

Fig. 11 *Antony House, Cornwall, the south front, possibly by James Gibbs and Thomas Edwards, 1711–21. This starkly simple house depends for effect mainly upon its fine proportions.*

Fig. 12 *Cound Hall, Shropshire, the north front, 1704. Cound Hall is the prototype for a group of tall, gaunt Shropshire houses built in the 1720s and '30s.*

Fig. 13 *Castle Howard, the entrance hall, by Vanbrugh. This soaring hall, its ground plan in the form of a Greek cross, was considered the most daring and original of its time.*

Gibbons was allowed to carve in wood the capitals of the Corinthian columns at the entrance to the 'bow' and the frieze above them; but the chimney-piece, designed by Vanbrugh, he carved in marble, as he did that in the Duchess's bedroom and the noble doorcases in the Saloon.

The windows throughout the house have Vanbrugh's massive sash-bars, some of them carved; each pane of glass has bevelled edges (Fig. 8). The shutters and the rest of the wainscot were made by Sir Charles Hopson and his son, who had worked with Wren at St. Paul's. Their craftsmanship was typical of the age; for whether one sought a clock from Tompion or a key from the Queen's locksmith, Josiah Kay, one could be certain of getting something superb. To benefit from this craftsmanship was of course a matter not only of means but also of taste; and the accounts of Sarah's furnishing of Blenheim make at times odd reading. A good start had been made with such perquisites from her offices as a crimson damask bed, bound with rich, bold, stiff galoon, its tester and head-cloth bearing the royal arms; and silver chamber-pots. Hangings and covers were tasselled or fringed or both, some of the fringe being 'of the Duchess of Marlborough's working'. More surprising were the bedroom and closet furnished throughout with

1

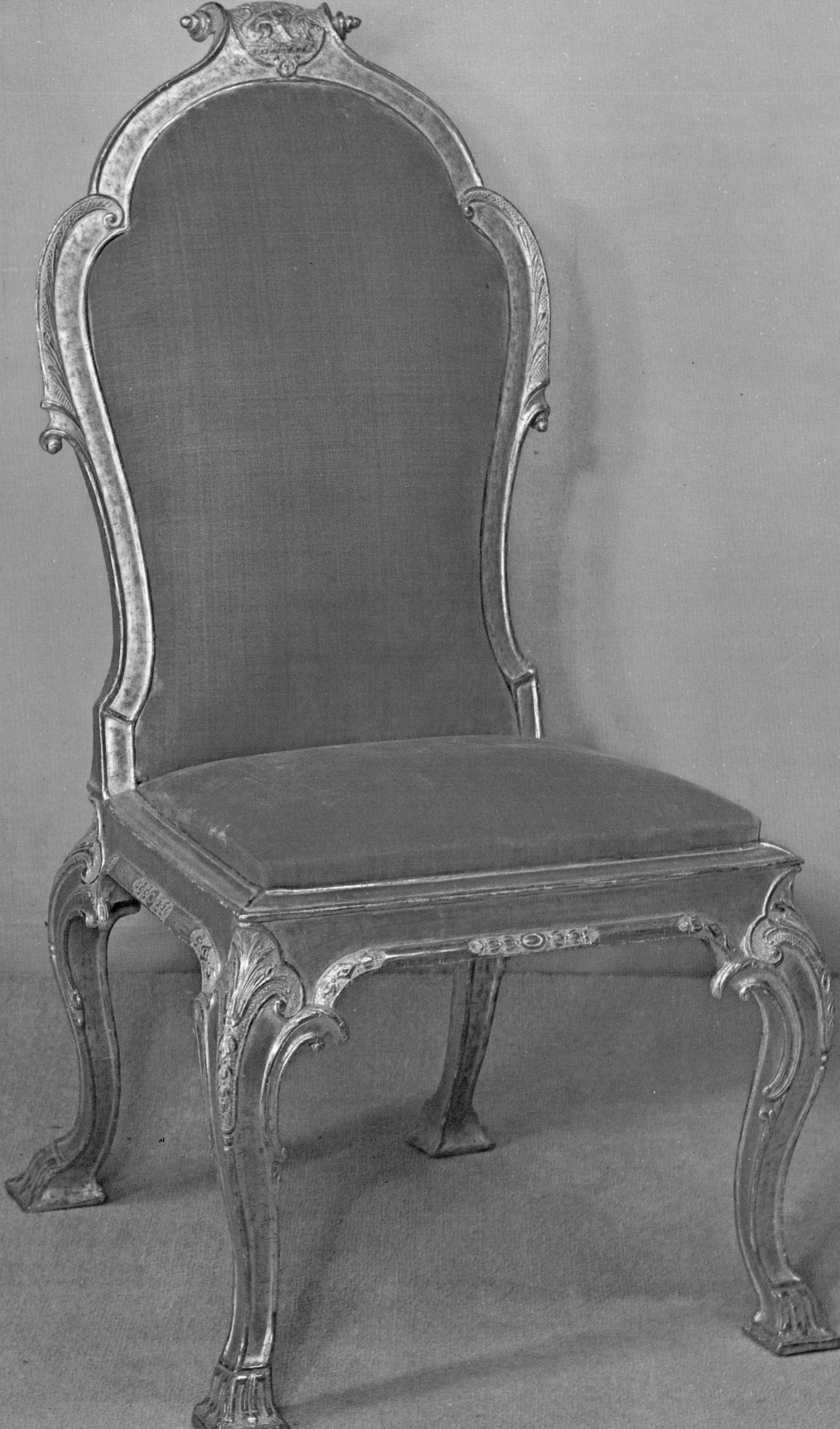

Furniture for style and comfort

John Kenworthy-Browne

Fig. 1 **Dining-chair**, *after 1717.*
Gilt gesso, with the crest of
Humphreys.
Carved and gilt gesso was a
popular finish between about
1710 and 1730 for pieces of
furniture intended more for
luxurious display than for daily
use.
(Mallett and Son Ltd., London.)

Fig. 2 **Bureau-cabinet**, *1710–20.*
Burr-elm veneer.
One of the most subtle and
beautiful figures chosen for fine
pieces, burr veneer was cut from
a root or crotch of the tree.
(Victoria and Albert Museum,
London.)

Fig. 3 **Day-bed** by Giles
Grendey, *c.1730. Japanned*
beechwood.
The shape of the back and legs,
and the caned seat, preserve the
earlier fashion of c.1710.
(Victoria and Albert Museum.)

Fig. 4 **Dressing-mirror and**
desk on matching stand, *c.1710.*
Amboyna veneer with kingwood
and rosewood banding.
This charming piece, with its
pivoting mirror, is typically
English in style and convenience.
(Victoria and Albert Museum.)

Designed by the craftsmen of the period rather than by professional designers, Queen Anne furniture is distinctive for its functional, comfortable and highly decorative elegance that holds great appeal for modern eyes

Queen Anne furniture is generally the most popular of all English styles. Its pleasant walnut veneer, usefulness and air of comfort and affluence typify the very best in the English vernacular tradition. The style began as a simplification of its seventeenth-century inheritance, but after about 1712 ornamentation again became fashionable. As a whole, the style is characterised by refinement and artistry of design that shows a considerable advance over that of William and Mary.

Queen Anne was not distinguished for her lively personality, and her Court was probably the dullest that had been in England up to that time. The Queen herself did nothing to direct the progress of fashion, and about the time of her accession, if not before, one can detect a kind of pause in furniture design. The pause represents a moment when patrons and craftsmen alike wished to discard the foreign and generally useless elaboration of late seventeenth-century furniture and, by reducing it to practical forms, to retain only the essentials of the design. The campaigns that Dutch William

had successfully conducted against Louis XIV had the curious effect of weakening the economy of Holland while strengthening that of England. With growing confidence, therefore, the craftsmen in London, whether they were native or immigrant, could shake off their previous dependence on Dutch fashions.

The contours and carving on furniture became smoother. Fragile caned chairs and stools, and the hard, high settees that were made for posture rather than for comfort, were replaced by pieces more suited to the shape of the human body. Fall-front writing-desks survived for a little, but before long gave way entirely to the more convenient bureau. Cabinets and cupboards became less elaborate and fussy. All these pieces were economically designed with a view to their function rather than to the display of an abundance of material and crafts-manship. At the same time, cabinet-makers perfected the technical improvements that had started a few years previously, stronger case con-struction and better dovetailing helped to establish the superiority of English furniture over its Dutch counterparts.

It is curious that, in an age which saw the building of such houses as Castle Howard and Blenheim Palace, drawings of furniture by archi-tects are almost unknown. Essentially the Queen Anne style seems to have been dictated by the craftsmen themselves. To them we may attribute the domestic character and gentle contours. There was a general lack of classical detail. During the reign of William III most furniture, whether chairs, bureau-bookcases or beds, had the height empha-

5

6

7

Furniture of the
Queen Anne period

Fig. 5 *Settee*, *c.1710. Walnut veneer with marquetry panels. Contemporary needlework, showing the Fall of Phaeton. (Christie's, London.)*

Fig. 6 *Bureau, possibly by Coxed and Woster, c.1700–10. Stained figured elm inlaid with pewter banding. (Christie's.)*

Fig. 7 *Side-table, c.1715. Gilt gesso with the crest of Lord Cobham. Originally from Stowe House. (Victoria and Albert Museum.)*

8

Fig. 8 *'Bended-back' chair, c.1710. The arms are of the over-scrolled type called 'shepherd crook' arms. (Mallett's.)*

Fig. 9 *Dining-chair, c.1710. Walnut veneer with scrolled back and relief scallop shells and husks. (Mallett's.)*

9

sised by elaborate crestings or pediments topped by finials. From 1700 there was a tendency to bring down the height and to make a piece appear more stable by directing the eye to an apparently low centre of gravity. This difference is parallel to that between the high gabled terrace-houses of Amsterdam and those built in London at the same time.

Their new sense of proportion allowed the London makers to dispense with much elaboration. The splendid marquetry tradition dwindled almost overnight to the occasional use of small panels of inlaid arabesques. After 1700 such panels were only incidental to the decoration and contributed nothing to the form of furniture (Fig. 5). Parquetry, too, was restricted. The overpowering and often startling contrasts of late seventeenth-century styles were unacceptable in the new century.

In general, the decoration of case furniture was limited to the choice of a single fine walnut veneer, or to two or more sheets of veneer cleverly matched with their reflecting patterns laid side by side. The wood was carefully chosen for its marking, the best having a burr figure, cut from the root or a crotch of the tree (Fig. 2). Normally, the veneer was bordered by cross-bandings and a narrow line of herring-bone pattern, all of the same material and identical colour. English walnut was the best variety, and its colour might be described as a warm grey-brown; but as the home supply became less, French and Italian walnut was imported. The continental variety has a darker colour tending towards olive, and a darker figure. Virginian walnut, imported from the American colonies, is a hard, dark wood without much figure. It was generally used for solid work, rather than for veneering.

Good quality elm furniture tended towards woodworm and is uncommon today

Yew, which today we find most attractive, never became really popular at this period. On the whole, elm had much better possibilities; it tends to be coarse in grain, but when cut at the root for a burr figure it can be so fine as to be almost indistinguishable from walnut. Elm was considerably cheaper, but soft, light and very appetising to woodworm. Consequently good quality elm furniture tends to be uncommon today. The burr elm veneer could be curiously stained in such a way as to produce a mottled figure like mulberry wood. The firm of Coxed and Woster in St. Paul's Churchyard, used this technique on bureau-bookcases (Fig. 6).

Olive and laburnum might still be used occasionally, both having a beautiful and delicate grain. Rosewood and kingwood, imported from Brazil, at one time used chiefly for cross-banding, soon became unfashionable. Generally, then, the choice of woods appears to be more restricted than during the seventeenth century. The former richness of surface and colour was replaced by a uniform but subtle texture.

Some new types of furniture were invented, all of them pieces that were typically English in their style and convenience. The dressing-mirror was now not merely a framed looking-glass, but was pivoted between two uprights; the stand included fitted drawers, and often a small writing flap (Fig. 4). These dressing-glasses appeared around

1700 and were made for over a hundred and twenty years. A knee-hole dressing-table about three feet wide, with nine drawers and a back cupboard for slippers, was also intended for use as a writing-table. The bachelor's chest appeared rather later. It was essentially a light, movable piece for a person of small personal needs; it would hold clothes and the folding top opened to make a table. When inns and lodgings offered little but discomfort, such an object was most useful. Although bachelors' chests are obsolete today, they have become valuable and interesting collectors' pieces.

Two other developments of about 1710–20 are by no means obsolete. The card-table grew around 1710 from the rather small seventeenth-century piece that was designed for piquet, into the Queen Anne card-table, about three feet wide, which was intended for four-handed games such as ombre and quadrille. It remains of ideal size for our own whist and bridge.

The tallboy, or chest-upon-chest, was also developed at this time as it was more capacious than the already existing chest-on-stand. By the eighteenth century the chest of drawers had been accepted in all fashionable circles as a more convenient clothes store than the coffer, though it is somewhat surprising that as late as 1726 Defoe wrote that the manufacture of these objects was centralised in London; but it is evident that most fine furniture must have been made there. Not only was it the metropolis of fashion, but only there could be found the concentration of skills needed to produce furniture at reasonable cost. The cabinet-maker, carver, gilder, chair-maker, upholsterer, glass-maker and metal-worker all enjoyed separate trades, and the quality achieved in furniture depended very largely on the degree of specialisation and co-operation between craftsmen.

Whereas in the seventeenth century chairs might still be made by the joiner and carver, soon after 1700 a new type of chair developed that made a specialist chair-maker absolutely necessary. The Queen Anne chair is one of the finest products of the period. Its curves give comfort to the sitter besides forming a pleasing and strong design. At the time, these were known as 'bended-back' chairs (Fig. 8). The back, rising from firmly splayed back legs, and the cabriole front legs, were best when carved out of solid walnut, elm or beech, despite the extravagant use of wood. The tenon and mortice joints which held the frame together achieved a much firmer chair than the William III type. Stretchers between the legs were soon dispensed with.

Not all chairs of the period had cabriole legs; but the cabriole leg is rightly regarded as a distinctive innovation of this period. On chairs and stools it was sturdy, but when supporting tables or stands for bureaux and cabinets it might be elongated and refined. Its origin is mysterious. It is said variously to be Dutch, Chinese, or derived from an animal's leg. In its early form, around 1700, it was of square section; this shape persisted and was often used with grandiose effect well into the 1720s. It lent itself to variations such as 'broken' knees or feet. When the leg is rounded, it has gentle curves that seem almost sculptural. The earliest examples retaining the 'Braganza', or flattened scroll, foot are rare. The deer foot, or *pied de biche*, is generally early, but similar pony-hooves can be found up to

10

K. Hoddle

11

A. C. Cooper

**Fig. 10 *Design for a garden* by
Daniel Marot. Engraving
c.1700.
Compare with Fig. 11.
(Victoria and Albert Museum.)**

**Fig. 11 *Table top*, probably
1723. Gilt gesso with the arms of
Cholmondeley impaling
Walpole. This elaborate table
top shows the influence of the
universal French style of Marot
and Bérain. Even two such
different objects as a table and a
formal knot garden (Fig. 10)
show the same vigorous strap-
work pattern softened by touches
of scrolled leaves and foliage.
(Christie's.)**

about 1730. The knees were carved with side mouldings, sometimes scrolled, or ornamented by turned bosses. Within certain limits the makers showed considerable invention in the decoration of the cabriole leg (Fig. 5).

Queen Anne's reign passed through war to peace, and in 1714 the Stuarts lost the crown to the Hanoverians. It is around 1713, the date of the Peace of Utrecht, that one detects a revival of ornament. While simple shells, carved in relief, and mouldings were in use quite early, more elaborate decoration is apparent during the second decade of the century. On the cresting of a chair a new kind of scroll-work appeared, suggesting that the frame was made not of wood but of curling-up leather or strap-work. Foliage sprouted at salient points. The carved shell became stylised, sometimes so much as to be confused with a stiff form of honeysuckle, and might be set on the elegantly scrolled hip of a chair leg, with husks trailing below it (Fig. 9).

These artificial motifs were of French origin,

and can be found on furniture up to about 1730; but during the 1720s another type of carved decoration appeared that was more naturalistic, even animated. The carved acanthus leaf found a vigorous freedom, and eagles' heads appeared on the arms of chairs. The eagle head might seem the logical extension of the claw-and-ball foot (Fig. 9), which had appeared earlier; some writers say it was used as early as 1710.

Two kinds of furniture show special richness of surface treatment: those in gesso and 'japan'. Gesso furniture had a magnificent revival up to about 1730 when the fashion for it lapsed. Between ten and twenty layers of chalk and parchment size were laid on a shaped or partly carved piece of furniture and, when it had hardened, the decoration was carved into it. Then the whole was gilt or, more rarely, silvered. Thus, the high relief carving had a wooden basis, while the low relief existed only in gesso. Differences in texture could be obtained by pouncing the ground, or by applying sand to produce a rough surface, and burnishing the raised ornament. The resulting furniture was fragile, intended for display rather than for use. It generally consisted of sets of mirrors, side-tables and torchères for state-rooms; sets of gesso chairs, too, were opulent luxuries, and were made with increasing elaboration up to 1730 (Fig. 1).

Such furniture implied pomp and circumstance, and it is not surprising that these pieces were often inspired by French patterns. In fact, a revival of Louis XIV influence in both form and decoration is obvious in the years following the Peace Treaty of 1713. The designs of Daniel Marot and Jean Bérain were once more taken as models, as they had been before 1700 (Fig. 7). The adaptable nature of this universal style can be appreciated by comparing, for instance, a table top with a design for a formal knot garden (Figs. 10 and 11). Both show the same vigour in an underlying strap-work pattern, which is softened by touches of scrolled leaves and other stiff foliate decoration.

Tall mirrors leafed with gold or silver had carved and pierced crestings which revived, but with a greater confidence of design, the fashions of William III in which the Marot influence had been paramount. Towards 1720, however, a distinct type of mirror appeared with a spreading flat frame, shaped and carved in relief. Here again the French style in the carved ornament was repeated with subtle variations; but at the same time it became mixed with the same naturalistic innovations that we have already noticed on the chair. Beside the interlaced strap-work, demon faces and shells, there appeared eagle heads, luxurious acanthus and other foliage. When set beside such animated details, the French patterns can look old-fashioned, artificial and 'precious'.

Japanned furniture continued in the tradition already set in the seventeenth century. The vogue for *chinoiserie* was steadily increasing up to 1730, and the patterns, with figures in pleasure gardens or mountain landscapes, tended to become rather stereotyped. Perhaps more attention was paid to the genuine lacquer imported from China, and rather less to Stalker and Parker's quaint adaptations from it in 1688. Japanning on black and dark green grounds was the most common, but the large and expensive bureau-cabinets decorated in gold on a brilliant scarlet ground somehow seem to us more typical of the period (Fig. 3). These pieces show a love of colour that one would not have suspected from a knowledge of sober walnut furniture alone.

MUSEUMS AND COLLECTIONS

Queen Anne furniture may be seen at the following:

London:	Hampton Court Palace
	Victoria and Albert Museum
Cornwall:	Antony House
Gloucestershire:	Dyrham Park
Hampshire:	The Vyne
Oxfordshire:	Blenheim Palace

FURTHER READING

The Shorter Dictionary of English Furniture
by Ralph Edwards, London, 1964.
English Furniture Styles 1500–1830 by Ralph
Fastnedge, London, 1955.
**Furniture Making in Seventeenth and Eighteenth
Century England** by R. W. Symonds, London,
1955.
Georgian Cabinet Makers by Ralph Edwards and
Margaret Jourdain, London, third edition, 1955.
The Dictionary of English Furniture by Ralph
Edwards, London, 1955.
English Furniture from Charles II to George II
by R. W. Symonds, London, 1929.

A new look in Traditional Textiles

Virginia Glenn Pow

An unmistakable mixture of quaint-ness and sophistication makes the textiles of the Queen Anne period some of the most beauti-ful and decorative ever made

The first twenty years of the eighteenth century saw no radical innovations in the English use of decorative textiles. The silk-weaving and tapestry industries had both been well established in England in the previous century and the most fashionable types of embroidery, both domestic and professional, were simply developments of old and favourite techniques. Nevertheless, there is about Queen Anne textiles an unmistakable character, reflecting the confident, prosperous stability of the age in which they were made.

Building was rapid and widespread, not only of great baroque palaces, but also of large numbers of town houses and comfortable rural mansions. Furnishing materials were in ever greater demand as upholstered chairs, settees and day-beds increased in number and comfort, all requiring richly woven or embroidered coverings.

Consequently, canvas work – both *gros point* and *petit point* – enjoyed a renewed vogue. Every possible source was ransacked for motifs and designs. Elaborate European woven stuffs were copied; *chinoiserie* figures gathered on little hummocks floating against dark backgrounds were taken either directly from oriental lacquers or from Vanderbank's *chinoiserie* tapestries (Fig. 2). Trees, flowers and birds from Indian printed cottons had already been deeply absorbed into the repertoire of the English needlewoman. More ambitious spirits even copied classical compositions, biblical scenes or peasants in the Teniers manner from engravings.

For example, there is in the Victoria and Albert Museum a very handsome wing chair made in the early eighteenth century, still with most of its original coverings of wool embroidery in *gros point* and *petit point* (Fig. 6). Amid rocky landscapes and fantastic classical architecture are scenes from the *Aeneid*. On the back of the chair Dido enter-tains Aeneas at a banquet beneath a chandelier and an imposing draped canopy, and on the seat cushion Aeneas rescues his father Anchises from the burning city of Troy. These scenes are taken from engravings then half a century old: Wenceslaus Hollar and Pierre Lambart's illustrations to the edition of Virgil published by John Ogilby in 1658.

More modest efforts, such as individual chair seats, pole-screens and tops for card-tables, abound from Queen Anne's reign. Clearly, however, major programmes of needleworking involving a great deal of labour and organisation must have been required to provide the furnishings for a large household. In the previous reign, Celia Fiennes had described Queen Mary's closet at Hampton Court where she saw 'the hangings, chaires, stooles and screen the same, all of satten stitch done in worsteads, beasts, birds, images and fruites all wrought very finely by Queen Mary and her Maids

Museum Photo

Fig. 1 *Nankeen curtains*, c.1720.
Worked in coloured crewels in the Chinese manner.
(Lady Lever Art Gallery, Port Sunlight.)

538

2

R. Todd-White

3

Museum Photo

4

Fig. 2 *Tapestry in the* chinoiserie *style of John Vanderbank, Soho, early eighteenth century.* (Vigo-Steinberg Gallery, London.)

Fig. 3 *Panel picture, 1708. Coloured silks in cross-stitch,* petit point *and chain-stitch on canvas, 8 x 9½ ins. This picture is an example of domestic needlework and can be contrasted with the large, ambitious examples in Fig. 4.* (Lady Lever Art Gallery.)

5

Andrew Houston

Fig. 4 *The Needlework Room, Wallington, Northumberland, containing ten panels worked by Lady Julia Calverley (probably with others) for Esholt, Yorkshire, in 1717 and transferred to Wallington in 1775.* (By Courtesy of the National Trust.)

Fig. 5 *Coat, c.1700–1710. Gold brocade. This coat shows the characteristic brown and gold used for costume.* (Castle Museum, Norwich.)

Fig. 6 *Wing chair, early eighteenth century. Wool embroidery in gros point and* petit point. *Embroidered with scenes from Virgil's* Aeneid, *this is an example of Queen Anne needlework applied to luxurious upholstered furniture.* (Victoria and Albert Museum, London.)

of Honour.' In the following generation under Queen Anne, the production of embroidery increased with the amount of upholstered furniture and fancy floral marquetries were replaced by plainer veneers, leaving textiles to provide the main areas of ornament.

A set of ten attractive and well-preserved floral canvas-work hangings now at Wallington in Northumberland were made towards the end of this period (Fig. 4). They are signed and dated 'Julia Calverley: 1717' and are mentioned in her husband's memorandum book of 27 February, 1716. Sir Walter Calverley (reputedly the prototype for Addison's jovial Sir Roger de Coverley) writes: 'my wife finished the sewed work in the drawing room, it having been three years and a half in the doing. The greatest part has been done with her own hands. It consists of ten panels.' As each panel is just under a yard wide and nine and a half feet long, and as Lady Julia led the busy life of a rich and sociable landowner's wife, one must regard the

6

K. Hoddle

statement that she completed all this work in three and a half years mostly with her own hands as something of a fond, husbandly exaggeration. The scale of the task makes it much more likely that she had about half-a-dozen helpers. However, the selection of the designs, the choice of the colours and the high standard of workmanship which make these hangings so remarkable must be attributed to Lady Julia herself.

The designs which she used are in the height of contemporary fashion. Sir Walter was a frequent visitor to London and it seems likely that he had the panels designed by one of the best cabinet-makers there. All the panels are filled with richly exotic Eastern blooms. The compositions are of two types: symmetrical and asymmetrical. The symmetrical designs, in their balance and pattern rather than their detail, immediately call to mind contemporary weaving, particularly the richly baroque effects of Genoa velvets. The asymmetrical panels, which foreshadow the lighter rococo style, owe much more to the painted Indian Palimpore.

These large painted calicos were first imported into England as expensive luxuries in the reign of James I. After various fluctuations in public taste, they began to arrive more cheaply in bulk by the later seventeenth century. Enterprising agents in Europe at this stage began to send out

patterns to be copied, so that homely fruits like the strawberry, unknown to Indian craftsmen, blossom gigantically on exotic Trees of Life. Chinese elements also entered the designs, both directly by way of Indo-Chinese trade and indirectly through the fashionable *chinoiserie* motifs which the European agents included in their designs. The charming and unexpected hybrid style became such a rage in England that early in Queen Anne's reign English textile manufacturers brought pressure to bear on the Government to have the import of Indian cottons banned. Nevertheless, the influence which the style had gained in the seventeenth century on canvas work, crewel work and woven textiles still permeated much early eighteenth-century design and was chosen by Julia Calverley, a rich, elegant young woman still under thirty years of age and presumably keenly aware of current fashion.

Pavilions, archways, diagonal screens and balustrades

In addition to the characteristic woolwork, needlewomen at this period also produced some very fine silk embroidery, the richest specimens including lavish silver and gold work. The favourite objects for embellishment in this way were matching sets of bed coverlets and cushions. The ground was usually a double layer of fine linen or, for the most sumptuous effects, white silk or satin. The designs normally consisted of a deep border with large motifs at the four corners and a central panel of decoration. This arrangement derives from oriental embroideries and the technique also recalls Chinese work in the use of long and short stitch, satin stitch, stem stitch and couched metal threads.

It is, however, not always easy to distinguish amateur from professional work in these cases, unless it is signed; normally only amateurs signed their work. We are told that one of the most impressive sets of bed furnishings of this type in the Victoria and Albert Museum was worked by Mary, wife of Sir Richard Vyvyan of Trelowarren when they were both imprisoned in the Tower of London in 1715 for suspected complicity in the Jacobite rising of that year (Fig. 9). Like almost all examples of this type, the background is criss-crossed all over with lines of stitching in pale silk. The main design is a masterpiece of exuberant flame-like shapes and rich, scrolling gold thread worked in an amazing variety of knots and stitches. The Vyvyans' incarceration must have been in unusually spacious and well-lit quarters, shared by a considerable staff with access to the most accomplished designers.

Large items of embroidered costume from the early eighteenth century are very rare indeed, but there do remain some charming accessories such as aprons, stomachers, pockets (Fig. 8), scarves, bags (Fig. 7) and shoes, to show us that both professional and amateur embroiderers worked on these, too. Quilting was a particularly popular form of decoration used on petticoats, waistcoats and robes (Fig. 14).

We now turn our attention from the skill of the needlewoman to that of the weaver. The English silk-weaving industry began in a small way in the early seventeenth century as an attempt to compete

540

7

8

Museum Photo

9

K. Hoddle

10

11

12

K. Hoddle

K. Hoddle

K. Hoddle

K. Hoddle

K. Hoddle

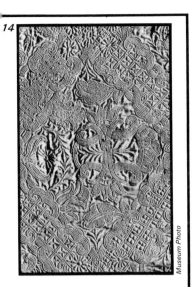

14

Museum Photo

Fig. 14 **Detail of a dress**, early
eighteenth century. Quilted
satin.
(Victoria and Albert Museum.)

Fig. 7 **Bag, or purse**, c.1700.
Embroidered with coloured
silks and gold thread.
(Lady Lever Art Gallery.)

Fig. 8 **Embroidered pocket**,
early eighteenth century.
The embroidery is executed on
fine linen.
(Victoria and Albert Museum.)

Fig. 9 Detail of **The Vyvyan
Bed Furnishings**, 1715.
Although this lavish baroque
embroidery looks professional,
it was reputedly worked by Lady
Vyvyan when she was
imprisoned in the Tower of
London in 1715.
(Victoria and Albert Museum.)

Fig. 10 **Brocade**, probably from
Spitalfields, c.1705–10. 'Bizarre'
patterned silk, with long repeats.
(Victoria and Albert Museum.)

Fig. 11 **Brocade**, English or
Dutch, early eighteenth century.
The Chinese motifs used here
are strongly reminiscent of
porcelain designs.
(Victoria and Albert Museum.)

Fig. 12 **Design for Spitalfields
silk** by James Leman, 1719.
This design shows the
progression towards a light
rococo style.
(Victoria and Albert Museum.)

Fig. 13 **Brocade**, part of a dress,
eighteenth century.
(Victoria and Albert Museum.)

with the very successful products of France, Italy
and the Low Countries. There are records of a silk-
weaving factory at Canterbury, but none of its
products have been identified and the industry
seems to have centred almost entirely on Spitalfields
in London. Louis XIV unwittingly gave a great
boost to the English manufacturers with the
Revocation of the Edict of Nantes in 1685; this
drove large numbers of highly skilled Huguenot
weavers to leave France and offer their services at
Spitalfields. In Queen Anne's reign the industry
made even greater strides during the War of
Spanish Succession. This dragged on from 1701
until 1713, during which time not only were the
products of the enemy French barred from the
English home market, but also the British navy
managed to disrupt French trade all over the world,
leaving new customers anxious to accept English
goods instead.

It is not easy to identify for certain which silks
are from Spitalfields, which French and which
Dutch. All the factories copied each others'
products, with France usually leading the fashion.
Generally speaking, however, English weavers
preferred pale grounds – light blue, mustard or buff
– while the French used darker shades. There are
also some very rare cases where designs which are
known to have been drawn at Spitalfields can be
linked with particular silks.

One very talented silk-designer, James Leman,
began his career at Spitalfields in the early 1700s.
We are fortunate that a large number of his designs
have been preserved (Fig. 12). His first dated design
of 1706 is in a style very characteristic of the first
two decades of the eighteenth century. Although
apparently loosely oriental in inspiration, there
is such doubt about the source of this style that it is
referred to simply as the 'bizarre' style. Its chief
feature is the use of strange, jagged, abstract shapes
which appear alongside the more usual flowers and
scrolls (Fig. 10). The repeat used is also peculiar to
the 'bizarre' style; it is very long and vertical, giving
a serpentine emphasis to the stems of the plant
forms. These designs first appeared in about 1700,
reached their peak of popularity in 1705, were still
frequently seen around 1710 and did not disappear
until the 1720s. Another Leman design of 1707
gives us a possible clue to the source of the 'bizarre'
style. Here, instead of purely abstract shapes, are
pavilions, archways, diagonal screens and balus-
trades, with Chinese fret patterns and in Chinese
perspective. Surely this is Leman reverting to the
motifs which the 'bizarre' patterns had stylised out
of all recognition.

Far into the eighteenth century, weavers
continued to produce silks in a rather formless
flower style, based on the patterns of the previous
hundred years. However, small naturalistic flowers
increased in popularity from about 1705 until, by
1730, in common with most contemporary
decorative artists, silk-designers seemed to work
entirely in posies and ribbons. Only the baroque
love of ostentatious gold and silver thread, hardly
lending itself to realistic representation of plant
life, prevented an even more rapid and wholesale
spread of the naturalistic style. These naturalistic
flowers seem first to have developed between the
jagged shapes of the 'bizarre' style which gradually
shrank until they were mere rocky outcrops
supporting the plants which formed the principal
motif of the pattern.

A third and extremely attractive type of silk
pattern, popular just at the beginning and again
at the end of this period, was the 'lace' pattern, so
called because the flowers were framed by areas of
diaper design closely resembling lace or net. The
delicate charm of these fabrics provided a counter
to the slightly harsh 'bizarre' style. All these designs
were used for both costume and furnishing
materials.

Throughout this period, one of the most fashionable fabrics for hangings or upholstery was figured
velvet. This had more formal patterns than the
silks, and was almost always imported, usually
free from Italy; hence the name Genoa velvet.
There is one famous instance where the figured
velvet may have been English. In 1714 John
Johnson, a mercer whose company regularly
supplied the royal family, sent out a bill for furnishings now at Hampton Court 'for 321 yards ⅛ of
white, crimson, and yellow figured velvet for a
standing bedd compleat, three pairs of large
window curtains, vallance and cornishes, a large
arm chair and 8 square stools at 42/– per yard . . . '.
This velvet is very elaborate for English work at
this date but it is most unlikely that, had it been an
expensive import (a fact normally stressed in such
bills), John Johnson would not have mentioned the
fact. Perhaps the English weavers had finally caught
up with and surpassed their continental rivals.

The Queen Anne period is really too short a space
of time in which to trace any clear development in
an artistic field so bound by tradition and limited
by technique as needlework. The designs of
the woven fabrics, on the other hand, are perhaps
more closely allied to those of other contemporary
decorative arts. In conclusion, it must be remembered that it is difficult to date many textiles even
to within a particular decade. What we can say of
Queen Anne's reign, however, is that it saw the
useful textile arts of the Stuart period carried to
their most sophisticated and refined heights.

MUSEUMS AND COLLECTIONS

Queen Anne textiles may be seen at the following:

Bath:	The Museum of Costume, Assembly Rooms
Bristol:	Bristol City Art Gallery
Cambo, Northumberland:	Wallington
Edinburgh:	Royal Scottish Museum
Leeds:	Temple Newsam House
London:	Hampton Court Palace Victoria and Albert Museum
Manchester:	The Gallery of English Costume, Platt Hall, Rusholme
Port Sunlight, Cheshire:	Lady Lever Art Gallery
York:	Castle Howard

FURTHER READING

English Needlework by A. F. Kendrick, 2nd edit.
revised by Patricia Wardle, London, 1967.
Baroque and Rococo Silks by Peter K. Thornton,
London, 1965.
'Ten Floral Panels by Lady Julia Calverley' by
G. F. Wingfield Digby, **The Connoisseur**, April
1960.
'Origins of the "Oriental Style" in English
Decorative Art' by J. Irwin, **The Burlington
Magazine**, XCVII, 1955.

ARTHUR NEGUS COLLECTORS' ITEM

THIMBLES

Thimbles date back to Anglo-Saxon times and have been made in wood, leather, bone, brass, gold, silver, enamel and porcelain. Silver thimbles were first made in the sixteenth century but mostly these are only to be found in museums. However, Georgian and Victorian thimbles are plentiful.

An eighteenth-century thimble usually has a band encircling the rim which is chased or engraved with scrolls, a cartouche enclosing a small crest or cipher, wreaths of flowers or foliage, or other motifs. A rare series was made with wide bands of intricate filigree work above the thimble ring. Other thimbles were bordered with gems, and gold ones were sometimes set with precious stones. Until the invention of the 'nose machine' in the middle of the eighteenth century, by which time indentations were impressed symmetrically, all indentations were hand-punched and display irregular spacing. Painted enamel thimbles, decorated with flowers or tiny motifs and narrow rims of double gilt metal, were made in South Staffordshire and Birmingham from about 1770. Many had enamelled thimble cases resembling nutmeg graters.

Thimbles in bone china were strong and tough in comparison with earlier soft-paste porcelain. Thimbles were also carved in jade, ivory, bone, boxwood or mother of pearl. Towards the end of the eighteenth century, and during the early part of the nineteenth, presentation thimbles were enclosed in small cases made of precious metals. Some had places for needles and pins, together with the thimble. Cases of shagreen were fashionable in the eighteenth century. Heavy brass and iron thimbles were used in the sharpers' game of thimbling, which required three thimbles and a pen.

Collecting Hints

The vast majority of thimbles were made inexpensively in bronze and brass and occasionally in pewter. Thimbles were first made in England by John Loffing. In 1695 he obtained a patent and set up a thimble works in Islington.

Collectors may sometimes find heavy iron thimbles. These were known as 'dames thimbles' and were used by dames of small children's schools to tap sharply and vigorously on pupils' heads when correction was considered necessary. This was called 'thimble-pie making' and was much dreaded. The following points will help you date a thimble:

1. Early Georgian thimbles were often engraved with scrolls or crests; later ones have filigree work or gem-stones above the rim. Souvenir thimbles with engraved views of famous places are Victorian; those with a motto or line of verse around the rim have been made in all periods.

Right: *Collection of thimbles and cases.* Clockwise: *Tartan case, Mauchline ware,* c.1840. *Painted wood case. Ivory egg-shaped case* containing thimble set with marcasites. *Acorn case,* brass, mid-Victorian. *Ivory barrel case* containing different-sized silver thimbles.

Centre right: *Three thimbles,* all late nineteenth century. Left: *Silver thimble* set with turquoise. Centre: *Gold thimble* set with agate. Right: *Silver thimble* set with lapis lazuli.

Bottom: *Sewing case,* wooden, late nineteenth century, containing a silver sewing set.

Opposite: *Jubilee thimble,* celebrating the coronation of George V, 1911.

2. Not all silver thimbles are hall-marked and, even when they are, the mark is not always decipherable. As a broad guide, thimbles made between 1739 and 1790 were exempt from hall-marks and then, until 1890, the monarch's head duty-stamp was included in the hall-mark.

Prices

Generally speaking, prices range from about 25p to a couple of pounds – double the amount, if you like thimbles in novelty cases.

A silver thimble in a velvet-lined mother of pearl casket might cost £4.30. This would be a fair price providing the thimble fits the case exactly.

During the Cromwellian regime, there was a brisk demand for silver thimbles. In those days, one could buy one for anything up to 2s.

Where To Buy

Thimbles are to be found in many antique shops and markets. Certain silversmiths have gold and silver ones.

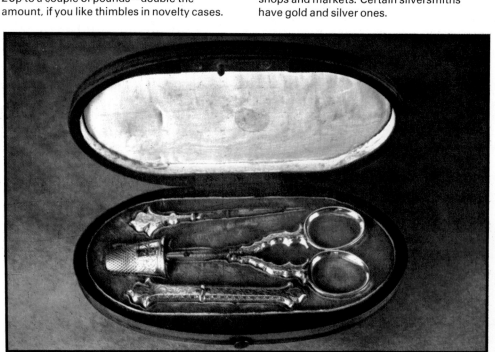

Pamela Clabburn Collection: Andrew Houston

ACCESSORIES TO MASCULINE FASHION

John Wallace

Fig. 1 *Three pendant seals, late eighteenth century. (Left) Gold, set with a cornelian, with an intaglio of a warrior's head. (Centre) Gold set with a flat bloodstone disk on a swivel mounting. Signed 'Parry'. The intaglio shows a triumphal procession taken from an antique model. (Right) Gold set with a crystal on which is engraved a coat of arms. (Victoria and Albert Museum, London.)*

SEAL: The Print of a Coat of Arms or some other Device made in Wax, and set to any Deed or Writing; also the Instrument or Piece of Metal Etc., on which the Figure is engraven that impresses the Wax.
Nathan Bailey: *Dictionarium Britannicum*, London 1730.

Anyone who becomes interested in sealing-instruments of the period between 1660 and, say, 1830 can look forward to building up a collection of considerable artistic merit. Within the confines of the three distinct types of sealing-instruments most likely to be available to the ordinary individual, there lurks astonishing variety. For the really enthusiastic and well-informed collector there are even greater pleasures in store. The print of the seal can reveal the identity of some long-dead notable, or display the virtuosity of a master engraver; the instrument itself can prove a minor social document, reflecting in form and decoration the fads and fashions of the period in which it was made.

The busy man of affairs, or the compulsive letter writer, must have found it convenient to keep a seal on his desk (Fig. 4). In the late seventeenth and early eighteenth centuries, these used to have a bulbous handle, chiefly of wood or ivory, that resembled a mushroom in shape. The end of the 'stalk' was mounted with a silver cap, on the base of which the seal matrix was carved. Sealing-instruments of this kind continued in use throughout the eighteenth century and into the early part of the nineteenth, although as time went on their handles took on more slender proportions. In addition, jasper, agate and other semi-precious stones became suitable and fashionable mountings for seal matrices of silver or, more generally, of steel, stone or coloured crystal.

On another kind of desk seal, the handle was made hollow, to form a long box in which sealing wax could be kept (Fig. 6). Usually these box seals were made of silver, or some other metal, sometimes covered with shagreen (untanned leather, usually green in colour). The seal matrices are cut either directly into the metal, or on a stone mounted in the base of the sealing-wax container.

Seal, or signet, rings have been worn and used for thousands of years. In classical times the subjects were often heraldic (though not in the later armorial sense) as a means of identification; frequently they consisted of self-portraits or portraits of the makers' patrons. It was these portrait seals which particularly took the imagination of the eighteenth-century gentleman, fired with fashionable interest in the world of Greece and Rome, and some of the finest intaglio work produced at that time is of portraits 'after the antique', set into rings or, more commonly, fob seal mounts. They were, in fact, not always after the antique. In the seal record book of a jeweller and engraver, Robert Wray, under the year 1738, we find Richard Hoare spending five guineas on an intaglio seal of Milton's head. Mr. Pope's portrait was another of Wray's ready sellers.

Fashion decreed that seals should be suspended from the fob of breeches

These portraits, when set in rings, were purely decorative and did not usurp the importance or function of rings which had coats of arms, crests or badges engraved directly into the metal, or on stones set in the bezel. Nonetheless, eighteenth-century heraldic rings, which were worn on the forefinger, are comparatively rare. The chief reason for this is that armorial seal matrices were also worn on pendants. These came to be called fob seals soon after the Restoration of 1660, when fashion decreed that they should be suspended from a watch kept in the right-hand pocket, or fob, of breeches (Figs. 1 and 3).

Some of the best heraldic intaglio work of the late seventeenth and early eighteenth centuries was carried out on plain metal (usually silver) seal pendants. The earlier examples of this period resemble the medieval pendant seal in broad outline; these are trumpet-shaped, but have a simple loop for suspension and ridges around the stem to prevent the hand from slipping down. In the last quarter of the eighteenth century, an elegant version of this trumpet shape re-appeared, either as a concave 'cage' of gold in which the intaglio would be mounted, or in silver, jasper or agate. This shape was even copied in fine stoneware by Josiah Wedgwood and other potters, the subject matter of the matrices usually consisting of classical heads and figures.

Fig. 2 **Members of the Wilson family,** grouped around a memorial of William Pitt the Younger in the garden of Binfield, by John Downman (c.1750–1824). Oil on Canvas, 27½ x 36 ins. Late eighteenth century. The gentlemen wear fashionable fob seals. (Leger Galleries, London.)

Simple and businesslike seal pendants in silver or steel continued to be produced right up to the end of the eighteenth century (Fig. 3), though the profile of the matrix became more domed, and the handles displayed a flat openwork or vase-shaped design.

Such seals were probably for everyday use in sealing documents. Nevertheless, pendant seals for ornament also seem to have been worn quite soon after the Restoration. In *The London Gazette*

for October 1679, there appears a notice, 'Lost by a Person of Quality. Four seals hanging on a black Ribon, describeth as followeth; one a Cornelian Stone, graved with a man's head, one a blew Stone, graved with a naked man and a little Diamond on each side, one a red Stone graved with two letters S.X. and two Angels holding a Crown over it, these three were set in Gold and Enamelled, the fourth a little gold Seal shap'd like a Dog, and graved with an Ostrich.'

The little gold seal 'shap'd like a Dog' is an early mention of a long-surviving fashion for having the handle of a fob seal in the likeness of an animal or bird. Mrs. Delany, in a diary entry for January 1756, noted about Mrs. Spencer that 'her watch and etuy suited to the rest [of her attire] and a seal of a Mercury cut in a very fine turquoise stone, set as a standing for a spaniel Dog, the body of pearl of the size of the Duchess of Portland's dolphin, the head and neck made out with gold finely wrought, two little brilliants for its eyes, and a brilliant collar: it cost 70 guineas.'

It was not the form of the seal that attracted Mrs. Delany's attention, but the sumptuousness of it – and the price. Considering that one of Horace Walpole's letters of about the same time informs us that sixteen guineas was the going rate for a pair of good seals, Mrs. Delany had good reason to comment.

Although the unfortunate 'Person of Quality' in 1679 lost four seals on a ribbon, the habit of wearing more than one or two fob seals did not catch on widely until the dictates of fashion around the

the 'Jessamies' (their imitators lower down the social scale) and after them, the 'Fops', did not spare the seal when deciding how they could take – to our eyes, at least – good taste to absurdity. Fashion plates of this period show great clusters of seals hanging down from fob chains or ribbons (Fig. 7). There was even a moment when *two* watches were carried '. . . with a watch in each pocket, one lent by his mother, To prove that one leg should keep time with the other'; so ran a verse in *The Gentleman's and London Magazine* for March 1776. Although quite frequently one of these watches was a sham, this bizarre fashion naturally resulted in two clusters of seals hanging down over the stomachs of the Fashionables. Even the women entered into the spirit of things. 'Among other fashions lately introduced from Paris is the brace of gold watch chains now sported by our fashionable females. Some economical men may wish their wives were less imitative' (*Morning Post*, January 1789). One can be quite sure that seals were worn as well.

Triangular seals in gold, silver-gilt, crystal, stone

Fig. 3 *Four pendant seals.*
(Left to right) Silver with the arms of Scowles Co., Berkshire, late seventeenth century. Silver, second half of the eighteenth century. Agate with a gold loop bearing the arms of Baker of Battle, Sussex, late eighteenth century. Cut-steel with a three-sided swivel, early eighteenth century. (Victoria and Albert Museum.)

1740s led to a shortening of the waistcoat. This started a trend that culminated in the late eighteenth century in the double-breasted waistcoats that barely covered the midriff. It is easy to imagine how the sharp dressers of the time would pay closer attention to this article of jewellery, now that it had, quite literally, come out into the open for all to see (Fig. 2).

Clusters of seals hanging over the stomachs of the Fashionables

'A repeater by Graham, which the hour reveals, Almost overbalanc'd with knickknacks and seals' is how the author of a satirical poem Monsieur A-La-Mode (published in *The Salisbury Journal* in 1753, and blithely plagiarised by the *London Magazine* in the same year) saw the contemporary man of fashion. Friendly and not-so-friendly rivalry as to the quality and originality of fob seals must have been rife. Certainly Robert Wray had several customers who allowed few weeks to pass without their purchasing yet another seal.

Towards the end of the century, fashion ran riot. Its exaggerators, notably the 'Macaronis' and

and steel are numerous, as they continued to be in vogue for many decades. They were mounted within a half hoop that allowed them to swivel – a form of mounting that was also given to flat seals intaglio-cut on both sides. The dating of these 'turning seals', as they were called, is reasonably straightforward; the earlier ones incorporated a generous expanse of finely pierced and chased openwork design in an appropriate metal; later turning seals swivelled within a relatively simple half loop, though this might be moulded, enamelled or enriched in some other way. Some well-heeled gentleman used *The London Gazette* for April 1701 to mourn the loss of 'a three square turning seal with 3 stones'. These stones were no less than a topaz (cut with a coat of arms), an emerald (cut with a cipher), and a sapphire (cut with a crest). In 1739 Robert Wray supplied Sir John Barker, Bart., with a triangular topaz set in gold, the faces of the stone cut with Queen Elizabeth's head, a coat of arms and a 'fancy' of two loving doves, all for seventeen guineas.

Fine fob seals continued to be made through the Regency period, and had a renewed popularity in the 1830s

The word 'fancy' was used by engravers and jewellers for stones shallow-cut with popular devices: ships, animals, birds, classical figures, lovers' knots and so forth. For fancies or for 'slight heads', Wray charged as little as a guinea. No doubt it was these cheap seals which made up the bulk of a would-be gallant's seal cluster later in the century. Certainly large numbers of them were made once the factory jewellers of Birmingham and elsewhere had perfected fast production methods to meet the great demand for attractive motifs. Inexpensively set, often in pinchbeck (the copper-zinc alloy which first became popular in the 1730s as a visual substitute for gold), fob seals became as cheap as they had ever been.

Fine fob seals, of course, continued to be made right through the Regency period, and had a renewed popularity in the 1830s. Not the least curious were the musical seals of the early nineteenth century, with mechanisms that were imported from the Continent. But the long-drawn-out Napoleonic Wars had duly sobered people and the inclination to wear ornamental seals in large quantities gradually diminished. New fashions ran their consecutive courses, and by the middle of the nineteenth century even people with only a pretence to a coat of arms began to favour signet rings for sealing purposes once more.

HINTS FOR COLLECTORS

It is unusual to come across desk seals and eighteenth-century signet rings outside the Works of Art sales at the major auction rooms. Nevertheless, an increasing number of jewellers have a section devoted to antique pieces. Certainly they should have a number of fob seals to choose from, though probably most of these will be late eighteenth- and early nineteenth-century.

Prices vary enormously, as might be imagined. The price of fob seals is frequently determined by the richness and intrinsic value of mounting and stone rather than by the age of the piece. A large topaz intaglio of a warrior's head, set in a heavy chased mount of about 1820 will probably cost more than a silver armorial pendant seal, even though the latter might be a hundred and fifty years older, and harder to find. Beware! All that glitters is not gold: it could be pinchbeck.

MUSEUMS AND COLLECTIONS

English seals of the seventeenth to nineteenth centuries may be seen at the following:

London: Guildhall Library
           Victoria and Albert Museum

Fig. 4 *Four silver desk seals. (Top and bottom) late seventeenth century. (Left and right) Second half of the eighteenth century. The example at the bottom shows the seal socket engraved with hounds pursuing a stag. (Victoria and Albert Museum.)*

Fig. 5 *Designs for silver* by D. Marot (c.1663–1752), *illustrated in his* Oeuvres, *printed in Amsterdam, 1744. The designs show patterns suitable for engraving and embossing. (Victoria and Albert Museum.)*

Fig. 6 *Two sealing-wax cases. (Left) Silver, late seventeenth century. The lid is set with an antique onyx intaglio. (Right) Silver, c.1720. The lid is set with a crystal. (Victoria and Albert Museum.)*

Fig. 7 *Watch with chatelaine and seals* by William Webster, *London, c.1715. Gold with intaglio seals. The profusion of decoration and the elaboration of style is typical of the state of exaggeration which gentlemen's fashion reached in the eighteenth century. (Fitzwilliam Museum, Cambridge.)*

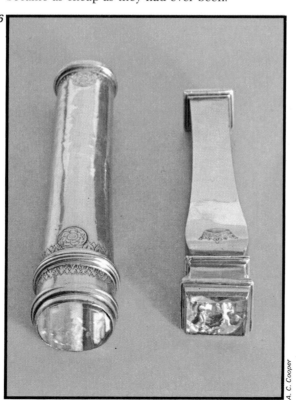

THE BRITANNIA ST

Douglas Ash

Fig. 1 **Teapot, kettle and chocolate-pot,** *all on matching stands, by Joseph Ward, London, 1719.*
Octagonal shapes were very popular in the early eighteenth century. This superb matching set uses them with a characteristic pear-shape on the teapot and kettle.
(Worshipful Company of Goldsmiths, London.)

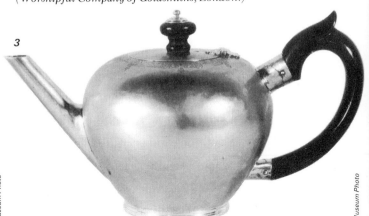

ANDARD IN SILVER

Fig. 2 *Tea-kettle stand in solid silver, unmarked, English, c.1725.*
(Victoria and Albert Museum, London.)

5

Museum Photo

Fig. 3 *Teapot by James Smith, London, 1719–20. Height 4 ins. Bullet-shaped teapots, as pots of this sort were called, were very popular later in the reign of Queen Anne, and well into that of George I. They were made very small in recognition of the high price of tea.*
(Victoria and Albert Museum.)

Fig. 4 *Tea-canister by Nathaniel Roe, London, 1713. These attractive containers for a very expensive commodity, tea, were not called caddies until late in the eighteenth century.*
(Worshipful Company of Goldsmiths.)

Fig. 5 *Candlestick by David Tanqueray, London, 1720. Height 7 ins. This design was current before 1700.*
(Victoria and Albert Museum.)

With the introduction of the Britannia standard in 1697, English silver design entered a period of unrivalled simplicity, dignity and beauty

The Queen Anne style is considered as having begun in the last decade of the seventeenth century, and a number of important factors affecting the craft of silversmithing were at work in the Queen's reign and that of her successor, George I. One was the quality of the silver itself. From 27 March, 1697, until 1 June, 1720, English silversmiths were compelled by statute to work metal of a higher standard than sterling. This is generally known as the Britannia standard, because the lion-passant mark was replaced by a figure of Britannia, which denoted the presence, in 12 oz. (Troy) of metal, of $11\frac{1}{2}$ oz. of pure silver as against the $11\frac{1}{10}$ oz. of the sterling standard. For much of this period, therefore, English domestic silver was of the Britannia standard and bore the appropriate marks.

Another important factor was the arrival in England and Ireland of large numbers of Huguenot craftsmen, among them plate-workers. These immigrants were refugees from the persecutions instituted by Louis XIV against their co-religionists after the Revocation of the Edict of Nantes in 1685. The great trouble they took with their work forced the native silversmiths to emulate both their industry and their mannerisms in order to compete with them. This brought about a general raising of standards.

Of small size, in recognition of the price of tea

One form of decorative technique which was popular in the early eighteenth century on hollowware of all kinds is known as cut-card work. The Huguenots were much addicted to it, but they had neither invented nor introduced it to England, where it had been used to a limited extent since quite early in the reign of Charles II. It consisted of thin sheet silver, cut into patterns such as leaf-forms and soldered on to various parts of a vessel.

It is now necessary to consider some of the more important items of domestic plate of the period.

From early in the reign of Queen Anne, silver teapots began to be made in comparatively large numbers, after appearing sparsely in the time of Charles II. They were of two main kinds. The more characteristic was shaped like a pear with a high, domed lid, and was of either circular or polygonal section (Fig. 1). The handle, which was of wood, or occasionally of ivory, was at right-angles to the swan-necked spout, or on the opposite side, the latter arrangement being more usual in the reign of George I. In wealthy households, they were sometimes accompanied by large silver kettles of much the same shape but with swing-handles, mounted on stands, with spirit-lamps to heat the water. These massive, expensive objects were beyond the resources of many people, whose teapots were furnished with their own small stands and lamps, possibly so that the water could be boiled in the pot itself.

The other type, which increased in incidence later, was of more or less spherical form and is consequently known as bullet-shaped (Fig. 3). These pots were nearly always plain and of small size in recognition of the high price of tea. Late in the reign of George I, kettles began to be made in the same form and remained popular long after the pear-shape had fallen into disuse.

A large baroque cartouche for the owner's arms

In considering the rest of the tea equipage, it must be remembered that the later conception of a matching tea-set was less popular in the first half of the eighteenth century (Fig. 7). Many people bought the various components separately as finances permitted, and they were not necessarily in precisely the same style. The teapot and covered sugar-bowl might be of circular section, the slop-basin might be vertically ribbed, and the milk or water jug and the tea-canister of long octagonal shape (Fig. 4). The last, incidentally, were not called caddies until the late eighteenth century. Some people owned no more than one; others had sets of two or three which were locked away in cases to prevent the pilfering of the contents by servants.

Coffee-pots and chocolate-pots were similar to each other, the only essential difference being that the latter had removable finials on the lids which enabled a rod to be inserted immediately before pouring, to stir the contents. For many years the lids were mostly domed like those of pear-shaped teapots (Fig. 8), but a lower form became

550

prevalent in the second quarter of the century. There was great variation in the shape of the bodies; some consisted of upward-tapering cylinders, some curved inward at the base just above the foot-ring, while others were of a fully-developed baluster shape. This became increasingly popular with the passage of time and persisted throughout the eighteenth century despite the introduction of other types.

Drinking-vessels had suffered a grievous loss with the almost total disappearance of the silver winecup, supported on a stem and foot, in the middle of the seventeenth century, but this had been chiefly replaced by two-handled cups of various kinds. The remote ancestor of them all was the ancient Greek *kantharos*. In the early eighteenth century some were purely functional and of simple shape, while others were of such important and monumental aspect that, although they were capable of being used, and almost certainly were on special occasions, one cannot but think of their purpose as being chiefly ostentatious. This is especially true of covered two-handled cups in which Huguenot influence is discernible.

The commonest household variant, used at breakfast and on other informal occasions, had an expanding U-shaped body which rested not on a foot-ring but on a slight downward extension of the base, and a pair of scroll handles which might be cast, or consist of narrow ribbons of sheet silver (Fig. 6). Very few were plain. Most were ornamented with a circuit of embossed spiral gadroons alternating with hollow flutes, rising from the base of the bowl and terminating in the lower half. This decoration was usually, though not invariably, answered by an embossed cable-moulding a short distance below the rim, and there might also be a large baroque cartouche for the owner's arms, crest or monogram. The same kind of decoration appeared on many other vessels.

Like their seventeenth-century predecessors, cups of this kind are often miscalled porringers, but it has been proved beyond doubt that this designation is incorrect and that they were, in fact, drinking-vessels. They were typical not only of the

reign of Queen Anne, but of that of her successor also. After George I's death, however, although they continued to be made to a decreasing extent and embellished with ornament which had long been obsolete, their proportions were gradually spoilt by their becoming too narrow in relation to their height.

Most tankards of the early eighteenth century held about two pints and involved the use of a great deal of silver but, despite the increased cost resulting from the imposition of the Britannia standard, there was no apparent diminution in the demand for them. They had already begun to be slightly narrower in the last decade of the seventeenth century than those of the Charles II period, when these pots reached their maximum width; but a further modification became almost universal after 1700. The hinged lid, which formerly had a flat or nearly flat top, now developed a low dome which became a more or less standard feature (Fig. 9), while a few of them were surmounted by finials, which had scarcely been seen since the reign of James I.

Various kinds of thumb-piece – also known as the billet or purchase – persisted from the late seventeenth century, including a type with voluted ends which continued after 1750. One of the more striking was in the form of a couchant lion cast in the solid, but this barely outlasted the reign of Queen Anne.

Handsome proportions and the sheen of silver in candlelight

The majority of tankards were cylindrical, sometimes with a narrow, applied moulding running around or beneath the centre of the body; but a new variety appeared in the form of a squat baluster, and this, with a more curvaceous outline, was destined to be especially popular in the second half of the century.

Not everyone could afford a silver tankard, and the production of cans or mugs burgeoned in a remarkable fashion after 1700. These miniature tankards without lids had first come on the scene just after the Restoration in 1660, the earliest type looking something like a common form of pottery vessel, with a globular body and a short cylindrical neck. The scrolled handle was cut out of sheet silver. A few of these were made in the reign of Queen Anne, but as they were uncomfortable to hold and inconvenient to drink from, they enjoyed no great popularity and quickly disappeared.

More numerous than these were mugs of cylindrical shape, with hollow wrought handles of D-section like those of tankards, but provided with a thumb-rest at the point where the top of the handle joined the body. All these handles had a notch at the bottom, to permit the escape of hot air when they were being soldered to the body, and thus to prevent their bursting open (Fig. 11, right). The myth that this notch was intended for use as a whistle is still widely believed; in fact, no such thing as a whistling tankard or mug has ever existed.

Some of these cylindrical mugs were quite plain; a few were spoilt by closely-spaced fluting in the Huguenot fashion, but a great many had a narrow moulding applied around the body a short distance below the rim (Fig. 12, left). This feature continued only for a year or so after 1714, and may be

Fig. 6 *Two-handled cup by John Sutton, London, 1705. Height 4½ ins.*
This common household variant of the two-handled cup was probably used at breakfast and on other informal occasions. The choice of this humble domestic vessel by the Company of Porters suggests that they were one of the poorer guilds.
(Victoria and Albert Museum.)

6

A. C. Cooper

Fig. 7 *A family at tea*, *attributed to Richard Collins (d.1732),* c.1730.
The principal objects of silver represented are a teapot, stand and canister of 1705–20, sugar bowl and tongs of about 1730, and a bowl and dish which could be either English or Scottish of about 1730.
(Victoria and Albert Museum.)

Fig. 8 **Chocolate-pot,** *maker unknown, London, 1722–23. Height 9¼ ins.*
The finial is removable to allow a stirring rod to be inserted.
(Victoria and Albert Museum.)

Fig. 9 **Tankard** *by Robert Timbrell and Benjamin Bentley, London, 1714–15.*
The hinged lid with a low dome was a standard feature.
(Victoria and Albert Museum.)

K. Hoddle

K. Hoddle

Fig. 10 *Monteith* by John Smith,
London, 1702.
*These bowls were originally
intended for cooling wine
glasses, suspended from the
notches. But this example has a
detachable rim so that the bowl
may be used for punch as well.
(Worshipful Company of Coach-
makers, London.)*

Fig. 11 *Punch-bowl and ladle* by
William Darker, London, 1729.
*In about 1720, the elaborate
Monteith with its detachable rim,
as in Fig. 10, fell out of favour.
Silver bowls about a foot in
diameter replaced them, which
relied on handsome proportions
and smooth gleaming surfaces for
their effect.
(Christie's.)*

Fig. 12 *Two mugs,* that on the
left by Timbrell and Bentley,
London, 1713; that on the right
by Nathaniel Locke, London,
1716.
*Cylindrical mugs of this sort,
either with or without a narrow
moulding applied just below the
rim, were quite common in the
early years of the eighteenth
century. At the base of the handle
of the right-hand mug can be
seen the notch which allowed
hot air to escape while the handle
was being soldered to the body,
thus preventing it from exploding.
(Private Collection.)*

considered highly typical of the actual years of
Queen Anne's reign. A baluster shape was also
used but became more frequent later, as in the
case of tankards.

Connected with more ceremonious forms of
drinking were silver punch-bowls and monteiths.
According to the diarist Anthony à Wood, the latter
first appeared in 1683. Their original purpose was
purely to cool wineglasses, which were suspended,
bowl-downward, in cold water from notches in the
rim of the monteith. Bowls intended solely for the
brewing of punch had level rims, but in the last
decade of the seventeenth century, a dual-purpose
vessel was devised, with a detachable monteith rim
looking somewhat like a crown (Fig. 10). The
production of these increased enormously in the
early eighteenth century, but the monteith fell out
of favour in about 1720, and thereafter large silver
bowls were devoted entirely to the brewing of
punch and had normal fixed rims without indentations. Surface decoration of any kind became rare,
and punch-bowls relied for their effect on handsome
proportions and the sheen of silver in candlelight
(Fig. 11).

The candlesticks of the Queen Anne and early
Georgian period are among the most satisfying ever
made. The columnar variety of the Charles II
period, with a shaft of thin, pressed silver filled
with amalgam to resist denting, was made for a
short while after 1700, overlapping a greatly
superior design which had first occurred in the
reign of William III, at the opening of the stylistic
phase designated by the name of Queen Anne. This
type, which was of heavy, cast metal and had a shaft
which comprised bold, simple mouldings of great
artistic assurance, had a self-confident dignity
characteristic of the period. Some were polygonal
like much other contemporary plate, the angles
running over the pyramidal base up to the socket.
Most were of circular section, the bases, of a
modified square shape, generally having a shallow,
saucer-like depression in the centre (Fig. 5). Even
when divorced from their function, these candlesticks are superb objects in their own right.

MUSEUMS AND COLLECTIONS

Queen Anne silver may be seen at the following:

Leeds:	Temple Newsam House
London:	Victoria and Albert Museum
Norwich:	The Castle Museum

FURTHER READING

English Silver Drinking Vessels, 600–1830 by
Douglas Ash, London, 1964.
English Domestic Silver by Charles Oman,
London, 1947.
Old English Silver by W. W. Watts, London, 1924.
An Illustrated History of English Plate by
Sir Charles Jackson, London, 1911.

Fig. 1 *Entrance Hall at Holkham Hall, Norfolk, by William Kent (1684–1748), 1734–59. Here the Palladian dependence on Roman architecture is unambiguously stated.*

The Grand Manner of the Palladians

Tim Rock

The Palladians conceived a style of architecture based on the principles of Andrea Palladio, seen through the English eyes of Inigo Jones, which shattered the canon of baroque taste

'Although variety and things new may please every one, yet they ought not to be done contrary to the precepts of art and contrary to that which reason dictates . . .', stated Andrea Palladio in his *Quattro Libri dell' Architettura* (1570). It might have been the first salvo fired in the Whiggish rejection of Wren. Indeed, it might have come from the pen of the Earl of Shaftesbury himself, who, as one of the most vocal of the advocates for the Rule of Taste, wrote in 1712 from Italy: 'Thro' several reigns we have patiently seen the noblest publick Buildings perish (if I may say so) under the Hand of one single Court Architect; who if he had been able to profit by Experience, wou'd long since, at our expence, have prov'd the greatest Master in the World. But I question whether our Patience is like to hold much longer. Hardly as the Publick now stands, shou'd we bear to see a Whitehall treated like a Hampton Court, or even a new Cathedral like St. Paul's'. (A letter concerning the Art and Science of Design, 1712.) It was to Palladio that

the text rendered in English by Nicholas Dubois.

The two books were complementary. They were unanimous in their views on Palladio: 'the *ne plus ultra* of his art', adumbrated Campbell; 'the fount of the true rules, unknown even to Michel Angelo and Brunelleschi', affirmed Leoni. They extolled the virtues of Inigo Jones – it was no accident that they both appeared in 1715, the centenary of Jones' return from Italy with Palladio's original designs ready to sow Palladianism on English soil. They bore their Whig allegiance proudly on their frontispieces. And they were judiciously dedicated to George I – from the architects of reformed Britain to the architect elect of reform.

Vitruvius Britannicus provided, at exactly the right moment, a unique conspectus of English country houses considered as architecture and not as mere topography. Campbell was self-appointed expositor of the new Palladianism, and the country-house boom of the 1720s came at just the right moment to provide him with his platform. With a nice sense of salesmanship that would make today's Royal Institute of British Architects turn pale at his scarce-concealed self-advertisement, Campbell followed his eulogies of past mastery with his own design, Wanstead House, then just nearing completion. It was pure, it was classical, it was large and it was conveniently near London. As such, it was much visited and much admired. It is no exaggeration to say that this one classical building changed the course of country-house design in England for half a century. Sir John Summerson

*Fig. 2 **Palladian Bridge** at Wilton House, by the ninth Earl of Pembroke and his Clerk-of-Works, Roger Morris, 1736–37. The Earl of Pembroke, known as the 'Architect Earl', was a gifted amateur. The extent of his activity is, however, hard to assess and most of the credit for this beautifully proportioned bridge must go to Morris.*

*Fig. 3 **Marble Hill**, Twickenham, possibly by Lord Herbert. Built 1724–29 for Henrietta Howard, mistress of George II.*

those reforming the 'architecture of Whig Britain' turned.

If Shaftesbury, the politician, expressed accurately the Whig case for diverting English taste from the French, Dutch and baroque models of Wren, Hawksmoor, Vanbrugh and Archer (who were all old or retiring by the time that he wrote), it was the publication of two books in 1715 that established the direction the architectural revolution should take – that of heroic revival.

The first was by a Scotsman – Colen Campbell. One hundred superbly elegant engravings of British classical buildings appeared, bound together and given the classical title of *Vitruvius Britannicus*. A second and a third volume appeared over the next decade. The second book was an annotated translation of *Quattro Libri*, the work of their chosen hero, Palladio. The plates and the introduction were by Giacomo Leoni and

has rightly called it 'a key building of its age'.

The façade of Wanstead – now demolished – was an unaffected reinterpretation of Inigo Jones. The portico comprised 'a just Hexastyle, the first yet practised in this manner in the Kingdom'. The pediment was borne on a lofty, elegant Corinthian order and the hall inside echoed it. 'No previous English house had displayed such spectacular and rational loyalty to Rome'.

The inspiration of Wanstead radiated far and wide: Moor Park in Hertfordshire, designed by James Thornhill, was among the first of a 'crop of fine porticos'; next came Wentworth Woodhouse, by Henry Flitcroft; next, Nostell Priory by James Paine; followed by Prior Park, Bath, by John Wood the Elder. To a man, these architects were all young, and to them Wanstead was 'the finest classical house in Britain' – in short, the apex of innovation. They were all to be the architectural

Fig. 4 **Wanstead House, Essex,** by Colen Campbell (d.1729), c.1715. (Now demolished.) Engraving by T. Simpson. Campbell was the father of Palladianism and author of the great Palladian work Vitruvius Britannicus (1715). Wanstead became the model for the English Palladian country house.

Fig. 5 **Staircase** at 44, Berkeley Square, London, by William Kent, 1742–44.
This impressive staircase is one of the most spatially exciting examples of Palladian design.

leaders of the next generation but, for the time being, Campbell was their star.

He moved on to design Houghton for Sir Robert Walpole – a leading Whig and a man of taste with purse to match. But Houghton was less Palladian, more Inigo Jones. Its model was Wilton House – a favourite of Campbell – and he unflinchingly stole the Wilton corner towers for Houghton. With its ravishing staircase and its cubic hall, in imitation of Jones' Queen's House at Greenwich, it is a totally Campbellian version of Palladianism.

Lord Burlington – the patron of the Palladian movement

But Campbell was capable of a much purer form. At Mereworth and at Stourhead, the Palladian villa was interpreted with a fine sense of translation from the gentler climate of Italy to the ruder, wetter weather of England – hence the dome-incorporated flues of corner fireplaces, and the closing of the dome itself. Mereworth closely resembles the Villa Rotonda, marginally enlarged.

If the books by Campbell and Leoni served to inaugurate the Palladian movement, Richard Boyle, third Earl of Burlington and fourth Earl of Cork (1694–1753) was its guide and theoretician. As a result of his zeal, Palladianism became the national style.

As a subscriber to *Vitruvius Britannicus*, his

ton House during much of this time. Their great work together was Chiswick. Here, the inspired amateur, Burlington, was responsible for the architecture and the landscape, Flitcroft for the draughtsmanship, and Kent for the interiors. Like Mereworth, it was modelled on the Villa Rotonda. But Burlington reduced the plan where Campbell had enlarged it. 'The dimensions in Palladio's book of sixty-eight Venetian feet were used exactly for English feet'. As Sir John Summerson has pointed out, 'the result is a toylike unreality and, in the richer parts, an extreme delicacy of detail'. The rooms encircle *en suite* a central octagon and the Thiene Palace at Vicenza, which had influenced Campbell at Houghton, produced at Chiswick a long apsidal-ended room approached from two circular or octagonal rooms. This innovation was later to enter the mainstream of English country-house architecture, *via* the Adam brothers. Chiswick was not merely innovatory, in a subtle but influential way; it was an architectural hot-house. When finally finished in 1736, the villa was adorned with Burlington's rich collection of paintings, sculpture and architectural drawings and was furnished by Kent and possibly Flitcroft; Pope described it as 'the finest thing the sun has shone upon'. Horace Walpole, who like Pope was a near neighbour of the Earl, more guardedly pronounced the house 'a model of taste, if too little to live in, too large to hang on a watch'.

Burlington, meanwhile, had passed on to the Assembly Rooms at York, where he had skilfully adapted the master's classical theme for an Egyptian Hall and Kent, under Burlington's patronage, had in the same period been appointed Master Carpenter to the Office of Works.

The spread of Palladianism owed much to the spate of architectural publications

By 1729, when Campbell died, leaving no acknowledged Palladian successor, Kent had firmly gravitated towards architecture. In 1735, he was appointed Master Mason. The commissions continued to flow: Devonshire House, London; the Royal Mews; the White House at Kew; and Stowe. But this high peak of Palladianism was dominated by his palatial designs for the Houses of Parliament. Here, Palladianism became a far cry from Palladio – a reassertion of the English gift of picturesque pragmatism. The designs found favour with Burlington. Indeed, their monumental eloquence must owe much of their inspiration to Burlington as a collaborator. Their splendour is all Kent. They were, alas, never to reach fruition. Enough of Kent's official designs were built to make it almost as much a matter for regret as the abandonment of Inigo Jones' grandiose Whitehall designs a century earlier. Nonetheless, Kent's Treasury (1734) and Horse Guards (1751) remain as elegant memorials to the Rule of Taste.

The spread of Palladianism into every corner of England owed much to the spate of architectural publications – not least Kent's own *Designs of Inigo Jones* (1727) (a Burlington-appointed task), Ware's translation of Palladio's *Quattro Libri* (1736), and Burlington's edition of Palladio's

Mansell Collection

A. F. Kersting

extensive tour of Italy in search of the true Palladianism in 1719 was undertaken with Campbell's enthusiasm in mind. He had, in any case, by this time employed Campbell to re-model Burlington House (unpicking the then-unfashionable Gibbs' work). His visit confirmed his own interest. On his return, he purchased original drawings, by both Palladio and Inigo Jones, from John Talman. He befriended William Kent and used his powers as a nobleman to open up the Office of Works to confirmed Palladians. Campbell became Deputy, and Nicholas Dubois Master Mason, in 1719. Thus, Palladianism became first the architecture of influence, and later the official style.

William Kent, so far, had a reputation as an 'heroic' painter and an interior decorator – at Kensington Palace, at Ditchley, at Houghton, at Chiswick, at Mereworth and at Raynham Hall, Norfolk. And Burlington had kept Kent at Burling-

6

8

9

7

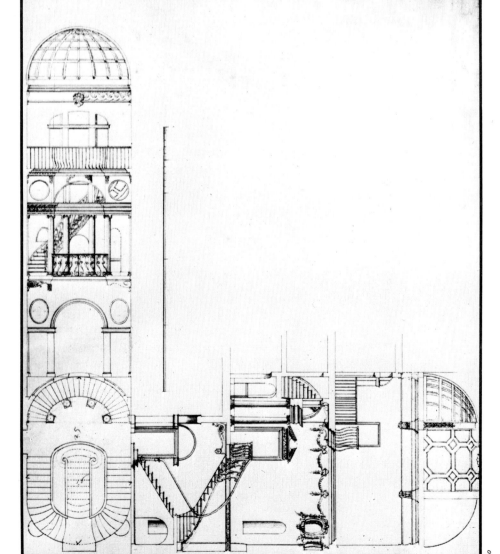

drawings from antiquity, *Fabbriche Antiche* (1730).

Inevitably these books were bought and used by the growing band of architectural amateurs of whom Burlington was the greatest. The eighteenth century was, after all, the age of the amateur, Palladianism the plaything of the dilettante.

The second generation of Palladians continued to refine the style

Coke of Holkham, Lord Herbert, ninth Earl of Pembroke, and Sir Rowland Winn were all amateurs and they were all gifted. Coke directed and inspired Kent and Burlington in his Holkham projects, and Herbert took personal charge of the restoration of Wilton with Roger Morris as his Clerk-of-Works, and may even have designed Marble Hill and White Lodge, Richmond. But outstanding among them all was Sir Thomas Robinson of Rokeby, who designed bridges, the west wing of Castle Howard and the main front of Claydon, Buckinghamshire. Kent's influence is to be seen in his Castle Howard, with which the abortive design for the Houses of Parliament has some affinity, and his Claydon design is even more grandiose. His rococo personality, scarcely suppressed by his passionate pursuit of Palladianism, contained within it the dangers which Pope had earlier prophesied in his *Epistle to Lord Burlington* of 1731:

'*You show us, Rome was glorious, not profuse,*
And pompous buildings once were things of use;
Yet shall (my Lord) your just, your noble rules,
Fill half the land with imitating Fools'.

After Campbell, Kent and Burlington, the second generation of Palladians – Henry Flitcroft and Isaac Ware – gave the movement a new lease of life. It was they who successfully married the greater house and the villa. And their successors, Sir Robert Taylor and Sir William Chambers, con-

Fig. 6 *Mereworth Castle, Kent, by Colen Campbell, 1722–25. Mereworth is perhaps the most successful of the Palladian designs based on the Villa Rotunda.*

Fig. 7 *Drawing for the Staircase at 44, Berkeley Square by William Kent, 1742–44. (Royal Institute of British Architects' Collection.)*

Fig. 8 *Clandon Park, Surrey, by Giacomo Leoni (c.1686–1748), 1731–35. Born in Venice, Leoni settled in England. He published a translation of Palladio's writings in 1715.*

Fig. 9 *Ceiling of the Entrance Hall (detail), Clandon Park by Leoni.*

Fig. 10 *Stourhead House, Wiltshire, the portico, by Colen Campbell, 1722.*

Fig. 11 *Houghton Hall, Norfolk, by Colen Campbell, 1721. Houghton Hall was built on a vast and imposing scale. The rusticated ground floor lifts up the main design, adding to its grandeur.*

Fig. 12 *Portrait of Lord Burlington (1694–1748) by Jonathan Richardson, c.1717–20. Oil on canvas, 57 x 46 ins. (National Portrait Gallery, London.)*

tinued to refine the English Palladian style. Their plans broke the bounds of Palladian precedent, while their façades became more fastidious and weaker. But they were at the end of the line. While Burlington was directing the Palladian movement (he continued by the sheer force of his intellectual lead to influence it long after his death), Horace Walpole was directing a different revival from a nearby camp, Strawberry Hill, and, a century after Palladianism had been born, England became a stylistic free-for-all. Burlington would have found it a world impossible for the flowering of his rational revival.

And yet, it was his intimate (and in the eighteenth century, this bond between Kent and his aristocratic master must have been rare) and most original pupil, Kent, who had himself indulged in Gothic at Esher, Hampton Court, Laughton Place, Rousham, Westminster Hall and Gloucester Cathedral. Kent's excursions must in some sense have added fuel to the fire that later consumed the classical canons of perfection, as intellectualised by the scion of the Whig aristocracy. In any case, the pendulum of fashion which had revived the ideals of Inigo Jones and Palladio was bound to move in the opposite direction once the Whig party, with which it had become inextricably identified, lost impetus. Political stability and architectural regularity had satiated English taste. The pendulum swung again. Out went Palladianism. In came the rococo style. Out went the Rococo, in Gothic, in Egyptian – in a host of styles. English Palladianism was the product of political stability. It was anti-novelty, pro-perfection. It was lucky in its perfectors, and it was engaging in its betrayers. What more can one ask of a style?

ARTHUR NEGUS
COLLECTORS' ITEM

HORSE BRASSES

It has been suggested that horse brasses are descended from the plate armour and heraldic harness carried by war-horses in the Middle Ages. Horse furniture with no associations with battle was also used, and the eighteenth- and nineteenth-century brasses so widely collected today are, in fact, descended from the iron and pewter decorations used by farmers and guilds.

Early brasses were worked by hand, and they can be distinguished by the hammer-marks which are likely to be most noticeable on the back of the brass, generally left unpolished. These brasses often carried designs of heraldic origin: the lion of Scotland and the leopard of England were popular motifs, as well as the bear of Warwick and the white hart of Richard II. Cast brasses appeared in the early 1830s and were made in enormous numbers. Old patterns such as wheatsheaves, elm trees, acorns or bunches of flowers were gradually superseded by more complicated designs of stars, diamonds and wheels.

There was a fashion in the 1840s and '50s for commemorative and portrait brasses depicting kings and queens, famous historical figures and politicians of the day, such as Cobden, Disraeli and Lord Derby. County symbols were also widely used: the Staffordshire knot and Suffolk windmill were among the commonest. After 1870, horse brasses were mass produced and machine stamped; these later brasses are much lighter in weight than the cast variety, and much less valuable. County and local motifs were swamped by crude representations of Kitchener and Gladstone, railway bridges and Derby winners.

It is important that the brasses should be mounted on the original leather straps. Most martingales, as the straps which prevent the horse from throwing back its head are called, have three or four brasses mounted on them; sets of five, two and one are sometimes found, and sets of six or more are very rare indeed. Usually these sets were bought complete from the saddler, although some farmers preferred to make up their own sets.

Hints to Collectors

There are so many fakes on the market that it has become something of a challenge to find and successfully to identify original brasses. Most fakes follow old designs, but they can usually be identified by their light weight, since they are machine stamped from sheet brass. One test is to examine the bottom edge at the back of the brass; there should be signs of wear here, where the action of the horse caused the brass to bounce against the leather.

Dr. B. Lloyd Bisley Collection: Angelo Hornak

Private Collection: Miki Slingsby

Prices

Prices depend largely on the knowledge and enthusiasm of the seller. Rare brasses of proven antiquity can cost as much as £20, while more common items fetch as little as £1.

Above left: **Martingales** with their brasses showing traditional pattern types, heart and shield motifs and a variety of horse designs. The latter include a horse's head in a horseshoe frame, the horse passant in a circular perforated frame and the 'Prancing Horse of Kent' — an old Saxon banner device. The centre martingale shows above its crescent brasses a ram motif which is a company trade-mark.

Above right: **Horse brasses** of a fairly common type. One, top centre, commemorates Queen Victoria's Golden Jubilee; that below is a portrait of Lord Nelson, and on the left is Noah's Ark and on the right a heraldic lion. Nelson seems to have been the most popular national figure as far as the brass-founders were concerned, outdistancing Wellington, Gladstone and the other notables whose profiles appeared on brasses.
(Harness by courtesy Young and Company's Brewery, Wandsworth, London.)

Below: **Shoulder-pieces and face-pieces** showing traditional heart, heraldic fleur-de-lis and geometrical shield designs. The brass on the right depicts King Edward VII in profile and the brass in the centre, above, was issued to commemorate the Treaty of Versailles (1919).

Opposite: **Flyers, swingers and unmounted brasses.** The Scottish 'double' flyer on the left, above, is in nickel. The brass in the centre, below, unusual heart motif while that on its left is one of more than twenty different locomotive designs known to have been issued, and that on its right is a merit brass which bears the inscription 'Kensington Horse and Cart Parade 1914'.

Dr. B. Lloyd Bisley Collection: Angelo Hornak

Chelsea Porcelain

John Raison

Chelsea, possibly the earliest English porcelain factory, produced fine and beautifully decorated wares, largely inspired by Meissen and the Orient

Fig. 1 *The Music Lesson,* marked with a gold anchor, Chelsea, c.1765. Height 16 ins. This delightful scene is based on a painting by François Boucher called L'Agréable Leçon. (Victoria and Albert Museum, London.)

Fig. 2 *La Nourrice,* also called *the Chellsea Nurs,* marked with a red anchor, Chelsea, c.1755. Height 7½ ins. Derived from a sixteenth-century earthenware model made near Fontainebleau, this famous piece has a wonderfully tranquil charm. (Victoria and Albert Museum.)

Fig. 3 *Goat and Bee Jug,* marked with an incised triangle, Chelsea, c.1745. Height 4½ ins. This jug is based on a silver design of the period. (Cecil Higgins Art Gallery, Bedford, by permission of the Trustees.)

Despite the long history of porcelain-making in China and Japan, it was not until the sixteenth century that an imitation was made in Europe. This so-called Medici porcelain, like the later manufacture at Rouen in the 1670s, was not the true hard-paste but a soft-paste, based primarily on glass rather than on rock. However, in the early part of the eighteenth century, J. F. Böttger at Meissen discovered how to make true, or hard-paste, porcelain. Böttger's court appointment was primarily to pursue the alchemist's dream of making gold, but from the large quantity and fine quality of porcelain produced for Augustus the Strong, it may be assumed that the latter was well pleased with the alternative discovery.

In England, the search for porcelain was backed by no such royal wealth and, indeed, the number of failures and bankruptcies among people involved in its production during the second half of the eighteenth century was distressingly large. That Chelsea in its early days may have had some sort of aristocratic backing is illustrated by the interest taken in its activities by Sir Everard Fawkener, secretary to the Duke of Cumberland (the 'Butcher of Culloden', and brother to George II). But, if this is a fact, Chelsea was alone in this among the early English factories, and any such direct support can only have been a marginal factor in its progress.

A Huguenot silversmith from Flanders, Nicholas Sprimont, provided the main inspiration for this new Chelsea factory in the 1740s, possibly aided by a chemist named Briand and a fellow Huguenot, a jeweller named Gouyn. Sprimont himself had registered his mark as a silversmith in 1742, but he turned his attentions at an early stage to the manufacture of porcelain, for his earliest dated pieces bear the date 1745. One piece even has a date which has been interpreted as 1743, but there is no agreement on this.

By about 1750, at least six soft-paste factories had sprung up in this country, and of these it is not unlikely that Chelsea was the first. Certainly no other porcelain of English manufacture carries a date earlier than 1745. Equally true is that the early Chelsea porcelain was of a very attractive quality, highly translucent and based on glass ingredients. A number of pieces which were produced in this first period, the 'Triangle Period', so-called because of the frequent use of an incised triangle as a mark, bear close affinities to Sprimont's silverwork. This was of high quality, in style not at all typical of the work of other silversmiths in this country at the time, and showing a particular emphasis on scroll-work and shell motifs. These features appear in some of his porcelain pieces such as sauce-boats and salt-cellars, although the curious cream-jugs, the bottom part of which were moulded in the form of a goat and which usually have a bee above the goat's head (Fig. 3), derive from the work of other silversmiths.

The majority of the products of this period, which takes us more or less to the end of the decade, were as attractive in shape as the porcelain itself is pleasing to handle, and include salts with a cray-fish modelled across one side of them, teapots, coffee-pots and beakers, with or without handles, moulded with overlapping leaves or with a tea plant motif, and shallow strawberry dishes with applied leaves and flowers and painted with butter-flies, insects and further floral decoration. Many of

4

5

6

7

8

Fig. 4 *Scent-Bottle, Gold Anchor
Period, Chelsea, c.1760.
Height* 3⅛ *ins.
Not only were scent bottles the
delight of London in the latter
half of the eighteenth century,
they were also exported in large
numbers to the Continent where
the gaiety and liveliness that
were such a hallmark of Chelsea
made them equally popular.
(Author's Collection.)*

Fig. 5 (Left) *Plate, Raised
Anchor Period, Chelsea,
c.1750–52. Diameter* 7½ *ins.*
(Right) *Plate, Chelsea,
c.1752–54. Diameter 9 ins.
The decoration on these plates
is in imitation of the Kakiemon
style. There are spur marks from
the kiln on the bases.
(Author's Collection.)*

Fig. 6 *Octagonal bowl and
saucer, possibly by J. H. O'Neale,
Red Anchor Period, Chelsea,
c.1755. Diameter of saucer 5 ins.,
height of bowl 2 ins.
O'Neale painted many animal
subjects for Worcester at a later
date, but never surpassed his
early work at Chelsea.
(Author's Collection.)*

Fig. 7 *Madonna and Child by
Joseph Willems, marked with a
red anchor, Chelsea, c.1755.
Height* 8⅛ *ins.
The probable source for this
design was a painting by Van
Dyck. Note the serpent emerging
beside the globe.
(Cecil Higgins Art Gallery.)*

Fig. 8 *Farmyard clock-case,
marked with a red anchor,
Chelsea, c.1755. Height* 8¼ *ins.
The figures of the Red Anchor
Period were the glory of Chelsea
porcelain. The modelling and
skilful attention to detail
reached a standard never
surpassed in English wares.
This delightful example still holds
its original clock, unlike a
similar case to be seen at the
British Museum in London.
(Author's Collection.)*

the pieces of this period are left in the white, but when enamelled the colouring and patterns are often in imitation of the prunus, bamboo and other plants normally found in decoration on the porcelain of the Kakiemon potters of Arita (Fig. 5), as well as their strange 'tygers' and weird birds.

Figures, invariably in the white, were also made during the early years, and these too derive largely from Oriental originals. Some remarkable, grotesque teapots consist of a Chinaman riding either on a parrot or on a serpent, which represents the spout. Pu-Tai, sometimes referred to as the Corpulent Monk, at other times as the God of Wealth and Contentment, is not so pleasing to Western tastes as, for instance, a fine figure of a fisherman, modelled after a painting by François Boucher. A French origin for the teapots with overlapping leaves, mentioned above, should also be noted, for soft-paste factories had been in existence for varying lengths of time at St. Cloud, Mennecy, Chantilly and Vincennes. This last, being transferred to Sèvres, became the great royal factory of France.

The trident and the anchor: both marks show an association with the sea

The ensuing period is characterised by the frequent use of a raised anchor, and in one form or another the use of an anchor as a mark was retained during and even beyond the life of Chelsea as an independent factory. Another mark, very rarely used in the Triangle Period, is a crown with a trident through it. This has, in common with the anchor, an association with the sea, but the reason for its adoption is equally obscure.

The porcelain used during the Raised Anchor Period contains less lead than the earlier creations, and in consequence is less glassy and more opaque. This change in composition was already under way during the Triangle Period, thus emphasising the fact that considerable overlapping of material, form and decoration takes place between the various periods known by their most frequently used marks. The quality of Raised Anchor products remained for the most part high, approximately covering the years 1749–53. Figure subjects include a series of birds, usually coloured, taken from the recently published *Natural History of Uncommon Birds* by G. Edwards (Fig. 9); imitations of Meissen artisan characters, such as the strongly modelled *Hurdy-Gurdy Player*; figures from the Italian Comedy, also largely inspired by Meissen; the famous *Chellsea Nurs,* or *La Nourrice* (Fig. 2), derived from a sixteenth-century pottery figure made at Fontainebleau; a pug dog, Oriental figures such as Kuan Yin, busts such as a child's head and that of the Duke of Cumberland (both in white), and a figure of a gardener's companion. Much of the decoration of these figures and of the contemporary wares appears to have been carried out in William Duesbury's London studio, prior to his becoming chief proprietor of the Derby factory.

The wares of this period continued to show strong Oriental inspiration in their decoration, but the influence of Meissen became increasingly more prominent. Certain kinds of flower decoration and landscape scenes are clearly of Meissen origin and indeed much of the Oriental type decoration had

picked up Meissen mannerisms in the process of being translated on to Chelsea porcelain.

However, the most interesting and attractive decoration is the fable painting which appears on cups, saucers, dishes, teapots and other wares. Two names in particular have been suggested as likely painters of these lively animal scenes: William Duvivier, from Tournai, and Jefferyes Hamett O'Neale, who much later did similar work on Worcester wares. If the original fable painter was indeed O'Neale, it can fairly be said that the matching of animal decoration to porcelain was never better accomplished than in his early Chelsea work (Fig. 6). Another type of decoration of purely English inspiration is known as the 'Hans Sloane plants'. These were largely taken from the drawings of Philip Miller, head gardener at the botanical gardens founded in Chelsea by Sir Hans Sloane.

The range of shapes for table wares also widened. Prominent among these are dishes in silver shapes, hexagonal bowls with everted rims, peach-shaped cups with or without stalk handles, all-white plates and beakers with prunus blossom in relief in imitation of *blanc de Chine*, hexagonal vases and other vase and bottle shapes.

During the latter part of this period the raised anchor is sometimes painted over in red, but by 1752, a red anchor, not in relief, but painted direct on to the glaze had become more common. The so-called Red Anchor Period lasted until about 1758, but its use continued occasionally for several years afterwards into the final era of Chelsea as an independent factory, namely the Gold Anchor Period of 1758–69.

Small, decorative items show skilful attention to detail

The figures of the Red Anchor Period are perhaps the chief glory of English porcelain (Fig. 8), derivative though many of them are from the work of Kaendler and Reinicke at Meissen. The Chelsea adaptations were probably created mainly by Joseph Willems from Brussels who stayed with the factory for most of its independent existence. The same Italian Comedy and artisan themes were favoured and developed, while classical, religious, animal and bird figures were also produced (Fig. 7). The modelling reached a standard never surpassed in English porcelain and the same skilful attention to detail is shown in the Red Anchor scent-bottles, in human, animal and bird form.

It may be noted in passing that scent-bottles had also been produced by the 'Girl in a Swing' factory between 1749 and 1754. The relationship between this factory and Chelsea is not clear, but it is at least possible that the bulk of the workmen employed came from Chelsea, and its guiding light was probably the jeweller Charles Gouyn. Besides the neatly made scent-bottles, there are also some much rarer figures, modelled in a unique and somewhat dainty style, as well as some still rarer wares, some of which were made for the dressing-rather than the dinner-table. Formerly, these products were often attributed to Chelsea, but whatever the connection between the two factories it now seems probable that the 'Girl in a Swing' establishment was altogether separate.

To return to Chelsea proper, table-wares of the

Red Anchor Period continued to display Oriental, Continental and fable motifs and are often recognised by the 'moons' which can be seen in the porcelain when held up to the light, and also by the small spur marks on bases where the pieces . rested in firing kilns. These features also occur in the earlier products of Chelsea, but the handsome animal and vegetable tureens with their stands are a new development. They may take the form of pineapples, melons, lemons, asparagus bundles, cauliflowers, rabbits, pigeons, ducks, swans, eels, boars and even carp or plaice.

Chelsea also produced a limited quantity of wares decorated with under-glaze blue in the Chinese style, sometimes marked with a blue anchor. Perhaps these products were not considered quite sophisticated enough for the relatively

9

A. C. Cooper

Fig. 9 *Great Spotted Cuckoo,*
one of a pair of which one is
marked with a red raised anchor,
Chelsea, c.1752. Height 7½ ins.
The design for this exquisite bird
was taken, together with many
other birds, from the Natural
History of Uncommon Birds *by*
George Edwards, a collection of
coloured engravings which was
published in London in 1743–47.
The decoration was probably
done by William Duesbury, who
was later to become proprietor of
the Derby factory.
(Author's Collection.)

wealthy customers whom Sprimont sought to attract, and far more blue and white of this period survives from Bow and Worcester. That there was no lack of quality in the Chelsea blue and white is illustrated by the continued use today of one of their few early Chinese-style patterns.

Sprimont's declining health and his frequent absences led to a lowering of standards in some, though by no means all, respects. The Gold Anchor Period is characterised by a change of taste towards the elaborate and the opulent. The coloured grounds which Meissen and Sèvres had developed became popular, while figures were likely to stand on rococo scroll bases and to be bedecked with bocage, a background of flowers and leaves. Gold was used frequently, on wares as well as figures, but the quality of the porcelain had in fact changed during the Red Anchor Period with the introduction of bone ash, an ingredient which, although rejected by Dr. Wall and his partners at Worcester, has generally survived in use in English porcelain to this day.

The range of wares widened considerably, and shapes, in particular in the case of vases and jars for purely ornamental purposes, became highly fanciful, often with flamboyant scroll handles. Sèvres became now the main influence behind these objects and much of the decoration of birds and fruit, often applied in James Giles' studio, took its inspiration from the French porcelain painters. Figure painting by John Donaldson on a number of vases derived likewise from Boucher.

Many small objects were exported to the Continent

White figures were by now very rare and the richness of colour generally used often, but by no means always, concealed less careful modelling. But the animals which adorned the fable candlesticks, for instance, were lively, if sometimes cruel, and liveliness is certainly a characteristic of the popular *Ranelagh Dancers.* Scent bottles (Fig. 4) continued to delight in London and elsewhere, and these and other small objects such as needle-cases, *bonbonnières* and seals were exported freely to the Continent.

By 1770 Chelsea had passed into the hands of William Duesbury of Derby and its history now became part of the history of that factory. The so-called Chelsea-Derby Period has more aptly been re-named Derby-Chelsea or Duesbury-Chelsea, but the finest days were over and little further in the way of significant innovation can be said to have emanated from the London factory. The main influences of the ensuing decade came from the Court of Louis XVI, typified by swags and urns on table-wares and rather sentimental figures.

By 1784, Duesbury concentrated the manufacture of porcelain in Derby and thus, about forty years after the beginning of its brilliant history, Chelsea came to its end.

MUSEUMS AND COLLECTIONS
Collections of Chelsea porcelain may be seen at the following:
GREAT BRITAIN
Bedfordshire: Cecil Higgins Art Gallery, Bedford
                      Luton Hoo
Cambridge: Fitzwilliam Museum
London: British Museum
             Victoria and Albert Museum
U.S.A.
Boston, Mass.: Boston Museum of Fine Arts

FURTHER READING
English Porcelain, 1745–1850, edit. by R. J. Charleston, London, 1965: 'Chelsea Porcelain' by J. V. G. Mallet.
Chelsea and other English Porcelain, Pottery and Enamel in the Irwin Untermyer Collection by Yvonne Hackenbroch, London, 1957.
The Gold Anchor Wares by F. Severne Mackenna, Leigh-on-Sea, Essex, 1952.
The Red Anchor Wares by F. Severne Mackenna, Leigh-on-Sea, 1951.
The Triangle and Raised Anchor Wares by F. Severne Mackenna, Leigh-on-Sea, 1948.
Chelsea Porcelain by William King, London, 1922.

1

K. Hoddle

Therle Hughes

FASHIONS IN FANS

Fig. 1 *The New Casino Fan,
English, late eighteenth century.
Pen, ink and water-colour.
The central inscription on this
useful fan reads, 'The New
Casino Fan Containing the
Laws, Rules, etc., of that
fashionable game as it is now
played in the Polite circles'.
(Victoria and Albert Museum,
London.)*

Ladies flirted and passed secret messages with them, blushed and protected themselves from 'unsuitable' sights with them — there were fans made for every occasion

In 1709 Queen Anne granted a charter to English fan-makers, whose Worshipful Company continues to this day. By that date, widespread demand for fans had ensured that the craft was well established in Britain, the native talent being enlivened and enriched by the influx of French Huguenots from the 1680s onwards. Indeed, the creation of a company was a direct result of the public's increasing demand for the fashionable toy.

Here, as in other crafts, there was alarm at the quality and quantity of imports from the Orient, where folding paper fans had originated over a thousand years before. In 1702, for example, an advertisement offered 'For sale, by the Candle, at the Marine Coffee House in Birchin Lane . . .

Forty Thousand Fans of Sundry Sorts . . .'.

Today, nevertheless, a Queen Anne fan is a treasured rarity. Far more collectors concern themselves with the changing shapes and styles of early and later Georgian fashion – always remembering that Victorians, too, loved the flash and flutter of a fan and borrowed freely from earlier modes.

Charles II and his Court, returning to England from the Continent in 1660, quickly popularised the folding fan. French influence established the fashion for the fan mount, or leaf of skin or paper, richly painted with boldly coloured figures, often enacting a classical scene in a dreary landscape setting to cover the whole sweep of the mount. Such a fan might have sticks of carved mother of pearl secured at the base or 'head' with a paste-mounted rivet and protected by guards or panaches, the more substantial end-sticks, inset with gold ornaments or jewels.

Collectors attempting to date eighteenth-century English specimens note not only a continuing love of magnificence but also details that changed over the years. It is a particular pleasure of the fan that it was produced in an immense range of

2

K. Hoddle

Fig. 2 (Above) **Painted Fan**, *English*, c.1730–50. *Paper leaf with water-colour, the ivory sticks and guards also painted.* (Below) **Painted Fan**, *English, eighteenth century. Paper leaf with water-colour, the ivory sticks decorated with red foil.* (*London Museum.*)

Fig. 3 **Painted Fan**, *English, late eighteenth century. Silk painted in water-colour and decorated with sequins. The guards are of wood, and the sticks are alternately of pierced wood and gilt ivory.* (*Victoria and Albert Museum.*)

Fig. 4 **Chapel Fan**, *English, 1796. Engraved paper mount and wooden sticks.*
Fans were made for every conceivable purpose in the eighteenth century, including church-going, for which the more frivolous subjects of everyday life were considered unsuitable. (*Victoria and Albert Museum.*)

qualities and prices. One maker could lavish superb materials and skill on a gift that would be treasured for years, while another chased after the briefest nonsense that happened to be in the news one day and forgotten the next.

In Queen Anne's day, fans were large and the finest mounts were of specially prepared vellum or kid, extremely thin and supple and known as chicken-skin. Others were of painted parchment, but more and more were of paper with outlines printed from an etched copper-plate which were then quickly hand-coloured. The paints used had to be elastic to avoid cracking: water-colours were given body and opacity with white and mixed with gum, which both ensured suppleness and contributed a delicate sheen.

Fans were smaller in the 1720s and 1730s but by the 1740s, they were in danger of becoming unwieldy. There were described by the *London Magazine* in 1744 as 'wonderfully increased in size from three-quarters of a foot to a foot and three-quarters or two feet'. By the 1720s, moreover, the mount had become narrower in proportion to the exposed part of the sticks. Early ornament consisted of a formal theme repeated on each stick, but this was gradually developed into a single unified pattern or picture over sticks that widened in square-shouldered outlines immediately below the mount to form a major part of the fan's ornament, carved, pierced or painted.

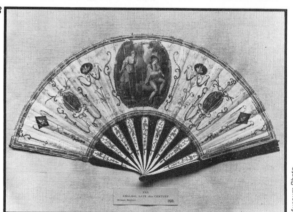

3

Museum Photo

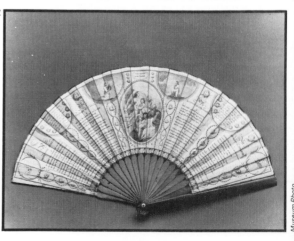

4

Museum Photo

5

Museum Photo

6

K. Hoddle

7

Museum Photo

8

K. Hoddle

Fig. 5 **Brisé Fan**, *English, late eighteenth century. Pierced and painted ivory, the sticks linked with silk ribbon.*
(Victoria and Albert Museum.)

Fig. 6 (Above) **Painted Fan**, *English, eighteenth century. Paper with water-colour, the ivory sticks painted and gilt.*
(Below) **Painted Fan**, *English, 1780–90. Painted paper leaf with carved and gilt-ivory sticks and guards.*
(London Museum.)

Fig. 7 **Fan Mount**, *English. Engraving depicting St. Bartholomew's Fair in 1721, published by J. F. Setchel.*
(Victoria and Albert Museum.)

Fig. 8 (Above) **Painted Fan**, *English, eighteenth century. Painted on perforated paper, the sticks of painted ivory.*
(Below) **Painted Fan** *depicting the Coliseum, eighteenth century.*
(London Museum.)

Some of the most costly sticks were of carved and pierced mother of pearl. This work achieved great scope later in the century when carved motifs and scenes were backed by thin shell in cameo effects of contrasting colour. Other sticks were of feather-light tortoise-shell given the metallic gleam of *piqué* work, or of resilient horn, now sometimes thought to be whalebone. Some were of sandalwood, sweetly scented and enriched with gold, or of white holly or pierced laburnum wood. And almost always, of course, wood was used for the stick blades concealed under the mount.

Carved guards encrusted with gold or studded with jewels

Ivory became especially popular for English fans following the French lead encouraged by Madame de Pompadour. Wafer-thin sticks of ivory would be pierced with daring elaboration and delicacy (Fig. 8, below), and the guards carved and encrusted with gold (Fig. 6) or studded with jewels. Sometimes one finds fretted patterns in the sticks echoing the theme of the mount, especially in such a collectors' delight as the Georgian marriage fan. Sometimes the ivory, too, was painted with the stipple touch of the miniature painter. It lent itself well to the absurdities of *chinoiserie* associated with the mid-century rococo ornament when

asymmetrical scroll-work might form cartouche effects around gay little figure scenes (Fig. 2).

Ivory at its finest is found in the *brisé* fan, a particular pleasure to many collectors (Fig. 5). Whereas the folding fan has a mount attached to sticks, to pleat into folds when closed, the *brisé* is composed entirely of sticks and guards, with as many as thirty blades exquisitely pierced or painted and linked around the perimeter with ribbons. It gained popularity in George I's reign and this increased towards the century's end. The delicacy of the fret-cut ivory or bone may remind the collector that some of the earliest, and latest, English fans bore mounts of filmy lace.

It must be acknowledged, however, that early Georgian fans in painted chicken-skin and fretted ivory seldom offer recognisably English characteristics. For these, the collector, like the vast majority of English women of their day, turns to the less pretentious printed fan. Once cheap paper fan mounts became acceptable for informal pleasure early in the eighteenth century, the fan mount printer-publisher came into his own. Collectors should look for the printed details giving his name and indicating that the fan mount was published in compliance with the copyright act of 1735 or a later variant (Fig. 7).

Mounts of hand-made paper could be sold for a shilling or two when the printed design was quickly finished by a group of girls around a table, each

K. Hoddle

K. Hoddle

Fig. 9 (Above) *The New Moralist Fan*, English, eighteenth century. Engraved on paper, with wooden sticks and guards.
The inscription on this attractive fan reads, 'The New Moralist Fan, or the Way to Wealth', and suitable scenes appear in the surrounding medallions.
(Below) *Miniature Fan*, English, late eighteenth century. Paper with water-colour, the sticks of painted ivory.
This toy fan was probably intended either to fit in a lady's purse, or to be used by a child. The loop of ribbon allowed the fan to dangle from the user's wrist, and was a common feature on fans at the end of the century. (London Museum.)

Fig. 10 *Fan Mounts*, English, eighteenth century. Paper with water-colour, the centre mount decorated with sequins.
These charming mounts are ready for use, but were never cut out and assembled. (Victoria and Albert Museum.)

adding a different colour. When the mount was pasted on plain sticks the complete fan might sell for half a crown. But the collector has to realise that a fan's sticks may be far older than a mount of this simple style, which was intended to last no longer than the popularity of the song it promoted, or the political cause it advocated. Etching, line engraving, stipple and even mezzotint printing might appear on mounts of vellum, paper or silk. The use of lithography dates a fan to the nineteenth century.

Every kind of occasion had its fan, from betrothal or baptism to military victory or the rise of Biaggini's air balloon, and it is intriguing today to try to decide the purpose of a specimen. Among costly fans some of the loveliest were marriage fans such as innumerable bridegrooms gave to their brides between about 1720 and 1800. In the 1730s and 1740s, especially, the finest would be commissioned from a master fan-maker, and would have jewelled guards of carved pearl or ivory, perhaps framing tiny portraits of the couple. The chicken-skin mount might be painted with a classical marriage theme among appropriate motifs or with some less specific idyll of lovers in a landscape. All kinds of symbolism proved acceptable from lovers' knots and nuptial torches to altars, doves and statues of Hymen.

Such a fan would be kept in a case covered in damp-defying shagreen (and it may be mentioned that such care is preferable to the too-prevalent display of old fans in glass cases at the mercy of light and damp or dry heat). Souvenir copies would be given to maids of honour and important guests, while still less costly but suitably ornamented fans with hand-coloured printed mounts might go to a wider circle of friends, some of whom might already have received fans to mark the pair's betrothal.

Anne, Crown Princess of England, daughter of George II, married Prince William IV of Orange in 1734. A splendid fan recording the event was painted with the Princess seated in a landscape surrounded by Cupids and Graces among trophies of Love and War. Fifty copies were ordered by George II. But cheaper fans for loyal souvenir hunters were also issued by such important London fan-makers as Gamble of St. Martin's Court.

Some fine Gamble marriage fans are on satin, the colours touched with gold. But by George III's day, marriage fans were for everybody. Mounts were printed with generally acceptable motifs such as views of churches. Many included blank spaces for the kind of individual naming that was then popular on loving-cups, plaques and other such objects.

Even for the mourner appropriate fans were devised, with sticks of grey-stained ivory, perhaps, and silver mounted guards to support leaves printed with weeping willows and memorial urns. Angelica Kauffmann is associated with some sentimental fan designs, but it is a mistake to imagine that important artists frequently engaged in commercial fan painting. This idea has arisen because fan printers knew the value of being able to attribute their designs to fashionable contemporary artists and decorators and the fan's hand colouring could obscure the printed outlines.

Church, fortune-telling or conversation fans

When a writer in the *Gentleman's Magazine* in 1753 complained that church-goers were being disturbed by fans showing Hogarthian scenes, more suitable themes were soon forthcoming. Church fans may be found printed with Bible illustrations or with the words of the Creed or the Psalms (Fig. 4). Indeed, one of the more curious aspects of the printed fan, especially in the second half of the century, is the endless flow of words, perhaps more to prompt conversation than to delight the eye. Much, of course, was childish nonsense, but it retains its interest still. Elaborate diagrammatical fortune-telling fans, for example, appear to have been popular throughout much of the century. The conversation fan offered a code of movements that enabled its user to spell out messages in defiance of her chaperone.

Often the theme of a printed fan gives a clue to its date, but the changes in style and treatment offer more general guidance. Thus the cabriolet fan was an innovation from France that may be dated from the introduction of the dashing little cabriolet carriage in 1755. The vehicle sometimes figures light-heartedly in the fan's painted decoration but the unusual feature here is the fan's shape, for its sticks support two or sometimes three narrow strips with space between them instead of a single leaf.

For more discreet peeping, this period approved

Fig. 11 (Below) **Fan Mount,**
*eighteenth century. Paper with
water-colour.*
*This lovely mount with its view
of St. Peter's Colonnade in Rome,
has been removed from its sticks,
the marks of which are still
visible. Fans depicting views of
scenic attractions were very
popular in the eighteenth
century.*
**Medallion from a Fan
Mount,** *English, eighteenth
century. Paper with water-colour.
The marks of the sticks are also
visible on this fragment, which
was probably one of several
medallions on a large fan.
(Victoria and Albert Museum.)*

the quizzing fan. This had inconspicuous peep-holes of transparent material such as net or mica among the border ornament of the leaf, so that a woman could modestly hide her face yet miss nothing of a *risqué* entertainment. Sometimes a fan's guards had tiny mirrors among their decoration, and there was obviously good sense for the short-sighted playgoer in the somewhat clumsy fan rivet containing a spy-glass. Inevitably, for play-goers, there were also fans printed with theatre and opera plans, indicating the seats or boxes taken by important subscribers.

The medallion fan can be easily recognised as belonging to the neo-classical style, which evolved in the 1760s, replacing rococo extravagance with gracious curves and ellipses (Fig. 11, below). A typical fan of this period would have plainer, narrower sticks, widely spaced, lacking the angular shoulders of earlier work or the rounded shoulders prevalent in the early nineteenth century. The medallions ornamented the leaf as three round or oval centres of interest, such as portraits, classical groups or scenes of pseudo-pastoral simplicity. The rest was more casually painted with trophies, wreaths or ribbons. Mounts of silk, which could glitter with tiny stitched-on metallic spangles whenever these were fashionable dress detail were also popular (Fig. 3). The favourite *brisé* fans, too, might have medallion ornament.

Another *brisé* design was the puzzle fan. In this, the many blades were so secured by their ribbons around the perimeter that only half of each could

be seen at a time and clever manipulation produced a succession of four different paintings. Even at the century's end, when the scantily dressed required muffs rather than fans, a small *brisé* fan might be squeezed into the tiny reticule along with handkerchief and smelling-bottle. Alternatively, like the flower posy, it might dangle on a ribbon from the wrist: hence the rivet loop for a ribbon which was introduced at this time (Fig. 9).

MUSEUMS AND COLLECTIONS
Collections of English fans may be seen at the following:
GREAT BRITAIN
Bath: Museum of Costume, Assembly Rooms
Birmingham: City Museum and Art Gallery
Glasgow: Art Gallery and Museum
Hereford: City Museum and Art Gallery
London: London Museum
Victoria and Albert Museum
Newcastle-Upon-Tyne: Laing Art Gallery and Museum
Nottingham: City Art Gallery and Museum

FURTHER READING
'English Fans' in **More Small Decorative Antiques** by Therle Hughes, London, 1962.
The Fan Book by MacIver Percival, London, 1920.
History of the Fan by G. Wooliscroft, London, 1910.

11

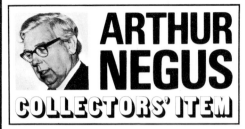

ARTHUR NEGUS COLLECTORS' ITEM

JACKFIELD POTTERY

There are records of potters working at Jackfield, near Iron Bridge in Shropshire, as early as 1560. Very little is known about the early products of the area, though, and they did not become widely known until the eighteenth century, after the arrival there of Richard Thursfield.

Thursfield came to Jackfield from Stoke-on-Trent in 1713 and started the manufacture of tea-sets, jugs and cow creamers of a red earth with a brilliant black glaze. These pieces were decorated in two ways, either with scroll-work and flowers in relief, or with flowers in oil paint; sometimes flat gilding was the only form of decoration. The bottoms of the pieces are often left unglazed, leaving the red body exposed. For most of the eighteenth century the ware was known by its local name of 'black decanters'; the appellation of 'Jackfield' did not come into general use until the nineteenth century. In 1780 the Thursfield family sold their factory to John Rose, who carried on the manufacture of the black-glazed pottery on a much larger scale. John Thursfield, Richard's son, established a second factory at Benthal in 1772, and this business flourished until Thursfield's successors, W. Pierce and Co., were bought out in 1818.

Hints to Collectors

Teapots, cups and saucers, teacaddies, jugs and mugs, are the easiest items to find. Despite the large output at the end of the eighteenth century, the ware is generally scarce. It should not be confused with Victorian black ware, which is coarser and does not have the red body characteristic of Jackfield. There are no marks on Jackfield ware, which is best identified by its lightness and crisp, simple shapes. The earlier pieces are noticeably smaller than the later ones, reflecting the scarcity and expense of tea.

Prices

There is very little variation in price between most pieces of Jackfield ware. Between £25 and £50 is the current price, although some of the larger jugs might cost more.

Above: *Jackfield Pottery* Left to right: a cream jug, a teacaddy with raised decoration which lacks its cork stopper, and a large beaker.

Below: *Three Jackfield Teapots.*

Opposite: *Jackfield wares* Left: *beaker with lid.* Centre: *cup and saucer, the cups following Chinese precedent and made without handles.* Right: *cream-jug.* Behind: *ewer.* Large wares of this type were used to carry water to the drawing-room to allow the lady of the house to wash her fine china herself. It has been suggested that this custom may have helped in preserving some of the fine china which appears in antique shops today from the clumsiness of maidservants in the last century.

Georgian Furniture Styles

John Kenworthy-Browne

Palladian furniture, like Palladian architecture, attempted to imitate in the fashionable mahogany specific shapes seen in Roman architecture

Fig. 1 Design for a table by William Kent (1684–1748), engraved by John Vardy (d.1765), 1744.
Designed for Lord Burlington's villa at Chiswick, this end view of Kent's table looks remarkably like an antique urn, demonstrating the Palladian preoccupation with the classical Roman mode.

Fig. 2 Card-table, c.1740.
Spanish mahogany. Finely carved with masks and vines, this table expands with a concertina action. (National Trust, Stourhead.)

Fig. 3 Architect's table, c.1730, Spanish mahogany.
This example retains the square-sectioned cabriole legs of the Queen Anne period. (Victoria and Albert Museum, London.)

Fig. 4 The Breakfast Scene by William Hogarth (1697–1764) from Marriage à la Mode, *a satirical series. 1743. Oil on canvas.*
This scene shows the interior of a Palladian room. Some of the furniture is rather old-fashioned considering the date and points to the fact that furniture in the Queen Anne style was being made well into the 1740s. (National Gallery, London.)

In 1743 Hogarth produced his six paintings called *Marriage à la Mode*. The second in the series, *The Breakfast Scene*, shows an interior in the classical, or Palladian, style of William Kent, thought to be taken from an existing house in Arlington Street, London (Fig. 4). Strangely, the furniture is very old-fashioned for the date. In the background there are card-tables and chairs very much in the Queen Anne tradition that was already more than thirty years old, and the scrolled legs of the tripod table derive from an even earlier period.

Walnut furniture in the Queen Anne style continued to be made at least until the middle of the eighteenth century. Fine tallboys and knee-hole tables in figured walnut veneer can be found, and these show themselves to be mid-Georgian productions only by small features like the shape of the feet or their original brass mounts. But from the 1720s other fashions were growing up.

The new fashions were governed mainly by two factors. First, there were the classicising activities of the Palladian architect decorators headed by Lord Burlington and William Kent. Their intentions were to restore the principles of ancient Roman architecture, and to displace the current baroque and French stylisations. Second, there was a change in the wood used for furniture, from walnut to mahogany.

Many features of the new style depend on the nature of mahogany. This red wood seems first to have been brought to England from the New World by Raleigh, and, known as Jamaica wood, to have been imported in the seventeenth century from that British colony. However, it was not until the 1720s that it was imported on a greater scale for general use in cabinet-making.

There were several varieties. First, there was wood from San Domingo, known as Spanish mahogany. It was very heavy, hard, dark and close-grained. This did not lend itself well to veneering, and was generally used in the solid. The best cabinet-work in Spanish mahogany shows great precision of construction and excellent carving. The surface, darkening with age, took on a fine polish and was sometimes compared with patinated bronze (Figs. 2 and 3).

At first, mahogany was used as an alternative to walnut. Accordingly, a fashion was quickly established for red-coloured furniture and certain kinds of walnut were stained red with bulls' blood. In such cases, the two woods can look amazingly alike.

Around 1740, a different variety was imported from Cuba which was rather lighter in weight and brighter in colour. Moreover, it often showed a fine curl or flame figure that encouraged the revival of the art of veneering (Fig. 5). Cuban mahogany was easy to work with the chisel, but was still hard and strong enough to take carving in higher relief and with greater vitality than was possible in walnut. Dark Spanish mahogany, then, tends to be characteristic of the earlier Georgian furniture, while the mid-Georgian period generally used Cuban wood. Mahogany was an extremely expensive material, and it is one of the curiosities of English furniture that this wood should have been employed universally and lavishly throughout the whole Georgian period.

The ancient trees of the West Indies were ruthlessly felled, and around the end of the century the supplies were almost exhausted. From them could be made wide planks, and so table-tops might be in single pieces instead of being formed, as previously, of narrow boards joined together. Around 1730, the dining-table began its evolution from the gate-leg table. There are many surviving gate-leg tables in Spanish mahogany which are mostly of a very plain design. At first oval, they developed into a rectangular shape; from this, it was a simple move to have two flap tables which might fit closely together when necessary for extension. Later on, additional leaves were

Hawkley Studio

A. C. Cooper

Museum Photo

Fig. 5 **Tripod Table**, c.1750,
*Cuban mahogany, height 27 ins.,
diameter 31 ins.
Antique motifs incorporated in
this piece include acanthus
leaves and shells on the urn at
the base of the fluted pillar,
which supports the table top.
(The Greater London Council as
Trustees of the Iveagh Bequest,
Kenwood.)*

Fig. 6 **Mirror**, c.1740. Gilt-wood.
*While essentially of classical
architectural form, the cartouche
and carving indicate the
beginnings of the rococo style.
(Victoria and Albert Museum.)*

Fig. 7 **Side-Table**, *attributed to
Matthias Lock (d.1769), c.1740,
in the classical manner.
(Temple Newsam House,
Leeds.)*

Fig. 8 **Pier-glass**, *in the manner
of Benjamin Goodison, c.1745.
This extremely ornate pier-glass
characterises the rich decoration
of the period. The base may have
been restored at a later date.
(Victoria and Albert Museum.)*

Fig. 9 **Upholstered chair**, *in the
manner of William Kent, c.1730.
Soft-wood painted bronze.
(Lady Lever Art Gallery, Port
Sunlight, Cheshire.)*

clipped in. The mahogany dining-table was
peculiar to England; on the Continent, the tradition
remained for formal meals to be set up on
temporary trestle tables covered by damask cloths.

When there was no formal party, meals might
be set upon small tripod tables, not more than
two-and-a-half to three feet wide. One such table
is shown in Figure 5 and a large number of these
are found today. They are often quite plain but
can be elaborately carved. When mahogany
furniture was carved, the ornament was vigorous
and monumental, as can be seen on cabriole legs of
chairs that are boldly cut with lion-heads and feet.
But when it is plain, early Georgian furniture
appears to be even more simple than that of Queen
Anne, for the mahogany lacks the variegated figure
and banding that had enlivened walnut chests
and tables. The architect's table, otherwise known
as a reading- or drawing-table, is an innovation of
this period which is usually very simple in design.
The reading-stand rises on a double easel, and the
whole piece is of a massive construction, for this
was a functional piece of furniture and had to be
strong enough to hold the heavy folios from a
gentleman's library (Fig. 3).

During the 1730s, the scale of living among the
wealthy, and especially among the Whigs, was
expanding fast. A nobleman's true home came to be
his country seat, and his London house, used only
for entertainment during the London or parlia-
mentary season, was regarded as the less
important. We read of the ideal Whig aristocrat
in the writings of the third Earl of Shaftesbury
(1711). He should be a man of wealth and fine
manners, learning and culture. He was not to be
subject to caprices and enthusiasms, but a senator
combining modest virtue with an Olympian
detachment from trivialities. The Whigs attempted
to recover the lost excellence of antiquity, and
Lord Shaftesbury's sentiments found their
expression not only in Palladian architecture, but
also in the furnishing of houses.

The most representative room is perhaps the
library. Book-cases, befitting a man devoted to

Fig. 10 **Chair**, c.1740. Carved
mahogany.
*The decorative motifs are
Palladian while the back
anticipates a later style.
(Lady Lever Art Gallery.)*

the cultivation of antiquity, now took on a monumental appearance. They were plain, generally with solid doors below and glazed doors to the upper part. Crowning the centre, there would generally be an architectural pediment. Thus furniture, like Palladian architecture, aspired to the definite and clearly defined shapes of Roman buildings. Ponderous columns or more delicate pilasters were surmounted by a cornice and pediment, and the plinths and mouldings, carved in solid mahogany, took on many of the classical details found in temple architecture.

Furniture for state-rooms included tables and frames for looking-glasses of carved gilt-wood, massive shaped coffers and chests of drawers, chairs and settees in heavy mahogany, herm pedestals carrying marble busts (which therefore had to be stronger than the customary *torchères*), and ponderous library tables.

We must now consider the architect's part in the development of Palladian furniture. The third Earl of Burlington (1694–1753) was among the first and most influential leaders of the movement that restored Palladian taste to England. With his friend and protégé, William Kent, he designed his own villa, Chiswick House; but as regards furniture, clearly it was Kent who was the inventive genius. William Kent (1684–1748) lived in Italy studying to be a painter from 1712 to 1719. After Lord Burlington had brought him back to England, he practised architecture, landscape gardening, interior decoration and furniture design. His originality in all these fields is amazing, and his achievement has not yet been properly assessed.

William Kent was the first architect in England to make a regular practice of furniture design. His interiors at such great houses as Houghton and Holkham, and, on a smaller scale, at Rousham, remain intact and form complete units. The monumental doors, fireplaces and ceilings were based upon antique buildings, the walls might be hung with Italian velvets and silks of strong colours; the furniture was designed on a correspondingly palatial scale.

Kent was, above all, an artist in the real and most general sense of the word, and his complete interiors show an infallible and instinctive sense of design. The sources for his inventions are not easy to discover. When he was in Italy, he wrote condemning 'this damned *gusto* [taste] that's been for this sixty years past'. It was the French taste of Louis XIV to which he took exception, and which, by then, had affected Italy as well as England. He wished for a return to a less affected, purer, classical style. All the same, his furniture designs show even more clearly than his architecture that he was not content simply to practise the correct simplicity of the acknowledged masters, Inigo Jones, Palladio and the ancients. Of course, there was little precedent for Palladian furniture as such. Strictly correct classical details and mouldings abound in his furniture, but these are set together in a fantasy that must surely be called baroque. The ever-prominent scallop-shells and sculptured figures may well be derived from Bernini's fountains in Rome and Tivoli; and the profusion of motifs seems not far removed from interiors by Pietro da Cortona and the designs of the French decorators that Kent despised.

At the same time, Kent's work does not bear much similarity to contemporary furniture in Europe.

There certainly seems to be no furniture comparable to it in France. It perhaps approaches most closely certain carved and gilt side-tables that Kent must have seen in Turin, Genoa and Rome. In such pieces the sculptural element is very strong. From these are derived the familiar side-tables, with supports carved as eagles or dolphins. These, and fine tables made for great houses, carved with lions, sphinxes or cherubs, flanked by luxuriant acanthus leaves, are essentially a sculptor's work in wood. Even the typical Kentian supports in the form of cusped S-scrolls show a sculptor's inventive treatment of the usual console scroll.

Palladian furniture, in a rather simpler form than that designed by Kent, became general during the 1730s and 1740s. Architects of his school, such as Flitcroft and Vardy, designed pieces to stand in their houses. John Vardy's drawings made towards 1750 show a lightening of the bold masses which were typical of Kent. Mirror-frames became narrower and less dependent upon bold architectural detail; foliage, garlands of flowers and drapery were introduced more as attractive decoration than as essentials to classical structure. For by then, even though these designers might be preserving the Palladian tradition, they could not help being affected by the rococo movement, from which they learned a lightness of touch and greater freedom of decoration.

It is from the Palladian period that we begin to receive more particular information about the London furniture-makers. Benjamin Goodison worked in Long Acre, Covent Garden, throughout the reign of George II and supplied furniture to the royal palaces, to Longford Castle and elsewhere (Fig. 8). John Channon, of St. Martin's Lane, is familiar on account of his speciality of inlaying furniture with engraved brass plates and lines and of using heavy, gilt-bronze mounts. William Hallett, also of St. Martin's Lane, made book-cases, cabinets and chairs. His known work is of excellent design, combining a simple, classical form with a stable appearance. William Vile was one of the finest cabinet-makers England ever produced, and is thought to have executed pieces for Chiswick from Kent's designs as early as 1730. Vile is best known for his work of between 1750 and 1765, which coincides with the rococo period. Yet, more than his contemporaries, he seems to have preserved to the end the Palladian traditions of design, proportion and detail.

MUSEUMS AND COLLECTIONS
Palladian furniture may be seen at the following:
GREAT BRITAIN
Cheshire: Lady Lever Art Gallery, Port Sunlight
Derbyshire: Chatsworth
London: Marble Hill, Twickenham
    Victoria and Albert Museum
Norfolk: Holkham Hall
Oxfordshire: Rousham House
Wiltshire: Wilton House

FURTHER READING
Georgian Cabinet Makers by Ralph Edwards and Margaret Jourdain, London, third edition, 1955.
The Work of William Kent by Margaret Jourdain, London, 1948.
Some Designs of Inigo Jones and William Kent, London, 1744; reprinted 1967.

Fig. 1 *Plain stem glasses* (left to right): *Toasting glass*, 1740. *Height* $7\frac{1}{2}$ *ins. Firing glass*, 1740. *Height* $3\frac{1}{2}$ *ins. The thick base is designed for hammering on the table. Pan-topped wineglass with a tear in the stem*, 1740. *Height 6 ins. Wineglass*, 1740. *Height 6 ins. Engraved around the rim with a continuous band of leaves. Large wineglass, probably Newcastle*, 1740. *Height* $7\frac{1}{2}$ *ins. Deceptive double glass, probably for use as a gin measure*, 1745. *Height* $4\frac{7}{8}$ *ins. Wineglass*, 1740. *Height 6 ins. Wineglass*, 1740. *Height* $5\frac{3}{4}$ *ins. The pale green colour is associated with export glass. (Author's Collection.)*

Fig. 2 *Plain stem glasses* (left to right): *Ale glass engraved with hops and barley*, 1740. *Height* $7\frac{3}{4}$ *ins. Tall flute*, 1740. *Height* $7\frac{1}{2}$ *ins. Goblet*, 1745. *'Wood green' glass. Height* $6\frac{3}{4}$ *ins. Probably for export. Cordial glass*, 1750. *Height* $6\frac{3}{4}$ *ins. Cordial glass*, 1730. *Height* $6\frac{3}{4}$ *ins. Ale glass*, 1730. *Height* $7\frac{3}{4}$ *ins. (Author's Collection.)*

Plain, Pedestal and Air Twist Stems

Peter Lazarus

Fig 3 *Pedestal sweetmeat glasses* (left to right): *Quilted ogee bowl*, 1740. *Height* $5\frac{7}{8}$ *ins. Double ogee bowl flared into eight panels*, 1730. *Height 7 ins. Double ogee bowl with an everted dentil rim*, 1750. *Height 6 ins. Flared double ogee bowl with Silesian stem*, 1730. *Height 6 ins. Saucer bowl with Silesian stem*, 1740. *Height* $4\frac{3}{4}$ *ins. Double ogee bowl*, 1740. *Height* $6\frac{1}{2}$ *ins. Double ogee bowl*, 1740. *Height* $6\frac{3}{4}$ *ins. (Author's Collection.)*

Fig. 4 *Plain stems* (left to right): *Goblet with gilt decoration of fruiting vine*, 1750. *Height* $7\frac{1}{4}$ *ins. Excise wineglass engraved with fruiting vine*, 1745. *Height* $6\frac{1}{4}$ *ins. Very rare. Newcastle drawn trumpet bowl engraved with a gentleman toasting a lady*, 1730. *Height 8 ins. Wineglass*, 1730. *Height* $5\frac{1}{2}$ *ins. Electioneering goblet, engraved 'Success to Sir Francis Knollys'*, 1750. *Height* $7\frac{1}{2}$ *ins. Wineglass*, 1750. *Dark green glass. Height* $6\frac{1}{4}$ *ins. Trumpet bowl wineglass with unusual domed and plain foot*, 1745. *Height 8 ins. (Author's Collection.)*

Fig. 5 *Silesian stems* (left to right): *Baluster wineglass*, 1725. *Height* $7\frac{1}{4}$ *ins. Baluster wineglass, pedestal variety*, 1725. *Height* $7\frac{1}{4}$ *ins. Excise Silesian sweetmeat glass, with hollow stem*, 1745. *Height* $5\frac{3}{4}$ *ins. Wineglass*, 1745. *Peacock green. Height 6 ins. Sweetmeat glass*, 1740. *Height* $6\frac{1}{2}$ *ins. Wineglass*, 1725. *Height* $5\frac{1}{2}$ *ins. Baluster glass, with a thistle bowl and a solid ball at the base*, 1720. *Height 7 ins. (Author's Collection.)*

Due to the heavy taxes imposed on certain alcoholic drinks, and the consequent popularity of different types of beverage, eighteenth-century glasses took on a corresponding variety of new shapes and sizes

With the death of Queen Anne, the last of the Stuarts passed from the English scene. She was succeeded by George I of Hanover. With 'German George' and his Court came many new Continental ideas to transform the English taste. Among them was a new design for glass which was known as the Silesian, or moulded pedestal, stem (Fig. 5). This became popular and remained so, particularly with regard to sweetmeat glasses, tapersticks and candlesticks, until the latter half of the eighteenth century, together with the plain stem glass which superseded the heavy and light baluster stem glass. The rarest of these Silesian stems was four-sided; this was followed by the hexagonal stem and then, the most common, the octagonal stem. There were many variations on this particular type, including the star-studded Silesian stem which was quite often, and particularly on sweetmeat glasses, heightened by the addition of rings or collars at the base or shoulder. In many cases, decoration on the bowl was carried through into the foot.

Plain-stemmed glasses were the most common

It is the plain stem that constitutes by far the largest group of eighteenth-century glasses, accounting for between twenty and twenty-five per cent of all glasses still in existence. The plain stem glass (Figs. 1, 2 and 4), which by the 1730s was in every house and tavern, was extremely cheap and easy to produce and by this date had become popular at all levels of society superseding earthenware, pewter, silver and horn as the universal container.

One important factor in the development of new glass styles at this period was the popularity of a variety of different drinks. The earliest type of heavy baluster had been designed for wines to be consumed in considerable quantity. By the end of the first decade of the eighteenth century, however, there was a heavy tax levied on all French wines by the passing of two acts; the first, in 1703, was 'An Act for Incouraging of the Consumption of Malted Corn and for the better preventing the running of French and Foreign Brandy' The second was the famous Methuen Treaty by which the wines of Portugal were admitted into England bearing a tax of only seven pounds per tun whilst the importers of French wines had to pay fifty-five pounds per tun (large cask). Naturally, because of the rates of duty, there was a considerable decline in the popularity of all French wines and the consumption of port rose steadily as did the consumption of 'strong spirits'.

By 1735, drunkenness had become so widespread

Fig. 6 *Composite stems,
multi-ply air-twist* (left to right):
Drawn trumpet bowl, 1750.
Height 6¾ ins. *Sweetmeat glass*,
1750. Height 6 ins. *Wineglass*,
1745. Height 7 ins. *Ale flute*,
1750. Height 8½ ins. *Wineglass*,
1740. Height 6¾ ins.
(Author's Collection.)

Fig. 7 *Air-twists* (left to right):
Wineglass, 1750. Height 7 ins.
Wineglass, 1750. Brilliant green
glass with air-twist stem, height
6½ ins. *Trumpet bowl wineglass*,
1750. Height 6¼ ins. *Wineglass*,
1740. Height 6¾ ins. *Wineglass*,
with rare domed, plain foot.
Height 7¼ ins. *Goblet*, 1750.
Height 8¼ ins. *Cordial glass*,
1745. Height 5½ ins. *Large
wineglass* with multi-ply column
surrounded by double mercury
twist of air, 1750. Height 7 ins.
Large wineglass, 1745.
Height 7½ ins.
(Author's Collection.)

Fig. 8 *Knop stems* (left to right):
Wineglass with five knops, 1750.
Height 6¾ ins. *Wineglass with a
quadruple knop multi-spiral
air-twist stem*, 1750. Height
6¾ ins. *Wineglass with a triple
knop air-twist stem*, 1750.
Height 6¾ ins. *Wineglass with
double knop multi-spiral
mercurial stem*, 1750. Height
8 ins. *Wineglass with
hammered moulding and a
shoulder knop*, 1750. Height 7 ins.
(Author's Collection.)

Fig. 9 *Two engraved glasses.*
Left: *Hanoverian glass* inscribed
'To the glorious memory of King
William. Battle of the Boyne,
1690'.
Right: *Jacobite glass* engraved
with a picture of Bonnie Prince
Charlie, the Young Pretender,
and the inscription, 'Hic Vir Hic
Est' – This is the man.
(Cecil Higgins Art Gallery,
Bedford.)

that the ministers of George II put forward a bill which was supposed to come into operation on 29 September, 1736, banning the sale of gin and other strong liquors. Ballads at the time lamented the death of 'Mother Gin' and a contemporary newspaper announced the 'Funeral of Madame Geneva who died September 29th 1736'; all the signs from liquor shops were put into mourning and many dealers made a parade of mock ceremonies for 'Madame Geneva's lying in state' which in many cases led to disturbances, and Justices of the Peace were obliged to commit the 'chief mourners' to prison. Far more important was the rise in the consumption of port to the extent that, from early in the eighteenth century, port had become the most popular wine in England and was virtually regarded as a national wine.

The Gin Act did very little good, as spirits and 'strong cordials' were sold under various headings by hawkers in the streets and there were many brandy shops in every town. Some of the names by which these alcoholic beverages were sold are amusing enough in themselves: Sangree, Cuckold's Comfort, Parliament Gin, Makeshift, The Last Shift, The Ladies' Delight, the Baulk, King Theodore of Corsica, Cholic and Gripe Water and many others. Quite often the spirit was coloured and on the outside of the bottles were the words 'take two or three spoonfuls of this four or five times a day, or as often as the fit takes you'. Even chemists would sell 'cholic' water and 'gripe' water, which were very different in content from present-day brews of the same name. All this led to new designs in glass, in particular smaller and more delicate bowls, and predominantly the ogee bowl with its many variations (Fig. 3).

Engraving often signified the drink for which the glass was intended

One of the earliest types, which remains unsurpassed in its simplicity and beauty, was the simple drawn trumpet wineglass (Fig. 6, left). These glasses were made by the simplest method, that is to say that the bowl and stem were made in one piece, the stem frequently having no air tear; the foot, which up to 1745 was almost invariably folded, was made separately. They were the plain two-piece glasses which could be made to a general pattern and at great speed.

It is often possible to find enormous varieties in the type of bowl set on to plain stems, as this cheaper glass was made long after the advent of both the air-twist and the opaque-twist stem glasses. Probably the most interesting for collectors are those plain stem glasses which are engraved and decorated in some way. More often than not, engraving on plain stem glasses signified the use of the glass: for example, hops and barley often decorated ale glasses; apples, glasses intended for cider; and fruiting vine, wineglasses.

The most important event with regard to English eighteenth-century glasses was probably the Excise Act of 1745–46. From this one Act, the whole of the English glass industry changed its pattern, style and indeed the very make-up of its glasses. The Act taxed not so much the glass itself, but the quantity of material that went into the manu-

facture of the glass, and this at the rate of one penny per pound weight for all ingredients used in its manufacture. In consequence, the glass-makers had to try to find a way of making more glasses from the same quantity of raw materials. They set about this in several ways. By reducing the size of the glass generally, they were able to produce far greater quantities from the same weight of glass. This in itself, however was not enough and so they attempted to solve the problem in two ways.

First they experimented by blowing the stems completely hollow, which was not a great success as the hollow blown stems tended to be weaker at one point than another and seldom lasted; this idea was soon dropped and few of these 'excise' glasses exist today. The second, and regrettably the more drastic measure which has remained with us ever since, was that the glass-makers dispensed with the folded foot. This resulted in considerable saving on the part of the glass-makers with regard to the amount of material used, but it, too, weakened the glass. In a roundabout way, however, the lowering of the standards of the product actually helped the glass industry considerably, as glasses were broken and damaged far more easily than in earlier decades.

It is amusing to think that the most important period of English glass might have begun as the result of poor workmanship, for, more often than not, air bubbles were trapped in the plain stem glasses and it was the dedicated craftsman who, realising how much they enhanced the beauty of the glass, started to experiment with the introduction of air into the stems by design and not by chance (Figs. 6, 7, and 11).

The earliest of the air-twist glasses were the two-piece variety; these were made up to about 1740. They showed many flaws; strands of air might be thin or weak and the spirals often did not extend to the full length of the stem, or were too far apart. In several cases, where the stem was knopped, they might even break at the knop. Most air-twist glasses were of simple multiple spirals (Fig. 6, left), but from the middle of the eighteenth century glass-makers started to concentrate on silvery brilliance, uniform spacing and thickness.

It was customary to hold the glass by the foot

The glasses of really silvery brilliance are known as 'mercury twists' (Fig. 11, second from left). Prior to this, the composite stem glass made a short but interesting appearance. These glasses are basically associated with Newcastle, because of their form of stem, the majority having a simple waisted trumpet bowl above a stem consisting of an air-twist section over a ball or baluster knop, usually with small air tears inserted into a short plain section above a foot. The small baluster ball knop with air tears is the one most strongly associated with Newcastle (Fig. 6, right).

Although foreign influence was obvious in English glass at an earlier date, the air-twist was strictly an English design which was later exported to the Continent with great success.

These glasses were both fashionable and popular, but it is from this period that the glass-makers incorporated the full range of bowls and stems, advancing the general design of these by the

D. Balmer

D. Balmer

D. Balmer

D. Balmer

10

D. Balmer

Fig. 10 *Engraved wineglasses* (left to right): **Waisted trumpet bowl** with engraved Jacobite emblems, 1750. Height 7¼ ins. **Funnel bowl** bearing Jacobite emblems, 1765. Height 6 ins. **Waisted bell bowl** with a carnation and a bee, both of Jacobite significance, 1765. Height 6¾ ins. **Hanoverian funnel bowl** engraved with 'The White Horse of Hannover' beneath a ribbon inscribed 'Liberty'. **Bell bowl** engraved with an oak leaf and a rose, Jacobite emblems, 1750. Height 7½ ins. **Jacobite flared bucket bowl** with a sunflower and a butterfly, 1760. Height 5⅞ ins. **Trumpet bowl** engraved with buds and an oak leaf and the word 'Fiat' – Let it be done – the Jacobite motto, 1745. Height 7 ins. (Author's Collection.)

11

Fig. 11 *Air-twists* (left to right): **Ale glass** engraved with hops and barley, 1760. Height 6½ ins. **Cordial glass** with two thick mercurial air-twist corkscrews, 1750. Height 6¾ ins. **Wineglass** with a very fine double knopped air-twist stem, 1750. Height 6½ ins. **Ale glass** engraved with hops and barley, and a fine air-twist stem, 1750. Height 6½ ins. **Ale glass**, 1750. Height 6 ins. **Ale glass** engraved with hops and barley set on a knopped multi-ply air-twist stem, 1750. Height 7¾ ins. (Author's Collection.)

introduction of the three-piece glass. In nearly all cases, the foot was no longer folded but in some of the earlier specimens both folded and domed feet can be found.

Almost invariably the diameter of the bowl was smaller than the diameter of the foot; the two basic reasons for this were, first, that it was far easier to set the glass down and far more difficult to knock it over, and second, that it was customary to drink from the glass by holding the foot rather than the stem; this is borne out by contemporary engravings and paintings.

This was the period when glass engraving of all descriptions really came into its own (Figs. 9 and 10). The commemorative glasses of the two Jacobite rebellions, the Hanoverian clubs or, quite simply, the hops and barley of the ale glasses (Fig. 11), together with other simple decorations such as swags and flowers, all add to the charm and beauty of the glass of this particular period.

MUSEUMS AND COLLECTIONS

Plain, pedestal and air-twist stemmed glasses may be seen at the following:

Belfast: Ulster Museum
Bristol: Bristol City Art Gallery
Harvey's Wine Museum
Cambridge: Fitzwilliam Museum
London: Victoria and Albert Museum
Manchester: City Art Gallery
Oxford: Ashmolean Museum
St. Helens: Pilkington Glass Museum

FURTHER READING

A History of English and Irish Glass by W. A. Thorpe, London, second edition, 1969.
The Collectors' Dictionary of Glass by E. M. Elville, London, second edition, 1965.
Glass Through the Ages by E. Barrington Haynes, Harmondsworth, second edition, 1959.

Eighteenth-century
Room Arrangement

Peter Thornton

2

Museum Photo

3

A. C. Cooper

Georgian furniture was considered to be part of the architecture of a grand house. It stood in its allotted space in the room for which it was designed

Environment is a concept that is claiming increasing attention nowadays. It has even begun to affect the study of antiques. In the case of eighteenth-century furniture, the question of how it was related to the way people lived at the time is engaging historians ever more widely, and the subject is now being approached from a new angle. A great deal of pioneering work has been done in Scandinavia and, to a lesser extent, in the United States; but this facet of furniture-history is now being taken up with considerable energy in England. Two recent articles in *Country Life* on the furniture at Osterley Park, where each piece now stands in what is believed to be the correct position, exemplify the new approach.

It is not always realised that grand furniture was usually commissioned for a particular room in a particular house, and that each piece had its appointed place in the room concerned. The style, decoration and colouring of the furniture was made to agree closely with the décor of the room and, while such matters might be left to the upholsterer or cabinet-maker, a conscientious architect would often take some pains to see that the furniture agreed with his conception of the room as a whole.

It is clear from a study of contemporary inventories and illustrations that certain general principles governed the placing of furniture in a room. The principles changed radically around 1800 when what many people regard as a characteristically Victorian arrangement, in which a large amount of furniture was placed haphazardly about the room, came into fashion. In the seventeenth and eighteenth centuries, on the other hand, rooms were generally rather sparsely furnished and the furniture was placed against the wall in order to leave the floor clear. People still spent a large proportion of their wealth on their clothes and, although furniture had become elaborate and expensive during the late seventeenth century, they still felt obliged to adhere to the earlier tradition of displaying the finery they carried on their person as conspicuously as possible. They therefore wanted space in which to parade themselves and be seen. The furniture was merely part of the décor – a setting, not the principal feature. When Madame de Maintenon pulled a chair forward from the wall, she was reprimanded by Louis XIV for upsetting the architecture. This particular chair was obviously designed to stand just in that one place, by the wall; it was not meant to be free-standing.

A desire for symmetry governed the arrangement of furniture

In those eighteenth-century rooms where all the original furniture survives, it is of course possible to replace the pieces of furniture in their original positions, and it will usually be found that there is only one possible way of arranging them if the backs-to-the-wall principle is adopted. In some cases, the backs actually fit the space beneath a wall-panel, while the decoration of a carved chair-back may echo that of the plaster-work or carving above.

During the seventeenth and early eighteenth centuries, a whole row of chairs was frequently set close together along the wall. Later, it became common to have a sofa flanked on each side by one, or sometimes two, armchairs. A desire for symmetry of course governed all such arrangements, even during the High Rococo. There might therefore be, say, a sofa on each side of the fireplace, each with its accompanying chairs, or there might be similar groups against the end walls. The walls which did not have the sofas would then have groups of chairs instead. The upholstery of such an array of chairs produced a band of colour round three sides of the room and this was often continued along the window side by similarly upholstered window-stools, although one could also place chairs in the window-recesses. If there were an odd number of windows, it was customary to have an even number of window-stools (or chairs) which left the central window-recess empty.

In dining-rooms, also, the chairs were always placed against the wall, never in the centre around a table as they are so frequently today. Dining-chairs, especially English ones, had open, carved wooden backs. The carving is on the front only, for the simple reason that one was not meant to see the back, since it was against the wall. Earlier in the century, dining-chairs often had seats upholstered with Turkey-work, which had a pile surface and cannot have been very practical; later, it was usual to have leather or horsehair cloth which could easily be wiped clean.

It was not normal to have a dining-table in an eighteenth-century dining-room. If it was decided to eat there – or in any other room, for that matter – the servants brought in a table of the sort one often sees in obscure corners of country houses today. They are gate-legged and have two large

flaps. They may be oval, but rectangular ones had the advantage that they could be placed side by side to form a large dining-table. Such tables lived in passage-ways and were therefore humble pieces of furniture with little or no decoration; in use, they were entirely hidden by linen table-cloths which reached to the ground. Unencumbered as an eighteenth-century dining-room thus was, with the tables removed and the chairs against the wall, it often served as a picture gallery where family portraits might be seen to advantage.

There would normally be one or more side-tables with marble tops, for serving food; these might be set against the piers with mirrors above. There would also be a side-board, at first just a rather more imposing table, but later an elaborate affair flanked by, or fitted with, urns. A wine-cooler was often provided *en suite*. This ensemble was intended not only for serving wine and other beverages, but provided the base for an imposing display of silver plate; for the side-board was a descendant of the old 'cupboard' on which the cups and other silver were set out.

In a drawing-room or in ante-rooms, it was usual to hang elaborate pier-glasses between the windows, with console-tables or commodes (both essentially decorative items) below. The chimney-glass, if there was one, might echo the pier-glasses

584

Developement de l'entresol et du premier Etage.

Fig. 5 **Section through a house at Bayonne** by J.-A. Meissonnier, 1733. Engraving.
This overall decorative scheme shows chairs set beside each other in the accepted formal manner of the day.
(Victoria and Albert Museum.)

Fig. 6 **Design for the side of a room** by J. M. Hoppenhaupt, c.1750. Engraving.
This German rococo interior includes chairs specially designed to fit the shape of the wall-panels.
(Victoria and Albert Museum.)

and always stood near the wall.

The use of tapestry for wall-hangings declined after about 1725; gilt-leather was rarely used on the walls after the beginning of the century, except in Holland. Velvets were used by those who could afford them but again largely went out of fashion after about 1740. The most popular material for the fashionable rooms throughout the eighteenth century was silk damask; it did not harbour dust as did velvet or tapestry. Wallpapers with flocked patterns provided a rather cheaper and quite hygienic substitute. Ordinary wallpapers and also printed cottons were more suitable for bed-chambers, dressing-rooms and the like, but would hardly be suitable in reception rooms.

Curtains, wall-hangings and chair covers were often of the same material

The window-curtains were usually of the same material as the wall-hangings. Two principal types existed: divided curtains which pulled to the two sides of a window but had the disadvantage that they tended to obscure the frames of the pier-glasses and might upset the candelabra when pulled back too violently, and pull-up curtains which might be of the 'Venetian' sort which pulled straight up, or of the 'festoon' type which were pulled up and sideways by cords running through pulleys at the top corners. Pull-up curtains made a decorative finish to windows especially if not pulled up too tightly. The chairs in the room might be upholstered in the same material as the walls and the curtains. At very least, it was normal practice to upholster them in a material of the same colour. Moreover, if the carved mirrors, tables and so forth were not gilt, they might be painted in colours harmonising with that of the walls.

in their decoration, and there might also be sconces or girandoles on the side walls, in the same taste. Girandoles provided more light than ordinary sconces because the candles were reflected in the mirror forming the back. Candelabra were also placed on the console-tables, or on decorative commodes, so that their lights were reflected in the pier-glasses behind, although the pier-glasses sometimes had their own candle-branches instead. There might also be two-branch (and therefore flat) candlesticks on the narrow mantelpiece. This was all the light one probably had in a normal drawing-room, although one could bring in more candles, just as one could bring in a supper-table, card-table, or work-table. None of these extra items remained in the room all the time, however. In larger rooms, instead of girandoles, one might have candle-stands (*torchères* or *guéridons*) on which candelabra could be placed. These were decorative but rather easy to knock over; for this reason, they were often placed in the corners of the room,

Carpets were comparatively rare until the middle of the century; people were not shy to expose their floors of polished oak or sand-scrubbed deal. Robert Adam and his successors were able to order carpets that suited the other colours and the décor of the room but, before that, Oriental carpets had to do, and their colouring might easily form more of a contrast than a complement to a room. However, such an exotic object was so highly prized that one was apt to put up with this deficiency. After 1770 or so, fitted carpets, made of strips of carpet sewn together, were not unknown. Painted floor-cloths – the ancestor of our linoleum – were much used in subsidiary rooms and even found a place in some dining-rooms of the less grand sort, especially in America, for this material was of course exceedingly practical and easy to keep clean.

Fig. 7 *The Eating-room* by *Robert Adam, Osterley Park, Middlesex, designed in 1767. This end of the elegant dining-room contains a sideboard flanked by urns and chairs. Note how the pattern in the chair-backs echoes that in the plasterwork above.*

Good furniture was protected by loose covers

Costly furniture was always protected by loose-covers, often of serge or of a checked linen, and sometimes of leather, when a room was not in use. The easy-going English country gentry frequently kept the loose-covers on their chairs even when they

were using a room, as many conversation pieces show. Presumably they removed the covers for grand occasions. For parties, extra chairs were brought into rooms and seem to have been placed in rows, facing each other well out from the walls. The French reserved the chairs set against the wall (*chaises meublantes*) for royalty and the like, and ordinary people sat only in the chairs standing out on the floor (*chaises courantes*). Probably the latter were removed at the end of the evening.

Some exceptionally grand houses had a State Bedchamber in which, of course, the bed was the principal piece of furniture. The chairs in a bed-chamber were more likely to be upholstered with the same material as that used for the bed-hangings than that used on the walls. There might be a chest of drawers in the room, and a pair of night-tables flanking the bed became obligatory. Clothes, however, were kept in a clothes-press in an adjoining room, which might also be a dressing-room. This was often decorated with much fantasy and charm. There needed to be a dressing-table, wash-stand, towel-rail and a night-table in such a room.

This subject is a vast one and the study of this aspect of furniture-history is still in its infancy. It is, however, worth remembering that there must have been many people in the eighteenth century who simply ignored the 'rules' set out here.

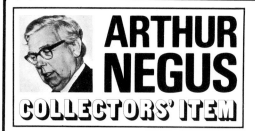

ARTHUR NEGUS
COLLECTORS' ITEM

TOBY JUGS

Although Ralph Wood the Elder (1715–72) was credited with the introduction of the Toby jug in the middle of the eighteenth century, jugs bearing human faces were fairly common from medieval times, a bellarmine being an obvious example. The first Toby jugs, in the form of a man seated holding a tankard of beer and a pipe, were apparently inspired by the character of Uncle Toby from Lawrence Sterne's novel *Tristram Shandy*, published in 1759, although it has also been suggested that the idea came from the character of Toby Fillpot who features in a country song, *The Brown Jug*, published in 1761. These jugs were made in very large numbers in Staffordshire, by several manufacturers. Although Ralph Wood began the fashion, his nephew Enoch (1759–1840) and son Ralph (1748–1795) were more prolific producers. There were innumerable variations on the original bucolic figure, including historical characters like Henry V and Admiral Lord Howe, literary figures such as Falstaff and types such as *The Irishman, The Highwayman* and the inexplicably popular *Welshman with his Goat*. In the nineteenth century, military and naval heroes such as Nelson, Lord Duncan and the Duke of Wellington were used on Toby jugs, together with the usual assortment of milkmaids, sailors, planters and fat men. Their popularity continued until the beginning of the twentieth century when jugs were still made, now including Lord Kitchener and King George V.

Nearly all Toby jugs were decorated with coloured glazes, although a few of the later nineteenth-century pieces were plain. Although most of the figures were made in Staffordshire, examples were also made at the Belleek factory in Ireland and in lustreware in Sunderland. Toby jugs of brown salt-glazed stoneware were made in the second half of the nineteenth century. These figures, made in Derbyshire, were usually impressed with their makers' name; Bourne and Son, Derby, and J. Oldfield and Co., Chesterfield, were the two most prolific manufacturers although Mathew Knowles and Son, Brampton, were popular makers as well.

Toby jugs were used for the many varieties of strong ale commonly drunk during the eighteenth century. These ales were very potent and expensive to buy, sometimes costing as much as ten guineas a gallon; they were always served from a jug. The merit of Toby jugs was that the detachable crown of the figure's hat served both as a lid and a measure, containing a gill of liquor. The tricorn hat worn by most of the figures also acted as a pouring device.

Hints to Collectors
A large number of Toby jugs have been reproduced; these copies were often made of porcelain, unlike the originals, and are therefore easy to detect. Earthenware copies are less easy to spot. In general, the patriotic figures were those most often reproduced in this way.

Prices
The commoner types generally cost around £10, rising to £20 or considerably more for rarer items. Do not pay much for a damaged jug, for so many examples are available.

Above, left: *Jug, possibly Belleek* c. 1860. £6. Centre: *Staffordshire jug* depicting *Mr. Pickwick* c.1860 £11. Right: *Lustre jug* of a Dickensian character £11.

Below, left: *Staffordshire jug* in the form of a highwayman, c.1850. £14.50. Right: *Staffordshire jug* depicting Mr. Punch, c.1860. £14.

Opposite: *Staffordshire jug* depicting Lord Nelson, 1850. £25.

Bow Porcelain

John Cushion

Fig. 1 *Plate*, c.1770. *Painted in enamelled colours and gilt, diameter 8½ ins. (Victoria and Albert Museum, London.)*

Fig. 2 *A selection of marks found on Bow porcelain:*
1 and 2: Marks on blue-painted wares, 1750–70. In under-glaze blue.
3–7. Marks of figures and other late pieces.
3. In red and under-glaze blue and red.
4. In under-glaze blue.
5. In under-glaze blue and red.
6. In under-glaze blue.
7. In red.
8. Marks on blue and white cups, in blue.

Fig. 3 *Sauce-boat*, c.1755. *Length 8 ins.*
This sauce-boat is fashioned after a slightly earlier silver shape decorated in the famille rose *colours frequently used at the Bow factory.*
(Victoria and Albert Museum.)

Bow, though not of such high quality as Chelsea porcelain, was both stronger and cheaper to produce and could, therefore, compete more successfully with imported Oriental wares

On 6 December, 1744, a patent was granted to 'Edward Heylyn of the parish of Bow in the county of Middlesex, merchant, and Thomas Frye of the parish of West Ham, in the county of Essex, painter'. This patent has since been found to refer to the making of materials for the production of porcelain rather than to the actual wares, and so, to the best of our knowledge, Chelsea still appears to be the earliest English soft-paste porcelain manufactory. Examples of this early undertaking bear the date of 1745. A later patent for actual production of porcelain at Bow was granted to Frye independently on 17 November, 1749.

The Bow factory does not appear to have produced porcelain on a commercial scale until about 1746–47, despite the fact that land and buildings

were purchased in the vicinity of Bow by Heylyn and an Alderman, George Arnold, in 1744. This new enterprise appears to have been financed by Arnold, a wealthy Cheapside linen draper. He died in 1751, too early to have reaped the full benefit of his investment. The 'Bow China Works' was not actually within the bounds of Bow, but across the bridge over the River Lea into the ward of Stratford, in the county of Essex, to where the concern seemingly moved in about 1746. Daniel Defoe, writing in 1748, refers to Bow as 'a new Manufacture of Porcelaine', where, 'They have already made large quantities of Tea-cups, saucers, etc. which by some skilful persons are said to be little inferior to those brought from China. If they can work this so as to undersell the Foreign Porcelaine, it may become a very profitable

business to the undertakers, and save great sums to the Public, which are annually sent abroad for this Commodity'.

Following the death of Alderman Arnold, the factory flourished under Thomas Frye alone. The name 'New Canton', which appears to have been adopted from about 1750, was, according to the factory decorator Thomas Craft, chosen because the works was modelled after a Cantonese factory. Following the retirement of Frye, the factory seems to have been run under the direction of John Bowcock (d.1765), the clerk of the concern, who had also managed the 'Bow China Warehouse' in Cornhill, where the stock was kept. This warehouse was later under the proprietorship of Weatherby (d.1762) and of Crowther (d.1790). The later history of Bow is rather vague; Crowther appears to have continued his interests, despite being bankrupt in 1763, until the concern was finally taken over in 1776 by William Duesbury of the Derby porcelain works, who immediately closed the concern.

Bow was without doubt the first English porcelain factory to have used calcined animal bones as an ingredient to their paste, enabling them to produce wares which, though perhaps not as beautiful as either Meissen or Chelsea, was certainly both stronger and cheaper; in consequence, they were more able to compete with the quantity of hard-paste porcelain which was being imported from the Far East by the East India Company.

The colour and quality of early Bow varies a great deal but, according to Josiah Wedgwood, the soft-paste porcelain made there was comprised of '4 parts bone ash; 4 parts Lynn sand; a ¼ part gypsum plaster or alabaster; a ¼ part of blue ball clay'. This recipe almost tallies with that quoted in the 1749 patent. Underfiring of the glaze often resulted in a surface made up of minute bubbles, and where the glaze tended to gather in pools, as within the footrims of vessels, a distinct greenish-blue tinge is often apparent.

The inkwell illustrated in Figure 6 bears the inscription 'Made at New Canton 1751', and is

4

J. Cannings

5

J. Cannings

6

J. Cannings

7

J. Cannings

8

J. Cannings

9

J. Cannings

Fig. 4 *Figure in Turkish Costume*, c.1765. *Decorated in enamelled colours, height 9 ins. (Victoria and Albert Museum.)*

Fig. 5 *Teapot*, c.1753. *Decorated in the Chinese style with under-glaze blue, height 5½ ins. (Victoria and Albert Museum.)*

Fig. 6 *Inkwell*, 1751. *Painted with enamelled colours, diameter 4 ins. One of the earliest dated Bow pieces, it is inscribed 'Made at New Canton 1751'. (Victoria and Albert Museum.)*

Fig. 7 *Pot-pourri*, c.1760. *Diameter 5⅝ ins., height 11 ins. This pot-pourri is painted in gay colours typical of the Bow palette. The flowers and masks are applied in high relief. (Victoria and Albert Museum.)*

Fig. 8 *Porringer*, c.1755. *Painted in enamelled colours, diameter 6 ins. This porringer, in the form of contemporary silverware, is painted in the Kakiemon style. (Victoria and Albert Museum.)*

Fig. 9 *Mug*, c.1760. *Decorated with enamelled colours on a transfer printed design, height 3¾ ins. (Victoria and Albert Museum.)*

Fig. 10 *The actor Henry Woodward playing the role of the Fine Gentleman in David Garrick's farce* Lethe, *c.1750. Undecorated, height 10¾ ins. Such figures often had enamel decorations added by decorators such as William Duesbury. (Victoria and Albert Museum.)*

Fig. 11 *Figure of Erato*, c.1750–55. *Height 6⅞ ins. One of a set of Muses, this figure is inscribed 'Eraton for the Love'. The complete set appears to be the work of one modeller as all the figures have similar facial features. (Victoria and Albert Museum.)*

Fig. 12 *Female Cook*, c.1756. *Height 7 ins. This view shows the square hole, so often present on Bow figures, which was intended to take a metal bocage. (Victoria and Albert Museum.)*

decorated in the so-called palette of the *famille rose*, after the name given to Chinese porcelain decorated in a similar manner from the early part of the eighteenth century. The pinkish-crimson enamel is derived from chloride of gold, a colour first used by European enamellers from about 1680. This inkwell has the typical wax-like glaze which is so easily scratched. There are a few similar inkwells decorated in under-glaze blue with the same inscription and the earlier date of 1750.

Bow catered especially for the interests of the Londoner

In addition to producing wares which could be sold cheaply, Bow catered especially for the interests of the Londoner, and we have such figures as actors and actresses of the day in their well-known roles. Figure 10 shows a fine figure of Henry Woodward playing the part of the Fine Gentleman in Garrick's farce *Lethe*; this figure was modelled, as was often the case at Bow, from a mezzotint by James McArdell. There is a companion figure of Kitty Clive as the Fine Lady in the same farce. Nearly all the early Bow figures were seemingly the work of one modeller. Figure 11 shows a figure of the same period.

Ceramic figures were usually made from one of two popular methods: slip-casting and press-moulding. In the first case, the watered-down clay, or slip, was poured into the hollow plaster-of-Paris moulds, but at Bow they preferred the second method and pressed the sheets of dough-like clay into the walls of the mould by hand, with heavier and somewhat clumsier results. This same method was also used for table-wares which could not be 'thrown in the round' on the potter's wheel. Such early Bow figures are often found to have the mark 'T' or 'T°' impressed into the clay, said to be the mark of the 'repairer' (assembler of the various moulded pieces), a mysterious 'Mr. Tebo' or 'Thibaud'. Similar marks are later seen on some of the wares made at Worcester, the hard-paste factories of Plymouth and Bristol, and Wedgwood.

The blue and white teapot (Fig. 5) is a fine example of early Bow; it has the typical translucency of the well-fired body, showing a pale greenish to straw-coloured hue by artificial light. The glaze has probably been deliberately under-fired in order to prevent it running, thus marring the Chinese style under-glaze blue decoration. The pattern in this instance shows the well known 'banana-tree, fence and bird' on a distinctive globular shape, with a similarly shaped knop. Note how the spout curves as compared with the usual straight spout seen on the original Chinese pots. On many of the later wares, the body, rather than the glaze, appears to have been fired at a lower temperature, resulting at times in an almost opaque, earthenware-like material. These later wares also show a distinct tendency to stain brown where the footrim is insufficiently protected by glaze, or where cracked or chipped, a feature to be found on the bone-porcelain of the English Lowestoft factory.

Sauce-boats were a very popular line with all eighteenth-century English porcelain factories. Their forms were usually taken from slightly earlier silver shapes. The substantially moulded sauce-boat in Figure 3 again illustrates the popularity of the Chinese *famille rose*, showing to advantage the rich enamel colours so typical of the Bow wares made from about 1754–60. The bright translucent green, a colour peculiar to this factory, is apt to run into 'tears' when applied too liberally in order to obtain a depth of colour.

The Bow factory produced even more wares decorated in the so-called Japanese Kakiemon style than Chelsea. Their version of the 'parteridge pattern', as illustrated in Figure 8, shows their treatment of this subject at its best. The shape is again that of a silver porringer. The decorators of Bow were probably less talented than those employed at Chelsea, which is likely to be the reason why the Bow versions of Kakiemon are painted much more closely to the free, careless fashion of the original Japanese Arita porcelain than the rival factories, where painstaking imitations of the early eighteenth-century Far Eastern porcelain is much more obvious.

All ceramic bodies shrink by approximately one seventh during the initial firing. As all the figures made by moulding were to some degree hollow, a small hole had to be provided to allow the air trapped within to escape. The figure in Figure 12 has an additional square hole at the back; this is a feature found on many Bow figures and was

Fig. 13 **Plate**, c.1760–65. Under-glaze blue painting on a ground of powder blue, diameter 7 ins. The ground colour is applied in the same manner as on the Chinese porcelain of the K'ang Hsi period (1662–1772). The marks are also in imitation of Chinese characters. (Victoria and Albert Museum.)

intended for the additional fitting of a bocage (a background of modelled leaves or flowers) or candle-holder. Whilst this is a feature which is normally found only on figures made at Bow, it can occasionally occur on those made at Derby. The female cook (Fig. 12) and her male companion were obviously popular models. John Bowcock, the factory clerk, records sixteen such models being ordered in 1756 by the dealer Fogg.

Bow was the earliest English porcelain factory to decorate its wares by transfer-printing in enamel colours from engraved copper-plates. The earliest and rarest examples are from engravings made by the famous Robert Hancock, prior to his working at the Worcester factory from about 1756. There are various explanations suggested of just how Bow wares of about 1755 were decorated with such fine

Museum Photo

prints, one being that they were purchased in the white and decorated at the Battersea enamelling concern at York House. The mug illustrated in Figure 9 has only the outlines of the decoration applied by transfer-printing, after which the enamel colours were added by unskilled decorators, rather in the style of a child's painting book. This mug also shows a common feature of a heart-shaped terminal, often used at Bow as a means of tidying up the join of the lower part of the handle to the body. This device is also seen at times on wares made at Liverpool. Note also the typical, opaque, light blue enamel, again a colour peculiar to the palette of Bow.

Figure 7 illustrates a type of rococo pot-pourri that was also popular at Derby and Worcester. Bow versions may be identified by the typical greens and blues previously mentioned, whereas Derby would have the so-called 'dirty turquoise' enamel

and the well-known 'patch-marks' on the base. Worcester can be clearly identified by the soapstone porcelain.

Under-glaze blue is a colour which cannot successfully be applied as a ground colour by brush. From about 1759, Bow adopted the same method as the Chinese. The plate shown in Figure 13 is a typical Bow form with a countersunk base, rather than a footrim, which bears four imitation Chinese characters as a mark. The panels to receive painted decoration were masked while the surface was sprayed with the powdered cobalt. These reserve panels are usually either circular or fan-shaped on Bow. Wares decorated in a similar manner at Lowestoft used more fussy rococo shapes.

The growing popularity of the rococo style did little to improve the appearance of porcelain figures. Models which had looked so animated on simple flat mounds or unpretentious slab-like bases began to be perched on precarious wave-like pedestals, or, in the case of Bow, distinct four-footed table-like bases. The figure of the Turk in Figure 4 is typical and dates from about 1765. Bow was now obviously endeavouring to compete with the extravagant wares made at Chelsea during the Gold Anchor period (c.1758–70). The glaze on these later wares is usually tinted blue with cobalt in an attempt to imitate the cold colour of the hard-paste Continental porcelain, such as Meissen, resulting in an altogether unhappy conclusion.

The plate in Figure 1 is of the same period. Here an attempt to imitate both the 'Mazarin' blue and the painting of the exotic birds of Chelsea has failed, and leaves us in little doubt that the wares of Bow are at their finest in the earlier periods when we can best appreciate the simple charm of its slightly clumsy soft-paste wares.

It was not until about 1762 that Bow adopted a factory mark, the 'anchor and dagger' which was often painted on wares from this date in red enamel. However, new collectors should be warned that this mark is frequently seen on hard-paste imitations of this factory's wares, almost certainly made during the nineteenth century by the well-known concern of Samson of Paris.

MUSEUMS AND COLLECTIONS
Bow porcelain may be seen at the following:
GREAT BRITAIN

Leicester:	Museum and Art Gallery
London:	British Museum
	London Museum
	Victoria and Albert Museum
Edinburgh:	Royal Scottish Museum

U.S.A.

Providence,	Rhode Island School of Design,
Rhode Island:	Lucy Truman Aldrich Collection

FURTHER READING
English Porcelain, 1745–1850, ed. by R. J. Charleston, London, 1965.
English Blue and White Porcelain of the Eighteenth Century by B. Watney, London, 1963.
English Pottery and Porcelain by W. B. Honey, London, 1962.
Eighteenth Century English Porcelain by G. Savage, London, 1952.
Old English Porcelain by W. B. Honey, London, 1945.
Bow, Chelsea and Derby Porcelain by W. Bemrose, London, 1898.

Costume in the Classic Mode

Stella Mary Newton

Fig. 1 *Mr. and Mrs. Andrews by Thomas Gainsborough (1727–88), c.1750. Oil on canvas, 27½ x 47 ins. Mrs. Andrews' skirt is supported by the huge flat hoops of the 1750s. She wears a hat over her cap, a peculiarly English custom, thought by the French to account for the beautiful complexions of English women. (National Gallery, London.)*

Symmetry led to virtual anonymity and the fashions for both men and women reflected the harmonious measure of antiquity

To our eyes, the fashions of the first half of the eighteenth century seem, once Queen Anne was dead, to lack drama. To the news-hungry journalists of the day, however, just enough happened, if not from week to week, certainly from month to month, to provide them with material for stirring up the little storms that were expected of them.

With the death of Queen Anne in 1714, the Georgian age began; a year later, with the death of Louis XIV, the thunderous, convoluted, grandiose seventeenth century had become a memory.

England settled down to twenty years of prosperous peace and a much longer span of relative but equally prosperous calm, and men and women, as was natural, adjusted their looks to the new climate. They had, in fact, begun the process not as a result of the event but, unconsciously prophetic as always, in preparation for it. The adjustment itself provided the first tiny scandal of the period in the world of fashion; it was pounced on in 1711 by the *Spectator*, which must have been driven to a remote part of Cornwall in search of news:

'. . . *a Lady who is the chief Woman of the Place and had passed the Winter in London with her husband, entered the Congregation in a little Head-dress and a Hoop'd Petticoat. The People, who were wonderfully startled at such a sight, all of them rose up . . .*'.

And so the great towering *fontange* was abandoned and the first hoop (a very modest one)

Fig. 2 *Series of Drawings from 'The Exact Dress of the Head'* by Bernard Lens, 1725–26. *Different occasions, different ages and different stations in life demanded varying ways of dressing the hair or modifications of the cap, the significance of which could be read like a language.* (Victoria and Albert Museum, London.)

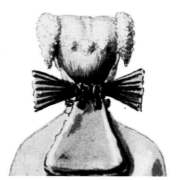

Fig. 3 *Marlborough's Funeral,* 1722. *It was usual for funeral processions to be commemorated in engravings, which are very useful as dated material. In this engraving, the size and form of the hoop is clearly visible.* (British Museum, London.)

Fig. 4 *Portrait of a Gentleman* by Joseph Highmore (1692–1780), 1747. *The gentleman's velvet coat is in what was known as 'murray brown', a colour very fashionable at that period. His waistcoat is edged with an elaborately hand-knotted fringe sewn with sequins. This was worn only with full formal dress.* (Tate Gallery, London.)

assumed. Some people stared, the *Spectator* goes on, 'at the prodigious Bottom and some at the little Top of this strange Dress', and these were the proportions that were to become ever more pronounced until they reached the ultimate in prodigiousness of bottom and narrowness of top in almost exactly 1750. As proportions they were, though exaggerated, natural – heads really are smaller than hips though from time to time fashion attempts to prove that they are not.

It was partly on an insistence on this natural relation of the parts, partly on symmetry and partly on uniformity, that the true classicism of eighteenth-century fashion lay. When, at the century's end, it was abandoned in favour of an imitation of the actual dress of the Greeks and the Romans, classicism had given way to a romantic conceit; but by that time the peace was broken and the French Revolution had intervened.

Early Georgian men were a little slower than their women to modify the design of their dress, but they too gradually reduced the size of their heads by thinning out, flattening down and tying back the enormous built-up wigs that had covered their heads and draped their shoulders at the end of the

K. Hoddle

R. B. Fleming

John Webb

Fig. 5 *The Strode Family* by William Hogarth (1697–1764), c.1738.
Correct but informal dress of the period is illustrated here. The man on the left is clearly wearing clerical dress and an appropriate wig.
(Tate Gallery.)

Fig. 6 *Satirical fantasy,* 1748.
Engraving.
This fantasy illustrates the huge hoops of the mid-eighteenth century and the problems involved in handling them.

B. T. Batsford, Ltd.

7

K. Hoddle

seventeenth century. Without changing the basic form of their dress – coat, waistcoat and breeches – gentlemen pared down not only their great periwigs but also the heels of their shoes, and raised their pockets and shortened their coats until, by 1720, they barely covered the knee. The ponderous baroque amplitude of the beginning of the century was neatened to a stricter and more precise form, an effect which slowly and almost imperceptibly increased until, by 1750, breeches were so tight that true elegance prevented an acute bending of the knee. Heads, even when covered by wigs (Fig. 2), were hardly enlarged at all, and the skirts of coats were set into pleats which swung out only when the

equivalent, not an imitation, of contemporary law-abiding classical architecture was achieved.

Fashion was not, of course, arrested, but in the years between 1720 and 1750 it moved at a leisurely pace. The hoops which had caused such a sensation in that Cornish church in 1711 had been extremely small; by the end of the 1720s they had grown, and women's torsos now rose from a gently swelling pyramid. At the end of the 1730s they were larger, but not much; but five years later still they had grown so big that through sheer necessity they were flattened front and back (Fig. 6). By 1750, still flat, they had reached their ultimate size and become rectangular; thereafter

8

K. Hoddle

9

Author's Photo

10

Author's Photo

Fig. 7 **Study of a dress**, *attributed to William Hogarth. Oil on canvas.*
(Victoria and Albert Museum.)

Fig. 8 **Brocaded Dress**, *English, 1745–50.*
The meandering pattern of a naturalistically treated spray of leaves and flowers is a movement away from the formality and heaviness of silk brocades common in the earlier part of the century. The yellow ground was popular in the middle of the century.
(London Museum.)

wearer moved.

While they naturally differed in composition, in the sharp precision of their outlines the clothes of men and women were alike. Unbroken by a diagonally slung bandolier, a carelessly draped scarf or even a single curl falling on one shoulder, the dress of both sexes observed a symmetry as strict as a classical portico.

With this precision appeared an almost unprecedented uniformity. Decoration was confined to certain approved areas of dress (as it is confined to the capital of the classical column), and with the decision tacitly taken round about 1720 that on all full-dress occasions every head should be greyed, uniformity must have verged on anonymity. No such simple decision could have more successfully ensured the elimination of individuality and when to these features was added the fact that the hooped petticoat extended both the thin and the fat – below the waist at least – to virtually the same size, an

they rapidly shrank away.

Less obvious but more interesting was the gradual change in the shape of women above the waist. Pushed upwards by the skilfully stiffened corsets of the 1720s and '30s the bust – 'neck', in polite eighteenth-century parlance – blossomed cosily behind the chemise's rising frill of lace. By 1745, however, only the most vulgar women still exhibited the upper hemispheres of their swelling breasts. Fielding's lovely Amelia is censured by an envious Colonel's wife who, trying to destroy her reputation, remarked:

'*her neck, likewise, is too protuberant for the genteel size especially as she laces herself; for no women, in my opinion, can be genteel who is not entirely flat in front*'.

Amelia was published in 1751.

Since the extension of the skirt was dictated by the size of the hoops beneath it and the position of the bust by the corset, and since their under-

Fig. 9 *Tea-party at Lord
Harrington's* (detail) by
C. Phillips, 1739.
*Tea was drunk in the evening and
this illustration shows the party
in formal evening dress. Both
men and women wore their hair
powdered.*
(Mellon Collection, New York.)

Fig. 10 **Detail of an embroidered
dress,** first half of the eighteenth
century.
*Rich embroidery on a satin
ground in silk, bullion, chenille
and sequins with velvet* appliqué
flowers.
(Collection of Miss M. Usher,
London.)

structures almost invariably no longer exist, specimens of women's dress which have survived from the first half of the eighteenth century are not easy to date. Men's dress is a little easier because the spacing and placing of the buttons and pockets and the shape and size of the pocket-flaps and the cuffs are minor details which, taken together, usually reveal a reasonably precise date. The brocaded silks of which waistcoats and trimmings were made also had their own chronology.

By the beginning of the eighteenth century, silk weavers, especially those working in France, had become so skilled that, as new designs poured from the looms of Lyon, the names of some of the most successful designers began to be known. England had her own silk-weavers, many of them Huguenot refugees and their descendants who, by 1700, already had a well-organised industry in Spital-fields. When it could afford it, however, the fashionable world preferred to buy from France.

The rich and luxuriant colour-schemes of the end of the seventeenth century were still popular during the first three decades of the eighteenth century and designs were still large. Mrs. Pendarves described the Duchess of Richmond as appearing at Court in 1729 wearing the French mode: 'very fine and handsome – silver tissue ground and velvet flowers'. In 1733 the same correspondent, who herself always dressed in the fashion, wrote to her sister about the brocade which she was to wear at a royal wedding as having 'a white ground with great ramping flowers in shades of purples, reds and greens'. But the taste for such bold patterns was not to last much longer and by the end of the 1730s, as hoops were rapidly expanding, more delicate colours and smaller, more widely spaced designs prevented the great areas of skirt from looking too heavy.

Superb embroideries adorned men's waistcoats and women's gowns

As always happens when luxuries become too readily available, however, even the costly, crisp and sparkling brocaded silks from Lyon, distributed in new designs every few months, became too banal for the grandest social occasions. On these occasions the most splendid gowns were, like the superb waistcoats worn by men, embroidered. At the coronation of George II in 1727, the Queen is said to have worn jewels embroidered on her petticoat amounting to a value of nearly a quarter of a million pounds sterling. The princesses who carried her train wore silver-tissue dresses entirely covered with silver embroidery, and most of the guests wore embroidery rather than brocade. A year later, on one of the royal birthdays, the gown of the Princess Royal was described by an eye-witness as looking 'poor' for, although the petticoat was richly embroidered, the robe was embroidered down the front edges of the skirt and bodice only.

Although heavy in the earlier years, by the middle of the century embroidery, like patterned silks, had grown lighter in design. Samuel Richardson describes the heroine of his novel, *Clarissa*, published in 1748, as being abducted in a gown of a 'primrose paduasoy; the cuffs and robings embroidered in a running pattern of violets and their leaves; the light in the flowers silver; gold in

the leaves'. With her primrose gown Clarissa wore a Brussels lace cap with matching ruffles at her elbows, another very expensive part of the fashionable wardrobe. Mrs. Pendarves had paid £50 for a similar 'suit' of Brussels lace not long before *Clarissa* was published.

Men, too, wore Brussels lace for their ruffles and cravats. The linings of their coats, often of silk in a contrasting colour that could show a brilliant flash as the wearer moved, were sometimes more costly still. In 1740, for instance, Lord Baltimore appeared at Court in a light brown coat embroidered in silver and lined entirely in ermine.

Styles were followed by rich and poor in the materials they could afford

Such was the clothing of the rich on ceremonial occasions, but simpler people could still follow the fashion in clothes of less expensive stuffs. The most usual form of women's dress was an open robe over a petticoat, which was often protected by a pretty apron. If the robe were of wool, the petticoat might be of quilted cotton or plain silk and the 'robings and facings' down the front might be of printed calico or chintz. Most middle-class men wore cloth coats and breeches, sometimes braided, and decorative waistcoats. But both men and women could appear with perfect decorum dressed in a 'nightgown' which carried with it no suggestion of the bedroom. A nightgown was often worn by men instead of the coat, informally, indoors, while women's nightgowns, being closed all the way down, were comfortable since they demanded less in the way of lacing beneath.

Like all the terminology of the past, terms used of eighteenth-century fashion can be employed only with caution for even contemporary sources do not always agree in the names they attach to garments and parts of garments. The truth is that both terms and their meaning varied, as they do today, and what can be identified with reasonable certainty at one moment may well have changed its name or its character the next.

MUSEUMS AND COLLECTIONS
Early Georgian costume, and pictures in which costume of the period is represented, may be seen at most major museums and country houses in England. There are particularly good collections at:
Bath: Museum of Costume, Assembly Rooms
Liverpool: Walker Art Gallery
London: Iveagh Bequest, Kenwood
National Gallery
Sir John Soane's Museum
Tate Gallery
Victoria and Albert Museum
Manchester: City Art Gallery
Gallery of English Costume, Platt Hall
FURTHER READING
The Cut of Women's Clothes 1600–1930 by Nora Waugh, London, 1968.
Baroque and Rococo Silks by Peter Thornton, London, 1965.
The Book of Costume by Millia Davenport, New York, 1965.
The Cut of Men's Clothes by Nora Waugh, London, 1965.

Fig. 1 *Candlestick*, one of a pair
by Paul de Lamerie (1688–1751),
London, 1748.
De Lamerie was strongly
influenced by the work of the
French designer,
J-A. Meissonnier, and was
one of the first English
silversmiths to use Meissonnier's
exaggerated and exuberant
rococo forms.
(Ashmolean Museum, Oxford.)

Fig. 2 *Sugar-castor* by De
Lamerie, London, 1734–35.
From his Huguenot master,
Pierre Platel, De Lamerie learned
the techniques of French
decoration which became so
popular in England. On this
castor are seen the characteristic
details of Huguenot silver, but
the piece is far less flamboyant
than would have been demanded
by a wealthy French patron.
(Victoria and Albert Museum,
London.)

Fig. 3 *Pair of tea-caddies*,
unmarked, probably by De
Lamerie, with engraving by
William Hogarth, London,
c.1720. Silver-gilt.
Dating from De Lamerie's years
at the sign of the Golden Ball in
Windmill Street, Soho, these
superb caddies are examples of
his work in a simple style. His
attention to detail is as great as
that of Hogarth to the complex
engraving.
(Victoria and Albert Museum.)

Fig. 4 *Cup and cover* by De
Lamerie, London, 1723.
Fairly restrained in its decoration,
this cup follows the fashion for
elaborate silver which
continued throughout the
eighteenth century. The
proportions are faultless, and the
decoration is typical of
De Lamerie's superb
technical skill.
(Ashmolean Museum.)

Fig. 5 *Newdigate centre-piece*
by De Lamerie, London, 1743.
Height 9⅞ ins.
An example of rococo work of the
very finest quality, this imposing
centre-piece was made as a
wedding present for Sir Roger
Newdigate. It is highly
decorative, but De Lamerie has
not forgotten the practical aspects
of such a large piece; the four
branches and waiters are
detachable.
(Victoria and Albert Museum.)

The work of Paul de Lamerie, sometimes simple, sometimes highly decorative, exemplifies the highest achievements in English rococo silver

Paul de Lamerie (1688–1751), who 'was particularly famous in making fine ornamental Plate, and has been very instrumental in bringing that Branch of Trade to the Perfection it is now in', as was stated is one of his obituaries, is among the most celebrated of the great English goldsmiths, certainly the greatest in the eighteenth century, and is known today as the prime exponent of the rococo style in English silver.

Although a great craftsman, highly esteemed in his own day, and a prominent member of the Goldsmiths' Company, Paul de Lamerie never became a crown goldsmith, Samuel Smithin and Thomas Minors holding this position during De Lamerie's long working life. Very little is known about his life, despite the presence of a number of remarkably well-documented facts. An eighteenth-century goldsmith, however talented and successful – and Paul de Lamerie has seldom been surpassed in ingenuity of shape and richness of ornament – was regarded merely as a superior tradesman and of no social importance whatsoever. As far as is known, there are no surviving engraved or printed bill-heads of his, there is no portrait, and about the only personal relics to survive from his long and active life, apart from his will and various signatures in a very beautiful and distinctive hand, are a group of handwritten invoices dating from the 1720s.

De Lamerie lived in Soho, a Huguenot refugee district

Paul de Lamerie was born on 9 April, 1688, and was a second generation Huguenot refugee. Despite his name, he was only French in so far as his parents were both of French origin. It is not known where his parents came from in France, but most of the Huguenot refugees came from the French provinces. He himself was almost certainly born in the Netherlands and never lived in France. His father, also Paul de Lamerie, a member of a minor aristocratic family, was an army officer in the service of William of Orange in 1686.

In 1689 the De Lamerie family left for England and by 1691 they were living in Berwick Street, Soho, a district filled with French Huguenot refugees at this period. The father De Lamerie probably lived on what money he had brought with him, and on the minute pension he may have received from the Crown. As a member of an aristocratic French family, however minor, he would have regarded earning his own living as being below his personal dignity, and was possibly too poor to obtain naturalisation, even if he had wanted it. He died, a pauper, in 1735.

One of the few professions a French aristocrat could follow without losing social caste altogether was that of a goldsmith, and in the records of the Goldsmiths' Company for 6 August, 1703, there

occurs the following: 'I, Paul De Lamerie, son of Paul De Lamerie, of ye Parish of Saint Anne's, Westminster, Gent., do put myself apprentice to Peter Plattell, Citizen and Goldsmith of London, for the term of seven years from this day'.

By this time the family was, obviously, very poor, as Pierre Platel, a Huguenot from an aristocratic French family in Lorraine, and a leading goldsmith of the day, was never paid for De Lamerie's apprenticeship, as was customary.

Pierre Platel was probably himself apprenticed in London, registering his mark in 1699. He made some of the most splendid pieces of early eighteenth-century silver, including a service of plate for George, Prince of Wales, who became George II. Paul de Lamerie would have lived with Platel during his apprenticeship, in Pall Mall, one

Paul De Lamerie

1

Museum Photo

K. Hoddle

Museum Photo

The Silver of Paul de Lamerie

Sylvia Coppen-Gardner

K. Hoddle

Fig. 6 **Sideboard dish** by De Lamerie, London, 1736. Diameter 27¼ ins.
The balance between plain and ornate surfaces on this dish is one of the marks of De Lamerie's genius. The armorial decoration in the centre is unusual in that it is raised rather than engraved. (Sotheby and Co., London.)

Fig. 7 **Box, waiter and casket** from the Treby Toilet Service by De Lamerie, London, 1724. The most complete set of its kind, the famous Treby service has over twenty pieces. It was made for the marriage of one of De Lamerie's most important clients, and cost £370 13s 10d, a vast sum of money in 1724. The superb use of flat chasing is a Huguenot speciality. (Ashmolean Museum.)

Fig. 8 **Set of four trencher salts and spoons** by De Lamerie, London, 1727. The interiors gilt. As a concession to English taste, and for poorer patrons, Huguenot goldsmiths, including De Lamerie, often made absolutely plain pieces.
The charm of these salts lies not in De Lamerie's usual flamboyant decoration, but in their perfect line and proportions. (Ashmolean Museum.)

Fig. 9 **The Walpole Salver** by De Lamerie, London, 1728. Diameter 19⅛ ins.
Made for Sir Robert Walpole, First Lord of the Treasury, upon the accession of George II in 1727, this famous salver is one of the finest examples of De Lamerie's work. (Victoria and Albert Museum.)

Fig. 10 **Ewer and basin** by De Lamerie, London, 1741. Height of ewer 14¾ ins., diameter of basin 31 ins.
Of elaborate rococo design, these superb pieces were made for the Goldsmiths' Company to perpetuate the memory of benefactors to the Company, whose presentation plate had been melted down in 1667 and in 1711. They are indeed 'performed in a very curious and beautiful manner', as was stated in the Court minutes for 9 December, 1741. (Worshipful Company of Goldsmiths, London.)

Peter Parkinson

Museum Photo

Fig. 11 *Rubbing of the central engraving on the Walpole Salver shown in Figure 9. The discarded matrix of the Exchequer Seal of George I was melted down and reworked to form this salver. On the accession of George II in 1727, Sir Robert Walpole, formerly First Lord of the Treasury, would have received the matrix as a perquisite of office following his retirement. (Victoria and Albert Museum.)*

flamboyant than those which would have been demanded by a wealthy French patron (Fig. 2). It must be remembered that eighteenth-century goldsmiths did not think in terms of individuality, but in terms of producing, to order, the finest fashionable work made by the workshop, using the mark of the master goldsmith.

At the same time as they produced flamboyant and highly decorative silver, the Huguenots made some simpler and plainer pieces as a concession to English taste and poorer patrons (Fig. 8). Paul de Lamerie himself did precisely this throughout his working life, and his earliest recorded piece of work is plain. In 1712 he became a Freeman of the City of London and registered his first mark with Goldsmiths' Hall, a mark very like that of Platel, his master, and similar to that of a French goldsmith of the period – LA, the first two letters of his surname, as was obligatory under the Act of 1697, incorporating a crown, as in Paris.

The Act of 1697 established the New, or Britannia, Standard for silver, a silver of greater purity than that used prior to 1697; this was very expensive and difficult to work. De Lamerie worked in the Britannia Standard for twenty years, although under the Wrought Plate Act of 1719 goldsmiths were allowed to revert to the so-called Old Standard if they so wished. Most goldsmiths after 1719 preferred to do so, as the Old Standard was probably easier to work.

He set up his own business and had a considerable stock-in-trade

By 1716 Paul de Lamerie was well enough established in his own right to set up his business at the sign of the Golden Ball in Windmill Street. The premises would have included a shop, and he is known to have dealt in jewellery. In 1717 he married Louise Juliott, a member of an old Huguenot family from Poitou. They had two sons and four daughters. In a fire insurance policy of 1728 his stock-in-trade, probably weighing about 3,000 oz, is mentioned as being worth about £800, a considerable sum at that time. It is from the Windmill Street period that the Hogarth tea-caddies, the Treby Toilet Service and the Walpole Salver date.

The Hogarth tea-caddies are an example of De Lamerie working in a simple style, but with superb attention to detail on a small scale (Fig. 3). Hogarth, who, like most English engravers working on silver, never signed his work, was apprenticed in 1712 to the goldsmith Elias Gamble, to learn to engrave plate. He set up on his own in about 1717. He did very little work on silver, as he had great success as an engraver and probably found engraving on silver too limited.

The famous Treby Toilet Service of 1724 was commissioned by one of De Lamerie's most important clients at this time on the occasion of his marriage, and is the most complete service of its kind (Fig. 7). There are over twenty pieces and an existing invoice states that it cost £370 13s 10d, a vast sum of money in 1724. Some of the pieces probably came from existing stock, as the ornament varies, but it is typical Huguenot work showing a superb use of flat chasing.

The Walpole Salver, named after Sir Robert

of the most exclusive streets in London. Pierre Platel died in 1719 and it is to him that De Lamerie owed his technical skill for which the Huguenot goldsmiths were renowned, particularly in their use of cast decoration which was not customary in England at this time.

French Huguenot goldsmiths were familiar with the complicated technique required to make the fashionable silver of the day (silver with sculptural decoration in what was basically the Louis XIV style) and, because of their desire to emulate Continental fashion, made most of the important pieces of silver in England at this period, although the styles in which they worked were often far less

Walpole for whom it was made in 1728, is another fine example of the quality of De Lamerie's work (Fig. 9). The piece was made from the discarded matrix of the Exchequer Seal of George I, which Walpole, as First Lord of the Treasury, would have received as a perquisite of office on the accession of George II.

In 1731 Paul de Lamerie became a member of the governing body of the Goldsmiths' Company, which was a high honour. By this time he was very successful indeed, was investing in property and was lending money on mortgage. It is from this period in his life that his most elaborate and magnificent pieces date.

In 1732 he registered a new mark, specifically stating on registration that it was for use on silver of the so-called Old Standard. All goldsmiths reverting to the previous standard were obliged to alter their marks after the Wrought Plate Act and his second mark (P.L., incorporating a crown) coincides with the use of altogether heavier and more decorative silver in the rococo style, for which the Old Standard was probably more suitable.

The exuberant, flamboyant and highly decorative forms of the rococo, coming from France and greatly influenced by the work of the architect Juste-Aurèle Meissonnier (who was made a master

Fig. 12 **Hallmark of Paul de Lamerie**, *registered in 1732 for use on silver of the Old Standard.*

Fig. 13 **Blade of a fish-slice** *(detail) by Paul de Lamerie, London, 1741. Pierced and engraved, width 4 ins. It was common practice in the eighteenth century for the decoration of a piece to reflect its purpose, as in the captured fish on this fish-slice. (Ashmolean Museum.)*

Museum Photo

of the Paris Goldsmiths' Guild in 1725 on the personal order of the Crown), were superbly exploited by De Lamerie (Fig. 1). He was one of the first to use this exaggerated and heavily ornamental form of decoration in England, which did not become widespread until after his death.

As a leading member of the Goldsmiths' Company, Paul de Lamerie was on the committee instrumental in drawing up the Plate Offences Act of 1738, whereby all goldsmiths had to change their marks. His third and last mark, registered according to the Act, is the only one that did not resemble that of a Paris goldsmith (P.L. in script, incorporating a crown).

In the same year he had moved to Gerrard Street, where he lived until he died and where he dealt in jewellery and watches as well as running his work-

shop. Some of his most notable works were produced in Gerrard Street and he took as an apprentice Peter Archambo, who was the son of another Huguenot goldsmith, and who himself became well known. Meanwhile his daughter Susannah married Joseph Debaufre, a member of a well-known family of Huguenot watchmakers.

De Lamerie's later work in the full rococo style, with its wonderful detail and elaborate and overall decoration, is superbly illustrated in the great ewer and basin of 1741 (Fig. 10). These pieces were made for the Goldsmiths' Company to perpetuate the memory of benefactors to the Company, whose presentation plate had been melted down in 1667 and in 1711. In the Court Minutes for 9 December, 1741, it is stated that 'All the new plate lately made for the Company having been now viewed by the several Members present at this Court it was the General Opinion that the same is performed in a very curious and beautiful manner'. After the viewing, the accounts were dealt with.

In 1743 De Lamerie became Fourth Warden of the Goldsmiths' Company, the same year that he made the famous *épergne*, or centre-piece, as a wedding present for Sir Roger Newdigate (Fig. 5). It is not only highly decorative, but also very practical, as the four branches and waiters (small trays for holding sweetmeats, etc.) are detachable. This centre-piece is characteristic rococo work of the very finest quality.

After his death his 'entire stock of curious patterns and tools' was sold

In 1747 De Lamerie became Second Warden of the Goldsmiths' Company and on 2 August, 1751, he died after an illness which had lasted for some months. In his will he asked that his business should be closed down, as his two sons, Paul and Daniel, had died in infancy and there was nobody to carry it on. The stock, including jewellery and watches, was to be sold by auction and on 4 February, 1752, 'All the genuine and entire stock of curious patterns and tools' were also sold.

The work of Paul de Lamerie, illustrating as it does, with supreme technical skill and superb quality of design, the current and fashionable styles in silver of nearly forty years of the early eighteenth century, is amongst the finest silver ever produced by a goldsmith and is worthy to rank with any other great work of art of the period.

MUSEUMS AND COLLECTIONS
The silver of Paul de Lamerie may be seen at the following:
London: Victoria and Albert Museum
Oxford: Ashmolean Museum

FURTHER READING
Paul de Lamerie by P. A. S. Phillips, London, 1968.
English Domestic Silver by Charles Oman, London, 1965.
Huguenot Silver in England 1688–1727 by J. F. Hayward, London, 1959.

K. Hoddle

Early Rococo Furniture

Felicity Mallet

Fig. 1 *Design* from A New
Book of Ornaments *by*
H. Copland, 1752.
Copland, a shadowy figure, was
at one time credited with most
of the designs in Chippendale's
Director.
(Victoria and Albert Museum,
London.)

The serpentine line of beauty seen
to perfection in nature was the
underlying theme of the Rococo.
Arriving in England from France,
it was interpreted freely in light-
hearted contrast to the order
and symmetry of Palladian
classicism

Rococo, a word first coined in Paris in 1796 as a
term of abuse to describe the decoration of the
time of Louis XV, retained derisive overtones
until well into the present century. In 1909,
the Oxford Dictionary definition of the word ends
'meaningless decoration, excessively or taste-
lessly florid or ornate', and as late as 1943 Fiske
Kimball wrote that 'in common English parlance
the word is still loosely applied in a derogatory
sense', and speaks of 'a belief, still widespread,
that any art called by that name can only be trivial
and debased'.

In France, the style had been slowly germinating
and evolving for thirty years before it reached
this country. Its roots and growth alike were alien
to the English; in the 1720s Lord Burlington was
leading a campaign to revive the classical splen-
dours of Palladio and Inigo Jones – his villa at

Fig. 2 **Drawing of a girandole** by *Matthias Lock, c.1750.
Girandoles, or branched candle-brackets backed by mirrors, were particularly suited to the adaptations of rococo designers.
(George Lock Collection.)*

Fig. 3 **Design** from The First Book of Ornament *by De la Cour, 1741.
This design illustrates De la Cour's grasp of the Rococo which is not evident in his designs for furniture.
(Victoria and Albert Museum.)*

Fig. 4 **Design for a pier-table and mirror** by *John Vardy, c.1745.
Vardy's furniture designs are generally in the Palladian style but here we can see an example of developing rococo taste.
(Royal Institute of British Architects, London.)*

Chiswick was begun in 1725 – but in France in the 1720s the swirling surrealistic designs of Meissonnier were affecting the whole field of decoration, and by 1732 Pineau had completed his designs for the Hôtel de Rouillé. It is doubtful whether English attempts at the Rococo were ever taken seriously abroad. Cochin wrote in 1755 of English classicism as a citadel, threatened by the ornaments of Gallic picturesqueness, but a citadel nonetheless. Blondel, writing in 1772, spoke of England as having followed most closely 'the good example of the Ancients; less ambitious to create something new than to imitate the excellent productions of the Greeks, and the handsome monuments of Ancient Rome'.

Fishes, fountains, icicles, crawling crabs and scaly monsters were the motifs of rococo design

It is necessary at this point to examine what the style was and how much of it crossed the Channel in order to see where English furniture designers found their ideas, how far they were successful or novel in translating these ideas into an English vernacular, and whether in the process they added anything.

Rococo decoration eschews the straight and formal line, and relies on continuous curves: the serpentine line of beauty, embellished by naturalistic ornament. Its roots go back into the seventeenth century. As early as the 1630s Stefano della Bella and Agostino Mitelli had published designs for cartouches (armorial shields) in which they attained balance without symmetry, and from the evolution of these cartouches there developed, over the years, an essential motif of the rococo – an amorphous, unformed substance, a cross between a jellyfish and the human ear, which could be moulded into any shape. Equally important were rock and shell forms known as *rocailles*, which originated in the garden grottos fashionable since the sixteenth century. From these basic motifs the great French *ornémanistes* of the 1720s and '30s – Pineau, Meissonnier, Cuvilliés – produced their extraordinary designs, sometimes gay and fanciful, often bizarre, where familiar objects lose their well-known outlines and

　　*...suffer a sea-change,
　　Into something rich and strange,*

now swirling and disappearing, now advancing, now retreating, now melting and dissolving, while all around and in and out is displayed the vast naturalistic vocabulary of rococo ornament: C- and S-scrolls, fishes, fountains, dripping water, icicles, undulating curves of serpents and creeping plants, rocks, shells, eels, crustaceans, crawling crabs and scaly monsters, primeval Calibans – a fancy bred neither in the heart nor the head, but in the subterranean caverns of the mind. Everything in this world curves and moves and writhes, but keeps its balance. It comes as no surprise to find figures perched on curling waves, or swinging light-heartedly from garlands. No anxiety is felt for them; the dull rules of commonsense are suspended.

Some aspects of the French Rococo scarcely reached this country. As Mr. Ward-Jackson, in the preface to his book on English furniture designs,

has pointed out, that essential part of the French style which relied on linear patterns and slender strap-work borders, having its origin in the sixteenth- and seventeenth-century grotesques and mostly used as a frame for wall-panels, doors and mirrors, seen to such advantage in the works of Pineau and Cuvilliés, was never understood here at all. The wilder aspects crossed the Channel, leaving the more subtle manifestations behind.

London in the 1730s was a small, closely-knit world; one of the centres of its artistic life was St. Martin's Lane, which was also the centre of the furniture-making industry. Here artists and craftsmen gathered, and foremost among them was Hubert François Gravelot (1699–1773), 'endowed with a great and fruitful genius for designs', a Frenchman who, arriving in England in 1732, probably did more than any other single man to introduce the rococo style to England. Best known as an engraver of delightful book illustrations, he had his own drawing school, and also, according to Vertue, the English engraver and antiquary, designed for silversmiths; Pye, the landscape engraver, writing a hundred years later, says that he designed for joiners and cabinetmakers. That his influence over artists and craftsmen was profound is clear from contemporary writings. Another disseminator of the Rococo was Georg Michael Moser, a German Swiss, who had the reputation of being 'the best chaser of the age', and who also kept a drawing school and taught at the St. Martin's Lane Academy.

It is through engravings and the works of silversmiths and goldsmiths, many of them of Huguenot extraction, that the Rococo first manifested itself in England in the early 1730s. Furniture remained solidly Kentian, but with increasing frequency the mounts began to reflect the new style. One of

Fig. 5 **Fireplace**, *Stedcombe Manor, Devon, designed by Matthias Lock. Carved wood and marble with looking-glass. This magnificent chimneypiece was made from the design by Matthias Lock seen in Fig. 7. It appeared in* A New Book of Ornaments *by Lock and Copland in 1752.*

Fig. 6 **Etching** *by Matthias Lock from* Six Tables, *1746. This design shows Lock's brilliant draughtsmanship and mastery of the* rocaille. *(Victoria and Albert Museum.)*

Fig. 7 **Design for a fireplace** *by Matthias Lock from Lock and Copland's* A New Book of Ornaments, *1752. This was the only pattern book on which these two designers collaborated. (Victoria and Albert Museum.)*

7

the first great assertions of the new fashion in this country was the centrepiece and two tureens designed for the Duke of Kingston by Meissonnier and executed in 1735, swirling asymmetrical masterpieces which must have ruined the taste of the soup for the Duke's more Burlingtonian-minded guests. There is no reason to think, however, that they were part of a rococo scheme of decoration; they may well have been an isolated exception in a solid Palladian room.

It is hard to guess how much effect the pattern books had on style in furniture-making. Almost certainly, the effect was mainly confined to London. The majority of cabinet-makers and joiners throughout the country probably never saw a pattern book in their lives, but went on making simple, practical furniture, the basic essentials of the house, neither knowing nor caring for the vagaries of fashion.

In 1736, Gaetano Brunetti, an Italian artist, published in England a book entitled *Sixty Different Sorts of Ornament invented .by Gaetano Brunetti, Italian painter. Very useful to painters, sculptors, stone-carvers, wood-carvers, silversmiths, etc.* Although these designs, which include six plates devoted to furniture and show tables, chairs, and mirrors, make use of rococo ornament – C- and S-scrolls, shells, curved legs – they are heavy and ponderous, and belong to the school of late Italian Baroque. It is doubtful whether these designs had much influence in England, although a pair of chairs exists which has strong affiliations with one of them.

William Jones, an architect, published in 1739 *The Gentleman or Builder's Companion*, which contains twenty designs for tables and mirrors. On the whole, these designs look back to Kent's Palladian classicism, but several of the tables show some rococo influence and an awareness of the designs of Pineau. Batty Langley, an architect, landscape gardener and designer, with his brother, Thomas, an engraver and draughtsman, published in 1740 *The City and Country Builder's and Workman's Treasury of Designs*, which included twenty-five designs for furniture. Mr. Ward-Jackson points out that Thomas' contribution consists almost entirely of plagiarisms; a dressing-table stolen from Schübler, a clock from Lauch, and six designs for tables lifted wholesale from Pineau's *Nouveaux Desseins de Pieds de Tables*. The designs not stolen from more competent masters are in the old Palladian taste.

John Vardy, although chiefly a follower of Kent, was a convincing exponent of the Rococo

Abraham Swan, a carpenter and joiner, wrote several architectural hand-books. His designs are Palladian, with a few modern ornaments added hopefully to keep up with the times; but a little tentative asymmetrical detail on a solidly classical looking-glass frame does not constitute Rococo. De la Cour, an engraver working in England, who published eight books of ornament in the rococo style between 1741 and 1747, was clearly capable of mastering the idiom in cartouches (Fig. 3), but when he came to apply it to furniture design the results, although robust and sympathetic, hark back in spirit to the Baroque (Fig. 8). To apply the style to furniture clearly demanded a mental leap needing considerable agility. Someone capable of making that leap was John Vardy, an architect in the Office of Works and

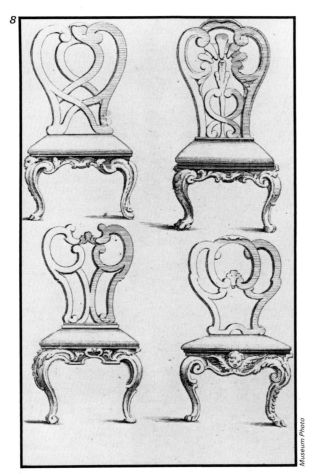

8

Museum Photo

Fig. 8 **Design for chairs** by
De la Cour from The First Book
of Ornament, *1741.*
*In spite of the use of rococo
motifs, the feeling is still baroque
in comparison with the design in
Figure 3.*
(Victoria and Albert Museum.)

follower of Kent. In 1744 he published a book entitled *Some Designs of Mr. Inigo Jones and Mr. William Kent.* A few furniture designs by him survive, mainly in the Kentian style, but, when he chose, his mastery of Rococo was totally convincing. His design for the pier-table and mirror illustrated in Figure 4 is doubly interesting; first because of the quality of the design, but also because the design was carried out with no loss of the original strength and spirit. Vardy had a brother, Thomas, who was a carver in Park Street, off Grosvenor Square, so it is even possible that the making of the furniture from this design was a family concern. We can only regret that the number of designs in the rococo style left by Vardy amount to the merest handful.

Lightness, pleasure and gaiety – the qualities of Lock's designs

The outstanding English interpreter of Rococo was Matthew (or Matthias) Lock, a carver and designer about whose life virtually nothing is known. His working dates were roughly 1740–69; he had workshops at different times in Castle Street, Long Acre and in the Tottenham Court Road. His designs in the Palladian manner and in the later neo-classical vein do not concern us here. His first book, *A New Drawing Book of Ornaments*, 1740, was one of the earliest collections of *rocaille* motifs published in England. It was followed by *Six Sconces*, 1744; *Six Tables*, 1746, and *A New Book of Ornaments*, 1752. (This last he published with H. Copland, whose contribution remains unknown but whose merit is clear, as Figure 1 shows.) These works are all of primary importance, and are imbued with those qualities so seldom understood in English furniture design, and,

indeed, in English life – lightness, pleasure, and gaiety. Lock was a superb draughtsman, and stood supreme as an interpreter of the French manner.

Lock's world, revealed particularly in his designs for mirrors and girandoles, is one of spontaneous delight; friendly goats confront surprised foxes; monkeys, precariously perched, blow insouciant bubbles; squirrels admire flowers; Chinamen with drooping moustaches cling to trees, the roots of which dissolve into icicles; owls stare with drunken dignity; cocks peck garlands; all among a riot of fountains and shells and running water. Although the birds and animals may sometimes be exotic, and the motifs may stem from Gravelot, the feeling is English.

As a designer and interpreter of the rocaille, Lock was unequalled

When we come to the very few pieces of furniture known to have been carried out by Lock as a carver from his own designs, it is hard to avoid a sense of disappointment. The Hinton House suite made for Earl Poulett (a mirror and table now in the Victoria and Albert Museum, London) are splendid pieces of craftsmanship, but little of the spirit which inspired the original designs for them is evident. Lock himself is known to have spent twenty days on the mirror and fifteen on the table that went with it; his assistants spent a good many more. But as Mr. John Hayward has written: 'evidently Lock the designer was more progressive than Lock the carver, and though his hand, when holding the pencil, produced the raciest designs, when he took up the chisel, reminiscences of the Baroque kept his fantasy in check.' There are, of course, grounds for wondering whether anyone of Lock's importance would have held a chisel at all at this stage of his career; his work may well have been confined to designing, overseeing, and business management. One piece of furniture which does keep the spirit of the original Lock design is the magnificent fireplace and looking-glass frame above it at Stedcombe House in Devon (Fig. 5). There is no evidence to connect Lock or his craftsmen, however, with the carving of this piece.

A fitting epitaph for Lock is the verdict of a contemporary, referring to some of his furniture designs: 'the enclosed drawings are valuable being designed and drawn by the famous Mr. Matt Lock recently deceased who was reputed the best Draftsman in that way that had ever been in England'. As a designer and interpreter of the *rocaille*, Lock remained unequalled in this country, even with the publication in 1754 of the first edition of Chippendale's *Director*.

FURTHER READING
The Shorter Dictionary of English Furniture by Ralph Edwards, London, 1964.
English Furniture Designs of the Eighteenth Century by Peter Ward-Jackson, London, 1958.
Georgian Cabinet Makers by Ralph Edwards and Margaret Jourdain, London, revised 1955.
The Creation of the Rococo by Fiske Kimball, Philadelphia, 1943.
'Furniture designed and carved by Matthias Lock for Hinton House, Somerset' by J. F. Hayward, **The Connoisseur**, December 1960.

Carpets of the 18th century

Bertram Jacobs

Fig. 1 *Queen Charlotte and her Children* by John Zoffany (1733–1810), 1765. Oil on canvas. The Queen is seen in this charming portrait seated in her boudoir, which has a Wilton carpet in a Persian design. (By gracious permission of H.M. the Queen.)

With the influx of skilled Huguenot craftsmen, English carpet manufacturing techniques were vastly improved. During the course of the eighteenth century the industry arrived at the sophistication seen in the carpets of Moore and Whitty, designed by Robert Adam

During the eighteenth century, British machine-made carpets passed from infancy to early manhood. The few treadle-operated looms in existence at the beginning of the century had increased to thousands at its finish. The carpet trade became firmly established, to continue its progress and to maintain its world leadership to this day. On the other hand, the craft of knotting on great upright looms, which started in 1520, thanks to Wolsey, and which had languished under the Protector, was revived early in the eighteenth century, during which it flourished and reached a glorious zenith, slowly to decline in the nineteenth century.

Fig. 2 *Saloon, Saltram House, Devon. The carpet designed by Robert Adam (1728–92) and made by Thomas Whitty at Axminster, c.1770. 46 x 22 ft. Reflecting the ceiling decorations by Zucchi, this carpet is one of the greatest made by Whitty, and one of the most beautiful objects in Saltram House. John Parker paid £126 for it on 3 October, 1770.*

Fig. 3 *Carpet (detail) in the Saloon, Audley End, designed by Robert Adam and made at Axminster, 1785. 55 x 22 ft. Adam worked on Audley End for Sir John Griffin for twenty years. He left the earlier gothic ceiling in the upstairs saloon, and had the carpet made in a soft-coloured tudor style to reflect and complement it.*

Fig. 4 *Carpet (detail) designed by Robert Adam for the Library at Audley End, made at Axminster, 1785. This Turkey carpet is of a style much appreciated in the eighteenth century.*

The two branches of the craft had quite separate histories, the upright looms coming from the East via Spain and France, while the horizontal automatic looms were descended from the English cloth loom. The slow method of the so-called 'Turkey work' was too expensive for the less wealthy who wanted to emulate the nobility by carpeting their floors, so enterprising cloth weavers evolved a cheaper form of floor-covering known as 'fote cloth', using coarse wool unfit for clothing. This is mentioned in early records as 'Kitterminster' stuff, for Wilton's daughter town had stolen a march on her mother.

The Huguenots improved techniques and the 'fote cloth' acquired designs by additional heddles (which lift the yarns) operating frames of coloured warps and various coloured weft shuttles. In 1735, Pearsall & Broom started making multi-coloured ingrain or Kidderminster carpets. Five years later, the ninth Earl of Pembroke brought over Anthony Dufosee and Peter Jemaule, two master-weavers from the Royal Savonnerie factory. They erected the first horizontal Brussels looms at Wilton, producing pile instead of ingrain. The following year, Dufosee patented his Wilton velvet pile. This was first achieved by cutting along a groove in the wire, but possibly the idea of fixing a knife on the end of the Brussels wire came from the knifed rod used by hand-knotters at Savonnerie.

The flat-surfaced ingrain carpets were made one yard wide, like cloth, but the Brussels carpets were the width of the Frenchman's ell, twenty-seven inches, and such narrow looms remain today. The piece of Wilton owned by Mr. H. Dufosee of Stalbridge Park bears an inscription to the effect that the maker, his ancestor, was brought to England in 1700, but as the ninth Earl of Pembroke was then only seven years old, this is hardly possible. Wilton records say that the two weavers were smuggled out in empty wine barrels in 1720, but this date is also apocryphal. For years, this story has been perpetuated, but Dufosee was a master-weaver when he arrived, and did not marry until 1745, and it seems unlikely that a mature man would have waited twenty-five years for a bride. He died in 1785, so that a date of around 1740 is more likely to be true.

Wilton quickly prospered and there is a record of £159 4s. paid for three hundred and ninety-eight yards of Wilton carpet, supplied by William Masters to the Earl of Cardigan in 1741. In North Carolina, Tryon Palace Restoration still has a Wilton carpet of about that date on the floor of the Governor's Bedroom in an attractive stylised floral pattern. The Royal Wardrobe accounts of 1750 show Wilton bedside carpets supplied by William Trolten, Upholsterer. Four years later, Dr. Pococke wrote that he saw the factory make carpets 'like those of Turkey but narrow, about three quarters of a yard wide', and in 1767, Chippendale accounts for '29 yards of real Wilton' for Sir Rowland Winn at Nostell Priory; later, he supplied Wilton for nearby Harewood House. In 1765, Zoffany painted the Queen in her boudoir, which is shown carpeted with Wilton in a Persian design (Fig. 1). Three other firms started making carpets when 'The Great Factory' was burned down in 1769; only two of the four survived after it was rebuilt, and they achieved sales of £20,000 and £15,000 a year. A German visitor wrote that by that time Wilton carpets were the best made.

Meanwhile, Kidderminster forged ahead. In 1749 John Broom built his first Brussels loom with the aid, it is said, of a master-weaver from Tournai, but it is suspected that two of his weavers, Foster and Tanner, were Wilton men. The other factories are said to have spied on the men while they erected their loom, so that they, too, had Brussels looms. By the end of the century, there were a thousand carpet looms there, eclipsing the cloth trade and dominating the carpet trade, though Dufosee's invention carried the name of the Royal Borough of Wilton round the world.

Brintons, who are still flourishing, started in 1783, Benjamin Grosvenor in 1790, and the year before, William Pebody Cooke left Kidderminster to start the industry in Yorkshire, from where it spread to Scotland. At Kilmarnock, the 'wabsters', famed by Burns, made flat ingrain weave, which they had the temerity to call Scotch carpet. Despite all this progress, it was the hand-knotted British carpets which became world famous.

Père Norbert, a French priest, fled to London and became naturalised as Peter Parisot, having ingratiated himself with the Court. In 1749, two master-weavers from Savonnerie arrived and appealed to him for help. They set up a loom at his lodgings in Westminster and the Duke of Cumberland bought their first carpet for Princess Charlotte. He helped them to start a factory in Paddington and orders poured in. Weavers came from France and youngsters applied for apprenticeship, so it was necessary to move to larger premises in Fulham. Parisot prospered and made some beautiful carpets. His prices were high, but he had the field to himself. By 1753, he had a hundred weavers and many apprentices.

By finding a way of visiting Parisot's factory, Whitty was able to learn his secret

In 1754, Thomas Whitty, cloth weaver of Axminster, was looking for ways of increasing trade so that he could keep his large family. His account of his dramatic success, though rather pious, makes good reading. He visited his friend, Freke, an ironmonger of Cheapside, who had imported some Turkey carpets. He laid out one, thirty feet by twenty-four feet, and Whitty could not fathom how it could be made so large without a seam. It worried him, and hearing that his wife's friend, Mrs. Forward, had one, he examined it and, on 25 April, 1755, made a sample eight inches square on a fifty-four inch loom, but could not see how it could be made twenty-four feet wide.

He took his sample to London, where friends encouraged him to persevere. Seeing an advertisement by Parisot, Whitty left to have breakfast at The Golden Lion, Fulham, where he met a man whose son was apprenticed to Parisot. The boy took him around the factory, pretending he was a relative, and that visit taught him all. The problem was solved. As he did his own spinning and dyeing, it was simple to erect an upright loom and prepare the materials. On Midsummer's Day, 1755, he started making the first Axminster carpet. He had trained his five daughters to tie the Ghiordes knot and, with their aunt, Betty Harvey, as overseer, they were his first weavers.

Many of the gentry came to watch this marvel,

18th Century English Carpets

Fig. 5 **Carpet** (detail) in the Tapestry Room, Osterley Park House, Middlesex, designed by Robert Adam and made at Moorfields by Thomas Moore, 1775–78.

Fig. 6 **Design for the carpet** at Osterley Park House seen in Fig. 5, by Robert Adam, c.1775–78. (Sir John Soane Museum, London.)

Fig. 7 **Design for the carpet** at Saltram House seen in Fig. 2, by Robert Adam, c.1770. The soft green contrasting with chocolate and red of this superb carpet have remained truer to the original colours of the design than the colours of the carpet in Fig. 5, which have altered considerably with age. (Sir John Soane Museum.)

offering orders, and a Mr. Cook secured the first carpet. This was seen by the Earl of Shaftesbury's steward and the Countess persuaded Cook to let her have it. She ordered many more and there are still four beautiful examples in the reception rooms of St. Giles' House, Wimborne St. Giles, Dorset.

Whitty's carpet trade soon outstripped his cloth business. Using the cheap labour of young women instead of men as weavers, his prices were low, as his competitors found to their cost. In fact, it appears that high prices brought about the bankruptcy of Parisot in 1755. His plant was bought by Claude Passavent, a wealthy Swiss serge merchant, who moved it to Exeter to give employment to Protestant refugees there. He had also taken the best of the French weavers, and their influence can be seen in the beautiful carpets he produced. The example in the Victoria and Albert Museum in London, dated 1757, bears a distinct resemblance to a Savonnerie carpet of the previous century in the Catan Collection, Paris, for both show tables covered with scalloped cloths with three red and gold tassels, carrying flowers. Whereas the French carpet has a shell-shaped shield in the border bearing a lion's face, in the Exeter carpet the face is human. It also has a spaniel reclining on a cushion in the centre. Another, at Petworth, dated 'EXON 1758' has a classical design with a sunflower centre, similar to one at Winterthur in the U.S.A., dated 1760. No doubt Exeter carpets were too good and the costs too high, for the following year Passavent went bankrupt.

In 1756, Thomas Moore opened his factory at The Bishop Blaze in Chiswell Street, Moorfields. He seems to have started with a hotch-potch of trades, advertising as Hosier and Manufacturer of materials for making hose, waistcoats, breeches, silk mitts, etc. but 'He being the first in England engaged in making Royal Velvet Tapestry, after the manner of Persians, has now with many improvements brought the manufacture of carpets, screens, seats of chairs, etc., to the greatest perfection Both for Beauty and Cheapness'. Some exaggeration perhaps, but the competitions held between 1757 and 1759 by the Society for the Promotion of Arts and Sciences secured the fortunes of both Whitty and Moore, but the latter could not compete in price with Whitty, who was a good business man, colourist, dyer and keen botanist, as can be seen by

his perfect floral effects.

However, Moore was a friend of Robert Adam, who found it convenient to supervise personally the production of his designs at Moorfields. Thus, Moore's carpets are meticulous reproductions of Adam's drawings in the Soane Museum, as can be seen by the carpet in the Red Drawing Room at Syon House, made in 1769 and surely one of the most beautiful ever made. Between 1775 and 1778 Moore made at least three carpets for Osterley Park to Adam's designs (Fig. 8). These can still be seen there, in the Drawing Room, Tapestry Room (Fig. 5) and State Bedchamber. There are also three fine examples in the Round Drawing Room of Culzean Castle, the Tapestry Room at Newby Hall, and at 19 Arlington Street, London.

Although Moore prospered and was able to extend his premises down City Road, there are more Axminsters than Moorfields carpets in existence today, for Thomas Whitty was more prolific. His prices were so low that Chippendale, Foskett and other suppliers preferred him, and Axminster grew in size and importance, whereas Moorfields declined after the death of Adam and closed three years later. William Crompton, a London dealer, bought Whitty's prize-winning carpet, and offered to take as many as he made. Sale of his output thus assured, within ten years Axminster was famous at home and overseas, and the plant had to be constantly extended. His carpets, with their riotous displays of floral bouquets and festoons, were popular among the wealthy planters and merchants of America. This encouraged Whitty to export his craft in the person of his apprentice, William Peter Sprague of Kidderminster, husband of Mary Whitty. They emigrated in about 1778, starting America's first carpet factory in Philadelphia, and in 1790 obtained the order for all the carpets in the new Congress House.

Whitty left a personal account of the great day when, with only two days' notice, George III brought his Queen and family to visit the factory on 13 August, 1783. The royal party was suitably impressed and naturally this event brought trade, including an order for several carpets from the Crown Prince, one of which is in the Victoria and Albert Museum. Eventually, the vast carpets for his fantastic pavilion at Brighton were made at Axminster but, before that, the nobility had followed the royal example and orders had poured in.

Many of Whitty's greatest carpets were made between 1770 and 1790. Those designed by Robert Adam for the saloon (Figs. 2 and 7) and dining-room of Saltram House in Devon are the most beautiful things there. They glow with colour, reflecting the ceiling decorations by Zucchi. The saloon carpet, its soft greens contrasting with its chocolate and red, is forty-six by twenty-two feet, and John Parker paid £126 for it on 3rd October, 1770. The dining-room carpet, with its soft greens and delicate shading, was only twenty feet by fifteen feet six inches. This has a twin in the Rijksmuseum, Amsterdam, which is slightly different in colouring.

This is the first indication of 'pot-boiling' by Whitty, for it was obviously an order taken while the first carpet was still in the factory. The most blatant example of this occurred between 1775 and 1780 when Sir John Duntze, liking the Saltram Axminsters, commissioned Thomas Leverton to design one for the saloon at Rockbeare House, near Exeter. This famous carpet has a smaller sister in the Victoria and Albert Museum. A third is now at Stourhead House and these three are similar in colouring, beige with pink centres, panels and borders, and decorated with baskets, bouquets and sprays of flowers. Two other similar carpets in the U.S.A. have blue grounds. They grace the Metropolitan Museum, New York, and the Philadelphia Museum of Art. Both are attributed to Adam and one to Moorfields but there is no doubt that they were both made at Axminster, adapted from Leverton's Rockbeare design.

Flowers and musical instruments on a rose ground

Obviously, accurate documentation is often lacking. Passavent and Moore 'signed' their carpets on the selvedge 'EXON 1758', or 'by Thomas Moore, 1769', but Whitty never bothered; it was not necessary. His skill with vegetable dyes ensure that his colours are as crisp as ever today, and his knowledge of botany is demonstrated by his lifelike flowers. He usually used natural cream wool for warps, whereas Axminsters made after the move to Wilton in 1836 have hemp or linen for warp and linen or coarse wool for weft. It is amazing that he could spin wool to such strength that it could bear the weight on loom of such great carpets as that in the saloon at Audley End.

For twenty years, Adam worked on that great palace for Sir John Griffin and transformed it into the lovely house it is today. He completely changed the ground floor and one of his Moorfields carpets is in a sitting-room, but he left the gothic ceiling of the saloon upstairs and Axminster made the huge carpet in a soft-coloured tudor style to reflect the ceiling (Fig. 3). It was made in 1785 and is fifty-five feet long by twenty-two feet wide, and the window stairs are covered with the same carpet. The library carpet (Fig. 4) made at the same time, an ugly Turkey, is in store.

The great architects of the period designed the interior furnishings as well as the structure, and thus the great houses were each one harmonious entity. The foundation of the furnishing scheme, the carpet, was their particular care, and even Chippendale concerned himself with this. Thus, when the Reverend E. J. Clarke visited Axminster

in 1791, he found them weaving carpets designed by Adam to the order of Chippendale for Mr. Lascelles' music-room and saloon at Harewood House, where they can still be seen. Clarke also saw one on loom for the Empress of Russia.

Perhaps one of the loveliest examples of a carpet designed as an integral part of the room can be seen in the Music Room at Powderham Castle, seat of the Earl of Devon. It is said that the extravagant young Viscount Courtenay and his sisters designed the room and painted the wall panels, but it is most likely that the architect James Wyatt designed the carpet and had it made at Axminster in 1789. Rose predominates and it glows with colour, with musical instruments, flowers and palm sprays. It is a lovely thing in a gracious house. The two Axminsters owned by Earl Spencer, at Althorp, are of the same period and style, so were no doubt produced by Wyatt, while another of his Axminsters recently came to the Victoria and Albert Museum. Made by Whitty in about 1790, for the Jervoise family at Herriards Park, it is in excellent condition. It can be seen in a period room, near the main entrance, a deeper rose than Powderham, with three medallions and overflowing with flowers. Similar carpets of the same period are still in use at Achamore House on the Isle of Gigha, and in the White Drawing Room at Buckingham Palace.

One of the last eighteenth-century Axminsters was recently acquired by S. Franses of Knightsbridge. Made for the Drawing Room of Felton Park, Northumberland, seat of the Riddell family, it is a deep blue, with Ralph Riddell's monogram on the family crest in the centre. The field is covered with multi-coloured acanthus scrolls and floral sprays, while the border is light green. The pile is perfect and it has many years of good life.

Such a carpet is well authenticated and a sound purchase. The few sold by Sotheby's in recent years have, undoubtedly, been genuine, but they rarely come on the market. Bargains cannot be expected, for the history of each piece is widely known. Those who proudly own an eighteenth-century Axminster, Moorfields or Exeter carpet, know its worth, and cherish it accordingly. 🐚

8

Museum Photo

Fig. 8 **Design for the carpet** in the Drawing-Room at Osterley Park House, by Robert Adam, c.1775.
This fine carpet, meticulously reproduced from Adam's design, may be seen to this day in the drawing-room of Osterley. (Victoria and Albert Museum, London.)

FURTHER READING
Axminster Carpets – Hand-made, 1755–1957 by B. Jacobs, Leigh-on-Sea, 1970.
European Carpets by M. Campana, London, 1969.
Story of British Carpets by B. Jacobs, London, 1969.
A History of British Carpets by Tattersall and Reed, Leigh-on-Sea, revised 1966.
'The Architecture of Robert and James Adam' by A. J. Bolton, in **Country Life**, London, 1923.

Vogue for

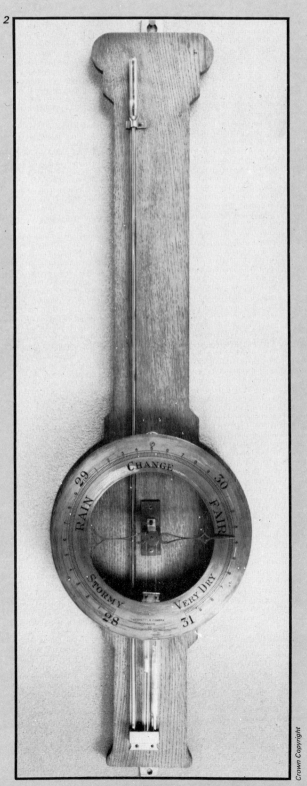

Crown Copyright

A. G. Thoday

Torricelli's barometer of 1644 was gradually modified and improved. By the eighteenth century, it had become a sophisticated piece of scientific equipment

In the spring of 1644, Evangelista Torricelli (1608–47), while working in Florence on investigations into the pressure of the atmosphere, devised the instrument known today as the mercury barometer. Figure 1 shows a model of the experiment based on a drawing in his letter dated 11 June, 1644, addressed to M. Ricci. Torricelli lived for only another three years, but others carried on investigations with this apparatus and showed that the level of the mercury in the tube changed with the weather. After 1660 the main centre of study of the barometer was associated with the Royal Society and such men as Robert Boyle and Robert Hooke. It was Boyle who gave the name barometer to the instrument, which, up until then, was known as the Torricellian tube.

By 1700 barometers had become items of furniture

By 1664, Hooke had shown the clear relationship between the weather changes and the rise and fall in the mercury level in the tube, and this led to the weather indications on barometers from the very beginning of their commercial production. The range of the change is from about twenty-eight inches to thirty-one inches of mercury and, during the second half of the seventeenth century, attempts were made to modify the barometer in order to enlarge this variation. In 1663 Hooke devised the wheel barometer; this is a U-tube or siphon barometer with a weight on the mercury in the shorter open limb. A cord from this weight passed over a pulley-wheel to a counter-poise weight; a pointer attached to the pulley-wheel showed an enlargement of the change in the mercury level. Figure 2 shows a cut-away example of a wheel barometer.

Sir Samuel Morland is generally considered to be the inventor of the diagonal or signpost barometer, in about 1680 or just before. Here, the upper

the Barometer

Fig. 1 **Copy of the first Torricelli barometer with stand.** *Torricelli (1608–47) devised the instrument known to us as the mercury barometer, which measures atmospheric pressure in 1644. (Science Museum, London.)*

Fig. 2 **Wheel barometer** *by Negretti and Zambra, nineteenth century.*
This cut-away example allows us to see the workings of the wheel barometer. It was originally devised by Robert Hooke in 1663 and consists of a U-tube barometer with a weight on the mercury in the shorter open limb. A cord from this weight passes over a pulley-wheel to a counterpoise weight and a pointer attached to the pulley shows an enlargement of the change of the mercury level. (Science Museum.)

Fig. 3 **Wheel barometer** *by Thomas Tompion (1639–1713), c.1700.*
Few barometers by Tompion are still in existence. This example bears the royal cipher of William III, which dates it to before 1702. (By Gracious Permission of H.M. the Queen: Hampton Court Palace, London.)

3

portion of the tube is inclined sharply towards the horizontal, thereby producing a magnification of the change of pressure by a factor of as much as ten. A third form is the folded or double barometer in which the mercury column is split into two, with a lighter liquid, usually an oil, between the two mercury columns, and above the open mercury level. This form also resulted in a shorter and more portable barometer, and was invented in 1688 by Guillaume Amontons (1663–1705).

Barometers suitably mounted as items of furniture first began to appear about 1680, or shortly afterwards. Three makers whose work covered the closing decade of the seventeenth century and the early years of the eighteenth century were Thomas Tompion, Daniel Quare and John Patrick. All were clock-makers, like many makers of barometers throughout the eighteenth century, and the instruments they produced were elegant and of exquisite workmanship.

Daniel Quare was an outstanding and prolific maker of barometers

Only a few barometers by Tompion appear to be extant; two are exhibited in Hampton Court Palace. He appears to have made only the siphon type; in one the scale, together with the weather indications, is set against the lower limb of the instrument, while the other is a wheel barometer. Figure 3 shows the latter example of Tompion's work, and the royal cipher of William III below the finial urn shows that it was completed by 1702.

Daniel Quare was an outstanding and prolific maker of barometers, many of which still survive. In 1695, he obtained a patent for a portable barometer, in spite of much opposition from his fellow members of the Clockmakers' Company.

All his barometers seem to be of the Torricellian or cistern type, mounted in a pillar form, the casing being either ivory or walnut. Many of the latter have the walnut column in two parts, the lower section being spirally reeded and the upper portion fluted, while the cistern is contained in a square-sectioned base which is supported on four hinged metal legs. Some have serial numbers engraved on the bottom of the metal surround to the scale, at either the front or the side. A few have the weather indications in both English and French, as in the one illustrated here (Fig. 4), which is also at

4

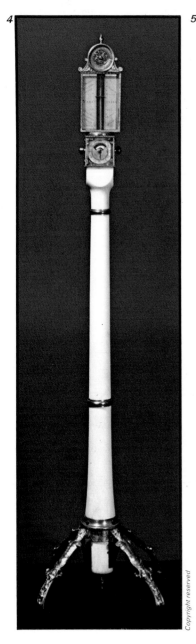

5

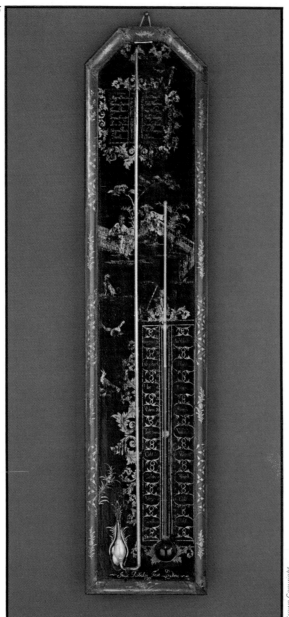

6

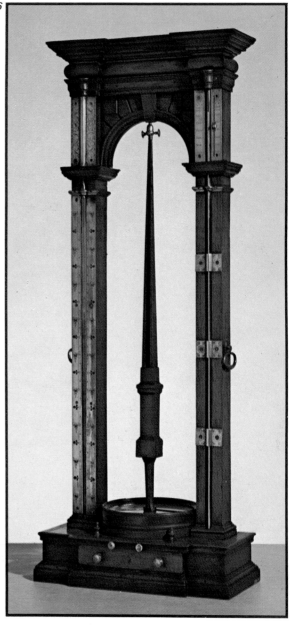

Fig. 4 *Siphon barometer by Daniel Quare (1649–1724), after 1695.*
It is interesting to note that the weather indications are marked on this barometer in both English and French.
(By Gracious Permission of H.M. the Queen: Hampton Court Palace.)

Fig. 5 *Siphon barometer by Isaac Robelou, 1719.*
(Science Museum.)

Hampton Court Palace. Most of Quare's barometers were designed for portability and have a closed boxwood cistern with a leather base; below it is a circular plate-ended screw which, when screwed up, forced the mercury up to the top of the tube, thereby reducing the risk of damage during transportation. In the latter part of the nineteenth century, a number of forgeries were made, and these still appear on the market.

John Patrick, unlike the two previous makers, was not a clock-maker, but primarily a barometer-maker. He was known as the 'Torricellian operator', and illustrated pamphlets published by him show a wide range of barometers. It is rather strange that so few of his instruments are in existence today compared with those of his contemporary, Quare. In the British Museum there is an example of Patrick's work similar to our illustration of Quare's ivory-columned barometer.

Few barometers bear dates; the earliest dated instrument is one acquired in 1695 by the Company of Watermen and Lightermen. This is of the cistern type, mounted on a frame of walnut-veneered oak, but there is no maker's name. An unusual one, now in the Science Museum is by Isaac Robelou, and dated 1719 (Fig. 5). The tube, of the siphon type, is unusually narrow and is exposed throughout its length; the weather indications are given in Latin

and English. Alongside the barometer is a spirit thermometer such as appears on a number of barometers of the period; the zero on the scale corresponds to temperate temperature. The tube and thermometer are mounted on a board covered with japanning; such decoration appears on a number of barometers of the period.

George Graham, who took over Tompion's business in 1713, produced a few barometers all possessing unusual features. The one in the Science Museum (Fig. 6) has a wooden frame with a cistern barometer on the right-hand pillar, and a spirit thermometer on the left-hand pillar, the temperature scale being similar to that of Robelou's instrument. In the centre is suspended a catgut cord which operates as a hygrometer, the pointer on the base moving over a scale as the catgut twists and indicating the humidity.

A number of diagonal barometers were made during the first half of the century; there is one by Quare in Hampton Court Palace, and Patrick, Sisson, Knie of Edinburgh and Whitehurst of Derby also made them in this form. One maker who seems to have made this type exclusively was Charles Orme of Ashby-de-la-Zouch, who also appears to have dated all his products. Some of his barometers were composed of two or three tubes, giving an even greater elongation to the rise and

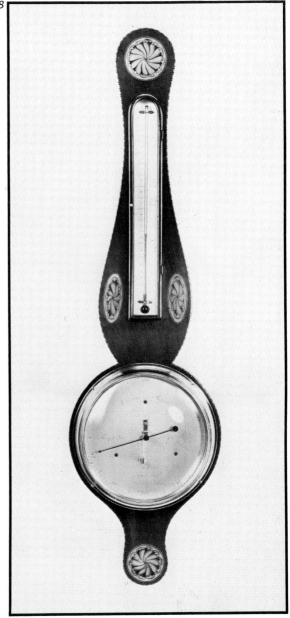

Crown Copyright

R. Fortt

Fig. 6 **Barometer** *by George Graham, c.1730.*
George Graham took over Tompion's business in 1713. This unusual example has a cistern barometer on the left-hand pillar, a spirit thermometer on the right-hand pillar, and a catgut cord which operates as a hygrometer.
(Science Museum.)

Fig. 7 **Diagonal barometer** *by Watkins and Smith of London, c.1765.*
Incorporated into this barometer case are an oatbeard hygrometer which measures humidity and an almanac for the years 1753 to 1852 in the central panel.
(Science Museum.)

Fig. 8 **Banjo-form barometer** *by Joshua Springer of Bristol, late eighteenth century, the case of veneered mahogany.*
(City Museum and Art Gallery, Gloucester.)

fall of the mercury level. There is an example in the City of Gloucester Museum. Orme, in 1735, introduced the practice of boiling the mercury when it was in the tube to rid it of any air and impurities. Another extremely interesting one is illustrated in Figure 7, made by Watkins and Smith of London about 1765, and now in the Science Museum. The baseboard is mahogany, a wood increasingly used for such a purpose from the middle of the century. Other interesting features are the oatbeard hygrometer, which measures the humidity in the air, below the inclined portion of the tube, and the almanac for the period 1753 to 1852 in the centre panel. The oatbeard hygrometer was invented by Robert Hooke in 1663, and is to be found on many barometers from this time until well into the nineteenth century.

So many early barometer-makers were also clock-makers that it is not surprising to find a few of them incorporating barometers in long-case clocks. There is an example by John Ellicott, which dates from 1760, in the Victoria and Albert Museum, and in the Wallace Collection, London, there are several French clocks with mercury barometers of the same period. Alexander Cumming not only added barometers to some of his clocks but also made them recording instruments, or barographs. He made one for George III, another for the Earl of

Bute and one for himself, which in 1814 was acquired by Luke Howard, the father of English meteorology; this instrument is dated 1766 and is still in the possession of the Howard family. All these barograph clocks are still in existence. Figure 9 shows the one made for George III in 1763, which stands today in Buckingham Palace. The case is of kingwood with ormolu decorations; the barometer is of the siphon type with the tube concealed in the ivory Corinthian column seen on the left-hand side. In the shorter limb is an ivory float to which is attached a framework of wooden rods, and the recording pencils are secured to this. Around the clock-face are two dials, operated by the clock, on which the barograph charts are placed. The inner dial makes a complete revolution in six months, and the outer one in a year. The pencils record the pressure on the charts on these dials. The lower dial is that of the barometer operated on the wheel principle.

From about the middle of the century, instrument-makers and opticians became the main makers of barometers; the rise in importance of such makers was due partly to the beginnings of the industrial revolution, but also the developments in navigation, astronomy and surveying. Sisson, Adams, Bird, Heath, Martin, the Dollonds, Ramsden and Nairne were some of the instrument-

Fig. 9 **Barograph clock** by
*Alexander Cumming, 1763.
This clock incorporating a
barograph (self-recording
barometer) was made for
George III.
(By Gracious Permission of
H.M. the Queen: Buckingham
Palace, London.)*

Fig. 10 **Cistern barometer** by
*James Ayscough, c.1760.
The mahogany mounting is in an
elaborate rococo style.
(Victoria and Albert Museum,
London.)*

inlaid *paterae*; it can be seen in the City of Gloucester Museum, where other barometers with Sheraton style mountings are also on display.

The early makers were all established in London, but as the century progressed an increasing number were to be found in the provinces. Orme and John Hallifax of Barnsley were in business before the middle of the century, and by the end of the century Balthazar Knie of Edinburgh, who made diagonal barometers of an unusual form, J. Springer and John Russell of Falkirk were also making excellent instruments. The barometer by Russell, displayed in the Victoria and Albert Museum, was made later, during the regency period.

The double barometer mentioned earlier seems to have had a short period of popularity late in the century. Although more compact and portable, it was difficult to construct, and certainly never became an attractive item of furniture. The form was a modification of that devised by Amontons, but the difficulties of construction, together with the evaporation of the oil in the open tube, no doubt largely contributed to its failure.

English barometers were handsome and imposing pieces of furniture

Many old barometers retain neither their original tubes nor their cisterns, and renovators have been unaware of, or paid little regard to, the original form. In some cases, it is possible to see how the cistern has been modified or replaced by one of another form.

The styles of English barometer mountings throughout the eighteenth century were both varied and handsome, making them attractive items of furniture. The same cannot be said of those produced in the following century, at the beginning of which immigrant Italian glass-blowers came in increasing numbers and satisfied the market for cheap domestic barometers. The vast number of dull, stereotyped banjo barometers to be found in the salerooms today testify to this fact.

makers who made barometers. These barometers tended to be more austere and were generally of the cistern type with silvered scale plates, and mounted on mahogany bases. A number, including Jeremiah Sisson and J. Ramsden made barometers with open mahogany cisterns fitted with semi-hemispherical covers, though the type with the closed boxwood cistern and leather base was still the more popular. There is an open cistern barometer by Sisson dating from *c.*1765 in the Science Museum. Two interesting features are the reading microscope for setting the vernier (the movable scale which marks the sub-divisions on a fixed scale) and the ivory scale which was adjusted so that the tip rested on the mercury in the bowl; this scale reading gave the correction to be applied to the reading of the barometer. Probably one of the earliest barometers to incorporate a vernier with the scale is that by J. Ayscough, made about 1760. The mahogany casing, in the rococo style, is unusually elaborate (Fig. 10). From this time onwards, verniers were fitted to the scales of all the better barometers of this form.

An interesting barometer, shown in Figure 8, is an early example of the banjo-form and was made by Joshua Springer of Bristol towards the end of the century. A vertical scale is engraved on the dial below the pointer arbor; the reading, in whole inches, is taken from the top of the weight suspended from the arbor, the pointer giving the decimals of an inch to 0.01 inches. The case, in the Sheraton style, is veneered mahogany with

MUSEUMS AND COLLECTIONS
Collections of barometers may be seen at the following:
GREAT BRITAIN
Cambridge: Whipple Museum of the History of Science
Edinburgh: Royal Scottish Museum
Gloucester: City Museum and Art Gallery
London: Hampton Court Palace
National Maritime Museum, Greenwich
Science Museum
Victoria and Albert Museum
Oxford: Museum of the History of Science

FURTHER READING
English Barometers, 1680–1860 by N. Goodison, London, 1969.
The History of the Barometer by W. E. K. Middleton, London, 1964.
Dictionary of English Furniture by P. Macquoid and R. Edwards, London, revised 1954.
Old English Barometers by B. H. and E. F. Bell, Winchester, 1952.

Collector's Corner

SUNSHADES AND UMBRELLAS

BY WILLIAM ALLAN

Thomas Coryat, an Englishman visiting Florence in 1611, noted that 'many Italians carry fine things, which they commonly call in the Italian tongue umbrellaes, that is, things that give them shelter against the sun and are made of leather and hooped on the inside with divers wooden hoops that extend the umbrella in a pretty large compass'. Coryat was the first to try the experiment in England, but the fashion was slow to catch on. It was not until the early eighteenth century that the umbrella began to play a part in everyday life. In *Robinson Crusoe*, which Daniel Defoe published in 1719, the hero 'spent a deal of time and pains to make me an umbrella . . . for I had seen them made in the Brazils'. By the middle of the century the umbrella was almost as common in the streets of London as it is today. The philanthropist Jonas Hanway carried his umbrella from the day he bought it in 1748 until he died in 1786.

Alongside the umbrella, with its severely utilitarian appearance, the sunshade also made its way into the catalogue of fashionable necessities. Popular in the eighteenth century, it reached its apogee in the nineteenth; no woman of fashion was complete without her battery of parasols.

Stifled sighs, austere behaviour

The half century before the Great War was the high period of inventiveness and originality for both parasol and umbrella; swans necks, heraldic beasts and comic masks were usual forms of decoration for the handle. Bone, glass and many different varieties of wood were in common use for the haft. Umbrellas were generally covered with silk or cotton, although the older oil skin survived outside hotels and restaurants; parasols were covered in every conceivable fabric from damasked satin to coloured crepe. Milliners' shops and fashionable ladies' tailors vied with each other in the extravagance of their materials and the names given to them. In 1880 a shop in Sloane Street, London, was selling colours called 'stifled sighs' or 'useless regrets' and one shop carried a form of blush rose entitled 'agitated nymph's thigh'—rendered, of course, in French.

The parasol was above all things the accessory of the coquette, 'a light and graceful ornament, serving to arm an attitude of charming reverie or make an avowal of abandon'. The umbrella, on the other hand, began to shed its ornamental function. From the 1870s onwards a gold ringed malacca was generally the most exotic pattern to be had in London. The umbrella became, in Parisian parlance, more *'constitutionnel'*: 'the Englishman carries his umbrella as a symbol of his austere and citizen-like behaviour,' noted one French visitor.

In the markets

It is still quite an easy matter to find old umbrellas and parasols; Tory bazaars and Church fêtes are a good source, as are most of the London markets, both indoor and out. It is more fun, however, to buy an old handle, or complete frame if one is to be had, and recover it. Many of the appropriate fabrics are to be had at Liberty's in London or any similar store; I would be a little wary, though, of asking for a yard of agitated nymph's thigh in Harrods.

Centre: *Crusoe's umbrella, as depicted in an edition of 1870, published by Cassel.*
Right: *Jonas Hanway, whose umbrella surprised eighteenth-century London. Early twentieth-century engraving.*

Below: Early sunshades and umbrellas in contemporary settings.
Left: Fashionable sunshade, 1810.

MANSELL COLLECTION

CRUSOE SLEEPING IN HIS BOAT

FRANK PHILLIPS

MANSELL COLLECTION

Care and Repair of upholstered furniture

Major upholstery repairs are strictly for the expert and there is no point in attempting them unless you have had special training. But some jobs are worth considering for the amateur, so long as the piece of furniture is not too valuable.

Getting Rid of the Sag

If the seat of a chair sags, the cause may be that the webbing has stretched or even broken. You can find out by turning the chair upside down and taking off the bottom cover of hessian, black cotton or linen. To remove the tacks use a hammer and an old screwdriver or special tack remover, remembering always to drive out the tack along the rail, not across it, since this may cause the wood to split. Pine is particularly vulnerable, but almost all upholstered chair frames are of either birch or beech. These are even-grained hard woods which hold tacks well.

Next, knock out the tacks which hold the lengths of webbing to the frame. You will probably have to remove the tacks which hold the bottom of the chair cover (see Fig. 1). When all the webs are free of the frame, cut the twine which ties the springs to them. Now test all the springs to see that they are firmly tied at the top and that they are not badly bent or twisted. If new ones are required, take an old one with you to make certain of getting an exact replacement. Use upholsterer's spring twine to tie new or loose springs back in position.

To re-web the chair you will need a light hammer and plenty of ⅝-inch improved upholstery tacks and a webbing stretcher. You can either buy a stretcher or make a simple and effective one from an odd piece of wood; there is a blueprint at the top of Fig. 1. Use the best webbing you can get. Black and white

cotton or cotton and jute is stronger than the plain brown jute webbing. If you want to match up with webbing typical of the eighteenth and early nineteenth centuries, a saddler's webbing is best.

Look carefully at Fig. 1 to see how the webbing should be spaced out, and at Fig. 2A to see how the webbing stretcher is used and the webbing tacked down. First double the webbing over and tack it to the frame with five ⅝-inch tacks. Bring the webbing to the other side of the chair and wrap it around the stretcher as shown—the stretcher should start at an angle of about 45° and finish horizontal. Now drive in three tacks, remove the stretcher and cut the webbing, allowing 1 inch for folding over and fixing down with two tacks.

It is very important that all the webs are as tight as you can pull them. Do not flinch from using your full strength. Tight webbing not only makes for long-lasting upholstery, but is also a big help in holding together the frame.

You will find that the springs get in the way and want to poke through between the webs as you work. So long as none of the webs are going through the springs, this does not matter.

When you have finished webbing the chair, sort out the springs into their correct positions and tie them to the webs. Use spring twine and a suitable upholsterer's needle, stitching through and tying with single knots to give three fixings to each spring. I have drawn in how to do it in Fig. 1.

To finish off, re-tack the bottom edges of the chair cover in position, then tack a new bottom of hessian or black cotton over the webbing, turning it in as you tack so that there are no raw edges showing.

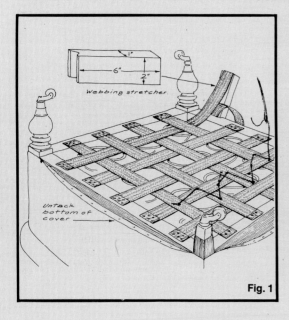

Fig. 1

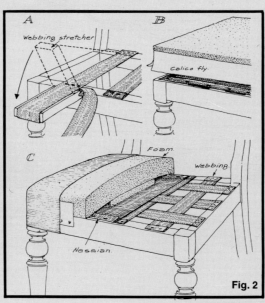

Fig. 2

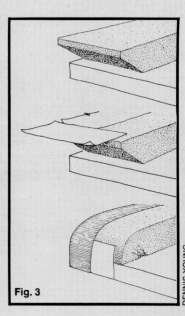

Fig. 3

DENNIS YOUNG

Strictly for the expert. Not only is this sofa in need of major repairs; it is also quite valuable. Regency in period, it would be worth about £200 when re-upholstered.

Re-Upholstering a Small Sprung Chair

The simplest and most effective way to re-upholster a small sprung chair is by using polyether foam which can be bought in almost any do-it-yourself shop. The first thing is to remove all the old upholstery padding, springs and webbing. It is a good idea to do this out-of-doors. Unless you have done this job before, you will be amazed at how much dirt and dust is inside. Re-web the chair by the method I have already described, but this time on the top of the seat rails (**Fig. 2C**). Over the interlaced webbing, stretch and tack a piece of hessian. This is to stop the foam slipping between the webs.

Cut out a template of thick paper to fit the seat, making sure it fits exactly, and take it to your local foam supplier. The foam should be of a medium firm density and either 2 inches or 1½ inches thick, and about ¼ inch larger all round than the template. If you have to cut the foam to size yourself, use a bread knife dipped in water and cut with a sawing action along lines drawn with a ball-point pen on the foam. You will also require a piece of foam about 9 inches square and from ½ inch to ¾ inch thick to stick to the underside of the main piece so as to give a dome to the finished seat (see **Fig. 2C**).

Take strips of calico 2 inches wide and the same length as the sides of the chair. Apply a thin coat of rubber adhesive such as Evostik along half the width of all the strips. Now apply a film of adhesive 1 inch wide all around the sides of the thick piece of foam. When it is dry, press the strips of calico on to the foam: this gives you the flies for attaching the foam to the seat frame with ⅝-inch upholstery tacks. There is, of course, the cut-out in the foam to fit around the back legs, but no fixing flies are needed there.

The seat is now ready for covering. Lay the upholstery cover over the seat, tacking temporarily at first and then finally driving the tacks home when the cover has been properly adjusted. Make sure that it is pulled evenly all over and that it is tight enough to compress the foam to give a clean firm line. All the tacking for the cover is, of course, down on the underside of the seat rails, except around the legs where the cover is cut and tucked in. Gimp pins in a colour matching the cover are used here. To finish off, a bottom cover of hessian or black cotton can be tacked on.

Re-Upholstering a Dining-Room Chair

To re-upholster a dining-room chair loose seat, follow the same instructions given above, but use foam 1 inch instead of 2 inches or 1½ inches thick. One point to remember. If you are thinking of using a thicker covering material than the old one: test first to see if the loose seat will still fit into the chair frame. If you wish to have a more rounded edge to either of the foam upholstered seats the sides of the foam are cut back at an angle of 45° and the calico flies stuck to the top edges as shown in **Fig. 3**.

Everyday Care

Use a vacuum cleaner with great care when removing dust and dirt from old covers: broken threads can be sucked out very easily.

Cats' claws and the buckles of children's sandals take first prize for causing havoc to upholstery fabrics. It is probably easier to keep the sandals off than the cats from clawing. A scratching block of soft wood is supposed to be the answer, but it is not foolproof.

Strong light and high humidity cause upholstery fabrics to rot, while an atmosphere which is too dry makes the fibres brittle. Plenty of green plants can raise the humidity in centrally heated rooms, which is a help for fabrics as well as for wood.

Moths prefer wool and silk to linen and cotton—you may have seen wool embroidery eaten clean away from its canvas backing. Always remove all the dust, dirt and moths' eggs that you possibly can before treating upholstery with an insecticide. There are many on the market.

If you need to remove grease from woven covers, first get the worst off by laying a piece of blotting-paper over the mark and pressing down with a warm iron. Continue until no more grease shows on the blotting-paper. Finish off with a dry-cleaning fluid. For very delicate fabrics the safest cleaning method is a light dusting with fuller's earth and then brushing with a soft brush. If you want to use warm water and a dry-cleaning fluid for cleaning a cover, try out the mixture first on a piece of the cover which is hidden, to see if the colours are going to run or 'bleed'.

DENNIS YOUNG

THE PORTOBELLO MARKET

Portobello Road of a Saturday, when the regular antique shops are augmented by street stalls and arcades, is at least as much a people show as a trading mart. Visitors and natives are many and colourful. But the main business of Portobello Road is, was, and hopefully ever will be, selling antiques.

The antique-sellers divide into four categories, according to tenure. Best off are the shop-owners, who have a whole shop to themselves, and usually open for at least a few hours during the week. Rents vary widely, but everyone agrees they have risen astronomically within the last ten years—perhaps as much as 500%—and it would be difficult to find a new lease now with a weekly rental of less than £35. Most of the shop-traders are leaseholders: freeholders prefer to turn their shops into arcades.

The arcade system is a fairly recent development, but now more and more shops are being turned into arcades to give the highest rent yield. The arcades usually open only on Saturdays and a stall in one costs £4 to £6 a week, though in the most recently opened arcade a front pitch costs £9 a week. Some arcades, such as the Red Lion where rents are £6, have an arrangement whereby the stall can be blocked off with a board and padlocked, so that the stallholder can leave his stock there through the week, and if he doesn't turn up for some reason, the stall is simply left closed.

But the less expensive arcades do not have any lock-up provisions and the stallholder must take his stock home with him each week. If he doesn't turn up by 10 a.m. on Saturday, the carpetbaggers can move in. Carpetbagging is a very casual system open to all comers: you simply turn up in Portobello Road between 9 and 10.30 a.m. with your goods and rush round the unlocked arcades asking if there are any vacancies. The charge for borrowing a booth for the day is about £3. People usually do it while they're on waiting lists for arcade-stalls, and the wait can be as long as six months.

The hard core of the market is the stretch from Talbot Road up to Henekey's pub; this is the original street market with stalls licensed by Kensington Borough Council. Licenses are issued to named stallholders and cannot be transferred. Since this is by far the cheapest way of trading in Portobello, most stallholders tend to hang on to the licenses, and many of them have been in the road for at least ten years. The licensed pitch costs 29 shillings a week and the stall is hired separately, for 15 shillings, which includes putting up and dismantling.

All the traders agree that **prices have been rising steadily** since the war, with an even sharper increase in the last ten years. The pattern of appreciation follows much the same pattern as The Times—Sotheby Index, but, since the goods are poorer quality, they are more dependent on fashion. Recently there was a craze for Victorian music boxes, Art Nouveau artefacts, and Hester Bateman silver; it was followed by an interest in maplewood frames and Baxter prints.

But how long can the boom continue? Silver prices have already dropped from their incredible peak of 1967. All dealers complain that goods are getting harder to find. Mrs. Dale of 'Chip and Dale' told me: 'My husband is out buying six days a week to keep the shop full, and it's not a very big shop'.

Dealers are, of course, cagey about what they consider a 'fair profit', but **a 40-60% mark-up seems average.** One arcade stallholder who just does it as a hobby told me that he reckoned to write things up by 100%, but then he usually had to come down. His average takings on a Saturday were £20-£30, but a good day in the summer would bring £50-£60, and he had been known to make £100 in a day—not bad going for a spare-time activity.

Where do the Portobello traders buy their stock? Almost every dealer I spoke to assured me that country shop and sale prices were often higher than London prices. The main source seems to be Bermondsey market in the small hours of Friday morning, and other East End markets on Sunday. Rather surprisingly—in view of the huge number of visitors to Portobello—the residents reckon to sell as much as 80% of their stock to other traders, at a special discount. This bartering is done between 8 and 10 a.m. on Saturday, before the tourists arrive, and it is quite common for a shop-owner to buy something from a stallholder at 9 a.m. for £5 and sell it in his shop at 11 a.m. for £7 or £9. Mrs. Dale told me: 'If you wait till you get a private customer, your business is going to be very slack. We buy from other shops in London, and then someone from Chelsea might come and buy from us; they might sell it to someone in Bond Street, who might sell it to an American dealer'.

This inbreeding, the fact that an item might have passed through ten dealers' hands and been seen by another hundred dealers before it finds its way into private hands, rather spoils

the chance of any great *trouvailles*. However, we will finish with an encouraging story, a true one which happened to a stallholder, Bill Lonsdale: 'It was in the winter, five or six years ago, and I was down one of the East End markets at 6 o'clock, before it got light. There was a cake basket on the ground which had probably been there an hour at that stage, and I had my torch with me so I looked at it with the torch, and it was yellow in the centre. Now silver plate when it's worn shows the base metal underneath, and if it's nickel it looks yellow, so I assumed this was nickel. But it was quite a pretty, showy style of old cake basket and the chap only wanted 10 shillings for it, so I thought, 'Well, I'll get it replated, and it'll be cheap at that'. So I bought it and took it away. When I got it in the daylight I rubbed away some of the dirt on the bottom—it was quite black with dirt—and I saw a mark. I could hardly believe it, but it was Georgian silver by a very famous maker called Paul Storr. And what had happened—why it was yellow in the centre—was that it had originally been goldplated, and the yellow was the remains of the gold, not nickel underneath. So I put it in Sotheby's and it fetched £147.

But, remember, this was an exception. It's never happened to me since and it'll probably never happen to me again'. . . .

LYNN BARBER

Antiques
as an investment

Antiques are good investments. Inside most collectors there lurks the subconscious urge of the investor. As the demand for antiques is constantly rising throughout the world and the supply of them is naturally limited, it follows that they will continue to offer an excellent method of capital appreciation.

Besides being good investments, antiques have the added attraction of being a joy to their owner. Most people buy them for their personal pleasure as well as for investment. They are looking not only for the capital appreciation in value, but also for their own appreciation and, perhaps even more important, appreciation from their friends!

Deciding What to Collect
As in most other fields of investment, a shrewd investor will not put all his eggs in one silver spoon, but rather spread his money over several items. Possibly the wisest—and happiest—method of investment is to buy what appeals most to you. To some, antique furniture and silver are fascinating lines to collect; for others, pictures and porcelain, and for some, perhaps, French china bidets have the greatest attraction!

Purchase Quality Items
Having decided which categories of antiques will form the basis of your investment, it is essential to ensure that the items purchased are the best available in their price range. Some people will already have enough knowledge to enable them to make their selections without outside help, but for many the task could be a little daunting. The stories of forgeries and frauds, headlined in the newspapers, shake the investor's confidence in his ability to choose good items that are genuine antiques. Especially in the areas where there have been sharp increases in value, it is important to be wary. Georgian wine glasses, for instance, have multiplied their value by about ten times in the last fifteen years. Supply is limited, and one should look out for fakes, as there are many coming from overseas these days. This is where it pays to consult reputable, expert antique dealers, or one of the major auction houses who should have at their fingertips all the information required on availability, current prices and likely trends. He may possibly also have some interesting suggestions on future collectors' pieces so far neglected by the buying public, which could offer excellent capital appreciation. It is contrary to the interests of the great majority of genuine antique dealers to make false claims since they are intent on building up good will.

The Rise in Prices
It is interesting to study the table (compiled from The Times—Sotheby Index) which shows the number of times some categories of antiques have multiplied in price during the period 1951 to 1969. The devaluation of sterling, and the consequent mistrust in paper money, has turned the attention of many investors to antiques and works of art. This factor has more than sustained the previous rate of increase in the value of antiques since 1967. There are, however, certain points to note when considering the individual headings separately. It is worth bearing in mind that

what has increased most in value in the past is not necessarily going to be the best investment in the future. Within the overall picture, shown in the table, it is fair to say that an investor who bought, for instance, eighteenth-century silver early in 1968, held on during the boom of the following months and sold out early in 1969 would have done appreciably better than the index; whereas one who had bought at the height of the boom and then sold when the price had averaged out again would have suffered a corresponding loss. At the height of the boom several reputable, and astute, dealers were quite frank in voicing their mis-

Table of Capital Appreciation

The figure on the right is the number of times by which the value has multiplied between 1951 and 1969.

Pictures	Old Master drawings	22
	Impressionist pictures	18
	English pictures	$9\frac{1}{2}$
	Old Master paintings	7
	Old Master prints	$31\frac{1}{2}$
18th Century Furniture	Italian	7
	Dutch	$5\frac{1}{2}$
	French *Fine furniture/collectors pieces*	5
	American	$3\frac{1}{2}$
	English	3
Silver	Candlesticks	9
	Coffee and Chocolate pots	9
	Porringers	7
	Sauce boats	10
	Salvers	7
	Tankards	8
	Overall	$8\frac{1}{2}$
English Porcelain	Worcester Wares	7
	Chelsea Wares	$3\frac{1}{2}$
	Bow figures	3
	Chelsea figures	$2\frac{1}{2}$
	Overall	4
English Glass	Baluster stemmed glasses	7
	Beilby enamelled glasses	6
	Colour twist stemmed glasses	$7\frac{1}{2}$
	Early glass	7
	Engraved glass	$10\frac{1}{2}$
	Jacobite glass	7
	Newcastle glass	$13\frac{1}{2}$
	Overall	$8\frac{1}{2}$

Reproduced from The Times—Sotheby Index by kind permission of The Times.

givings. They felt that such high prices could not be substantiated and must in time settle at a more realistic level. The right timing— as in all other forms of investment—is an essential part of success. It is always foolish to buy anything following a sudden steep increase in price.

Useful Antiques

An aspect of buying antiques which is sometimes forgotten is the intrinsic usefulness of many pieces. For instance, domestic silver is invariably attractive to own and use, and, with increasingly high standards of living throughout the world, it is eagerly sought after. Similarly, with furniture. As will be seen from The Times—Sotheby Index, eighteenth-century English furniture, relying on simplicity and refinement of form, has not risen in value as much as the more elaborate French and Italian pieces. But, whereas the high prices of the latter category reflect its increasing rarity, the pieces in the more restrained and functional style of the English designers should prove to have a steadier rate of growth in value over the long term, because of their greater domestic practicality and their appeal to more classical taste.

£1 in currency in 1951 now worth about 10s. 6d.

With the ever-dwindling size of houses and flats, the greatest interest recently has been shown in the smaller pieces of furniture. As a result some of the bigger chests of drawers and tallboys are relatively under-priced. A small Georgian wardrobe may be picked up for less than its modern counterpart. Never forget that modern furniture—usually mass-produced in woods of inferior quality—depreciates the minute it leaves the showroom, just as a new car does. The investor who buys to furnish his home will have the pleasure of beautiful surroundings, coupled with a steady appreciation of his capital to compensate for any lack of 'go-go' performance!

What About Dates?

The recognised definition of a genuine antique is an object which was produced before 1830, and, in the main, investors should always bear this point in mind. But, equally, there is no

---

£1 in ordinary industrial shares in 1951 now worth about £2 13s.

---

need to discard all thoughts of investing in pieces produced after 1830. In fact nowadays, with the consistently increasing prices being obtained for many pre-1830 items, it is to the early Victorian age that investors, seeking good capital appreciation from lower-

priced articles, could well cast their eyes. In general, prices of Victoriana have risen noticeably in the past few years. In fact it was only recently that a member of a well-known country firm of antique dealers told me that he could see they would have to include Victorian items in their stock before long, since the quantity of genuine antiques on the market became less and less each year.

Victorian silver, for instance, has shown steady if unspectacular appreciation and the collector might do well in this field if he sticks to items that are in good taste and, of course, in good condition. The emphasis should, however, be on prudent buy-

---

£1 in antique English porcelain in 1951 now worth about £4

---

ing, as not all Victoriana has the universal appeal necessary to send the prices up. One other point worth remembering is that antiques over one hundred years old can be taken into the United States and many other countries free of all import duty.

There is a tendency these days for people to collect antiques for their historical interest. Prints of cricket scenes, naval, military, coaching, and sporting prints all have their devotees. Commemorative objects (e.g. coronation mugs) also attract a following. These facts suggest that any pieces with historical associations, presumably because they can be securely dated, will show a steady rise in value as they get older.

Damaged Articles

A major factor governing the value of any antique is its condition. This applies especially to glass and porcelain. No matter how expert the repair, the value is invariably reduced, sometimes

---

£1 in antique English glass in 1951 now worth about £8 5s.

---

as much as by 50%. Slight damage is acceptable only in the very rarest items. It is therefore very important to inspect closely any object you intend to purchase. Check very carefully not only for minute damage, but also for any signs of the repairer's work, a great deal of which is very skilled, and which, in some less reputable shops, has been cleverly concealed.

It is impossible to cover every category of antiques in which a judicious investment now should show a distinctive profit over a number of years. Outstanding possibilities undoubtedly lie in the field of, for instance, antique clocks and oriental carpets. Simple laws of supply and demand (and the supply is limited to what exists) should ensure that good antiques remain a sound investment.

JULIAN GIBBS

Market Trends

QUEEN ANNE ANTIQUES

CHRISTIE'S

This Queen Anne card table made only 280 gns. at Christie's in July 1970.

Early eighteenth-century English furniture of good quality is rare and has been so for some years. As a result the market has become increasingly international and competition remains strong in spite of a general lowering of value in many branches of the applied arts.

Many pieces catalogued as early eighteenth-century have been tampered with or are in need of repair. It is only on occasion that an unquestionably good-quality piece comes to auction and, when it does, the price is justifiably high. For instance, four George I burr walnut chairs, their cabriole legs carved with husks framed by eagles' heads, were sold for £2,500 in July 1968. In November that year an elegant open armchair with contemporary upholstery fetched 1,500 gns. at Christie's. Understandably, mediocre furniture of this period commands little interest. The Queen Anne walnut card table illustrated here made only 280 gns. at Christie's in July 1970.

Field for the Super Rich

The first thirty years of the eighteenth century saw the development and fulfilment of the Queen Anne style in silver. While enormous quantities of plate were produced, much has not survived the vicissitudes of time; yet more is available from those years than from any earlier period. It is therefore possible to form a comprehensive collection of Queen Anne silver, but it remains a field only for the super rich. In spite of the temporary and considerable fall in value of much eighteenth-century silver, a good pair of Queen Anne candlesticks still fetched as much as £3,000 at Christie's in July 1970.

As in nearly all branches of the applied arts (an exception is the later Chinese porcelain), the indifferent items have lost in value more heavily than those which have quality or rarity, or both. Indeed, some of the more exceptional examples have stood firm, if not actually increased in value. TOM MILNES-GASKELL

A pair of Chelsea bowls and covers, gold anchor marks, each 6¼ inches high. Sold at Christie's in October 1970 for 400 gns. Centre: One of a pair of Chelsea blue ground potpourri vases and covers, each 9¾ inches high. Sold at Christie's in October 1970 for 150 gns. These prices reflect the fame of the Chelsea factory.

EARLY GEORGIAN ANTIQUES

While there remains some uncertainty as to which English factory was the first to produce porcelain, Chelsea has indisputably become the most famous. With this prestige came the inevitable copying of their wares, especially on the Continent; copies were produced in considerable quantities and should act as a warning to all collectors. As one might expect, the price range is enormous. A white figure of an Arabian bustard, only 7¾ inches high, realised 5,200 gns. in 1969. In the same season, a red anchor pineapple tureen and cover was sold for 3,800 gns. The same piece was auctioned in 1959 and then fetched £800. Chelsea was prolific in its production of scent bottles and *bonbonnières;* some of the more exceptional examples, such as a rooster scent bottle (Sotheby's 1962, £2,200), are by any standards inordinately expensive. A less unusual scent bottle, formed as a pineapple, realised 420 gns. in 1969 and in the same year a *bonbonnière* formed as a woman's head, her hair coloured in a light manganese and surmounted by a small green hat, fetched £190. A single Hans Sloane botanical plate painted with a large leaf and various insects was auctioned in October 1969 and made £460. In 1970 a plate decorated in the manner of J. H. O'Neale with figures, trees and buildings was sold for £95; it is a rare occasion when a piece of Chelsea porcelain makes less than £100, provided, of course, that the condition is good.

Glass

English glass is much more within the reach of collectors. Individual examples illustrating the many different techniques employed can be purchased with a small outlay. An ale glass with slender bowl, the stem with an angular knop containing a tear (£75); a Newcastle wine glass engraved with the arms of the Prince of Orange and Nassau (£55); another wine glass engraved with a band of key pattern and supported on a multi-knopped faceted stem (£100); and a pair of Jacobite wine glasses, each on a double-knopped multi-spiral air twist stem (£180). These were auctioned in November 1969.

Furniture

Mahogany was expensive when first introduced into England. This in itself limited its appeal to the wealthier and helps to explain why most early Georgian furniture is of such high quality. Nor was it produced in large quantities, for it would have graced only the main reception rooms of the grander houses. A set of twelve side-chairs in the style of William Kent realised 2,800 gns. in 1969 and individual chairs of some distinction can be purchased for under £200. At present there is a shortage of such furniture on the market, a shortage which will maintain a high price level.

TOM MILNES-GASKELL

624

EARLY ENGLISH GLASS, GEORGIAN MIRRORS AND CLOCKS / by Tom Milnes-Gaskell

A Wildenstein fortune is not required by those who wish to start a collection of early English glass. Many examples, elegant in their simplicity, can be purchased for less than £100. But the collector must beware of a pitfall which is common to other areas of the applied arts: early English glass was extensively faked in the last half of the nineteenth century.

At the cheaper end of the market a fine wine glass made 80 gns. at Christie's in July 1970. It had a straight stem with annular knop and a folded conical foot. Another, with a bell bowl on an inverted stem, realised 65 gns. and a baluster air-twist goblet was sold for only 42 gns. Rare pieces with historical associations fetch far higher prices. For example, a Jacobite wine glass was sold for £1,700 at Sotheby's in November 1968. It was enamelled with a portrait of the Young Pretender garbed in blue balmoral and the ribbon and star of the Garter.

Although prices for early glass have soared in the last few years, they have held steady in the last season, in sympathy with the general malaise of the art market.

Georgian mirrors
In February 1958 a fine George I wall mirror catalogued as 'of exceptional quality' realised only £100. Its giltwood frame was bound with ribbons and carved at the sides with a pair of imposing mermaids. Today, one would have to pay several times that amount. Not unnaturally, it is size that largely determines the value of less exceptional mirrors; on the best pieces quality becomes a more important factor. A large, fairly standard William and Mary marquetry mirror inlaid with flowers made 300 gns. at Christie's in May 1968. The same firm sold a Queen Anne Vauxhall glass and giltwood upright mirror with plain gadrooned edge for 900 gns. in March 1970 (this style is very much in sympathy with current taste). A year earlier a gilt gesso pier glass of the same period realised 550 gns. A rarity was seen at Sotheby's in February 1968: a George I red japanned toilet mirror with a miniature bureau plinth beneath. This reached £680. During the past year auction prices for mirrors have fallen but the indications are that this corner of the market is now recovering.

Early clocks
We now expect a good bracket clock by a renowned maker dating from about 1700 to fetch several thousand pounds. Ten years ago it was more usual to count in hundreds. For example, a basket-top kingwood bracket clock by John Constantin with verge escapement and calendar and pendulum apertures made only £300 in December 1960. In April 1968, one by Richard Baker in a fine seaweed marquetry case, repeating the quarters on three bells, realised £3,400. The same trend is apparent in long-case clocks of the same date. There were some fine examples included in the S. E. Prestige collection dispersed by Sotheby's in April 1968. One, by Edward East, realised £7,000. It had a silverwood case and a silvered chapter ring. Clocks of slightly earlier date have not aroused the same enthusiasm or shown a similar appreciation in value.

Eighteenth-century English wine glasses sold in 1970. They fetched (left to right) 130 gns., 34 gns., 150 gns. and 200 gns. (set of four).

A seventeenth-century long-case clock which made 950 gns., 1969.

PHOTO: CHRISTIE'S

George I gilt gesso mirror which made 320 gns. at Christie's, 1970.